D0025926

Conflict Survival Kit
Tools for Resolving Conflict at Work

Second Edition

Daniel B. Griffith, J.D., SPHR
Cliff Goodwin, Ed.D.
Purdue School of Engineering and Technology
Indiana University–Purdue University, Indianapolis, IN

PEARSON

Boston   Columbus   Indianapolis   New York   San Francisco   Upper Saddle River
Amsterdam   Cape Town   Dubai   London   Madrid   Milan   Munich   Paris   Montreal   Toronto
Delhi   Mexico City   São Paulo   Sydney   Hong Kong   Seoul   Singapore   Taipei   Tokyo

Editorial Director: Vernon R. Anthony
Executive Editor: Gary Bauer
Editorial Project Manager: Linda Cupp
Editorial Assistant: Tanika Henderson
Director of Marketing: David Gesell
Marketing Manager: Stacey Martinez
Senior Marketing Assistant: Les Roberts
Production Manager: Laura Messerly
Senior Art Director: Jayne Conte
Cover Designer: Suzanne Behnke
Cover Art: Thinkstock
Manager, Rights and Permissions: Karen Sanatar
Image Permission Coordinator: Mike Lackey
Full-Service Project Management: George Jacob
Composition: Integra Software Services Pvt. Ltd.
Printer/Binder: Edwards Brothers
Cover Printer: Lehigh-Phoenix Color
Text Font: 10/12, ITC Century Std

Credits and acknowledgments for materials borrowed from other sources and reproduced, with permission, in this textbook appear on the appropriate page within text.

Photo Credits: Introduction: Thinkstock; Part I: Joel Goodwin; Part II: Fotolia; Part III: Joel Goodwin; Part IV: Joel Goodwin; Conclusion: Joel Goodwin.

Copyright © 2013, 2014, 2015, 2016 Pearson Education, Inc., publishing as Prentice Hall, One Lake Street, Upper Saddle River, New Jersey 07458. All rights reserved. Manufactured in the United States of America. This publication is protected by Copyright, and permission should be obtained from the publisher prior to any prohibited reproduction, storage in a retrieval system, or transmission in any form or by any means, electronic, mechanical, photocopying, recording, or likewise. To obtain permission(s) to use material from this work, please submit a written request to Pearson Education, Inc., Permissions Department, One Lake Street, Upper Saddle River, New Jersey 07458.

Many of the designations by manufacturers and seller to distinguish their products are claimed as trademarks. Where those designations appear in this book, and the publisher was aware of a trademark claim, the designations have been printed in initial caps or all caps.

Library of Congress Cataloging-in-Publication Data

Griffith, Dan (Daniel B.)
  Conflict survival kit : tools for resolving conflict at work / Daniel B. Griffith, Cliff Goodwin. — 2nd [ed.]
      p. cm.
  Prev. ed. entered under Cliff Goodwin.
  Includes bibliographical references and index.
  ISBN-13: 978-0-13-274105-7
  ISBN-10: 0-13-274105-9
  1. Conflict management.   2. Interorganizational relations.   3. Industrial relations.   4. Psychology, Industrial.
5. Conflict (Psychology)   I. Goodwin, Cliff   II. Goodwin, Cliff   Conflict survival kit.   III. Title.
  HD42.G66 2013
  658.3'145–dc23
                                                                    2011035613

10 9 8 7 6 5 4 3 2 1

ISBN 10: 0-13-274105-9
ISBN 13: 978-0-13-274105-7

CONTENTS

CHAPTER 3:
APPROACHES TO CONFLICT   33

CHAPTER 4:
WORKING TOWARD COLLABORATION   46

PART II: Interpersonal Communication Skills for Resolving Conflict   67

CHAPTER 5:
THE THREE CHANNELS
OF COMMUNICATION   68

CHAPTER 6:
LISTENING TO RESOLVE CONFLICT
AND BUILD LASTING RELATIONSHIPS   87

CHAPTER 7:
THE COMMUNICATION CONTINUA 107

PART III: Preparing to Resolve Conflicts 121

CHAPTER 8:
ARE YOU CAPABLE? 122

CHAPTER 9:
OPENING THE DOORS TO CONFLICT
RESOLUTION   142

CHAPTER 12:
OVERCOMING BARRIERS TO
INTEGRATIVE NEGOTIATION 206

CHAPTER 13:
MEDIATING CONFLICTS BETWEEN PARTIES 229

CHAPTER 14:
DECISION–MAKING CHOICES
FOR THE MANAGER   254

CHAPTER 15:
HANDLING CONFLICTS REQUIRING
DIRECT CONFRONTATION   278

CHAPTER 16:
SPECIAL SITUATIONS: "OPPORTUNISTIC"
EMPLOYEES, WORKPLACE VIOLENCE,
TERMINATIONS, AND BULLYING   303

CONCLUSION   327

CHAPTER 17: ACHIEVING EFFECTIVENESS AS A CONFLICT MANAGER   328

Give us the tools and we will finish the job.
          Winston Churchill

Unless you are a hermit, conflict is a reality in your life. If you are a leader or aspire to a leadership role, much of your success will depend on how well you respond to conflict among those you lead or serve. Whether you manage a staff of 2 or 200, you are expected to address and equitably resolve many conflict situations in the course of a month, a week, or even a day.

Are you prepared to manage these conflicts? Can you build rapport among battling parties and encourage their mutual cooperation? Do you have the finesse and problem-solving skill needed to achieve a workable resolution while preserving the parties' integrity and fragile relationship? Do you have the maturity and composure to persist with parties in conflict when they appear to have reached the limits of their willingness to bargain?

The ability to manage conflict is often viewed as more of an art than a skill, suggesting that you are best advised to leave the management of conflicts in the hands of "professionals." Yet while there is an art to a skillfully negotiated resolution, it is an art form that you can master with the right tools. Although some workplace conflicts may necessitate the involvement of a professional, such as a trained mediator or arbitrator, human resources representative, or labor relations specialist, many more conflicts depend on your intervention as a manager. To be successful, you need to build on your foundation of communication and leadership capacities and apply them to the kinds of conflict management strategies and methods this book provides.

This book is both a classroom text and an on-the-job guide for the individual who has received no formal preparation in managing conflict and needs "instant" skill building and practical methods for handling organizational and personal conflicts. It also offers insights for the aspiring professional who, though expert in the subject matter of his or her field and educated in conflict theory and negotiation strategy, needs grounding in basic interpersonal communication and management skills, such as rapport building, empathic listening, behavior modeling, reframing, problem solving, and decision making.

This text is divided into six sections. The Introduction (Chapter 1) discusses the Nature of Conflict. Part I (Chapters 2–4) examines the Theory and Context for Managing Conflict in the Workplace. Part II (Chapters 5–7) covers Interpersonal Communication Skills for Resolving Conflict. Part III (Chapters 8–9) addresses Preparing to Resolve Conflicts. Part IV (Chapters 10–16) provides Application and Practice. The book concludes with Achieving Effectiveness as a Conflict Manager (Chapter 17). Each chapter provides concrete information regarding the various aspects of conflict management in the workplace with plenty of examples and illustrations to promote learning. In addition, each chapter includes the following features:

- **Performance Competencies:** A succinct statement of what will be covered in the chapter

- **Tools to Add to Your Conflict Survival Kit:** Specific advice, activities, thought starters, challenges, and pointers to help you apply what you learn to real-world contexts

- **Performance Checklist:** Key points summarizing the basic content of the chapter

- **True/False and Multiple Choice:** Ten questions to test your knowledge

- **Discussion Questions:** Two to four focused questions on issues relevant to the chapter to encourage in-class discussion and reinforce learning

- **Personal Growth Exercises:** Additional optional activities and reflection exercises to help you continue your learning and application of concepts and skills beyond the classroom

- **To Learn More:** References and resources for individuals interested in exploring the chapter topic in greater depth

In addition, at the end of each chapter, *Conflict Survival Kit* includes a case or role-play to provide learners hands-on practice with handling conflict situations. Cases involve scenarios for class discussion, written assignments, or self-instruction. Role-plays are intended for use in the classroom or seminar. Specific instructions are provided for each. Role-plays can also be used as traditional case studies. Cases and role-plays are built around a number of roles in a fictitious company that are profiled at the end of the book. To receive the full benefit of these cases, become acquainted with this company and the characters before reading the cases. For many of the chapters, the case includes a section entitled, "Alternative Procedure for Online Learning Formats." Recognizing that many classes are taught either entirely or partially online, this section offers suggestions, when possible, for facilitating role-plays and case discussion through these alternative learning methods.

The second edition of *The Conflict Survival Kit* includes the following significant changes from the first edition:

- Additional discussion has been added to Chapter 1 (The Nature of Conflict) concerning the **imperative for managers and leaders to gain skills and competencies in managing conflict**.

- The discussion on preventing conflict at the organizational level in Chapter 2 (Preventing Conflict) has been expanded to include **insights on what managers and employees can do to prevent conflict at a personal level**.

- A section on **understanding cultural differences** in the interpersonal communication process has been added to Chapter 5 (The Three Channels of Communication).

- A section has been added to Chapter 13 (Mediating Conflicts between Parties) regarding the **distinctions between mediation of workplace conflicts and mediation of conflicts in more formal and legal settings**.

- **Principles of dialogue to encourage open communication** have been added to Chapter 14 (Decision-Making Choices for the Manager) to assist managers in facilitating collaborative and joint decision-making processes with employees.

- **Strategies for remaining calm and focused** have been added to Chapter 15 (Handling Conflicts Requiring Direct Confrontation) to assist managers in controlling their own emotions and tendencies to become reactive when confronting the negative and challenging behaviors of others.

- A section on **managing workplace bullying** has been added to Chapter 16 (Special Situations: "Opportunistic" Employees, Workplace Violence, Terminations, and Bullying).

- The section at the end of most chapters on "Alternate Procedures for Online Learning Formats," as noted above, is also new to the second edition. Users of the first edition will also notice that some of the end-of-chapter materials were formerly included in a separate student *Conflict Study Guide*. These include the true/false questions and personal growth exercises. As a result of this change, the *Conflict Study Guide* has been discontinued, as there is no longer a need for students to purchase this separate text.

Course instructors can request a *Conflict Survival Kit Instructor's Manual with Test Item File* by contacting their local Prentice Hall/Pearson representative or submitting a request on the Prentice Hall web site. PowerPoint slides outlining the key concepts and ideas from each chapter are also available.

Enjoy your journey as you learn about managing conflict in your organization and workplace. With knowledge and practice, you will develop mastery in managing conflict and do more than survive as a manager. You will thrive.

Special thanks to the reviewers, who provided helpful suggestions: Will Hodge, University of Alabama; Stacy Ball, Southwest Minnesota State University; Christina Wilson, T-Mobile USA, Issaquah, WA; and Mark A. Smedal, Smith & Helman, Philadelphia, PA.

DANIEL B. GRIFFITH, J.D., SPHR

Daniel Griffith is associate faculty within the Organizational Leadership and Supervision program at Purdue School of Engineering and Technology at Indiana University–Purdue University Indianapolis (IUPUI). In that role, he teaches courses in conflict management, leadership, and human resources. He is also manager of training and organization development at IUPUI. An attorney and mediator, he specializes in mediating employment, management, and higher education disputes and training lawyers, HR professionals, and managers in mediation, negotiation, and communication skills. He also facilitates workshops and provides consultation on conflict resolution and related topics for nonprofits, government agencies, colleges and universities, health institutions, HR professional associations, and other organizations. He previously worked for the state of Indiana as an attorney for the state's civil rights agency and as an attorney and administrative law judge for the state's transportation department.

Mr. Griffith holds a bachelor of arts degree in English from DePauw University and a doctorate of jurisprudence from Indiana University School of Law–Indianapolis.

CLIFF GOODWIN, ED.D.

Cliff Goodwin is on the faculty of the Purdue School of Engineering and Technology at Indiana University–Purdue University at Indianapolis (IUPUI). He teaches in the Organizational Leadership and Supervision program. His primary teaching emphasis is in the area of leadership skill development, sustainable leadership practices, and organizational longevity. In addition to his university work, Professor Goodwin has acted as a consultant to numerous businesses throughout Indiana. Prior to his university appointment, he was in management in the automotive manufacturing industry.

Professor Goodwin holds degrees from Purdue University and Ball State University in management and industrial training. He earned his doctorate of education at Indiana University.

Professor Goodwin and Mr. Griffith are also co-authors of *Supervisor's Survival Kit*, 11th ed., also published by Pearson Education, Inc.

To the man who only has a hammer in the toolkit, every problem looks like a nail.

Abraham Maslow

THE NATURE OF CONFLICT

PERFORMANCE COMPETENCIES

After you have finished reading this chapter, you will be able to

- Describe the general nature of conflict
- Describe the costs of unresolved conflicts in organizations and among individuals
- Articulate a definition of conflict
- Differentiate between *positional* and *interest-based* approaches to addressing conflict

When you think of conflict, what comes to mind? Imagine that you had a long day at work and everyone you encountered decided to grumble at you about something. Or imagine that you had an argument with someone with whom you are close. Are you thinking good thoughts? Do you really embrace the conflicts in your life?

If you are honest with yourself, the thought of conflict makes you uncomfortable. If the conflict is bad enough, you may wonder whether you are in the right job or whether you want to continue your relationship. The conflict may be making you feel tense. The tensions are manageable; you are not going to do anything drastic, but you know you will have to face the conflict eventually. You do not look forward to it.

What is it about the nature of conflict that often leaves people feeling tense and worried? Is conflict bad, or is there a healthier way to look at conflict and, therefore, a more positive approach to take?

I never did say that you can't be a nice guy and win. I said that if I was playing third base and my mother rounded third with the winning run, I'd trip her up.
Leo Durocher

How Does Conflict Affect Us?

When thinking about conflict, we often envision two or more parties holding mutually exclusive, wholly incompatible positions. Conflict is a contest of wills involving winners and losers. This win/lose paradigm pervades our culture and is so ingrained that it influences how we interact with one another. Consider some examples.

> When we think of conflict, we often think of winners and losers.

GLOBAL CONFLICT

Certain dates in history sear our national memory for their association with global conflict. December 7, 1941, when Japan attacked Pearl Harbor and triggered U.S. involvement in World War II, was aptly termed by President Franklin Roosevelt as "a date which will live in infamy."[1] The phrase "9/11" is all Americans need to hear to recall the tragic events of September 11, 2001 and the resulting so-called "War on Terrorism." Simple phrases capture our national conscience for their power in conveying sustained periods of global tension. For example, the phrase "Cold War," representing the U.S./Soviet Union build-up of nuclear armaments, triggers thoughts of a Titan clash of worldviews. These words provide powerful images and metaphors for classic pitched battles between the forces of good and the forces of evil. While we may be convinced that we stand on the side of good, our enemies are equally convinced that they stand on the side of what is good, just, and true.

POLITICS

Issues in politics are posed as choices between Republicans and Democrats, liberals and conservatives, fiscal responsibility and social awareness, pro-choice and pro-life, gun control and gun ownership, and on and on. Political partisans perpetuate this "either/or" thinking through their language. A socially progressive politician accuses a fiscal conservative's budget proposal as an "attack on the poor and middle class." An advocate for industry deregulation is cast as an "enemy of the environment." A pro-life advocate calls a pro-choice advocate "pro-abortion."

VISUAL MEDIA

The phenomenon of reality TV is rife with examples of cutthroat competitors vying to win a job, a performance contract, or even a spouse. On the sports channel, we expect winners and losers but don't always expect to see well-paid athletes behave like schoolyard bullies and brawl on the field of play. And in "sports" such as professional wrestling, spectators gleefully watch feigned brutality as one opponent bashes another. Children and adults play video games with which they can engage in virtual blood sport to defeat weaker opponents. Sadly, the thirst for visual imagery of violence doesn't end in virtual conflicts; it is not uncommon to find viral videos on the Web of actual school and street brawls that people have posted from their cell phones. Does it occur to them to try and stop the fight or call the police?

LAWSUITS

Lawyers advocate zealously for the interests of their clients against the interests of opposing parties. They use the fine art of persuasion and trial advocacy techniques to win their client's dispute at all costs. Even settlement negotiations can become contentious as lawyers posture and make arguments and counterarguments focused on winning as many concessions as possible from their opponent while conceding few.

NEIGHBORHOODS

If someone has been a little too noisy, has encroached on the property line, or owns a dog that barks late at night, a reasonable neighbor may call the police or animal control or, if things are not resolved, file a lawsuit. An angry neighbor may take more drastic measures. In our society today, many have become too busy to get to know their neighbors and deal directly with them to work through their disputes.

EMPLOYMENT

When managers lack the will to lead effectively and work collaboratively with the employees they manage, their solution to addressing employee conduct and performance concerns is to invoke discipline procedures, performance improvement plans, restrictive attendance policies, monitoring, and negative performance appraisals. Not surprisingly, employees counter with grievances, discrimination and harassment complaints, and lawsuits. The ensuing battle becomes costly, protracted, and inefficient and usually leaves both employer and employee dissatisfied.

DISCOURSE

Words become weapons. When discussing important issues, some are more intent on verbally attacking their opponent's positions than on engaging in thoughtful dialog. In the worst case, opponents become uncivil. They rant about whatever bothers them, stridently make their points, and vehemently discount their opponent's arguments. Openness and candor are risky. When feeling attacked, people become guarded and choose their words carefully lest their meaning be taken out of context and misconstrued.

SOCIAL MEDIA

Opportunity for dialogue is further put at risk when people engage in harmful personal attacks on others through social media. It is bad enough when individuals identify themselves when writing blog posts, text messages, and comments to other's blogs and write vitriol concerning a person or an opinion that offends them. It is quite another when they do so anonymously and feel all the more emboldened to slander others with hurtful comments.

RELATIONSHIPS

Many people have not learned effective means for constructively communicating through their conflicts. While professing love, they know how to hurt each other with cruel words and thoughtless argument. Two headstrong individuals will beat each other up with accusations and finger pointing. The more "mature" will simply stop talking and engage in passive-aggressive behaviors. At best, relationships endure despite dysfunction. At worst, we see divorce, abuse, and domestic violence.

> Many of us have not learned how to constructively communicate through our conflicts. While professing love, we know how to hurt each other with cruel words and thoughtless argument.

IS CONFLICT BAD?

When faced with conflict, we often respond in one of four ways that are not wholly constructive:

1. *Avoidance.* We avoid the conflict, either out of fear of confrontation or as a means of controlling the situation.

2. *Accommodation.* We concede arguments and issues to those with whom we are in conflict as a means of smoothing over our relationship, though often at the expense of satisfying our own needs and concerns.

3. *Competition.* We press to achieve our own goals in the conflict at the expense of having a positive relationship with the other party.

4. *Compromise.* Even when we face up to our conflicts, such as through negotiation, we often settle for compromise solutions. We give a little to get a little. Though this may be an appropriate strategy at times, it means that we end up only partly satisfied and, therefore, still somewhat dissatisfied.

While these responses can be appropriate under the right circumstances, they suggest our natural tendency to view conflict negatively. Yet, when viewed another way, the existence of conflict can serve as a positive indicator, signaling opportunities for change and growth.

A fifth and more constructive response to conflict is to *collaborate.* It is said that two heads are better than one, so when any two individuals engage in truly collaborative strategies, they are bound to realize improved communication and understanding, more creative solutions, increased productivity, and a healthier relationship. Through collaboration, individuals realize increased confidence in their ability to communicate, interact with others, and solve problems. By facing situations directly and maturely, rather than indirectly or not at all, their esteem grows. Teams encouraged to deal with conflict in this way experience improved morale and teamwork.

> The existence of conflict can serve as a positive indicator, signaling opportunities for change and growth.

Conflict, then, is neither good nor bad. In fact, it is often not the conflicts themselves or their root causes that bring so much consternation. Rather, it is the *perception* that conflicts are bad instead of opportunities for change and positive outcomes that leads to ineffective responses. And the more we engage in these responses, the more likely our conflicts may remain unsolved, further fueling our negative view.

Clearly, if we are to get a handle on our conflicts and realize positive resolutions, this view must change. Our conflicts will not go away, but our perceptions about them can change, and along with them, our responses.

> It is often our *perception* that conflicts are bad that leads to ineffective responses. The more we engage in these responses, the more likely our conflicts may remain unresolved, fueling our negative view.

A Deeper Look at Conflict

At its heart, conflict involves *competition* between two or more individuals or groups who have *incompatible interests* and who are *interdependent*. Let us examine this definition further:

> Conflict involves competition between two or more individuals or groups who have incompatible interests and who are interdependent.

- **Interdependent parties:** Each party in a conflict has needs that only the other party can satisfy. For example, an employee and her boss are interdependent. She has needs for income, job satisfaction, and other considerations that can be met only through her relationship with her boss. Her boss needs her to do certain work, which only she is available and capable to do. Conflict arises through their attempts to have their needs met. Without this mutual need, no conflict exists. If the employee finds a job that better meets her needs or her boss finds someone who will do the work if she will not, their interdependence ceases.

- **Incompatible interests:** Interests are the parties' wants, needs, values, and goals, which represent the source of the disagreement or conflict. It is why the parties are fighting. Conflict results from the belief by one or both parties that their interests are not compatible. If there are no incompatible interests—that is, the needs and wants of both parties are being met—there is no conflict because there is nothing to fight about. Put another way, each party perceives that his interests cannot be met except by exclusion of the other party's interests—more for you means less for me.

- **Competition:** Conflict occurs when one or more parties perceive that a need is threatened or that resources are insufficient to meet the need. This is often referred to as a "fixed pie" gambit in which parties perceive that there are finite pieces of pie available or, in other words, only a finite number of options that will satisfy the need. Conflict is thus seen as a "fight" as the parties compete to gain as many pieces of pie, or resources, for themselves and leave as few as possible for the other party.

In considering this definition, note that the existence of conflict is often based on perception, for it is often the belief that our interests are incompatible, rather than the reality, that sets the stage for conflict. What often causes conflicts to continue and escalate is this gap between what is *perceived* to be irreconcilable and what may be reconciled if the parties' perceptions about each other's interests can change. With the right approach, perhaps the parties can find common ground where their interests are not as irreconcilable as they first thought.

But what is the right approach? If parties have been in conflict for a long time over seemingly intractable issues, how will they come to realize they have many interests in common? How will a husband and wife, two neighbors, an employee and a supervisor, two coworkers, or two brothers realize they have less and less to fight about? The answer is both simple and complex: They must communicate.

A deeper look at any conflict usually reveals that the parties have legitimate underlying needs they want to express but have not found an effective means for doing so. If we dig deeper into why a husband and wife are not communicating and are on the verge of divorce, we uncover their underlying fears, hurts, and unfulfilled needs. If we can help each party understand the other's concerns—that is, take a proverbial walk in the other's shoes—we may see these concerns dissipate. As a manager, you may have to discipline an employee who lashes out in anger at you, but it may benefit you and the employee to first talk about what is driving such behavior. Is the employee suffering some personal loss or turmoil at home? Have you heard his cries of feeling overloaded and stressed? Does he feel threatened by recent organizational changes? As long as the employee is not intractable, asking the right questions and having the appropriate empathic response may save your relationship with the employee and begin the process of restoring him as a productive worker.

> How will parties with seemingly intractable issues come to realize they have many interests in common? They must communicate.

TWO APPROACHES TO ADDRESSING CONFLICT

Individuals generally take one of two distinct approaches to addressing conflict, which are referred to as *positional* and *interest based*.

POSITIONAL

In the positional approach, the parties, to varying degrees, treat the conflict as a contest of wills. They enter a conflict discussion with clear ideas of what they want to achieve and hold firm to these positions. An employee wants a salary increase of a certain amount and will leave if she does not receive it. The manager will pay only up to a certain amount in salary to keep the employee and not a penny more. If these amounts are incompatible, the lines are drawn. The positional approach does not take into consideration the underlying concerns, needs, or wants of the parties, which generally forecloses any examination on how the parties' positions might be reconciled. Rather, the parties lock into their positions. If resolution occurs, it is because the parties have weighed what they have to win against what they have to lose by not resolving the dispute rather than considering how each might achieve more by working together.

> When parties lock into positions, they do not consider each other's underlying concerns, needs, or wants, which generally forecloses any examination of how their positions might be reconciled.

The positional approach is the traditional model we have come to know and accept in our culture, which is not to say it is always the "wrong" approach. Indeed, accomplished lawyers, salespeople, and businesspeople have written eloquently on the subject. Look for titles such as *Negotiating to Win*, *Playing the Negotiation Game*, or *How to Negotiate What You Want in Life*, and you will learn from the experts on how to play the positional game to advantage. But it *is* game playing. You might take this approach if you are a customer wanting the best deal on a car or the salesperson wanting the best commission. In such circumstances, your relationship with the other party is superficial. However, do not expect positive outcomes if you use this strategy in your next argument with your spouse or coworker, where relationships matter greatly.

INTEREST BASED

The interest-based approach takes into consideration the underlying needs, wants, values, and goals of the parties. The seminal work on the interest-based model, also called *principle-centered negotiation*, is *Getting to Yes: Negotiating Agreement Without Giving In* by Roger Fisher, William Ury, and Bruce Patton.[2] The authors discuss the limits of the positional model and make the case that any meaningful conflict resolution must take into consideration the relationship between the parties with the view of preserving it, and perhaps even improving it. They set forth clear principles on which a negotiation should be judged. In addition to preserving or improving the relationship, any agreement should meet the legitimate interests of the parties, resolve conflicting interests fairly, be durable, and take the interests of others who may be affected by the agreement into account.[3] Fisher, Ury, and Patton argue that the interest-based approach is more efficient than the traditional positional model because it eliminates the associated game playing, time, and costs.

> Meaningful conflict resolution must take into consideration the relationship between the parties with the view of preserving it, and perhaps even improving it.

When relationships matter, focusing on interests rather than locking into positions makes sense. We value our relationships and, therefore, must consider both the short-term and long-term impacts of our agreements. We will not settle for agreements that may benefit our selfish interests in the short run if there are long-term consequences we would not like. Even our salesperson from the previous example may have a few things to learn using this approach. Does he badger, cajole, and manipulate the customer for the best price if it creates ill will in the process? Where will the customer purchase her next car? Will the customer return for service? While the savvy car dealer wants a sale, he values more a long-term relationship and the chance to sell the customer six cars over a lifetime, not just one. Even when positional bargaining appears to make sense, the positional bargainer often has an incentive for engaging in the interest-based approach.

The best methods for resolving conflict are generally those that focus on collaborative problem solving and meeting the interests and needs of all parties. Interest-based approaches hold the promise of resolving conflicts through less contentious, more amicable, and mutually satisfying means than positional approaches.

THE CHALLENGES, IMPERATIVES, AND GOOD NEWS ABOUT MANAGING CONFLICT

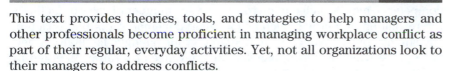

This text provides theories, tools, and strategies to help managers and other professionals become proficient in managing workplace conflict as part of their regular, everyday activities. Yet, not all organizations look to their managers to address conflicts.

Some organizations rely more on "professional" conflict management specialists operating within formal channels. In such organizations, many conflicts do not receive serious attention until some official action has been taken, such as the filing of a grievance, the initiation of a formal investigation of wrongdoing in violation of policy, or the filing of a complaint or lawsuit with a government agency or in court. Such matters are generally handled by human resources or labor relations specialists or by corporate counsel. Organizations operating in this mode tend to be reactive in their response to conflict and ignore or underutilize less formal mechanisms to resolve conflicts early on before they escalate. Such organizations would benefit from employing managers who are equipped to recognize conflict situations as they arise within their teams and empowered to resolve them.

Another reason some organizations do not fully recognize the need for managers who can effectively manage everyday conflict is their sluggishness in adopting new management practices for today's workforce. Management practice has experienced a significant paradigm shift through the late 20th and early 21st centuries. Earlier management models supported "command and control" practices whereby managers were expected simply to direct employees to behave in certain ways to achieve performance and production goals. Conflict resolution practices under this paradigm generally involve nothing more than ordering employees to "get along" and do not address the deeper emotional, social, or status needs of employees. Current management models contemplate these deeper needs and also recognize the change in how work is done. The economy continues to shift from an age of heavy industry wherein workers' "hands" were their principal asset to the current age of technology and information wherein workers' principal assets are their "heads" and the knowledge they bring to the job. Current management models call for managers to serve more as facilitators and team leaders who support employees at a more interpersonal level to guide them through communication challenges and conflicts. Accordingly, as described by Mark Gerzon in *Leading Through Conflict: How Successful Leaders Transform Differences into Opportunities*, the ideal managerial role has transformed from that of "demagogue," who harshly commands compliance through fear and intimidation, or generic "manager," who does not deal with conflict outside the boundaries of his self-interests or the interests of his team, to the role of "mediator":[4]

> [T]his model of leadership is able to turn conflict into a positive force for achieving our larger purposes. This kind of leader transforms conflict from a force that can be destructive and divisive into one that is healing and connecting. Since we human beings urgently need to make conflict work for *us* rather than *against* us, those who can lead through conflict hold the key.[5]

There is a clear need for informal, internal conflict resolution specialists who serve in such roles as part of their regular duties. Any leader, manager, or professional in the organization who demonstrates appropriate competence may be called upon to assume any number of roles to facilitate the resolution of conflict, such as managerial mediator, conflict coach or advisor, meeting convener, peer mediator, group dialogue facilitator, grievance peer review or appeal panelist, or grievance arbitrator. As noted by William Ury in *The Third Side*:

> Inside many organizations, facilitators are working with cross-functional teams to overcome interdepartmental issues. Managers are learning to mediate among their teammates, their employees, and often their multiple bosses. The success of a company is coming to depend on the ability of its people to resolve the innumerable conflicts that crop up between manufacturing and marketing, sales and headquarters, employees and supervisors, and to seek a "triple win"—a solution good for each side and for the company as a whole.[6]

This is good news. The aspiring manager who demonstrates effective conflict management skills and competencies has a "leg up" for hiring or advancement opportunities over managers who lack such skills or competencies.

As you explore the issue of conflict and how to address conflicts as a manager, realize that you are fully capable of learning and mastering the concepts, tools, and strategies necessary to effectively manage conflict in your organization. The same positive conflict resolution techniques used by the professional are accessible to any individual dealing with conflict. Developing the mastery to manage conflict will result in more effective and positive working and personal relationships and will build confidence. With the proper tools and the attitude that conflicts are imminently resolvable, you will survive and thrive in conflict situations. With the right mindset that conflict is not bad but rather presents opportunities for change and growth, you will find your efforts at managing conflict within your organization to be both challenging and rewarding.

Managers today are expected to serve in a mediator role and actively engage in efforts to resolve conflicts among employees, within teams, cross-functionally within the organization, and through external negotiations on behalf of the organization.

PERFORMANCE CHECKLIST

- If we are honest with ourselves, we will admit that we often view conflict negatively and most conflict situations as win/lose battles between adversaries who hold incompatible positions.

- The win/lose paradigm pervades our culture and is so ingrained that it influences how we interact with one another.

- Many people have not learned effective means for constructively communicating through their conflicts, leading to detrimental costs to working relationships, marriages, families, and communities.

- Conflict involves the perceived incompatibility of interests between two or more individuals or groups who are interdependent.

- Conflict is neither good nor bad, but our perception often makes conflict seem bad.

- Individuals take two distinct approaches to address conflict, referred to as positional and interest based.

- With positional approaches, the parties enter a conflict discussion with clear ideas of what they want and hold firm to these positions without taking into consideration each other's underlying interests.

- Outcomes based on positional approaches are generally not based on clear communication or concern for the parties' relationship, but rather they are more strictly based on a weighing of what the parties have to win against what they have to lose by not resolving the dispute.

- Interest-based approaches for resolving conflict place a value on clear communication and on preserving or improving the parties' relationships. They focus on durable outcomes that meet both parties' legitimate interests and resolve conflicting interests fairly.

- New management paradigms call for informal, internal conflict resolution specialists who serve in such roles as part of their regular duties. Any leader, manager, or professional in the organization who demonstrates appropriate competence may be called upon to assume any number of roles to facilitate the resolution of conflict.

TEST YOURSELF

True/False

For each statement below, check true or false.

TRUE   FALSE

_____   _____   1. When discussing important issues, some are more intent on verbally attacking their opponent's positions than on engaging in thoughtful debate.

_____   _____   2. The existence of conflict can never really serve as a positive indicator, signaling opportunities for change and growth.

_____   _____   3. At its heart, conflict involves competition between two or more individuals or groups who have incompatible interests and who are interdependent.

_____   _____   4. Individuals generally take one of two distinct approaches to addressing conflict, which are referred to as situational and interest based.

_____   _____   5. In the interest-based approach, the parties, to varying degrees, treat the conflict as a contest of wills.

MULTIPLE CHOICE

Circle the letter next to the best answer for each question. On a separate sheet of paper, state why you chose that answer.

1. Which response to handling conflict provides the *best possibility* for achieving a win/win outcome?

a. compromise

b. compete

c. avoid

d. collaborate

e. accommodate

2. Which statement is *most accurate*? Conflict is not bad, but
   a. our experiences cause us to often view conflict as bad and, therefore, avoid it.
   b. we should try to avoid engaging in conflict, especially with people we don't like.
   c. the world is a hostile place and we must try not to cause others to dislike us.
   d. it is best to act as though conflict is bad to protect ourselves.

3. The term *positional* refers to
   a. a technique used by a skilled negotiator to indicate that she is holding firm to her "position."
   b. the mind-set that conflicts involve a contest of wills rather than collaboration.
   c. negotiations in which the parties hold to narrow positions with little room for compromise.
   d. principle-centered approaches to addressing conflict.
   e. all the above.
   f. a, b, and c.
   g. a, b, and d.
   h. b and c.
   i. c and d.

4. Of the relationships and scenarios that follow, which *best exemplifies* a positional approach to addressing conflict?
   a. A husband and wife negotiating who will pick up their three-year-old from child care and who will fix dinner.
   b. A supervisor and an employee exploring options for the best way to accomplish a project.
   c. A used car salesperson and a prospective buyer making offers and counteroffers regarding the price of a used car.
   d. A mother asking her teenage daughter why she will be coming home after 11:00 p.m.

5. All the following are important aspects of *interest-based* approaches to addressing conflicts *except*
   a. open communication.
   b. consideration of needs and interests.
   c. game playing.
   d. concern for relationship.

DISCUSSION QUESTIONS

1. Think of a conflict you have had recently or that you observed among others that you think was resolved in a positive manner. Next, think of a conflict you have had or observed that did not resolve positively. What was the difference? Compare and contrast the characteristics that led to a positive resolution in one situation and a negative or no resolution in the other situation.

2. Some experienced negotiators believe that interest-based negotiation is not appropriate or useful and prefer to engage in positional negotiation strategies for most situations. Do you agree or disagree? In what situations would positional negotiation be appropriate?

3. The authors have provided examples of how society perpetuates a win/lose mentality in numerous fields of endeavor. However, society also offers examples in which the win/win mentality is more prevalent. What examples of the latter can you identify in your work, neighborhood, or community?

Recently, Joe Newcomer witnessed a squabble between a customer and one of the customer service representatives, Tina. The customer, Maria, was attempting to return what she claimed was a defective belt sander. She claimed the sander caused a serious abrasion to her husband's arm, resulting in a trip to the emergency room. There is no question that Tina was rude to Maria in her response. Not only did she curtly refuse to honor the return, claiming the return was beyond the 30-day "no questions asked" return policy, but she suggested that perhaps Maria's husband hadn't appropriately followed the directions. Specifically, she asked whether her husband could read English. Maria angrily responded that although she and her husband are Latino, they are U.S. citizens and fluent in English.

When Joe overheard this exchange, he walked up to the return counter and asked Tina to assist another customer. He then offered to assist Maria. Joe had a dilemma. Though he knew Maria had been wronged by Tina's conduct and offensive comment, he had to agree with Tina that the sander probably was not defective and that the return policy could not be honored. Joe was unsure how he should handle this situation. In an ideal world, he hoped he could restore Maria's goodwill while holding firm on the store's policy by refusing the return.

Case Questions

Should Joe take a positional bargaining approach by apologizing for the rudeness and inconvenience but holding firm on the store's policy? Or should he seek a win/win by accepting the return, even though it goes against store policy, in exchange for restoring Maria's goodwill and the hope of gaining repeat business? Is there a third approach?

Which approach would you use? Why? If you select an alternative approach or a combination of the two, defend your position.

Think about the conflicts you have had with others in the past year. For the most part, did you take a positional or an interest-based approach to addressing them? Was your tendency to avoid, accommodate, compete, compromise, or collaborate? Were you satisfied with the outcomes of these conflicts?

If you were not satisfied with the way these conflicts were resolved, think about how they might have turned out differently had you taken a more interest-based, collaborative approach to resolving them.

Write down the specific behaviors and skills you think you need to develop to be a better conflict manager. Further, write down your vision of a successful resolution to a conflict in general. Carry forward these thoughts and ideas as you read the remainder of the text and engage in the activities and discussions.

The following texts provide discussion of the definition, nature, and costs of conflict:

Budjac Corvette, Barbara A. *Conflict Management: A Practical Guide to Developing Negotiation Strategies.* Upper Saddle River, NJ: Pearson Education, Inc., 2007.

Dana, Daniel. *Conflict Resolution: Mediation Tools for Everyday Worklife.* New York: McGraw-Hill, 2001.

Levine, Stewart. *Getting to Resolution: Turning Conflict into Collaboration*. San Francisco: Berrett-Koehler Publishers, 1998.

Masters, Marick F., and Robert R. Albright. *The Complete Guide to Conflict Resolution in the Workplace*. New York: American Management Association, 2002.

Mayer, Bernard. *The Dynamics of Conflict Resolution: A Practitioner's Guide*. San Francisco: Jossey-Bass, 2000.

Tjosvold, Dean. *Learning to Manage Conflict: Getting People to Work Together Productively*. New York: Lexington Books, 1993.

Ury, William. *The Third Side: Why We Fight and How We Can Stop*. New York: Penguin Books, 2000.

Van Slyke, Erik J. *Listening to Conflict: Finding Constructive Solutions to Workplace Disputes*. New York: American Management Association, 1999.

The following texts provide discussion on the shift in management paradigms from an Industrial Age model to an Information Age model:

Covey, Stephen R. *The 8th Habit: From Effectiveness to Greatness*. New York: Free Press, 2004.

Drucker, Peter F. *Managing in the Next Society*. New York: St. Martin's Press, 2002.

NOTES

1. Franklin D. Roosevelt, Speech to the U.S. Congress on December 8th, 1941, http://www.pearlharbor.org/speech-fdr-infamy-1941.asp (accessed May 31, 2011).

2. Roger Fisher, William Ury, and Bruce Patton, *Getting to Yes: Negotiating Agreement Without Giving In*, 2nd ed. (New York: Penguin Books, 1991).

3. Ibid., 4.

4. Mark Gerzon, *Leading Through Conflict: How Successful Leaders Transform Differences into Opportunities* (Boston: Harvard Business School Press, 2006), 17–58.

5. Ibid., 50; emphasis in original.

6. William Ury, *The Third Side: Why We Fight and How We Can Stop* (New York: Penguin Books, 2000), 10.

THE THEORY AND CONTEXT FOR MANAGING CONFLICT IN THE WORKPLACE

Any jackass can kick a barn door, but it takes a carpenter to build it.
Sam Rayburn

PREVENTING CONFLICT

PERFORMANCE COMPETENCIES

After you have finished reading this chapter, you will be able to

- Describe the ideal environment for reducing the presence of conflict in the workplace

- Identify the signs of evolving conflicts

- Analyze conflicts and the level of response needed using a simple framework for knowing when to intervene

- Identify personal triggers to conflict and consider approaches for managing them

Managing conflict effectively begins long before conflict surfaces. It is naïve to take a wait-and-see mind-set about conflict, hoping conflict will not erupt in the work environment. In reality, it is not a matter of *if* conflict will occur, but *when*. And when conflict occurs, you must learn how to manage it and minimize its effects. The goal is to prevent conflict when you can and to contain it when prevention is not possible.

CREATING AND MAINTAINING AN ENVIRONMENT OF REDUCED CONFLICT

> Remove the environmental conditions that make people believe they have no alternative but to react negatively and you will remove the need to react.

Conflict cannot be avoided in every circumstance, but you can take proactive measures to diminish its presence. Conflict often occurs when conditions are created or allowed to fester in an environment in which people feel they have no reasonable alternatives but to react negatively, perhaps even belligerently. While such responses may not be justified, understanding the conditions that precipitate them helps explain the behavior. Remove the conditions and you will likely remove a person's need to react.

We've learned how to destroy, but not to create; how to waste, but not to build; how to kill men, but not how to save them; how to die, but seldom how to live.

Omar Bradley

MEETING BASIC HUMAN NEEDS

The battle for preventing or containing conflict lies first in our efforts as managers to ensure that our employees' basic human needs are met. Two well-known behavioral theorists provide insight into how to focus these efforts.

Frederick Herzberg observed in his *hygiene-motivation theory*[1] that when employees are dissatisfied with their work, they are mostly concerned about the environmental conditions. He refers to these conditions as *hygiene* (or *maintenance*) factors, which include policies and administration, supervision, working conditions, interpersonal relationships, money, status, and security. Herzberg found that these factors do not motivate employees to be more productive, but their absence can adversely affect productivity and motivation. Take them away and you risk de-motivating employees and fostering conditions for conflict.

Abraham Maslow postulated in his *hierarchy of needs theory* that an individual's most basic needs must first be met before he or she will spend significant time pursuing higher aspirations.[2] Thus, an individual will first pursue the fulfillment of *physiological* (or *survival*) needs, and then other needs in ascending order in the hierarchy (Exhibit 2-1).

In addition to physiological needs, the most basic human needs are for *safety and security* and *acceptance*. In the work environment, safety and security needs include environmentally safe working conditions; interpersonal relations that are free from threatening, violent, or harassing behaviors; and conditions that foster job security, reduced stress, and supportive managerial relationships. Acceptance needs include opportunities to foster relationships, engage in social interactions, and be part of a team. Similar to Herzberg's hygiene factors, if an employee is unsuccessful in fulfilling these needs in the workplace, then conditions are favorable for creating conflict.

PROVIDING MEANINGFUL WORK

Fulfilling employees' basic human needs will go a long way in preventing or reducing conflict. A second, higher goal to minimize conflict is to provide employees intrinsically valuable and meaningful work.

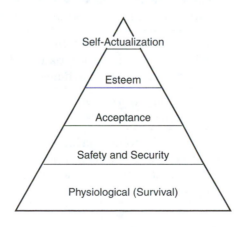

EXHIBIT 2-1
Maslow's hierarchy of needs (*Source*: Maslow, A; Frager, R., Motivation and Personality, © 1987. Adapted by permission of Pearson Education, Inc., Upper Saddle River, New Jersey)

The second part of Herzberg's hygiene-motivation theory involves *motivation* factors. Whereas providing the appropriate working conditions and environment keeps employees from becoming dissatisfied in their jobs, true motivation comes from factors relating to the work itself. That is, employees are motivated to increase productivity when they find intrinsic value in their jobs. Such motivators include achievement, recognition for accomplishment, challenging work, increased responsibility, and growth and development.

In the work context, the higher levels on Maslow's hierarchy of needs also relate to the needs that employees have for meaningful work. *Esteem* needs relate to an employee's need for challenging assignments, variety, professional development, career growth, autonomy, and recognition. *Self-actualization* refers to the opportunity to grow and develop to the fullest extent possible and to fulfill one's potential. An employee's need for self-actualization often transcends needs for money and status to foster a desire to seek personal and professional challenges inside and outside the organization.

The more an employer can help its employees find meaning and value in their work, the more it will realize a motivated workforce, increased productivity, and reduced conflict. Exhibit 2-2 offers a checklist to assess your workplace environment.

EXHIBIT 2-2
Work environment checklist

The following is a nonexclusive list of items for you to consider with respect to meeting basic human needs and providing meaningful work within your organization.

For each item, place a check (✓) under the column that applies for your organization. A check (✓) in the *yes* column means that your organization at a minimum meets the need to a satisfactory level so that it does not generally lead to conflict. If you cannot check *yes* with this level of confidence, place a check (✓) in the column for *yes, but needs improvement*. If your organization does not meet the need at all, place a check (✓) in the *no* column.

My organization:	Yes	Yes, but needs improvement	No
Provides pay and benefits that are competitive			
Supports employees' "creature comforts" while at work (e.g., appropriate facilities, break times, vending machines)			
Provides safe work environments (e.g., at a minimum, meets relevant OSHA standards)			
Has policies prohibiting harassment, violence, and other inappropriate conduct; enforces these policies; and supports employees when they have been victimized			

My organization:	Yes	Yes, but needs improvement	No
Provides employees avenues for redress when they believe they have been unfairly treated or disciplined			
Provides employees with a clear understanding of job duties and expectations, their role within the organization, and other support that gives them a sense of job stability and belonging			
Provides employees consistent and timely feedback, recognition, and praise			
Helps employees manage stress and provides avenues to seek help, such as an employee assistance program			
Encourages collegiality and teamwork			
Provides employees opportunities to socialize and form relationships			
Uses a participative management style where employees feel included in decisions that affect them			
Values inclusiveness, respects differences, and provides a welcoming culture			
Provides challenging work, variety in job assignments, and the chance to reach for higher personal and organizational goals			
Delegates responsibilities to employees so that they feel entrusted to manage their work and the methods for accomplishing tasks without being micromanaged or ignored			
Provides employees appropriate training and professional development opportunities			
Has systems in place for recognizing and rewarding accomplishment			
Provides coaching, mentoring, and other support to help employees achieve their potential to the fullest extent possible within the organization			
Respects and supports employees' need to balance the demands of their job with their need to enjoy a family life, meet personal and family obligations, engage in community and volunteer activities, and seek spiritual fulfillment			

EXHIBIT 2–2
Work environment checklist
Continued

EXHIBIT 2-2
Work environment checklist
Continued

After you have completed all items, consider what your responses mean with respect to your organization's success at meeting basic human needs and providing meaningful work. Further, consider any items not on this list that you feel also need attention in your organization. Then, consider what steps you can take to help the organization improve in these areas.

In some cases, you may feel there is nothing you can do because the conditions are the result of institutional and business challenges that extend beyond what you can affect in your work area or among the staff you manage. The intent of this overview is neither to overwhelm you nor to suggest that such factors are within your complete control. This overview merely provides a snapshot of your workplace.

You must decide whether there are measures you can take to address these issues. Can you work with other managers and staff to improve some areas? Are there ways to increase dialogue within the organization to focus on certain issues that have not previously received attention? Think creatively, yet be realistic. If you have identified situations that concern you and are beyond your control, you must decide the extent to which the concern is serious enough that you can no longer in good conscience continue working for the organization. Some circumstances may merely require patience as the organization gradually works to correct them. Other circumstances, such as serious problems with workplace safety, violence, or harassment, may present moral and ethical challenges that you are no longer willing to face. It is important to have a realistic assessment about your organization's effectiveness in preventing and managing conflict. The resulting choices you must make will not always be easy.

PAYING ATTENTION TO EVOLVING CONFLICTS

Conflicts evolve when individuals' needs have not been met or when interests are threatened. Individuals then attempt to satisfy the need or remove the threat. If they are successful, the potential for conflict lessens. If they are unsuccessful, this potential increases. Creating and maintaining a positive work environment by addressing needs is a baseline standard that organizations should adopt to lessen the potential for conflict. Many conflicts simply will not evolve because employees' basic needs are being adequately addressed.

Yet creating and maintaining such environments will not ensure against all conflict. Conflict is inevitable even in the most progressive environment. If it cannot be eliminated altogether, conflict can be contained. This involves two considerations: (1) look for triggers to evolving conflict and (2) respond appropriately before conflict escalates.

> If conflict cannot be eliminated altogether in the environment, it can be contained.

LOOK FOR TRIGGERS...

Conflict may evolve from multiple sources, or triggers, within an organization, and it is important to understand them before you can begin to tackle them:

Triggers over roles, goals, policies, and procedures occur when

- The roles individuals play within a team come into conflict, such as when employees appear to be working at cross-purposes

PART I: The Theory and Context for Managing Conflict

or when an employee's efforts run contrary to team goals and expectations.

- Changes in organizational or team policies, procedures, and expectations threaten personal interests, including deeply held emotional and psychological needs for security, acceptance, or respect.
- Employees disagree with the goals of their team or the organization and their responsibilities for fulfilling them.
- Employees do not trust the roles, goals, and expectations laid out for them and ask, "How does this impact me?" or "What's in it for me?"

Triggers over information occur when

- Individuals do not have the information they believe they need to do their jobs, believe the information is not accurate, or believe information is being withheld.
- Misunderstandings arise about the information provided, such as when the information has not been effectively communicated.
- Individuals receive the appropriate information or data but interpret it differently, disagree on its relevance or validity, or disagree on the impact of the information on their interests.

Triggers over relationships occur as the result of

- Individuals' ability, comfort, and effectiveness (or lack thereof) in communicating and interacting with others, especially with individuals who are different from themselves.
- Perceptions, filters, and biases based on differences in experience, background, culture, and other factors.
- Specific differences involving race, ethnicity, gender, age, religion, and sexual orientation as well as differences in personality; the way people communicate, learn, and work; social and economic status; job classification and duties; and a host of other factors.

Triggers over values occur as the result of

- Different values placed on work and the importance of work, such as the contrast between those who find intrinsic value in work and those who value work because it furthers other interests, such as the need to make a living or the desire to make more money.
- Different values concerning certain aspects of work, such as the importance of getting to work on time, participating in meetings, and working on a team in contrast to working alone.
- Different values concerning management authority, with some deferring to authority without question and others willing to challenge authority when they do not understand management expectations.
- Different values concerning the way individuals evaluate ideas or behaviors. For example:
  - Some are open to differing viewpoints while others are more rigid.
  - Some are tolerant of quirks and odd behaviors, while others are less tolerant.

- Differing values concerning lifestyle choices, ideology, politics, religion, and other deeply held beliefs and practices.

Triggers over structures occur when

- Structures in place for fulfilling the organization's business purpose and the means for doing so are not realistic, causing employees to feel time pressures, work overload, and stress.
- Power imbalances or an inequitable distribution of power and authority exists, causing others to feel disenfranchised and powerless.
- Employees do not have the degree of control they would like over their work and decisions impacting their work. This can occur when

  - Individuals would like more control, but management either disallows this control or minimizes it.
  - Management wants employees to exercise more control, but organizational and management structures create disincentives for doing so.

- Employees proceed with a "business as usual" mentality while more logical, effective, or innovative ways of doing things are never considered.

TOOLS TO ADD TO YOUR CONFLICT SURVIVAL KIT

To identify triggers, you must be sensitive to any suggestion that conflict may occur in the environment and proactively address any incident or situation that may potentially lead to greater conflict. This means

- Know the day-to-day happenings in your organization. Make a point of connecting with employees on a regular basis about what is happening.
- When a change has been implemented, openly communicate it and stand ready to respond to any reactions and concerns individuals may express.
- When you sense that a personal or organizational issue may cause a rift, offer your support up front rather than wait to see what happens.
- Be sensitive to individuals who are experiencing difficulties in their personal lives or working relationships and offer to help.
- Do not overlook customers. Stay in touch with customer needs and concerns about any product or service and respond quickly to any complaints.

> You must be sensitive to any suggestion that conflict may occur in the environment and proactively address any incident or situation that may potentially lead to greater conflict.

. . . THEN, RESPOND APPROPRIATELY

If you have done your homework, it becomes less of a guessing game to know when conflict is developing. But is a response always appropriate? Before addressing the question of *how* to respond to conflict, the first question is whether a response is warranted and, if so, *when*.

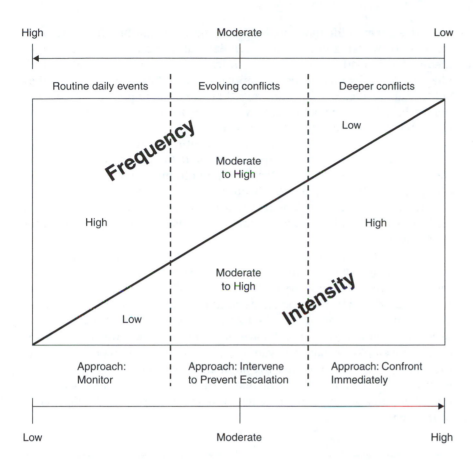

EXHIBIT 2-3
Routine daily events, evolving
conflicts, and deeper conflicts

Let us categorize the organizational conflicts you may encounter into three distinct stages. These stages are depicted in Exhibit 2-3.

This diagram provides a useful framework for thinking about conflicts in your organization. Numerous situations command your daily attention. Some situations require only that you monitor them in the event they evolve into greater conflicts. Other situations have increased in intensity and require you to intervene at some level so that they do not escalate into deeper conflicts. Conflicts at this level may or may not be within your competence to handle and may require assistance from others or may require a different response such as ending the employment relationship.

As depicted in this diagram, your response will depend on the level of intensity of the situations requiring your attention. Further, under normal organizational conditions when effective management and a positive work environment exist, more day-to-day activities will involve monitoring rather than direct intervention. Conversely, fewer situations should require your intervention either to prevent further escalation or to respond to conflicts that have fully evolved.

ROUTINE DAILY EVENTS (MONITOR STAGE)

Parties at this stage are in disagreement but are maintaining their relationship and appear to be working out their situation, at least for the moment. This is the most prevalent form of conflict in an organization.

Individuals experiencing routine daily conflicts are often
engaged in lively discussion and
are challenging one another to
achieve more creative solutions.

It is a fact of life that people "bump" into one another. It is part of the richness of working in a vibrant organization. Conflict at this level often means that individuals are engaged in lively discussion or debate and are challenging each other to achieve more creative solutions than either might achieve alone. It can be a healthy sign that two or more people with distinct personalities and viewpoints are trying to reconcile their positions so they can achieve outcomes that all can accept.

The best approach is to monitor the situation in the event the conflict escalates. If the parties are mature and the disagreement causing the conflict is manageable, there is no need to intervene. Even when the disagreement becomes a little heated, this does not necessarily mean that the parties are experiencing great turmoil. They may simply be passionate about their issues and attempting to make each other understand their views.

As a supervisor, you must be careful when either party comes to you for assistance regarding their issue. Empowering individuals to address their own situations is always preferable. This allows them to take personal ownership of the situation and builds confidence as they experience success. While you might offer advice, such as your opinion on the feasibility of a proposed solution, you should leave ultimate resolution for the parties to decide. An employee may also want you to intervene for him or her. Perhaps the employee lacks confidence to handle the situation and is looking for an easy way out. You might offer advice on how to better communicate with the other party but encourage the individual to address the situation on his or her own.

EVOLVING CONFLICTS (INTERVENTION STAGE)

Evolving conflicts may require some form of intervention to prevent the situation from escalating. Perhaps it is a routine matter that has gained steam and may soon be beyond the parties' control to handle, at least in a mature fashion. Or perhaps the conflict evolved so quickly that there was no opportunity to monitor the situation beforehand.

Someone at this state may be complaining about the situation but not attempting to address the individual with whom she is in conflict. These two people at this stage may be playing little games such as avoiding each other. Perhaps they are bickering or talking behind each other's back. They may have been working well together but suddenly are tense and aggravated when working together. Communication is breaking down. An employee may display a lot of nonverbal cues such as an angry or frustrated look, crossed arms, a red face, or walking away without saying anything but appearing upset. Symptoms such as these may indicate that a larger conflict may soon erupt.

On the other hand, conflict at this stage presents your best opportunity to step in and possibly eliminate the conflict or at least keep it from escalating. For example, before an employee's behavior worsens and requires discipline, counsel the employee on his behavior and the consequences for similar behaviors in the future. Offer support to address any personal issues that may be contributing to the problem. Before you lose a customer who may then complain to friends, recognize the issues that are distressing her and attempt to resolve them equitably. And before communication completely breaks down between two employees, jump in to help them understand each other's concerns.

DEEPER CONFLICTS (CONFRONTATION STAGE)

Deeper conflicts are those that have escalated. The triggers have been pulled, and the battle has ensued. Such conflicts may or may not have been avoided through a proactive approach. Fewer of these conflicts should occur than those in the other stages precisely because you have been proactive and because it is in the parties' best interests to settle issues before they get out of hand. Still, not all conflicts can be avoided despite your best efforts, and some form of intervention will be necessary.

> When a conflict has escalated, you must decide whether you are capable of addressing the situation, whether you need outside assistance, or whether the situation is beyond repair requiring corrective discipline or termination for the employee or employees involved.

At this stage, meaningful communication and any hope that the parties can reconcile without help have broken down. If matters do not resolve, the consequences to the individuals and the organization can be costly. While workplace violence is an extreme yet possible outcome, loss of productivity, lowered morale, dysfunctional relationships, team disunity, and general employee turmoil and discontent are among the more common ills.

Your ability to handle conflicts at this stage is based on your skills in conflict resolution, your familiarity with the issues and parties involved, and your knowledge and expertise with underlying substantive and technical matters. Based on your skills and confidence in your abilities, you will need to decide whether you are the appropriate individual to intervene. Some situations may require a more experienced colleague, a qualified human resources (HR) representative, or perhaps an outside mediator. Yet, recognize that some situations may be beyond repair. Better to pursue formal measures such as corrective discipline or termination if the employee or employees involved remain unwilling to change their behaviors than to endlessly hope matters will improve.

CATEGORIZING CONFLICTS IS HELPFUL

The categorization of conflicts into these stages provides a framework whereby the conflict manager can triage conflicts in the organization, much like a patient receiving triage prior to surgery. The triage is simple:

- Routine daily events can wait.
- Evolving conflicts require preventative action.
- Deeper conflicts require immediate attention.

TOOLS TO ADD TO YOUR CONFLICT SURVIVAL KIT

As a manager, consider the following strategies and activities for preventing conflict in your organization:

- Perform an audit of the potential for conflict in your work environment. Using the motivational needs and conflict triggers identified previously, create checklists, employee satisfaction questionnaires, climate surveys, or other instruments that cover the broad scope of potential concerns for conflict applicable to your area. Work with other managers and the human resources department to develop the appropriate tool, assess the data obtained, and implement changes accordingly.

- Develop close relationships with all staff. Get to know them on a personal level, without being intrusive or violating their privacy, to identify their emotional and motivational needs, as well as the concerns, circumstances, and "quirks" that may trigger conflict. Be unconditionally supportive in seeking to address their legitimate needs. If in doubt about a particular need or situation that is troubling them, do not make assumptions—ask.

PREVENTING CONFLICT AT A PERSONAL LEVEL

Discussion to this point has focused on measures organizations can take to minimize the conditions that lead to harmful conflict and to respond appropriately when conflicts arise. But what can individuals do to prevent conflict at a personal level? What are the triggers and what are the appropriate responses?

At the most fundamental level, the trigger that initiates a conflict is simply an event that an individual perceives negatively to which he then reacts negatively. The basic theory to explain this is "stimulus and response," in which the individual's negative reaction can be explained and justified as the natural, predetermined response any individual would make under the circumstances. When a coworker makes a rude comment, the individual is justified in making a rude comment in return. When a boss puts a stack of work on an employee's desk toward the end of the day, the employee is justified in bad mouthing his boss with his friend whom he calls to cancel dinner reservations because his boss is "forcing" him to stay late. When we hear someone justifying his bad actions with comments like "you would have done just as I did if you were in my shoes" or "I had no choice but to yell back at him when he said that to me," he is adopting the mindset that his actions were justified and beyond his control.

In *The Seven Habits of Highly Effective People*, Stephen Covey notes in his discussion of Habit 1, "be proactive," that the response we have to stimuli is not as predetermined as we may want to believe. Instead, we have the "freedom to choose" our response.[3] To be proactive rather than reactive, we can reflect on the stimulus we received and choose a more mature, reasoned response. When hurt by a rude comment, we can refuse to be baited and avoid responding in a similar fashion. Instead, either we can attempt to maturely address the concern with our coworker, noting that the comment was offensive and hurtful, or we can walk away. When our boss puts work on our desk at the end of the day, we can inquire about when it is due or remind her that we had an evening appointment. We can negotiate an early morning due date and come in early the next day. Even if we must stay late, we can refrain from bad mouthing our boss simply because it does no good to complain and allow our anger to fester.

This change in response from reactive to proactive is easier said than done. When an unwelcome stimulus causes concern, it is natural to experience angry or upset feelings. Our emotions get the best of us, causing

PART I: The Theory and Context for Managing Conflict

us to believe we really had no choice after all in how we responded. One explanation for this is the "fight or flight" response. The natural tendency in both humans and animals is to either flee from a threat or danger or stay and fight in order to overcome the threat or danger. These responses are instinctual "gifts" of evolution ensuring our survival. Because they are instinctual, the same protective responses that keep us from physical harm are triggered to protect us in civil society from threats of psychological or emotional harm. Fight responses in conflict situations are aggressive behaviors such as arguing, belligerence, and raised voices, while flight responses are passive or dismissive behaviors such as avoidance and withdrawal.

In conflict situations, we may always feel strong emotions that tempt us to engage in fight or flight. However, through development of appropriate skills and strategies, and consistent practice, we can better manage our responses. Responding proactively is one means for doing this. In addition, the authors of *Crucial Conversations: Tools for Talking When Stakes Are High* discuss numerous strategies for managing the fight or flight tendency, focusing on a model that encourages individuals to remain in dialogue by thinking through their emotions and potential responses when confronting others and by approaching others about difficult issues in ways that will minimize their defensiveness and keep them from fight or flight.[4] Finally, many of the skills needed to manage fight or flight are also skills needed for emotional intelligence. As popularized by Daniel Goleman, some of the key competencies of emotional intelligence involve appropriately managing our emotions when communicating with others and appropriately managing our responses when dealing with the strong emotions of others.[5]

> You can reduce conflict at a personal level if you acknowledge your innate potential for reacting negatively to displeasing events and choose instead proactive responses that help keep personal triggers in check.

This text provides numerous skills and strategies that will assist you in managing emotional responses during conflict in various contexts. The lesson for now is to recognize that we can play a role at a fundamental level in preventing harmful conflicts from evolving and escalating by (1) acknowledging our innate potential for responding negatively to displeasing events in ways that contribute to the escalation of conflict and (2) choosing proactive responses that keep these triggers in check.

PERFORMANCE CHECKLIST

- To prevent conflict in the workplace, you must create conditions in which employees' needs for a safe, supportive, and accepting work environment are met and they can pursue meaningful work.

- By understanding what motivates employees, you can assess their needs and create favorable conditions that will minimize the likelihood of conflict.

- To prevent conflict, you must also look for its potential causes, or triggers, among individuals and within the environment and seek to address the underlying concerns.

- Triggers occur as the result of problems in communication and the sharing of information; difficulties in work relationships; differences in values; structural or organizational barriers; or struggles with roles, goals, policies, and procedures.

- When there is an evolving conflict, you must determine whether intervention is necessary by triaging conflict situations.

  - Individuals may disagree with one another but are able to maintain their relationship and work out their problem. These routine daily events can often lead to positive results such as improved relationships, productivity, and innovation. They do not generally require intervention but should be monitored in case the situation escalates.

  - Evolving conflicts could lead to greater problems if not addressed. They present the best opportunity to help parties resolve disputes before they get out of hand.

  - Deeper conflict develops when matters are ignored, allowed to fester, or have escalated so quickly that earlier intervention was not possible. They require deliberate and immediate action. As a manager, you must assess whether you have the skills to address the situation or need the assistance of others, such as a mediator or qualified HR professional. Some situations may be beyond repair and may require corrective discipline or termination.

- We can prevent harmful conflicts from escalating at a personal level by (1) acknowledging our innate potential for responding negatively to displeasing events and (2) choosing proactive responses that keep these triggers in check.

TEST YOURSELF

True/False

For each statement below, check true or false.

TRUE   FALSE

_____ _____ 1. In the work environment, *safety and security* needs include environmentally safe working conditions.

_____ _____ 2. Employees are motivated to increase productivity when they find intrinsic value in their jobs.

_____ _____ 3. *Evolving conflicts* are types of conflicts that have increased in intensity and require you to intervene at some level so that they do not escalate into true conflicts.

_____ _____ 4. The best approach to addressing a *routine daily conflict (or event)* is to monitor the situation in the event it escalates.

_____ _____ 5. A *routine daily conflict (or event)* is a conflict that has not fully erupted and, therefore, presents your best opportunity to step in and possibly eliminate the conflict, or at least keep it from escalating.

MULTIPLE CHOICE

Circle the letter next to the best answer for each question. On a separate sheet of paper, state why you chose that answer.

1. According to the hygiene-motivation theory, good pay will

   a. motivate employees to be more productive.

   b. motivate employees if the pay is increased on a consistent basis.

c. not motivate employees but will de-motivate them if the amount is reduced.

d. not motivate employees unless the pay is equitable with what others are paid for similar work.

2. When two employees are experiencing a routine conflict but are maintaining a good relationship, you should

a. let them figure it out on their own, unless the matter escalates.

b. intervene if requested at any time by either employee.

c. let them figure it out on their own, but only if the conflict is a minor one.

d. intervene as early as possible to prevent any possibility of escalation.

3. Which of the following is an example of a trigger over roles, goals, policies, and procedures?

a. Lucille isn't getting along with Ricky because he is gay and doesn't know how to do his job.

b. Charlie thinks he and Sumiko should complain to their boss about having to work overtime, but Sumiko disagrees and says they should not say anything.

c. Matt is upset with his boss because she always makes decisions that affect him without consulting him first.

d. June is uncomfortable about a recent change requiring her and the other customer service representatives to talk no more than five minutes on the phone with a customer.

4. The following statements about evolving conflicts are true, *except* that

a. they present the manager with the best opportunity to intervene before the matter escalates.

b. they require more monitoring than routine daily events but generally do not require intervention.

c. they require intervention because the parties are often no longer able to communicate effectively with one another.

d. they are generally beyond the employees' ability to address on their own without help.

5. All of the following are good examples of measures you can take to exercise vigilance to prevent conflict in the workplace, *except* to

a. ask employees on a consistent basis how their work is progressing.

b. express concern regarding an employee's personal family situation and offer to help.

c. inquire into the health, financial, and emotional concerns that you believe are causing an employee's erratic behaviors.

d. ask an employee to elaborate on his concerns about a stressful situation he is experiencing that he brought to your attention.

DISCUSSION QUESTIONS

1. Within your company or the team you manage, what are the unfulfilled needs of your employees? Are they basic survival or security needs, or are they needs for esteem, acceptance, or self-actualization? What measures can you take to assist in meeting these needs to minimize the potential for conflict?

2. Within your company or the team you manage:

a. Describe two or three routine daily conflicts you have observed among employees. Did you or your manager intervene in these situations, or were the parties allowed to resolve the issues on their own? How were matters resolved?

b. Describe two or three evolving conflicts that you have observed among employees. Did you or your manager intervene in these situations, or did they escalate? If you intervened, what were the results? How were matters resolved?

c. Describe two or three deeper conflicts you have observed among employees. How did they evolve to deeper conflicts? What could you or your manager have done (if anything) to prevent these conflicts from occurring? What measures were taken to address these situations?

CASE: TRIGGERS

OBJECTIVE

To gain insight into the kinds of triggers that can cause conflict in an organization and to learn ways to address them in order to prevent conflict or minimize its effects.

PROBLEM

In Joe's evening class on Managing Conflict in Work and Life, Professor Timothy Justice lectured on the causes of conflict in an organization. Joe started to consider all the possible situations at More Power that could be sources of growing conflict. In fact, there were a number of issues within the customer service, warehouse, and delivery functions he managed. Joe learned from Professor Justice's lecture of the importance of being proactive in identifying (1) the potential sources (or triggers) of conflict and (2) measures to address these sources to prevent or minimize conflict. Joe has a good idea about the most common issues within his group that could be sources of conflict, so he jotted these down quickly (see the following list). However, he wants advice on strategies for addressing these issues to prevent conflict.

Joe's List of Conflict "Triggers"

1. Tina Tumultuous has been experiencing a lot of personal problems lately. She can be volatile, which could affect her relationships with coworkers and customers.

2. There seem to be minor turf battles and skirmishes between the delivery and warehouse teams. Fred Staid's and Sally Ambitious's personalities and work styles are so different. This could lead to difficulties if I require them to work together.

3. The way we maintain inventory and store items in the warehouse is archaic. This leads to delays in retrieving items for pick-up by customers or delivery to their homes. It doesn't help that the warehouse and delivery teams are not communicating well.

4. I need a new team leader for the customer service desk. Customer complaints have increased. Jim Talent is telling me to fix the problem quickly. Yet, it's not that simple.

5. I sometimes wonder if Kim Khan is trying to undermine my efforts. Talent tells me I can learn a lot from Khan. Yet it's like pulling teeth to get information, and then I'm not sure I'm getting the full story. Does Khan resent me for some reason?

PROCEDURE

Break up the class into five teams. Assign one trigger each to the five teams. Each team then selects a spokesperson to summarize the team discussion. Have each team spend ten minutes doing the following for the assigned trigger: (1) Consider all possible options for addressing the issue so that conflict might be prevented or minimized and (2) come up with the best strategy for preventing conflict from the list of options.

Write each of the five triggers on separate areas of the whiteboard or on separate pieces of flipchart paper. Once the groups have finished discussing strategies for addressing their assigned trigger, each group should write the options it identified and its preferred strategy for the assigned trigger on the whiteboard or flipchart paper. Ask the spokesperson for each group to report out to the class the team's discussion and the options and preferred strategy it identified, and why. Ask the full class to address the questions below; then proceed to the next group.

Case Questions

In class discussion, address the following questions with respect to each strategy proposed:

1. How effective will the strategy be in addressing the "trigger"?

2. How will the proposed strategy prevent conflict?

3. What are the advantages and disadvantages of implementing the strategy?

ALTERNATIVE PROCEDURE FOR ON-LINE LEARNING FORMATS

Assign groups as discussed above and have them engage in appropriate off-line discussions regarding their assigned trigger. Have each group then post its collective response for all class members to view. Have each group also address the questions above with respect to its assigned trigger. Be sure to establish a firm deadline for posting responses.

Once all five team responses have been posted, have each student post critiques of at least two of the groups' responses *other than the group to which he or she was assigned*. With respect to each critique, have students identify what they agree and disagree with regarding the initial group's response, and why. Be sure to establish a firm deadline for posting responses.

PERSONAL GROWTH EXERCISE

Fill out the Work Environment Checklist. Examine the results and determine which are causing you a conflict at this time. Consider at least two of these, determine concrete steps you can take to address these concerns, and take action on them this week.

TO LEARN MORE

To read more about Abraham Maslow's and Frederick Herzberg's theories, refer to the following texts:

Herzberg, Frederick, Bernard Mausner, and Barbara Snyderman. *The Motivation to Work*, 2nd ed. New York: John Wiley & Sons, 1959.

Herzberg, Frederick. *Work and the Nature of Man*. New York: World Publishing Co., 1966.

Herzberg, Frederick. "One More Time: How Do You Motivate Employees?" *Harvard Business Review Classic* (September–October 1987): 5–16 (reprint, *Harvard Business Review* 46, no. 1 [January–February 1968]: 53–62).

Maslow, Abraham H. *Motivation and Personality.* New York: Harper & Row, 1954.

Maslow, Abraham H. *New Knowledge in Human Values.* New York: Harper & Row, 1959.

Maslow, Abraham H. *Toward a Psychology of Being.* Princeton, NJ: D. Van Nostrand Co., 1962.

Maslow, Abraham H. *Maslow on Management.* Hoboken, NJ: John Wiley & Sons, 1998. (Originally published as *Eupsychian Management.* Homewood, NJ: Richard D. Irwin, Inc. and Dorsey Press, 1965.)

The following texts discuss the causes, identification, and assessment of conflict in organizations:

Costantino, Cathy A., and Christina Sickles Merchant. *Designing Conflict Management Systems: A Guide to Creating Productive and Healthy Organizations.* San Francisco: Jossey-Bass, 1996.

Lipsky, David B., Ronald L. Seeber, and Richard D. Fincher. *Emerging Systems for Managing Workplace Conflict: Lessons from American Corporations for Managers and Dispute Resolution Professionals.* San Francisco: Jossey-Bass, 2003.

Masters, Marick F., and Robert R. Albright. *The Complete Guide to Conflict Resolution in the Workplace.* New York: American Management Association, 2002.

Mayer, Bernard. *The Dynamics of Conflict Resolution: A Practitioner's Guide.* San Francisco: Jossey-Bass, 2000.

Moore, Christopher W. *The Mediation Process: Practical Strategies for Resolving Conflict,* 3rd ed. San Francisco: Jossey-Bass, 2003.

NOTES

1. Frederick Herzberg, Bernard Mausner, and Barbara Snyderman, *The Motivation to Work*, 2nd ed. (New York: John Wiley & Sons, 1959); and Frederick Herzberg, *Work and the Nature of Man* (New York: Thomas Y. Crowell Co., 1966).

2. Abraham H. Maslow, *Motivation and Personality* (New York: Harper & Row, 1954); and Abraham H. Maslow, "A Theory of Human Motivation," *Psychological Review* 50 (1943), 370–96.

3. Stephen R. Covey, *The Seven Habits of Highly Effective People: Restoring the Character Ethic* (New York: Simon & Schuster, 1989), 67–72.

4. Kerry Patterson, Joseph Grenny, Ron McMillan, and Al Switzler, *Crucial Conversations: Tools for Talking When Stakes are High* (New York: McGraw-Hill, 2002).

5. Daniel Goleman, *Emotional Intelligence* (New York: Bantam Books, 1995); and Daniel Goleman, *Working with Emotional Intelligence* (New York: Bantam Books, 1998).

APPROACHES TO CONFLICT

PERFORMANCE COMPETENCIES

After you have finished reading this chapter, you will be able to

- Describe the power-based, rights-based, and interest-based approaches to addressing conflict
- Describe the negotiator's dilemma and how to overcome it
- Differentiate between distributive and integrative negotiation

People generally adopt one of three approaches when addressing conflict:

1. They exert *power* to impose a resolution over the other party.
2. They exert superior claims of *rights* and entitlements over the other party.
3. They focus on articulating their *interests* and understanding the interests of the other party to achieve a resolution that will meet mutual goals.

When parties negotiate to resolve their conflicts, they commonly use one of two negotiating strategies:

- *Distributive* negotiation in which the parties bargain in an adversarial manner and view a win for one party as a loss for the other
- *Integrative* negotiation in which the parties use a more open bargaining process to share their interests and needs and explore how a resolution that will satisfy both may be achieved.

Let us examine these negotiation strategies and their relation to power-, rights-, and interest-based approaches to addressing conflict.

I suppose leadership at one time meant muscles; but today it means getting along with people.

Indira Gandhi

POWER-BASED APPROACHES

Power-based approaches: Resolution to conflict is reached because one party can wield power over a weaker adversary and force compliance on its terms.

As implied by the name, a power-based approach to resolving conflict depends on who has the most power. A resolution to conflict, or at least an end to the dispute, is reached because one party is able to wield power over a weaker adversary and force compliance on its terms. The use of power to resolve a dispute can have mixed results. While a stronger party can force a weaker party to accept a resolution, the costs in terms of lost trust and damaged relationships do not generally make the exertion of power worth what can be gained. Power-based approaches are used in a number of contexts.

WAR

Rightly or wrongly, a country wages war based on a calculation that it can force concessions from a weaker opponent. This is not to say that such an approach cannot lead to positive outcomes, such as securing a lasting peace, ensuring national security, liberating people from oppression, and achieving other noble outcomes generally attributed to a "just" war. Of course, the goals for engaging in war are not always this clear-cut.

SOCIAL AND POLITICAL ISSUES

During times of political and social upheaval, some groups exert what power they have after less drastic means have failed. These methods may include both violent and nonviolent action. The labor and civil rights movements are just two examples where exertion of power through strikes, sit-ins, and violent action in the case of labor and boycotts, marches, and civil disobedience by civil rights activists resulted in social change. Current examples include groups that take action on issues such as the environment, abortion, and gay rights.

LABOR/MANAGEMENT

Some labor/management disputes remain issues of power rather than disputes over rights or interests. Labor can strike to force recognition of concerns regarding labor practices or provisions within the collective bargaining agreement that it could not persuade management to accept otherwise. Management can institute a plant lockout to force labor to accept the terms of a collective bargaining agreement and return to work or face the economic consequences of not working.

MANAGER BEHAVIORS

A manager uses the power approach to exert authority absent consideration of the employee's interests or participation in the decision. The exertion of power may be accompanied by threats, such as termination or loss of privileges, to enforce compliance. On one hand, such a "power play" may be deemed necessary because the employee is uncooperative. On the other hand, the manager may use power inappropriately in a contest of wills or to control, manipulate, or embarrass the employee. The manager is often able to achieve a power-based resolution in such cases because of the authority granted through his or her position.

EMPLOYEE BEHAVIORS

Employees can also use power-based methods. They can force acquiescence from managers by threatening to file a discrimination complaint, slowing down or passively refusing to do work assignments, or vociferously complaining. These methods will prove especially effective when exercised against a weak manager who is unwilling, unable, or unsure about enacting appropriate discipline.

RIGHTS-BASED APPROACHES

Rights-based approaches to resolving conflict depend on rules, policies, laws, procedures, or similar frameworks from which parties can make claims to equity, justice, procedural fairness, or other entitlements. Whereas a power-based approach involves a claim that a party should prevail because it has the power to reward or punish, a rights-based approach involves a claim that the party should prevail because such a conclusion is the correct one based on the law, policy, or other framework on which the party relies.

> Rights-based approaches: Parties depend on rules, policies, law, or other framework to claim they should prevail in the interests of equity, justice, or other entitlements.

Although rights-based methods generally lack the potential for violence that some power-based struggles can bring, they can still be contentious. Instead of hand-to-hand struggle, the battle is fought through appeals to what is right. Parties engage in a contest of wills to persuade a third party of the justness and correctness of one's position over the flawed position of one's adversary. Rights-based approaches occur in the following contexts.

LAW

In the legal setting, resolution is usually dependent upon a judge, arbitrator, or other third-party decision maker who reaches a conclusion based on a "correct" interpretation of the rights and other entitlements in question. The third party also decides how these rights and entitlements will be allocated. This, again, is not to say that such an approach is an inherently poor method for resolving conflict. Our democratic society is based on the rule of law.

Many rights-based structures came about as the result of power-based struggles. For example, from the civil rights movement, antidiscrimination laws have developed to protect individuals from discrimination in employment, public accommodation, housing, education, and other areas of life, along with procedures for determining when discrimination has occurred and the liabilities and penalties for such conduct. From the labor movement, laws, regulations, and procedures exist for determining when strikes, lockouts, and other practices are appropriate and how these practices will be managed.

EMPLOYMENT POLICIES AND PROCEDURES

Companies have numerous policies, rules, and procedures for ensuring proper conduct and protecting important rights and corollary processes for responding to complaints and grievances when violations have occurred. A progressive company maintains policies that ensure that the rights and protections afforded under federal, state, and local laws regarding discrimination and sexual harassment are enforced. Many companies, whether unionized or not, have internal grievance procedures that give employees the right to appeal punitive actions when they believe they have been unfairly disciplined or otherwise treated unfairly by their manager or others.

INTEREST–BASED APPROACHES

Interest-based approaches focus on parties' underlying needs, concerns, and desires and on finding solutions that will address them. The ideal context for facilitating interest-based conflicts is a collaborative model whereby the parties seek to understand each other's interests in the dispute and find ways to achieve an outcome that is acceptable and mutually beneficial. Unlike power- or rights-based approaches, wherein outcomes are achieved through superior force or superior argument, an interest-based approach focuses on the "why" of a dispute. Using this approach, parties discern the underlying issues that brought them to the point of conflict in the first place. The following contexts illustrate the use of interest-based approaches.

> **Interest-based approaches:** Parties seek to understand each other's interests and find ways to achieve an outcome that is acceptable and mutually beneficial to them.

THIRD-PARTY INTERVENTION

Courts, arbitrations, and other decision-making forums are ill equipped to address interest-based approaches because they focus on what the "correct" resolution should be as applied under the rule or standard in question, regardless of whether such an outcome will be satisfactory to the parties. In contrast, methods such as collaborative problem solving, mediation, and facilitation open up the possibility that a party will realize some satisfaction from resolving the dispute in contrast to the all-or-nothing gambit presented through litigation.

In the legal system, increasing emphasis has been placed on encouraging parties to consider such facilitated approaches to resolving their dispute because of the cost, time, and inefficiency of litigation. Such approaches afford the parties the opportunity to reframe rights-based issues into interest-based ones. In a rights-based model, which is typically exemplified by the legal posturing prior to and during a litigated dispute, the parties state positions and concede or fight only to the extent that their positions may not succeed in court. During mediation, these positional approaches can be reframed so that the parties can articulate their own interests and better understand those of their opponent and then work toward mutually agreeable solutions not normally available through a rights-based model.

GRIEVANCE AVOIDANCE

Similar reframing occurs in the work setting when parties work toward collaborative approaches to resolving conflict before resorting to traditional grievance procedures. A formal grievance process affords employees the opportunity to exert their rights and less opportunity to express their underlying concerns that prompted the filing of a grievance in the first place. Feelings of unfairness, a lack of respect, or a basic need to preserve one's dignity and status within the organization may not be adequately addressed through a formal process. A manager who is sensitive to conflicts among his employees and the underlying causes and needs driving the conflict can work to find solutions that a grievance procedure will not address. Further, even when a grievance procedure is used, a progressive company will provide intermittent steps in the grievance process that offer nonbinding interventions, such as mediation, to provide for a more open discussion of interests.

THE APPROACH PARTIES USE WILL FLUCTUATE

Any dispute may have elements of power-, rights-, and interest-based approaches the parties use to achieve desired outcomes. In the course of a negotiation, even the most open-minded individual seeking a win/win may seek to influence another party by claiming a proposed solution is the just thing to do (rights based) or by asserting she has the leverage to take a certain action (power based) if an agreement cannot be reached. There are not always clear demarcations signaling when a dispute has left the realm of one approach and entered another. The approach taken will depend on the nature of the conflict and the parties' perception of their options for having their needs met.

> The approach individuals take to resolve conflict will depend on the nature of the conflict and the parties' perception of their options for having their needs met.

DISTRIBUTIVE VS. INTEGRATIVE APPROACHES TO ADDRESSING CONFLICT

Students of conflict theory, on the other hand, study how these various approaches are assimilated into various negotiation models. In analyzing negotiation strategy, a distinction is drawn between what is called *distributive negotiation*, or traditional adversarial bargaining, and *integrative negotiation*, or interest-based bargaining.

DISTRIBUTIVE NEGOTIATION

Distributive negotiation: Parties view the potential outcome as limited to a fixed pie with only so many slices that may be distributed. A win for one party is a loss for the other.

Distributive negotiation is commonly considered the traditional model for handling negotiation, particularly as observed in the legal system or when negotiating a sale. It is more closely aligned with the power- and rights-based approaches to addressing conflict than to the interest-based approach. The term *distributive* is used because parties view the potential outcome as limited to a fixed pie with only so many slices that may be distributed between the parties. A distributive negotiator views the bargaining as a situation wherein any win for the other party is a loss for his side. The more pie one side concedes, the less pie it has won for itself.

Distributive bargainers generally frame negotiations with statements of positions. When two lawyers meet, a customer works with a salesperson, or a buyer and seller negotiate the price of a home, each party begins negotiations with an optimum solution in mind that is most advantageous to his interests. The parties then strategically leverage their positions for maximum gain. They withhold information regarding their bottom line or true motivations for reaching agreement. They are selective about when and how they will share information, revealing only what is necessary to persuade the other party to compromise or concede. And they are careful in making concessions of their own, agreeing to ultimate terms only at the point when further concessions are not possible and what has been achieved through agreement is better than any alternative, such as paying more elsewhere or the possibility of losing in court.

While a distributive negotiation process is not necessarily negative, harsh, or unfriendly, it is adversarial. Depending on the outcome at stake, the strength of the positions, and the skills of the negotiators, negotiations can become a matter of game playing, and the tactics used by the negotiators can be aggressive, manipulative, and domineering. Lawyers, salespeople, business leaders, politicians, and individuals in other competitive fields often expect to negotiate on this basis. In this form of negotiating, achieving the best possible result for one's side is the goal, while maintaining or building lasting relationships is secondary. If relationships are maintained at all, it is because each party knows it must depend on the other for future negotiations. It is part of a professional aura surrounding the relationship based on accepted business practices rather than respect for any sort of relationship built on lasting trust or commitment. Indeed, achieving the best result for one's side often comes at the cost of relationships, which is the principal weakness in this form of negotiation.

THE NEGOTIATOR'S DILEMMA

Is it possible for parties to foster relationships while seeking to achieve the best possible outcomes for themselves?

Negotiation theorists refer to the *negotiator's dilemma*, which focuses on the question of how a party can achieve the best result, or biggest piece of pie, she possibly can. To maximize her gains, a negotiator's natural instincts are to *claim value* by gaining as much as possible in the negotiation for herself and leaving as little as possible for the other party. To do this, she typically withholds information, assumes an aggressive posture, and adopts other strategies common in the distributive negotiation model. This approach naturally creates resistance in the other party, causing him to also withhold information and concede as little as possible.

In contrast, many negotiators realize that achieving the best possible outcome depends on *creating value* for both parties. To maximize gains, the parties recognize that they are interdependent and that cooperating is preferable to no agreement. Each party recognizes that it is in his or her best interests to see that the other party's interests are also met. Working together to achieve mutual gains requires them to communicate openly and to share information about their bargaining positions. This requires them to be vulnerable.

Thus, the dilemma is created, as illustrated by this example:

> A hiring manager believes that a particular candidate is not only the best candidate, but also the only qualified candidate currently available. She is prepared to offer a generous salary because she knows that the time and effort to find someone else will prove even more costly. Yet she must also keep the salary within a reasonable range to maintain pay equity among other individuals in the same position. She doesn't want to reveal these issues because she's concerned the candidate will press for every dollar and perk possible. Conversely, the candidate is willing to take less than he might for the same position in the city where he currently resides because he wants to move back to this city, his hometown, where his ailing mother lives. He still wants the best salary possible, though, and is afraid to reveal his personal interests in taking the job for less money out of fear that the company will "nickel and dime" him.

Clearly, each party has interests that the other party can readily meet, if only they were willing to share information. The negotiator's dilemma asks: How can the parties be brought to a level of trust where they can seek to meet each other's interests and foster a cooperative relationship without jeopardizing their own interests? The integrative, or interest-based, model of negotiating attempts to address this dilemma.

INTEGRATIVE NEGOTIATION

The integrative negotiation model begins with the premise that developing and preserving relationships is a key value of the negotiation process. Parties using this model educate each other about their needs and engage in problem solving to reach a resolution that will "integrate" their needs. This model suggests that when parties explore their interests, they will find they actually share interests and that solutions beyond fixed pie choices are possible. Parties who value their relationship and consider each other's needs are more likely to engage in creative problem solving and discover

> Claim Value:
> Get as much for yourself.
> Create Value:
> Get as much for yourself and the other party by cooperating.

> The negotiator's dilemma: How can I cooperate and be open with the other party without jeopardizing my position?

> Integrative negotiation: Parties educate each other about their needs and engage in problem solving to reach a resolution that will "integrate" their needs.

solutions that wouldn't be evident through distributive bargaining. The pie becomes expandable.

The classic example of how a distributive framework may be reframed into an integrative one to the delight of both parties involves the splitting of an orange:

> There are only a few oranges and two sisters each claim she needs all of them. They fight over who should get the oranges. Their mother asks why each needs the oranges. One sister says she needs the fruit to make orange juice. The other sister says she needs the rinds to bake a cake. Through integrative negotiation each sister receives what she needs from the oranges.[1]

The problem is solved, but only after an exploration of the parties' true interests and a realization that their interests are compatible. Though most bargaining is not so clear-cut, distributive bargainers fail to explore deeper possibilities available through this approach. Consider these two examples:

> A customer may pay a little more for a car once the salesperson realizes she wants a certain color, a reasonable monthly payment plan, the first oil and filter change free, and an extended warranty thrown into the deal. The salesperson may readily give these concessions on the hope that he may keep her as a customer for ongoing service and perhaps the purchase of her next car from his dealership. He may also have a pressing interest in clearing his inventory to make room for next year's models.

> An employee might agree to drop a union grievance and discontinue her fight for principles of justice and fair treatment once the employer realizes that issues such as respect, improved working conditions, soothing misunderstandings between the employee and her manager, and other easily grantable remedies reflect the true reasons for filing the grievance. The employer might more readily address the employee's legitimate concerns once the employee agrees to modify inappropriate behaviors, respect lines of authority, and refrain from pursuing other costly and time-consuming union grievances.

Such outcomes are achievable only when the relationship is valued as much as the outcome. This implies a level of trust, an understanding of the need for cooperation to satisfy all needs, the open and honest sharing of information, and working together at problem solving. While the integrative posture may suggest that the parties are naturally friendlier, nonaggressive, and non-adversarial, in contrast to the distributive model, this is not always the case. Integrative negotiation is not characterized by the level of toughness or kindness of the parties, but by the level of commitment to reaching mutually acceptable outcomes. Often, the parties' commitment to "staying at the table" to struggle through their differences for the sake of preserving their relationship is the key to success.

Ultimately, a party will choose the strategy that best meets his or her objectives. In the management context, a manager is probably best served in most instances by integrative, cooperative approaches to working with employees, customers, colleagues, vendors, and others. But reasoned consideration of other parties' interests may not always be in the best interests of the manager or the organization. Sometimes, hard-nosed bargaining, or a refusal to bargain at all, may be the strategy to choose. Should a manager be expected to deeply explore the selfish interests of a price-gouging vender, a customer who demands unreasonable price concessions, or an employee who is defiant over the simplest request? Is laborious, time-consuming collaboration necessary with an argumentative team over basic operational decisions when all that is needed is a clear, unequivocal decision from the boss?

There is a place for distributive bargaining. There is also a place for switching between integrative and distributive frameworks as circumstances change. And there are valid reasons not to bargain at all and adopt either a posture of competitiveness or avoidance. The challenge is identifying the best approach under the circumstances.

TOOLS TO ADD TO YOUR CONFLICT SURVIVAL KIT

When managing employees, consider the implications of using power-, rights-, and interest-based approaches before acting:

- Do not abuse your authority. You have the power to exert authority over an employee by virtue of your position. You will often have a rights-based rationale for compelling compliance, such as a policy or conduct code or the threat of discipline. This does not mean you should always exert such authority. Whenever possible, seek interest-based approaches to resolve disputes. While the exertion of authority may enforce compliance, interest-based approaches better ensure buy-in from the employee that working with you is in his or her best interests.

- Do not be swayed by the power- or rights-based tactics of others. Do not allow employees' use of tactics such as threats of legal action, claims of discrimination, or intimidating or manipulative behaviors to force you into making concessions. While legitimate rights claims must be addressed through the appropriate channels, you must take a principled response to addressing disputes. Work toward interest-based solutions whenever the employee can be persuaded that shifting his or her approach will prove mutually advantageous.

- Maintain control over your emotions. Be aware of situations that may cause you to become angry or upset. Such occasions may tempt you to exert undue authority. Take a step back and assess how to handle the situation more objectively. In many cases, this "space" to think will lead you to pursue interest-based approaches instead.

- Individuals deal with conflict by using one of three approaches:
  - They use power-based approaches to wield power over another party who is generally perceived as weaker to force compliance on their terms.
  - They use rights-based approaches when they rely on rules, policies, laws, procedures, or similar frameworks to make superior claims of equity, justice, procedural fairness, or other entitlements.
  - They use interest-based approaches when they desire to focus on the underlying needs, concerns, and desires of all parties and look for solutions that will address their mutual needs.
- When adopting a strategy to handle their conflicts, individuals generally use distributive negotiation strategies when they take a power- or rights-based approach and integrative negotiation strategies when they take an interest-based approach.
- Parties using distributive negotiation strategies tend to take the view that there is a "fixed pie" whereby the more one party gains, the less the other party can gain.
- A party that pursues distributive negotiation strategies faces a *negotiator's dilemma*—in order to persuade the other party to concede more, she must be willing to provide information regarding her bargaining position at the risk of weakening her position by revealing too much.
- Integrative negotiation strategies answer the negotiator's dilemma because they encourage openness and the mutual exchange of information in order to explore how the parties' mutual interests may be satisfied.

TEST YOURSELF

True/False

For each statement below, check true or false.

_____ _____ 1. *Integrative negotiation* refers to a more open bargaining process whereby the parties share their interests and needs and explore how a resolution may be achieved that will satisfy both.

_____ _____ 2. A manager uses the power approach to exert authority absent consideration of the employee's interests or participation in the decision.

_____ _____ 3. Rights-based approaches to resolving conflict depend on rules, policies, laws, procedures, or similar frameworks.

_____ _____ 4. The legal system does not have mechanisms to encourage parties to consider facilitated third-party approaches to resolving their dispute.

_____ _____ 5. The integrative negotiation model begins with the premise that developing and preserving relationships is a key value of the negotiation process.

Circle the letter next to the best answer for each question. On a separate sheet of paper, state why you chose that answer.

1. Which of the following is the *best example* of a power-based approach used by an employee?
   a. Jamal files a grievance for a disciplinary action he feels is unfair.
   b. Yvonne files a discrimination claim with the local civil rights agency.
   c. Yvette keeps asking to speak with her boss about a problem, but he never seems to have the time.
   d. Andrew tells his boss he will talk with his attorney if she continues to evaluate his performance negatively.

2. The *negotiator's dilemma* refers to
   a. deciding how much information to share concerning your position in order to explore mutual interests without jeopardizing that position.
   b. choosing between sharing information and refusing to do so.
   c. deciding what information to withhold because you do not want the other party to know how weak your position truly is.
   d. deciding how much information to share with the other party to show your goodwill to the other party.

3. Rights-based approaches to resolving conflict are common in the following contexts, *except*
   a. employment grievance procedures.
   b. labor strike protesting unfair labor practices.
   c. court proceedings.
   d. charge of sexual harassment with the company's equal employment opportunity office.

4. Tabitha filed a grievance with her company's human resources department, claiming that she has been unfairly disciplined. Wendy, the human resources representative, contacted Tabitha's boss, Leon, to inquire about the issue. Leon said he didn't really want to discipline her but thought he had no choice because "nothing else seems to get through to her." Believing that the issue involves a communication problem rather than a discipline problem, Wendy asks the parties to meet with her to talk about the situation. Wendy's request is an example of
   a. an effort to negotiate with the parties to get them to drop their respective claims.
   b. exerting one's superior position to force parties to comply with the rules.
   d. using rights-based methods to determine who is right.
   e. an attempt to explore the parties' mutual interests.

5. If you are "claiming value" in a negotiation, you are
   a. considering the other parties' interests and trying to meet them.
   b. arguing that your position has more value and merit than the other party's position.
   c. trying to gain as much as possible for yourself and to give as little as possible to the other party.
   d. considering the weaknesses in the other party's position and making claims that your position is stronger.

1. From your experience as a worker, would you say that management typically adopts a rights-based or an interest-based approach to responding to conflict? Defend your answer by providing concrete examples from your work experience that illustrate the management response you have typically observed.

2. Do you agree with the authors that distributive bargaining can be appropriate under the right circumstances? Under what circumstances (if any) have you observed distributive bargaining to be productive?

3. Think of a situation in which you were faced with the negotiator's dilemma. Did you resolve the issue successfully? If so, how did you and the other party manage to transcend your reluctance to reveal your positions and explore each other's interests to achieve a mutually agreeable solution? If not, what might you have done differently in order to explore these interests?

CASE: POWER, RIGHTS, AND INTERESTS

Tina Tumultuous tends to argue with customers when they complain about faulty products, want a refund, or do not adhere to More Power's refund and return policies. In the past, Joe Newcomer has issued written warnings for repeated instances of rudeness and unprofessional conduct. Although Joe has been patient, his tolerance gave out when he overheard an incident in which Tina was rude and made an ethnically insensitive comment to a Latino customer, Maria. Therefore, he issued a three-day suspension to Tina.

On her first day back from the suspension, Tina requested to meet with Joe. She immediately became argumentative and demanded the removal of the three-day suspension from her record. She also threatened to file a discrimination suit if Joe refused. She claimed that the discipline was unfair because she had observed other employees who were not disciplined after they were rude with customers. She was clearly upset and at one point resorted to tears. She said she was dealing with some stressful family situations but did not elaborate.

Tina seemed to know all the right buttons to push. Joe resented her challenge to his authority, her claim that he was discriminating, and her attempt to manipulate him through emotions. He responded curtly that he did not have to entertain her allegations of discrimination and that the discipline was just and would not be reconsidered. He said Tina was lucky to have a job and the best thing she could do was leave his office and get back to work.

Tina was shaken. As she left Joe's office, she said, "Well, I've got to do what I've got to do."

Joe was angry. Tina was so combative and, as much as he considered himself a calm, rational person, all Joe could do was respond in a similar combative manner. It led nowhere. Joe reflected that there had been a time when he and Tina worked well together. She had been a conscientious employee, and Joe had been a supportive boss. Did he not want that sort of relationship with Tina again? Didn't Tina?

Case Questions

What are the natural tendencies that Joe and Tina exhibited in handling their conflict? To what extent are these tendencies power based? To what extent are they rights based? What could Joe have done differently if he truly desired a cooperative relationship with Tina? How might he have explored an interest-based solution with her?

Interview a human resource specialist in your company and discuss the company's grievance procedure. Describe the procedure in detail. Explain how and when it is used and the role one's immediate supervisor plays in the process. Identify the nature of the grievances that are addressed through the process and the frequency in which employees pursue the procedure. Examine whether the grievance procedure provides alternatives for pursuing interest-based resolutions to disputes. If only rights-based resolutions are considered, why are interest-based processes not considered?

TO LEARN MORE

The following resources discuss the negotiator's dilemma, claiming vs. creating value, and the basic concepts of distributive and integrative negotiation:

Fisher, Roger, William Ury, and Bruce Patton. *Getting to Yes: Negotiating Agreement Without Giving In*, 2nd ed. New York: Penguin Books, 1991.

Lax, David, and Jim Sebenius. *The Manager as Negotiator: Bargaining for Cooperative and Competitive Gains*. New York: Free Press, 1986.

Mayer, Bernard. *The Dynamics of Conflict Resolution: A Practitioner's Guide*. San Francisco, CA: Jossey-Bass, 2000.

Raiffa, Howard. *The Art and Science of Negotiation: How to Resolve Conflicts and Get the Best Out of Bargaining*. Cambridge, MA: Harvard University Press, 1982.

Raiffa, Howard, John Richardson, and David Metcalfe. *Negotiation Analysis: The Science and Art of Collaborative Decision Making*. Cambridge, MA: The Belknap Press of Harvard University Press, 2002.

NOTE

1. Adapted from Roger Fisher, William Ury, and Bruce Patton, *Getting to Yes: Negotiating Agreement Without Giving In*, 2nd ed. (New York: Penguin Books, 1991), 56–57, 73.

WORKING TOWARD COLLABORATION

PERFORMANCE COMPETENCIES

After you have finished reading this chapter, you will be able to

- Identify the five strategic approaches for handling conflict based on the Thomas-Kilmann Conflict Mode Instrument
- Choose the appropriate approach for any given circumstance to achieve the most effective outcome
- Describe the circumstances in which each approach will prove ineffective

Is there a "best" approach to addressing conflict? Are there specific strategies for appropriately responding to conflict? Do individuals have preferred modes for responding to conflict that may help or hinder their effectiveness? Do the circumstances surrounding a conflict dictate the approach that will prove most successful?

THE THOMAS–KILMANN MODEL IN PRACTICE

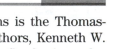

A widely accepted model for analyzing these questions is the Thomas-Kilmann Conflict Mode Instrument. Named after its authors, Kenneth W. Thomas and Ralph H. Kilmann, this instrument identifies five basic modes that individuals generally adopt when responding to conflict:

- Avoiding
- Accommodating
- Compromising
- Competing
- Collaborating

To fight and conquer in all your battles is not supreme excellence; supreme excellence consists in breaking the enemy's resistance without fighting.

Sun Tzu

This model, as depicted in Exhibit 4-1, provides important insight into our preferred styles for responding to conflict and helpful guidance in deciding the best strategy for addressing the conflicts that concern us.

CONFLICT STYLE

The traditional Thomas-Kilmann model illustrates the various styles or modes individuals adopt when responding to conflict. The five modes are identified based on the combination of two behaviors that an individual exhibits during conflict:

1. Degree of *assertiveness* (from unassertive to assertive)
2. Degree of *cooperativeness* (from uncooperative to cooperative)

This model is helpful in guiding people's understanding of their natural or preferred style for responding to conflict. Although we each possess qualities that support use of all five conflict modes, the Thomas-Kilmann Conflict Mode Instrument helps people identify the one or two dominant modes they are most comfortable using for most situations. Conversely, the model is useful in helping an individual identify the modes he or she is not accustomed to using and which, if developed, may prove beneficial to more effectively address conflict situations in the future.

CONFLICT STRATEGY

Savage, Blair, and Sorenson adapted the Thomas-Kilmann model (Exhibit 4-1) to illustrate the various strategies individuals use when addressing conflict.[1] The same five modes are identified based on the combination of two variables:

1. *Importance of outcome*
2. *Importance of relationship*

This model illustrates that understanding the five conflict modes is useful not only for analyzing individual conflict styles, but also for assessing the negotiation strategy a person may choose to take depending on the outcome he or she desires. Using this model, individuals choose their

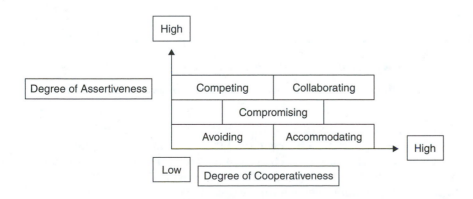

EXHIBIT 4-1
Conflict modes
(*Source:* Kenneth W. Thomas, "Conflict and Conflict Management," in The Handbook of Industrial and Organizational Psychology, ed. Marvin Dunnette (Chicago: Rand McNally College Publishing Company, 1976), 889–935. Reprinted with permission of Marvin Dunnette.)

approach to conflict resolution based on their interest in achieving a certain outcome and their interest in fostering or maintaining their relationship with the other party.

USE THE CONFLICT MODES TO CLARIFY YOUR VALUES DURING CONFLICT

How important is a particular outcome to you? How important is your relationship with the other party? You can gauge the response that would be most appropriate to take, such as how hard you push or how much you let go, based on the importance you place on these two considerations. Further, even though your tendency may be to adopt a particular mode for most situations, clarifying your values may compel you to step out of your usual mode so that your response appropriately reflects your values. A basic example will suffice:

> Josh and Anila value their marriage but feel differently about where to eat Saturday night. Josh could eat anywhere and is content to let Anila decide. Anila is more particular about where to eat, focusing on ambiance, dietary concerns, and a place that represents a true "escape" from the kids. She also likes to talk through such decisions with Josh. Josh is thus *avoiding* while Anila is attempting to *collaborate*. If they are not careful, this seemingly simple matter could result in conflict, with Anila pushing Josh to engage in a decision, causing Josh to respond with irritation.

> To step out of their usual modes, Josh needs to care a little more, realize that some aspects of the dining experience do matter to Anila, and support her in the decision-making process. Anila needs to care a little less, realize that where they eat is less important than enjoying an evening with Josh, and get on with a decision.

> Solution: Josh and Anila *compromise*.

Let us look at each of the five conflict modes in action and how to apply them in your work as a manager.

AVOIDING

Conflict Style: Low Assertiveness/Low Cooperativeness

Conflict Strategy: Low Interest in Outcome/Low Interest in Maintaining Relationships

People will adopt an *avoiding* approach to conflicts (Exhibit 4-2) that are trivial to them or for which they have little stake in the outcome or concern with the party with whom there is a dispute. It is a successful strategy when the costs of engaging in conflict are not worth the possible benefits to be gained, usually because the issues and relationships involved are

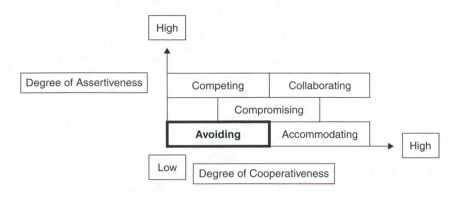

EXHIBIT 4–2
Avoiding

not important. An avoidance strategy also makes sense when an individual needs to buy time, such as to gather information or assess his or her resources before engaging in the dispute, to delay a decision, or simply to cut out from the dispute quickly. Avoidance also works for issues that the individual knows will disappear through inattention.

This approach is also referred to as *withdrawal* because an avoider is consciously withdrawing from dealing with a conflict, sometimes for good reason, though often out of fear, uncertainty, or a feeling of powerlessness. People may withdraw because of the following reasons:

> *Avoiding* works best when the costs of engaging in conflict are not worth the possible benefits, usually because the issues and relationship involved are not important.

- They realize they cannot change a decision made by some person or entity in power (a boss, a large institution, government, etc.) and, therefore, must either cope or quit.
- They lack the skill, experience, or confidence to effectively advocate for their interests against a more determined party.
- Past conflicts with the other party were not positive.

AVOIDING AND THE MANAGER'S ROLE

Managers might appropriately use the avoiding strategy in several situations:

- They want to sidestep dealing with employees, coequal managers in other departments, or a boss over matters that do not require immediate attention or affect day-to-day operations.
- The issues are trivial and the consequences for not addressing them are minimal.
- The issues involve matters that can be deferred to a subordinate or another manager who has more direct responsibility over the area in question.
- They disagree with a larger organizational decision and remain silent as the preferred option because no amount of persuasion or complaint will result in a change.
- They choose to avoid everyday squabbles, petty disputes, arguments, and minor bickering between employees when they know the employees will eventually work things out.

WHEN AVOIDING IS NOT EFFECTIVE

An individual who tends to avoid conflict may minimize issues that deserve more deliberation. The avoider is often a person who dreads conflict and wants to wish it away. Such "head in the sand" responses do not generally resolve conflict but merely delay the inevitable until the conflict becomes more egregious and protracted once it does surface. The avoidance of important conflicts, such as employee and customer complaints or matters affecting organizational effectiveness, often leads to escalation and a loss of trust, goodwill, and even revenue. The manager as avoider loses respect as those he leads become frustrated with his willingness to allow issues to be decided by default. In such contexts, avoiding brings more negative than positive consequences. Many conflicts, in other words, demand some attention.

ACCOMMODATING

Conflict Style: Low Assertiveness/High Cooperativeness

Conflict Strategy: Low Interest in Outcome/High Interest in Maintaining Relationships

People adopt an *accommodating* approach to conflict (Exhibit 4-3) when they value the relationship with the other party and are less concerned about the ultimate outcome of the conflict. This approach is also referred to as *smoothing* because an individual desires to smooth over any disruption or bump between the parties in the interest of harmony. Parties who accommodate generally concede any interest they may have in the outcome of the dispute and allow the other party to have a "win."

This approach is especially effective when individuals desire to foster long-term relationships through trade-offs over issues that are less important to them, but perhaps more important to the other party, in exchange for achieving more important interests through collaboration later. Accommodators often perceive continued competition over unimportant matters as detrimental to the relationship or their ultimate goal. In other circumstances, an accommodator will concede issues because she realizes she is wrong, is open to considering differing viewpoints, or simply wants to demonstrate that she is reasonable and fair minded. Accommodation doesn't necessarily mean weakness. Often, the person in power may accommodate

EXHIBIT 4-3
Accommodating

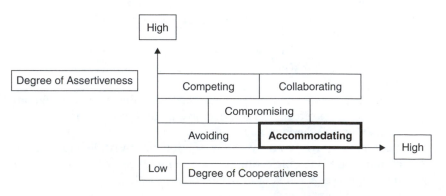

as a means of building someone up, providing opportunity for development and growth, or sharing power.

ACCOMMODATING AND THE MANAGER'S ROLE

Managers committed to empowering employees and developing leadership and decision-making ability will often accommodate them. Rather than micromanage every aspect of another's duties, they will let employees figure out the best way to accomplish tasks. At times, this accommodation leads to mistakes, which the manager will allow when they are not too costly and will promote learning. More often, such accommodation leads to successful completion of tasks in ways that the manager may not have considered, but which nonetheless result in achieving the appropriate ends.

> *Accommodating* can be an effective strategy when seeking to empower employees and develop their leadership and decision-making ability.

Matters involving tasks, duties, and day-to-day operations provide a great deal of fodder for accommodating employees, while larger organizational and planning issues provide less opportunity. Nonetheless, managers may concede small issues relating to aspects of the organizational and planning processes as a means of gaining concessions for weightier issues later. Wise managers know which issues they can concede and which issues cannot be compromised in the interest of organizational effectiveness. With respect to vendors and customers, the same analysis applies. To keep a customer from shopping elsewhere, a manager may accommodate over issues such as price and delivery. With vendors, he may concede some issues concerning cost now but will press for concessions later regarding quality, delivery, or volume discounts.

WHEN ACCOMMODATING IS NOT EFFECTIVE

The accommodating style may be appreciated in an organization because of its emphasis on promoting harmony and fostering relationships. Yet it may also be interpreted as pacifism. The classic accommodator is a giver, seeking always to put the needs of others in front of her own. A person relying too heavily on this style will often find that the issues she truly cares about are deferred, minimized, or ignored. Such an individual will not gain respect or influence as a serious contributor because her ideas will not see the light of day or will be co-opted by someone more aggressive and willing to take credit. When this ethic permeates an organization, a great deal of innovation and synergy is lost because gentle and kind, yet creative, individuals are suborned by more aggressive colleagues. A manager must truly believe an issue does not warrant greater attention or otherwise must gain skills in assertiveness to push for her ideas.

COMPETING

Conflict Style: High Assertiveness/Low Cooperativeness

Conflict Strategy: High Interest in Outcome/Low Interest in Maintaining Relationships

EXHIBIT 4-4
Competing

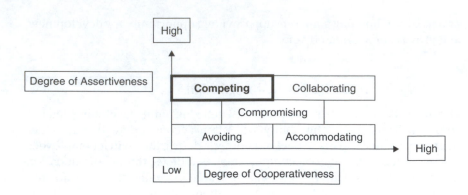

People adopt a *competing* approach to conflict (Exhibit 4-4) when they are more concerned about achieving a desirable outcome than enhancing or protecting a relationship. Such an approach may be appropriate when both parties expect a competitive mode of bargaining, such as long-term negotiations between tough-minded business competitors. People also adopt this mode when they are clear about their goals, including their bottom line, and are prepared to walk away if precise terms are not met. Perhaps they are confident they can achieve a better outcome elsewhere, such as a better price from a competitor or a better job offer from another employer. They may be willing to forgo the purchase of a product they want but do not necessarily need.

An individual might also pursue this strategy where he is willing to fight for a principle at any cost and does not care what the other party desires. For example, a consumer will fight for satisfaction when he feels he has been short changed or not provided the product for which he bargained. He will threaten to tell his friends, call the local consumer hotline, or shop elsewhere if he does not get satisfaction. Similarly, an ex-spouse in a child custody dispute will fight for non-visitation of the noncustodial parent when he or she thinks the other parent is unfit.

Effective use of the competing approach does not mean it must cost the relationship in order to be successful. Individuals who compete often have the power and authority to win against those who lack such power, yet they choose to exercise their power judiciously. For example, a weaker party (an employee, citizen, athlete, plaintiff or defendant, or child) will operate in a compete mode to persuade the individual in authority (a boss, political figure, referee, judge, or mom and dad) to accept his position. Yet the authority figure retains the power to render the ultimate decision. While the stronger party may press her advantage and insist on an outcome less favorable to the weaker party, she seeks to do so in a way that preserves the integrity of the relationship. A manager, for example, persists with an employee regarding completion of an assignment, suggesting corrective action may be necessary if the employee continues to miss deadlines, yet the manager still cares about helping the employee succeed.

COMPETING AND THE MANAGER'S ROLE

Managers will use the *competing* mode when quick, decisive action is needed. They may solicit input but will ultimately make the final decision,

PART I: The Theory and Context for Managing Conflict

whether or not others agree. They will also use this mode when making an unpopular decision, such as the following:

- Invoke the next level of progressive discipline
- Implement a new workplace rule, such as a stricter application of the tardiness policy, a requirement to wear a hardhat in areas where it was previously not required, or a stricter enforcement of the no-smoking policy
- Terminate, lay off, or demote an employee or conduct an unfavorable performance appraisal
- Implement budget cuts or other unpopular cost-cutting measures

While managers may create a few enemies, they will choose the competing approach in the interest of goals that are more important than immediate relationship concerns.

WHEN COMPETING IS NOT EFFECTIVE

While the natural tendency for some is to cower in the face of conflict and adopt an accommodating or avoiding approach, the natural tendency for others is to press for every advantage. People who adopt this approach for most issues will realize costs in terms of lost trust, severed relationships, and unfavorable outcomes. Because they have authority, managers may achieve compliance through this approach, but the employees they manage will become unmotivated and lack commitment to organizational goals. When a manager uses this mode, employees are not given opportunities to participate, provide input, or have control over issues affecting them. Where the situation calls for cooperation, teamwork, creativity, and enthusiasm, this approach is counterproductive.

> A manager who adopts a *competing* mode may achieve compliance, but employees will become unmotivated and lack commitment to organizational goals.

Competing is also inefficient where fostering goodwill is required. Two central tenets for organizational survival are maintaining customer relations and retaining qualified staff. People have choices where they will do business and work. An organizational ethic that supports a compete approach, such as a practice of never bargaining with customers or a hard-line position against all employee grievances, will result in diminished returns. A decline in repeat business and an increase in turnover are but two negative consequences for such an ethic.

COMPROMISING

Conflict Style: Moderate Assertiveness/Moderate Cooperativeness

Conflict Strategy: Moderate Interest in Outcome/Moderate Interest in Maintaining Relationships

People adopt a *compromising* approach (Exhibit 4-5) when they have an interest in achieving a particular outcome but not to a point at which they are willing to invest the time or effort to fully collaborate or compete. Parties

EXHIBIT 4–5
Compromising

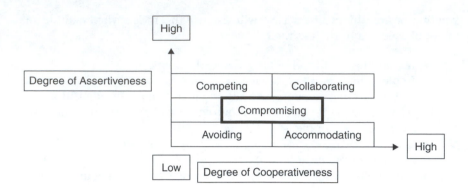

often compromise because neither party has an apparent advantage over the other, and each possesses mutually exclusive interests. For example:

> A homebuyer has accepted a job in a different city. He needs to move his family before the school year starts but cannot persuade the seller of a house he likes to come down on price. The seller does not have any other immediate prospects and must unload her house quickly because she must move to another city to be closer to her ailing parents, but she cannot persuade the buyer to meet her price.

If the pie has been sliced as much as it is going to be, it is time to settle, and both parties will achieve their goals, though not at their optimal positions.

Compromise solutions are also common in labor-management discussions when labor pushes for optimal benefits, pay, and other concessions, and management pushes back to maintain profitability and other business interests. But both parties need each other and, therefore, compromise at a point where each is neither completely satisfied nor completely dissatisfied. Parties also compromise when their relationship is ongoing and they must achieve intermediate outcomes in order to move forward while continuing to explore mutually beneficial, enduring solutions down the road. The mantra for compromise is, "Let's agree to disagree and move on." This mode is essential for many day-to-day disputes between employees and supervisors and among coworkers.

> The mantra for compromise is, "Let's agree to disagree and move on." Compromise is essential for many day-to-day disputes in the workplace.

COMPROMISING AND THE MANAGER'S ROLE

Managers interested in maintaining ongoing relationships with their staff will be motivated to compromise. Reaching complete agreement on any issue is something to hope for but is not guaranteed. While full cooperation is desirable, it is generally not required to achieve business objectives and complete tasks and assignments. Staff will not always agree with the direction the manager is taking, but when there is trust, they can arrive at mid-term solutions that at least go partway toward achieving goals. Mature parties can continue to work productively under these circumstances without friction.

In conflict situations, compromise is common. Employees will often press the manager for concessions on issues such as vacation and other leave time, modifications to work schedules, changes in duties, and opportunities for more challenging assignments. A manager may not be willing or prepared to grant such requests on the spot because of production demands, concerns with an employee's level of skill or competence, or concerns over the impacts such requests will have on others. However, when the requests are reasonable, the manager will want to compromise. The manager may, for example, convince the employee to take vacation at a different time or to take less time than desired now in exchange for priority consideration or opportunity to take additional time off once production demands ease.

WHEN COMPROMISING IS NOT EFFECTIVE

The manager as compromiser may become too accustomed to this approach as a means for getting the work done at the expense of achieving broader goals, developing staff, or compromising important individual or organizational values. Managers in this mode may find themselves constantly making deals. A weak manager may, in fact, be susceptible to employees' manipulation to wheedle concessions in exchange for cooperation. An appropriate compromise is one wherein the parties are mature and reasonable and seek to further positive working relationships. When employees behave otherwise, compromise is inappropriate, and the manager should reinforce the notion that cooperation is an expectation of work. Employees are not "owed" anything.

COLLABORATING

Conflict Style: High Assertiveness/High Cooperativeness
Conflict Strategy: High Interest in Outcome/High Interest in Maintaining Relationships

People adopt a *collaborating* approach (Exhibit 4-6) when they seek to foster an ongoing relationship with another party and want to achieve an outcome that will be mutually beneficial. This approach generally leads to the most productive and positive outcomes, assuming both parties are working to achieve a win/win solution. Parties pursuing this approach realize that there is no advantage to pressing for an outcome favorable to their interests if it results in damaging relationships. Therefore, a party seeking to collaborate will encourage the other party to engage in dialogue in which both parties are open about their interests, clear about their goals, respectful of each other's interests while expressing any reservations, and creative in exploring how their interests may be met.

The collaborative approach is a problem-solving, rather than a problem-generating, model. A typical collaborative process involves brainstorming multiple ideas that may resolve the conflict, analyzing the pros and cons of each idea, considering options and alternatives, and arriving at the best possible solution suitable to both parties.

EXHIBIT 4–6
Collaborating

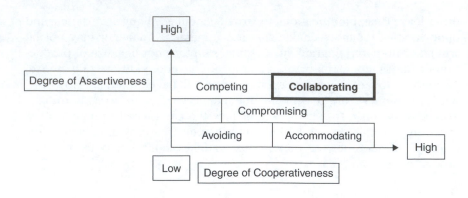

COLLABORATING AND THE MANAGER'S ROLE

Any manager focused on empowering employees should have a collaborative mind-set. However, it may be particularly important when a manager requires commitment to achieve long-term objectives. Whereas compromise may be effective for many day-to-day matters, and competing may be essential to compel compliance at times, a manager will be ineffective in the long run if she is unable to pull her team together, create cohesion, and get buy-in to larger organizational values. This will not happen unless the manager demonstrates an understanding that team members' needs are as important as her own and that she is committed to addressing their needs on a consistent basis.

More concretely, managers might consider collaborating when they

- Believe commitment to a decision will be greater if the team is made a part of the decision-making process.
- Believe the diversity of viewpoints will result in a more thought-out problem-solving process and a more creative solution than what they would achieve alone.
- Want to "win back" an employee with whom they have experienced a strained relationship.
- Need to make a difficult request of an employee, such as taking on an unpopular assignment, and want to involve the employee in a full discussion of any concerns.
- Want to help a staff member who is struggling with performance or conduct issues, provided the employee is open to considering the employer's legitimate concerns.

WHEN COLLABORATING IS NOT EFFECTIVE

Collaboration takes time, but it is worth the investment if the goal is to create enduring commitments while fostering long-term relationships. When these interests are less important, collaboration makes less sense. It would not be appropriate, for example, when quick and decisive action is needed, particularly over issues that are trivial. Collaboration is also not needed if the relationship is not worth preserving. When the opposing party has not demonstrated trustworthiness and is unlikely to change, an individual

Collaboration takes time, but it is worth the investment if the goal is to create enduring commitments while fostering long-term relationships.

would either compete or avoid the party depending on the importance of the issues involved. And when no matter of persuasion will convert an unreasonable individual toward a collaborative mind-set, such as a poorly behaved employee or a chronically unhappy customer, moving to sever the relationship may be the best recourse.

Exhibit 4-7 lists questions to consider about the different conflict modes.

You should consider many factors when deciding which conflict mode to adopt as a strategy for responding to conflict. Here are some questions to ask before engaging in any particular conflict and the possible modes you might consider:

EXHIBIT 4-7
Conflict mode questionnaire

Question	Answer	Conflict Mode to Consider
Is maintaining an ongoing relationship important?	Yes	• Collaborate • Accommodate (if the issues are more important to the other party than to you)
	Somewhat	• Compromise
	No	• Avoid (if the issues do not matter to you) • Compete (if the issues matter greatly to you)
Is achieving a particular outcome important?	Yes	• Collaborate (if you care about the relationship) • Compete (if you are less concerned about the relationship)
	Somewhat	• Compromise
	No	• Avoid (if you do not care) • Accommodate (if the issue is more important to the other party)
Is taking time to discuss the issues important?	Yes	• Collaborate
	Somewhat	• Compromise
	No	• Avoid (if issues are not important) • Compete (if issues are important and you must make a decision quickly)
Will failing to resolve the dispute affect organizational, team, or interpersonal relationship issues?	Yes	• Collaborate (if time) • Compromise (if less time)
	No	• Avoid

EXHIBIT 4–7
Conflict mode questionnaire
continued

Question	Answer	Conflict Mode to Consider
Do the costs of addressing the conflict outweigh the benefits?	Yes	• Avoid • Accommodate (if you have no choice)
	No	• Collaborate or compromise (if relationship is important) • Compete (if relationship is not important)
Does a decision have to be made quickly?	Yes	• Collaborate or compromise (if parties able to work together efficiently to reach a quick decision) • Compete (if you have authority and making decision is more important at the moment than concern about hurting the relationship)
		• Accommodate (if: (1) you do not have authority and must concede to the decision made; or (2) you have authority and are willing to agree to other party's decision)
	No	• Collaborate • Avoid (if issues do not matter to you)
Is there a power imbalance?	Yes	• Compete (if you have more power and relationship is not important) • Avoid (if you have less power and costs of addressing conflict outweigh benefits) • Accommodate (if: (1) you have less power and must address the conflict; or (2) you have more power and accommodating will benefit the relationship)
	No	• Collaborate or compromise (if outcome and relationship interests are important) • Other modes (depending on importance of outcome vs. importance of relationship)
Is lasting commitment to the outcome by the other party important?	Yes	• Collaborate or compromise (depending on level of commitment needed to move forward) • Accommodate (if the issue is not as important to you as the other party and it will engender greater commitment)

Question	Answer	Conflict Mode to Consider
	No	• Compete (if relationship is not important and you can force compliance on your terms)
Do you trust the other party?	Yes	• Collaborate or compromise • Accommodate (if relationship is more important than outcome and you trust party won't take advantage)
	No	• Avoid (if costs of addressing conflict outweigh benefits) • Compete (if benefits outweigh costs)

EXHIBIT 4-7
Conflict mode questionnaire
continued

TOOLS TO ADD TO YOUR CONFLICT SURVIVAL KIT

WHEN YOU ARE A MEDIATOR

Consider the questions in Exhibit 4-7 and similar questions and how each party would answer them. Do both parties have a mind-set for collaborating or compromising, and are they engaging in such behaviors? Is one party competing and the other avoiding? Are both competing or avoiding? Is one giving in, or accommodating, too quickly?

As a mediator, the ideal mode you will want to encourage in most situations, particularly as a manager mediating issues among employees, is collaboration. If the parties are not able to achieve a true collaborative outcome, the next preferred mode is compromise. In other words, you want to encourage the parties at least to come to some resolution so they can move forward in their working relationship, even if the outcome is less than ideal.

If there is an imbalance in the modes the parties are exhibiting, consider whether a party is taking undue advantage, giving in too easily, or trying to avoid the issues. You will then have to consider whether you can bring the parties to a more collaborative or compromising mind-set or whether you must disband mediation efforts.

WHEN YOU ARE NEGOTIATING A CONFLICT FOR YOURSELF

Carefully assess the conflict you are dealing with and weigh it against the criteria described in this chapter and suggested in Exhibit 4-7. While the collaborative approach is generally the most advantageous approach for resolving conflict, the circumstances surrounding the conflict must be conducive to realizing a mutually satisfying *outcome* while preserving and maintaining the *relationship* with the other party. Are both of these considerations important to you when you think about your conflict with the other party? Are they important to the other party?

Because circumstances will not always be favorable to collaborative resolutions, applying different approaches and strategies will be necessary. The process of choosing and implementing the appropriate strategy involves analyzing the conflict and having the savvy, skill, and confidence to apply the strategy most likely to achieve the desired ends.

PERFORMANCE CHECKLIST

- Based on the Thomas-Kilmann Conflict Mode Instrument, individuals tend toward a preferred conflict resolution style:
  - They *avoid* conflict if they are nonassertive regarding their own interests and uncooperative in considering the interests of the other party.
  - They *accommodate* if they are nonassertive and cooperative.
  - They *compete* if they are assertive and uncooperative.
  - They *compromise* if they are moderately assertive and moderately cooperative.
  - They *collaborate* when they are both assertive and cooperative.

- Although the ideal style for approaching conflict is the *collaborating* mode, success in collaborating depends on the willingness of both parties to approach the conflict with the same collaborative mind-set.

- While individuals have a preferred conflict resolution style, they may at times be required to adopt a strategy that is different than this style in order to be effective.

- While use of each mode can be appropriate under the right circumstances, *collaborating* is the best strategy for seeking an outcome that is favorable for both parties while maintaining or fostering their relationship.

- When choosing the appropriate strategy to use, you must consider your interest in achieving a particular outcome and your interest in fostering or maintaining your relationship with the other party.

- You need to keep in mind numerous considerations when deciding which mode to use; you will be challenged to evaluate these considerations to choose the most suitable approach each time you encounter a conflict in your organization.

TEST YOURSELF

True/False

For each statement below, check true or false.

TRUE   FALSE

_____   _____   1. According to the Thomas-Kilmann model, the five modes are identified based on the combination of one's degree of *assertiveness* and degree of *cooperativeness*.

_____   _____   2. The classic collaborator is a giver, seeking always to put the needs of others in front his own.

_____ _____ 3. A person will adopt a *compromising* approach when she has an interest in achieving a particular outcome but not to a point where she is willing to invest the time or effort to fully collaborate or compete.

_____ _____ 4. *Compromise* solutions are common in labor-management discussions when labor pushes for optimal benefits, pay, and other concessions and management pushes back to maintain profitability and other business interests.

_____ _____ 5. An accommodator often perceives continued competition over unimportant matters as detrimental to the relationship.

MULTIPLE CHOICE

Circle the letter next to the best answer for each question. On a separate sheet of paper, state why you chose that answer.

1. *Competing* is generally not a good idea when you are managing employees, *except when*
   a. you really don't care about an employee and would like to force him out.
   b. you need to exercise a strong hand so employees don't take advantage of you.
   c. an employee is inexperienced and needs clear direction.
   d. you have to make a decision quickly and must require a dissenting employee to comply.

2. Chanda has decided not to approach her coworker Gary about a disagreement she is having with him because she believes he needs time to cool down and may reconsider his viewpoint once he does. The mode Chanda is *most closely* exhibiting is
   a. accommodating.
   b. avoiding.
   c. collaborating.
   d. competing.
   e. compromising.

3. The traditional Thomas-Kilmann Conflict Mode Instrument identifies five conflict modes based on a consideration of which two variables?
   a. degree of assertiveness and degree of tolerance
   b. importance of being assertive and importance of achieving a particular outcome
   c. degree of cooperativeness and degree of consideration
   d. importance placed on cooperation and importance of relationship
   e. degree of cooperativeness and degree of assertiveness

4. Kendra wants to encourage two employees to talk through an incident in which one employee allegedly made a sexist remark to another employee. However, Kendra believes the remark was misinterpreted and that the speaker didn't intend to offend the employee. She hopes that she can get the employees to come to some sort of agreement so that a formal complaint can be avoided. If possible, she would like them to return to their prior cordial relationship. Of the possible modes she might encourage them to adopt, which are *most consistent* with her desired outcome?
   a. accommodating or avoiding
   b. compromising or collaborating
   c. compromising or avoiding

    d. competing or compromising

    e. collaborating or accommodating

5. *Compromising will not be* effective in which of the following situations?

    a. The parties need to make some progress on a project even if they cannot agree on every detail.

    b. The parties have worked together for years and compromise seems to work most of the time.

    c. The parties do not usually work closely with one another so compromise is acceptable this time.

    d. The issue is important to both parties, but maintaining a positive working relationship is equally or more important.

    e. a and b

    f. c and d

    g. b and d

DISCUSSION QUESTIONS

1. Realistically, in the business setting, are there ever situations when a manager should not be concerned *at all* about his or her relationship with another party as to warrant use of the *competing* style to address conflict? What situations come to mind?

2. Many people tend to adopt the *avoiding* style for addressing practically all conflicts in their lives. Why do you think this is? Discuss how using this style can be detrimental to successful conflict resolution when applied to all conflicts. What long-term consequences have you observed of individuals who routinely apply this style?

3. What is your preferred style when responding to conflict? Perhaps you have one or two preferred styles depending on the circumstances. When has using your preferred style been effective? When has it been ineffective?

CASE: CHOOSING YOUR APPROACH TO RESOLVING CONFLICT

OBJECTIVE

To evaluate the five approaches to responding to conflict from the Thomas-Kilmann Conflict Mode Instrument and choose the best approach for any given circumstance.

PROBLEM

Joe has so many fires to put out at work and could use a little help in choosing the best approach to respond to them. Here is a sampling of the issues confronting him:

1. Previously, Joe apologized to Maria, a customer, for an offensive remark Tina made. Now, Maria and her husband, Eric, have returned to the store and appear less concerned about Tina's offensive behavior and more concerned about getting satisfaction regarding the belt sander they claim is defective. They also want More Power to reimburse them for a small medical bill they incurred when the belt sander caused an abrasion to Eric's arm. While Joe feels badly about Tina's behavior toward

Maria, he also feels there is nothing wrong with the belt sander. More Power's attorney further advised Jim Talent that they should not reimburse the medical bill, as it could be interpreted as admitting to liability.

2. A customer named Charlie came in and wanted immediate satisfaction of a rebate offer for a pair of garden shears. He claimed that More Power's local advertisement was not in sync with the rebate program that the manufacturer of the garden shears offered. More Power's store advertisement said the rebate offer was good during the week Charlie purchased the product. However, Charlie later learned that the nationwide rebate offer from the manufacturing company had expired the week before. Joe expressed confidence that the manufacturing company would honor the rebate when Charlie submitted it with the appropriate explanation. But Charlie was doubtful and, at any rate, thought that going through such a process was inconvenient. The rebate was worth $3. Charlie wanted Joe to pay him $3 from the cash register.

3. Mr. Hassenfuss came in with a dirty, broken-down lawnmower. The mower clearly had not been maintained. Joe doubted that Mr. Hassenfuss had kept the appropriate maintenance schedule as required under warranty. The mower also had a severely chipped blade, probably from hitting a rock. Mr. Hassenfuss claimed that the mower broke down completely last Saturday. More Power should either do a complete overhaul of the mower or provide a completely new mower at no cost. Mr. Hassenfuss presented a warranty document that had expired a half-year before and claimed that the warranty should be honored anyway. He claimed that More Power knew its mower would break down at a prescribed time and deliberately contrived its warranty to expire well in advance. This was fraud, he claimed.

4. Vic Vendor, the new sales representative for Do or Dye Tools, has been complaining about the pricing structure that More Power has been using to sell Do or Dye Tools. He does not fault More Power for this since the problem lies mostly with Axel Rod, the former Do or Dye representative, who was in the habit of making informal handshake deals with More Power management regarding pricing rather than applying sound marketing principles. Despite this, Vic warns that if the pricing structure does not change, Do or Dye may have to discontinue business with More Power.

5. Jim Talent asked Joe to work with Kim Khan, assistant manager for tools, on negotiations with Vic Vendor regarding the pricing structure for Do or Dye Tools. However, Kim is livid about the veiled threats Vic has been making. Joe suspects that Kim is more offended because Kim was the individual responsible for the previous handshake deals with Axel Rod. Joe also feels Kim perceives Joe as a threat, representing the "new guard" within the More Power management structure.

PROCEDURE

Create tent cards with the words *avoid*, *accommodate*, *compete*, *compromise*, and *collaborate* on them. Place the tent card that says *compromise* in the center of the room and the other four tent cards in the four corners of the room corresponding with their placement on the Thomas-Kilmann Conflict Mode Instrument. If necessary, rearrange tables and chairs so that students can easily walk to each tent card.

Discuss each of the five scenarios and ask the students to walk to the tent card representing the approach they would take to address the conflict. In most cases, there will not be unanimous agreement regarding the approach. For each scenario, engage in a lively five-minute discussion regarding why the students chose the approach they did. Arguments should be based on the level of *assertiveness* and the level of *cooperativeness* (or the importance of outcome and importance of relationship) they believe is warranted for the situation. Students should attempt to persuade other students to come to their side.

Case Questions

In class, discuss the following:

1. Why can reasonable people draw different conclusions regarding the best approach to responding to various conflicts?

2. For any given conflict, are there approaches that are either clearly ineffective or clearly effective? Why or why not?

ALTERNATIVE PROCEDURE FOR ONLINE LEARNING FORMATS

Step 1: Have students review the five scenarios and submit online the approach (mode) they would recommend for each situation. If possible, do this in a confidential manner so that each student does not see how the other students responded and is, therefore, not influenced by other students' answers. Once all "votes" have been tallied, create a tally sheet or grid recording all the results. Post this tally sheet for all students to review. Be sure to time the process for collecting students' "votes" so that they have time to engage in online dialogue as specified in Step 2.

Step 2: Have students post their reactions and observations to the collective scores, including specifically their responses to the Case Questions posed above. For which scenarios did most students choose the same mode? For which scenarios were students' choices more varied? Why? Depending on available time and the online format used, encourage students to submit multiple posts so that they can respond to other students' initial posts, engage in dialogue, and build off of one another's ideas. If teleconferencing or videoconferencing formats are used, facilitate Step 1 as outlined above and then engage in live dialogue similar to the process identified in the in-class process outlined earlier.

PERSONAL GROWTH EXERCISE

Interview three people you know well and ask them how they generally resolve conflict. Analyze their answers based on the model presented in this chapter.

TO LEARN MORE

The Thomas-Kilmann Conflict Mode Instrument is available for purchase to help individuals identify their preferred styles and behaviors in handling conflict. It may be purchased from

Consulting Psychologists Press, Inc.
3803 E. Bayshore Road
Palo Alto, CA 94303
www.cpp.com

The Thomas-Kilmann model and similar two-dimensional models for assessing conflict modes are discussed in the following sources:

Blake, Robert, and Jane Mouton. *The Managerial Grid.* Houston, TX: Gulf Publishing, 1964.

Blake, Robert, and Jane Mouton, "The Fifth Achievement." *Journal of Applied Behavioral Science* 6 (1970), 413–26.

Covey, Stephen R. *The Seven Habits of Highly Effective People.* New York: Simon & Schuster, 1989.

Kilmann, Ralph H., and Kenneth W. Thomas. "Developing a Forced-Choice Measure of Conflict-Handling Behavior: The 'Mode' Instrument." *Educational & Psychological Measurement* 37 (1977): 309–25.

Patterson, James G. *How to Become a Better Negotiator.* New York: American Management Association, 1996.

Thomas, Kenneth W., and Ralph H. Kilmann. *Thomas-Kilmann Conflict Mode Instrument,* Copyright 1974 by Xicom, Inc. Xicom, Inc. is a subsidiary of CPP, Inc., Mountain View, CA 94303.

NOTE

1. Grant T. Savage, John D. Blair, and Ritch C. Sorenson. "Consider Both Relationships and Substance When Negotiating Strategically." *Academy of Management Executive* 3, no. 1 (February 1989), 37–47.

Part II

INTERPERSONAL COMMUNICATION SKILLS FOR RESOLVING CONFLICT

Communication is a skill that you can learn. It's like riding a bicycle or typing. If you're willing to work at it, you can rapidly improve the quality of every part of your life.

Brian Tracy

THE THREE CHANNELS OF COMMUNICATION

PERFORMANCE COMPETENCIES

After you have finished reading this chapter, you will be able to

- Describe three channels of communication and explain how they affect communication
- Select and use the tools for decoding messages accurately
- Describe how words model our reality and influence our behavior
- Explain how cultural differences affect communication

To practice effective conflict resolution, we must develop sound fundamental interpersonal communication skills. We begin our study of interpersonal communication by identifying the three channels of communication:

Channel I: **Nonverbal/Behavioral:** Includes all forms of body language, facial expressions, and gestures. We generally form first impressions and give and receive feeling and emotions using this channel.

Channel II: **Verbal:** Constructed of the words we use (written or spoken) to send information on thoughts, feelings, intentions, directions, and data.

Channel III: **Para-verbal:** How we say things. Grunts, groans, volume, pitch, speed, tone, and inflection of voice are examples. We can influence meaning by how we say things.

All communication comes through one or more of these channels. Effective communicators understand the characteristics of each channel. They develop a proper perspective and understanding of the limits of each channel.

What you do speaks so loudly that I cannot hear what you say.

Ralph Waldo Emerson

The nonverbal/behavioral channel includes all forms of data that are not spoken or written. Body language, looks, facial expressions, gestures, mannerisms, clothing, jewelry, and any sort of physical behavior are examples of nonverbal data. Data delivered through this channel are often used in forming first impressions, and we generally communicate and receive feeling and emotions nonverbally. We may choose to verbally tell another person how we feel, but often we send our feelings nonverbally. We may not say, "You hurt me," but instead act or behave in a manner that we think will communicate our anger.

Some people may give their spouses the silent treatment when angry. Some people make lots of noise, slam doors, or clank pots together while cooking. Some leave and go driving. Others clean. We communicate our anger in rather creative ways. How do you communicate anger? Think of the unfortunate fellow who says to his wife just before retiring for the night,

> "Gee dear, I've just realized that you haven't said a word to me in three days. Is something wrong?"

The nonverbal channel of communication is an active and complex one. In fact, it is the most active of the three channels. Studies have shown that we communicate a large majority of information nonverbally. To give you an idea of the complexity of the nonverbal channel, consider these nonverbal behavior areas:

> We communicate mostly through the nonverbal channel.

- **Personal appearance.** Body shapes, sizes, hairstyles, clothing, makeup, and jewelry send many messages. We wear wedding rings to let others know we are married. Some remove theirs when going out on the town. We bleach our hair because blondes supposedly have more fun. We pierce, tattoo, lift, tuck, and enhance our bodies to express our uniqueness or to appear more attractive to others.
- **Body movements.** Postures, gestures, head nods, legs crossed or uncrossed, and arms crossed or uncrossed are examples. We may sit in a way that others interpret as showing attentiveness. If we sleep in class, the instructor may conclude that we are rude.
- **Facial expressions.** We can give the concerned caring look or the "hate face" as needed. Sport commentators speak of athletes putting on their game faces. We can look pleased, certain, confused, or indifferent. We may roll our eyes to show our incredulity. Actors are skilled at putting on faces to create a mood or to communicate a feeling.
- **Touching behaviors.** Dignitaries from other countries kiss each other's cheeks. In our country, men shake hands, and women hug. We may think that touching customs of people from other countries are odd, but they are not odd to them.
- **Use of time.** Assume you are leading a meeting your staff is expected to attend, and one employee is always ten minutes late. In fact, you could set your watch by his tardiness. What would you conclude? Might you conclude that he has other more pressing matters than your meeting, he does not care to hear the information or

> Body language, looks, facial expressions, gestures, mannerisms, clothing, jewelry, and any sort of physical behavior are examples of nonverbal data.

participate in the meeting, he lacks discipline, he does not value your meetings and would rather stay away, or he just likes being "fashionably late"? All of these possible interpretations for his tardiness are reasonable. But, which is it? Other pressing matters, lack of discipline, or lack of caring are widely different conclusions.

The meaning we give to nonverbal messages guides and directs our attitudes and behaviors. We react to the meaning we give nonverbal messages.

INTERPRETING NONVERBAL INFORMATION

How good are you at reading people?

Think of all the information we send out to others in the nonverbal channel. The clothes we wear and how we wear them, our hair color and style, our jewelry, and our mannerisms all send out nonverbal data that are being interpreted constantly.

Sometimes those interpretations are correct or nearly so, and sometimes they are totally incorrect. Some people are good at what is often called "reading people." What they are actually good at is "reading" the nonverbal channel accurately. Others are not so good at doing this and are sometimes unpleasantly surprised when they find out that their initial interpretation of the person was totally incorrect:

> Cecil totally disliked a woman in his supervision class at the university. He loathed her from the minute he met her but could not figure out why. After several weeks of class, the answer came to him. He disliked her because she wore the same perfume as his ex-wife.

Unscrupulous people, such as con artists, are adept at "wrapping themselves in sheep's clothing" and are only later exposed as wolves after scamming an unsuspecting mark.

How good are you at reading people? To test your ability to read information received through the nonverbal communication channel, complete Exercise 5-1.

EXERCISE 5-1
NONSIGNIFICANT OTHER PERCEPTION INVENTORY (NSOPI)

Instructions:
Students who do not know one another form pairs and complete the NSOPI on their partner. Each student should take a few minutes to answer the following questions about the person with whom he or she is paired. Ask students to make a mental note of the reasons for their choices. When finished, have the students score their partner's guesses. Then, the instructor should lead a class discussion on how accurate the students were and discuss what influenced their guesses.
Circle the response that best describes this person:

1. This person is (married/unmarried)

2. This person is a (college grad/noncollege grad)

3. This person is (athletic/nonathletic)

4. This person is (under forty/over forty)

5. This person is a (parent/nonparent)

This person

6. is optimistic   is pessimistic

   1   2   3   4   5

7. is honest   is dishonest

   1   2   3   4   5

8. is a liberal   is a conservative

   1   2   3   4   5

9. is outgoing   is shy

   1   2   3   4   5

10. loves change   likes things to stay the same

    1   2   3   4   5

11. loves pets   dislikes having pets

    1   2   3   4   5

12. List a hobby you think this person has.

13. Give three traits or characteristics this person would say he or she has.

When you have completed making your choices, check out the accuracy of your guesses by discussing your answers with your partner.

THE AMBIGUOUS NATURE OF THE NONVERBAL CHANNEL

Often we will interpret the meaning of nonverbal behavior based on our past experiences. Our interpretations may or may not be accurate. Correctly interpreting nonverbal behavior is difficult. For example, how do we communicate our anger nonverbally? We may

- Give the silent treatment
- Go for a drive
- Make unusually loud noises while doing a chore, like cooking or cleaning the house

We may also do a great many other things. When our nonverbal messages are ignored or misinterpreted by another person, we may conclude that the other person does not care about our feelings or about us. Such a conclusion may cause conflict in a relationship.

Accurately decoding a nonverbal message is difficult because of the ambiguous nature of human behavior. For example, what might we conclude about someone who will not maintain eye contact when talking with us? We may choose any one of the following interpretations (or others not listed):

- He is disinterested.
- He is lying.
- He is shy.
- He is showing respect.

Which is the correct interpretation? If unsure, where do we go to find out? If someone uses a word we do not know the meaning of, we get a dictionary and look up its definition. Where do we go to look up the meaning of "lack of eye contact," or any behavior for that matter? To give another example, what does it mean if someone is sitting with her legs crossed, and her arms are folded tightly against her chest as you talk with her? There is no dictionary of nonverbal behavior defining "crossed legs and folded arms." We are left to guess. Conflicts often arise when we guess wrong.

We know that our interpretation of nonverbal data will influence our subsequent behavior and attitudes. Obviously, we will react to people differently if we think they are lying to us than if we conclude they are shy. The stakes can be high, so how do we choose which interpretation to believe? It is important that we correctly "decode" nonverbal behaviors.

COMMUNICATING OUR FEELINGS AND EMOTIONS

Studies on interpersonal communication show that most of us use the nonverbal channel to communicate our feelings and emotions. How do you typically communicate your feelings to others? How do you let others know you are angry with them or that they really hurt your feelings? We may verbalize how we feel, but most often we do not. We send our feelings nonverbally to others. Conflicts evolve or existing conflicts escalate when we fail to accurately interpret the feelings and emotions of others.

All languages are replete with words that refer to humans' inner feelings and emotions. We are empathic creatures. We have the ability to feel and the desire to express our feelings and emotions. We want and need others and to hear and respond to them. Expressing and having feelings heard and understood form the foundation for intimate relationships.

English is a fortunate language. It contains an enormous number of feeling words. We have a word for nearly every conceivable human feeling. Consider this brief list of negative and positive feeling words:

Negative feeling words

Doubt	Uncertainty	Confusion
Frustration	Loneliness	Guilt
Anger	Worry	Discouragement
Regret	Scared	Abandoned
Bored	Afraid	Fearful
Hateful	Inadequate	Resentful

Positive feeling words

Competent	Sure	Happy
Contented	Love	Optimism
Proud	Relieved	Glad
Grateful	Pleased	Appreciation

There are gross differences between some of these words, and only slight and subtle variations between others. Previously we read that many feelings are sent nonverbally and are open to an enormous number of possible interpretations, so accurately differentiating feelings is difficult. Gaining access to the feelings of others is a bit tricky too, because some people hold their feelings within themselves and close them to the outside world.

THE MEANING OF EMPATHY AND EMPATHIZING

Empathy means having, expressing, hearing, and responding to feelings. Those who can accurately interpret feeling from nonverbal behaviors are fortunate indeed because they can empathize. We empathize when we demonstrate that we hear and accurately decode or interpret the feelings of another person. Empathizing is operating at a high level of communication. It is a tool for building rapport and forming the foundation for intimacy within relationships. As a mediator, you may enhance communication by openly discussing any behavior that catches your attention. If one party seems to be acting angry, for example, it is best to ask the person if he or she is angry. Check out your hunch. If you are correct, the person may be relieved that his or her anger is being heard by at least one person in the room. If you are wrong, the person can correct you, and you can move on.

> Empathizing is operating at a high level of communication.

Saying something like "You seem angry" when you see the nonverbal actions of anger is called an *empathic response*. Empathic responses acknowledge that feelings are being received or "heard." Sending an empathic response like "You seem angry" may seem trite, but it is not. The more experience you gain with giving empathic responses, the more you will become convinced of their value. The empathic response is the most powerful communication tool in your Conflict Survival Kit. Using an empathic response with another person when appropriate can change, lessen, or even eliminate an emotion, especially anger, very quickly. We will discuss using this tool in greater detail later.

Messages sent in the nonverbal/behavior channel are more ambiguous than those sent in the verbal channel. Ironically, when someone's behavior belies his words, we believe the behavior. Ask anyone this question: "When people's actions or behaviors do not match their words, which do you believe?" Invariably, the answer is, "I believe the behaviors, not the words." Consider this scenario:

> Your life will be rife with conflicts when your actions contradict your words.

During a private conversation with your boss, she asks your opinion about a coworker. She says you can trust her and promises not to reveal what you say to anyone. The next day you overhear her telling the coworker what you said.

Which would you believe is true, her promised words or her behavior? Will you trust her in the future? Beware: Lives are rife with conflicts when actions contradict words.

TOOLS TO ADD TO YOUR CONFLICT SURVIVAL KIT

WHEN YOU ARE A MEDIATOR

Check out your hunches and follow your curiosity. When someone's behaviors catch your attention, for any reason, ask the person about it. Ask what the behavior means. If you have already formed your own interpretation of the behavior, check it for accuracy against what the person says. When someone's behavior contradicts his words, ask about it and probe for understanding. Bring the contradiction to a conscience level.

WHEN YOU ARE NEGOTIATING A CONFLICT FOR YOURSELF

Do not rely on your behaviors to send your thoughts and feelings; use words instead. Do not expect the other person to read your behaviors accurately. If you are angry, say so. If your feelings are hurt, then say so. Tempting others to read your mind or feelings is a setup.

CHANNEL II: THE VERBAL

The verbal channel is considered to be the most specific form of communication. Words, after all, have specific meanings. To define a word you need a dictionary. If someone says that you are acting *obstreperously* and you do not know what the word means, look it up.

Words are often inadequate at communicating everything we wish to communicate, however. When someone is trying to express a reaction to a witnessed tragic event, you will often hear, "There are no words to express what I saw or what I'm feeling."

You have heard the old saying, "A picture is worth a thousand words." This is true. But a word can easily be worth a thousand pictures. A word is an abstraction, the most abstract thing we encounter in our lives. Words are abstract because they are invented to model our reality and, ironically, have nothing in common with the thing the word describes. There are relatively few words in our language that in spelling and pronunciation resemble the things they represent. We invent words to communicate specific sounds, such as *bow-wow*, *splash*, *bang*, *boom*, and *whir*. These words are formed of letters in imitation of natural sounds. They are categorized under the group of words we call *onomatopoeia*. Apart from onomatopoeias, the likeness of a word to that for which it stands ends. All other words are gross abstractions. As such, the meaning of a word resides in the mind of

A word can easily be worth a thousand pictures.

the speaker and listener. Thus, abstract words often mean different things to each of us. Herein lies a root cause of misunderstanding and conflict. But words are what we have and we use them. We use them to communicate our thoughts, feelings, and intentions; to give directions; and to model our reality.

THE ABSTRACT NATURE OF LANGUAGE: WORDS AS ABSTRACT CONCEPTS

It is fairly easy to agree on the meaning of words that represent physical objects. For example, if you want to explain to someone what the word *apple* means or stands for, you can go get one, or a bushel basket, or buy $100 worth of them and hold them in front of the individual. Together you can fully experience *apple*. You can touch it, taste it, peal it, juice it, cook it in a pie, or examine it under the microscope. Because apples are real and exist in nature, we can easily learn all about the apple and easily associate the word *apple* with the physical object. But remember, the word *apple* is an abstraction of the physical object. And the word itself has no iconicity or likeness of any kind to the real apple. It is the name we have chosen to give the apple; that is all. It is obvious that looking at the word or studying it will not inform you about the object itself. You know what is meant by the word *apple* when you have experienced the physical object. For example, consider the word *manzana*. To what does this word refer? If you read Spanish, you will know the word means *apple*. If you do not know Spanish, the word *manzana* is meaningless to you. The word itself does not inform us about the object. Even so, words are all we have and, though they are abstract, they can be quite useful.

Humankind invented language for a practical purpose. Without words, we might have to carry around the objects about which we want to communicate. Without the word *apple*, you might have to carry one to the store, show it to the grocer, and grunt. The grocer would then look at the object and direct you to aisle #3. Carrying around an apple may not be too bothersome, but what if you wanted to purchase a concrete block? Can you imagine carrying one of those to your local stone center? Thus, words are practical and efficient and as such are perhaps humankind's greatest invention. Think of it: Words weigh nothing and take up no space, and they consume little energy to store and retrieve.

Accurate communication is difficult when our words do not represent a real physical object—that is, when they represent a concept and not a physical object. For example, if we wish to know what the word *justice* means, what might we do? We know that it is not a real physical object like the apple. We cannot go get a bushel basket full of justice to examine. We cannot experience the physical object because there is no physical manifestation of the word *justice*. It is not a real object. It is only a word, an abstraction. It resides not in the real world, but only in our mind. Unlike the apple, we cannot pick justice from a tree and bring it to our table to juice, peal, taste, and experience.

To further illustrate this point, consider the "ladder of abstraction" in Exhibit 5-1.

EXHIBIT 5-1
The ladder of abstraction

Concrete object

The real apple

Photograph of an apple

Wax apple

Still life painting of an apple

The logo of the Apple computer company

The word *apple*

Abstract conceptualization

At the concrete end, or at the top of the ladder, we have the real object, the real apple. At the bottom of the ladder, the abstract conceptualization end, we have the word *apple*. A word is the most abstract representation of any real object. When we want to comprehend what the word means in relationship to a real object, to fully experience the object, we simply move up the "ladder of abstraction" to find the object itself. To "experience and learn the apple," we go pick an apple. What happens, however, when we wish to understand or experience something that only resides at the abstract bottom of the ladder, like the word *justice*? No real tangible justice exists in nature. It is obviously not an object. So, what are we to do?

> A word is the most abstract representation of any real object.

DEFINING OUR WORDS

There is no real or concrete object called *justice* so we cannot go up the ladder to study the concept. Instead, we move horizontally across the bottom where other abstractions reside. When we go to the dictionary for its definition of justice, we see only other abstractions. For example, the dictionary will state the meaning using words such as *fairness*, *law*, *legitimacy*, *truth*, *correctness*, and *equality*. We may also rely on a poetic, philosophical, or religious definition for the meaning of abstract concepts. Any book of quotations will suffice for such sources. The *Oxford Dictionary of Quotations*, 3rd ed.,[1] lists the following examples under the word *justice*:

> *Justice is the means by which established injustices are sanctioned.*
> *Justice is truth in action.*
> *Revenge is a kind of wild justice.*

We may hear other metaphors, such as, "justice is blind" or "justice is only for the wealthy." Other concepts include "white man's justice" and "black man's justice." In any case, we are forced to use metaphors, examples, or other words (abstractions) to describe the word we call *justice*.

To fully comprehend the definition of justice, we must comprehend the meaning of the other abstractions used to describe it. If we say, for example, that justice is *truth*, we will need to ask the definition of *truth* in order to understand more fully. If we find that truth is a *constant*, we have to define and understand the definition of *constant*. This process goes on and on. How effectively we comprehend each other's abstract conceptualizations depends on the amount of shared agreement on the definitions of the words or concepts. The amount of agreement or similarity in definitions of concepts is influenced heavily by our culture, educators, family, and political and religious leaders. Some may offer an example of justice by pointing to something real like a fair trial or to some judge's decision. But as we know through experience, the examples of justice vary among people. Further, we cannot rely on behavioral examples because behaviors are open to multiple interpretations. An example of justice to one person may be an example of injustice to another. We may point to physical objects such as the statue of the blindfolded woman holding balance scales or to the courthouse. Whatever we use, however, is only a "sign" of the concept we call justice; it is not justice itself.[2]

QUESTIONING THE DEFINITIONS OF CONCEPTS IS TRICKY

Continually being asked to explain the meaning of their concepts can really irritate people. This is especially true when questioning goes on for too long. Constantly challenging people's definitions got the ancient Greek philosopher Socrates in serious trouble with his fellow citizens. In fact, they got so irritated with him that they voted to have him poisoned. Then and now, people get frustrated with this line of questioning because after a while they begin to realize that their words determine their beliefs and that their beliefs are concepts whose definitions reside within their own minds.

They may also realize that their definitions are heavily influenced by external forces, such as their culture, church, politicians, and teachers. They especially get upset when they realize that they may have "swallowed whole" someone else's meaning of a concept without any attempt to challenge its definition. This line of inquiry can challenge long-held, deeply ingrained beliefs. They may also realize that the process of interpreting reality is created from their own and others' meaning of words, and meaning making is socially constructed.

Even so, words provide us with wonderful potential and opportunity. With words, we communicate feelings and emotions, resolve conflicts, write laws that are just, create inspiring and beautiful poetry, and compose song lyrics that give us goose bumps when we hear them. We can say, "I love you" and be believed because it is true. We can say the most endearing thing that makes another feel really good about herself.

But then there is a dark side. The meanings of words have torn families apart. People have been killed over meanings of concepts. Nations go to war over them. Developers exploit and destroy the earth over their meanings of words such as *progress*. Words form our thoughts and our thoughts lead to behavior. Pro-life and pro-choice advocates will never end their conflict until they can agree on new definitions of the words *life* and *death*.

Our personal meanings of words have a profound and direct causal relationship on our emotions and behavior. Think of the confusion in the

> Words form our thoughts and our thoughts lead to behavior.

mind of a young soldier who, while being shot at in his desert foxhole, suddenly realizes that he does not believe in his leader's words anymore. His faith in the cause for which he had been fighting becomes a feeling that he has been betrayed. From that moment on, the leader's shouts of "march on" are no longer motivating. Or, contemplate how a young daughter might feel when she comes to believe that her father's definition of *love* is the same for his new car as it is for her.

The interpretive nature of language is a continuous source of wonder and illusion. We use language to model our reality. Our language is in a circular relationship with our deeds, our thoughts, our feelings, and our emotions. Each depends on the other. Conscious thoughts are words. Language allows us to move from raw apprehension to intellectual comprehension, thus giving us the possibility to know what is true from what is false, right from wrong, and beauty from ugliness. As Walt Whitman wrote, "Nothing is more spiritual than words."

Human language is a source of conflict, and yet language is the only way of getting out of conflict. How ironic that we must use the very thing that creates conflict to get out of conflict. Is it possible to do so? We must hope so, because words are all we have. They are absolutely necessary. Listen to them carefully and choose them wisely.

> The interpretive nature of language is a continuous source of wonder and illusion.

TOOLS TO ADD TO YOUR CONFLICT SURVIVAL KIT

WHEN YOU ARE A MEDIATOR

Ask for clarification for the meanings of abstract concepts. For example, if people say they seek a "fair and equitable" resolution to their conflict, ask what they consider to be a fair and equitable outcome. Be sure to write it down so you can refer to it at a later time. Sometimes people may change definitions, making them a moving target in order to manipulate the negotiations.

Helping people clarify their concepts in this way will help them recognize when they have achieved the resolution they seek.

WHEN YOU ARE NEGOTIATING A CONFLICT FOR YOURSELF

Be sure of your own definitions of abstract concepts. Write them down. Be as clear and concise as you can be as you work through the negotiations.

Ask others for their definitions of concepts. You already know your definitions, so seek out the other party's definitions.

CHANNEL III: THE PARA-VERBAL

Many times it is not only what we say but how we say it that listeners hear and to which they react. We want our message to be interpreted

PART II: Interpersonal Communication Skills For Resolving Conflict

correctly, so we use or modify the message with grunts; groans; and changes in volume, pitch, speed, tone, rhythm, and inflection. We may use a facial expression or other type of body gesture along with our words in hopes that listeners will decode the message as we intend, that they "get it." We add to or clarify our feelings, emotions, and intentions in this channel. The para-verbal channel has such a profound effect on communication and on our interpersonal relationships that we must attend to this channel carefully and with our full attention. This is especially true when dealing with conflict when emotions run high.

We add to or clarify our feelings, emotions, and intentions using the para-verbal channel.

It is difficult to give examples of the para-verbal channel using only the written word. When a writer wishes to have one of her characters say something sarcastically, for example, she will use both the verbal and the behavior channels to pull it off. She will try to have you see her words in your mind's eye. The writer gives the reader credit for having the ability to comprehend subtle nuances in writing and assumes that the reader will interpret the para-verbal message accurately. For example, when writing about a conflict mediation session between two people, the writer might have one of them say:

"Sure, I think George is a mature person."

The reader interprets this message. If the writer wishes the reader to hear more than the words and interpret the statement differently, she may write the following, adding para-verbal information:

"Sure, I think George is a mature person," hissed Helen, with daggers in her eyes.

The written message now, of course, means something quite different. The added words *hissed* and *daggers in her eyes* modify the written text and thereby help the reader grasp the meaning the writer intended. Of course there are no guarantees. Like the nonverbal channel, the para-verbal is fraught with ambiguity and open to diverse interpretations.

The nonverbal and para-verbal channels are fraught with ambiguity and open to diverse interpretations.

Sometimes people speak few words but wish to convey a great many feelings. To "hear" all that someone is saying or trying to say, the listener must attend to all three channels: the verbal, nonverbal/behavioral, and para-verbal channels. For example, consider the following conversation between a husband and wife:

"What's wrong, dear?" the husband asked.

"Nothing," she replied as she turned away and began to sob quietly.

"That's great, dear. I'm leaving for the golf course now. See you about six o'clock. Oh, and honey, don't forget, I'm going to the game tonight with Eddie."

If the husband continues to hear only his wife's words and ignores the nonverbal and para-verbal channel, he will continually miss the point of his wife's messages. Someday he may come home and find that his house key no longer works!

When you attend to messages from the para-verbal channel, you are helping others convey their intended message. They appreciate this. It shows that you care about them as people and value your relationship with them.

TUNING IN ON THE THREE CHANNELS OF COMMUNICATION WHEN RESOLVING CONFLICT

Unquestionably, a great deal of information is sent through the three channels of communication. Our interpretation of the message is heavily dependent on our ability to tune in the messages coming through these channels. Is it possible to accurately communicate when the nonverbal channel is missing altogether? Yes, it is. Telephones, letters, and e-mail would be useless communication tools otherwise. For example, resolving a customer service dispute is not always possible through face-to-face interaction. We must instead call or e-mail customer service to complain. We expect the customer service representative to interpret the content of our complaint, hear our feelings and emotions, and respond appropriately. To pull this off effectively, customer service representatives must receive special communications training.

Such training has limits. Resolving conflicts requires that we remain open to hearing and listening to messages sent in all three channels. It is *not* advisable to try to resolve serious conflicts over the phone, through letters and e-mails, or in any other way that leaves out the nonverbal channel. Conflicts are best resolved face to face. Human communication is abstract, open for interpretation, and complicated. Nonverbal information is missing when we talk on the phone or write letters or e-mails. We must listen to and use all three channels when resolving conflicts. To "hear all of me"—to hear and listen to all the content and feelings someone might send you—means that you as a listener must actively attend to the data sent through all three channels.

When Cultural Differences Exist: Minimizing miscommunication between people from different cultures is a serious challenge. The main cause of this challenge comes from the different languages and from using different sign systems of words to model reality. Language builds cultures and cultures define all the really important things. Because of differences in language, cultures give different meanings to concepts such as good and bad, right and wrong, pretty and ugly, just and unjust, freedom and slavery, and so on. Serious conflicts, such as wars and genocide, are the result of these differences. Language and cultural barriers have plagued humankind since ancient times, perhaps before the "Tower of Babel" from biblical times.

The interpersonal communication materials presented in this chapter have a certain degree of generalizability across cultures. Caution must be observed, however, because differences exist in all three channels of communications that may impact one's ability to fully understand others from a different culture. One cannot be expected to know all the nuances operating in other cultures. It is not possible to explain all the nuances impacting communication across or within a culture in a single book. But cultural differences matter greatly. Remember that norms of behavior are not universal.

PART II: Interpersonal Communication Skills For Resolving Conflict

If you find yourself in a conflict with a person from another culture, here are a few tips to consider:

- Remind yourself that your culture is not the only correct one. Expect that your communication techniques will not be universally practiced, understood, or valued by those from a different culture. Humility is an important virtue here.
- Seek out someone from the same culture as the person or group with whom you are having the conflict and explore how that culture generally approaches conflicts.
- Learn communications characteristics from someone from a similar culture. Explore the specific nuances within the three channels of communication.
- Read books or other material pertaining to cross-cultural communication. See the To Learn More section at the end of this chapter for suggested books to read.
- Learn a new language
- Immerse yourself in another culture for an extended period of time.

A FEW EXAMPLES OF CULTURAL DIFFERENCES

Frons Trompenaars, a Dutch theorist in the field of cross-cultural communications provides the following insight in how emotional reactions are perceived differently:

> In North America and north-west Europe business relationships are typically instrumental and all about achieving objectives. The brain checks emotions because these are believed to confuse the issues.… But further south and in many other cultures, business is a human affair and the whole gamut of emotions deemed appropriate. Loud laughter, banging your fist on the table or leaving a conference room in anger during a negotiation [are] all part of business.[3]

According to Geert Hofstede, Mexico's culture has a low level of tolerance for uncertainty.[4] In an effort to minimize or reduce this level of uncertainty, strict rules, laws, policies, and regulations are adopted and implemented. The ultimate goal of this population is to control everything in order to eliminate or avoid the unexpected. As a result, the society does not readily accept change and does not like to take risks. One might expect a person from Mexico to appreciate a concise explanation of what is likely to take place during a conflict resolution session, especially if the experience is new.

What are some processes available to us that help us understand another's language and culture, to help us find shared meaning? Learning another's language and immersing oneself into another's culture over an extended period of time are two commonly mentioned processes. However, experience has shown that while these may help, they are not guaranteed. Persons from the same culture who share the same language experience conflicts over the meaning they give to words and behaviors, that is, signs. In *Men Are from Mars, Women Are from Venus*, John Gray illustrates this point when he writes: "Just as a man is fulfilled through working out the intricate details of solving a problem, a woman is fulfilled through talking about the details of her problems."[5] Here, the difference is gender, not culture or language. Yet this one difference has important impacts on the expectations that American, English-speaking men and women have as they attempt to resolve their conflicts.

TOOLS TO ADD TO YOUR CONFLICT SURVIVAL KIT

WHEN YOU ARE A MEDIATOR

Listen for changes in tone of voice, pitch, volume, and so forth. Attend to *how* something is being said. If participants' words belie their behavior, openly talk about the difference. Ask questions about what people are trying to say. Ask questions for clarification for all to hear. Make every attempt to help the person effectively communicate to others. Help others to "hear all of the person."

WHEN YOU ARE NEGOTIATING A CONFLICT FOR YOURSELF

If *how* you say something is not getting through to the listener, become more specific in *what* you are saying. Tell the person how you feel or what you are thinking or trying to say. Do not expect the listener to read your para-verbal tones correctly. That is like asking someone to read your mind. The listener may not get it even if he or she desperately desires to do so.

PERFORMANCE CHECKLIST

- Communication affects conflict so directly that many people will often cite the lack of communication as the cause of their conflict.

- Interpersonal communication is a complex phenomenon.

- Sound fundamental communication skills can be learned, and the better you are at using them, the more beneficial and appropriate the outcomes of your negotiations will be.

- Nearly all that we communicate to another person or group of people is sent through the nonverbal, verbal, and para-verbal channels of communication.

- Our interpretation of any message is heavily dependent on our ability to listen to the messages coming through these channels.

- To "hear" all that someone is saying or trying to say, the listener must attend to all three channels.

- Studies have shown that we communicate the majority of our feelings through the nonverbal channel.

- It is *not* advisable to try to resolve serious conflicts over the phone, through letters and e-mails, or in any other way that leaves out the nonverbal channel.

- Those who hear feelings and demonstrate that they have heard them accurately are using their ability to empathize.

- The verbal channel is considered to be the most specific form of communication. Accurate communication is difficult when our words do not represent a real physical object—that is, when they represent a concept.

- We define abstract conceptualizations using other abstract conceptualizations. Seek clarification on the meanings of abstract concepts.

- Our personal meanings of words have a profound and direct causal relationship on our emotions and behavior.

- We use language to model our reality. Our language is in a circular relationship with our deeds, thoughts, feelings, and emotions. Each depends on the other.

- Many times it is not only what we say but *how* we say it that listeners hear and to which they react.

TEST YOURSELF

True/False

For each statement below, check true or false.

TRUE   FALSE

_____   _____   1. The nonverbal/behavioral channel includes all forms of data that are not spoken or written.

_____   _____   2. Studies have shown that we communicate the large majority of information nonverbally.

_____   _____   3. Correctly interpreting nonverbal behavior is easy.

_____   _____   4. Studies on interpersonal communication show that most of us use the verbal channel to communicate our feelings and emotions.

_____   _____   5. Empathy means having, expressing, hearing, and responding to feelings.

MULTIPLE CHOICE

Circle the letter next to the best answer for each question. On a separate sheet of paper, state why you chose that answer.

1. Which of the following is *not* one of the three channels of communication?
   a. verbal
   b. nonverbal
   c. abstract conceptualization
   d. para-verbal

2. Through which channel do we communicate most of our feelings?
   a. nonverbal channel
   b. para-verbal channel
   c. visual channel
   d. verbal channel

3. Having feelings, expressing them, hearing them, and responding to them are included in the meaning of which of the following words?

   a. understanding

   b. concrete object

   c. sympathy

   d. empathy

4. The most abstract "step" on the ladder of abstraction is a

   a. word.

   b. concrete object.

   c. physical representation of a concrete object.

   d. photograph or painting of a real object.

5. Our language is in a circular relationship with

   a. our deeds.

   b. our thoughts.

   c. our feelings and emotions.

   d. all of the above.

DISCUSSION QUESTIONS

1. How can you become more effective in communicating your feelings and emotions to others? How can you demonstrate that you have heard and understood the feelings and emotions of another person?

2. With the ladder of abstraction in mind, how can you be sure that you understand another person's meaning of abstract concepts such as *justice* or *fairness*? Be specific.

CASE: "READING" OTHERS

OBJECTIVE

To practice "reading" another's verbal, nonverbal, and para-verbal messages.

PROBLEM

After his lecture on the three channels of communication during his Managing Conflict in Work and Life class, Professor Timothy Justice proposes a real-life demonstration of the verbal, nonverbal, and para-verbal messages people send and a "test" of the students' ability to "read" other people. He asks for a volunteer who would be willing to share aspects of his or her life and work. Joe volunteers. Before beginning the demonstration, Professor Justice asks Joe to briefly describe the matters he will be discussing and the feelings associated with them. Joe describes five matters:

1. He feels angry with an employee, Tina, for accusing him of treating her unfairly and for not performing up to the expectations of her job.

2. He feels badly about yelling at Tina concerning these matters.

3. He feels stressed about the angry customers he must deal with at times. For example, a customer yelled at him for refusing to replace an old lawn mower with a brand new one, even though the mower had been abused and the warranty had expired.

4. He is excited that his wife will soon give birth to their second child.

5. Though stressed by his job, he likes the growth potential it provides.

Professor Justice proposes that Joe talk freely about these matters. As he does so, Professor Justice will ask appropriate questions to help Joe clarify and expand on them and his feelings. He further asks the class to focus on the verbal, nonverbal, and para-verbal messages that Joe sends.

PROCEDURE

Ask for a volunteer to assume the role of Joe. The instructor should either assume the role of Professor Justice or ask another student to take on that role.

The selected student discusses his or her work and life as Joe based on the issues identified and his or her understanding of Joe's role profile. The student should feel free to expound on the matters identified and interject his or her own personality into the character to the extent he or she feels comfortable. If a female student is selected, she should feel free to modify the factual situation to adapt the role to a female perspective. The student should be seated and should speak, use body movements, and engage in other natural communication patterns, as appropriate. The instructor or selected second volunteer should ask appropriate clarifying questions as needed to encourage the student to "open up."

Divide the remainder of the class into three groups. Ask the first group to observe Joe's verbal communication, the second group nonverbal communication, and the third para-verbal communication. Students should take notes of particular messages, communication patterns, and other aspects they consider to be significant.

Joe and the instructor should spend no more than fifteen minutes in discussion.

Alternative procedure: Rather than have a student assume the role of Joe, ask if anyone would be comfortable talking about his or her own work and life. If so, engage in the same process of inquiry and observation as outlined previously.

Case Questions

In class, discuss the specific messages that Joe sent through the three communication channels.

1. What were the verbal, nonverbal, and para-verbal messages?

2. Were nonverbal and para-verbal messages consistent or divergent from the verbal messages sent?

3. Did the groups "read" Joe correctly, or were the messages received different from the messages Joe intended to send?

4. What do these observations tell you about the challenges and complexities of communication or about the challenges you might encounter when addressing a conflict?

ALTERNATIVE PROCEDURE FOR ONLINE LEARNING FORMATS

Facilitating this case will be possible only if some form of videoconferencing is used for the course. If so, the instructor can engage in the interview process with the selected student while other students observe remotely from their computers. Afterward, have students respond to the questions and engage in other conversation about what they observed.

Alternatively, the instructor can ask for a volunteer to engage in this conversation beforehand, record it, and post the video online for all students to review. Then, have students prepare written responses to the questions above and post them online. If desired, engage in further online forum discussions or chats as time allows.

Optional discussion: Even with the use of video capabilities as outlined above, many of the nuances and subtle messages inherent in nonverbal and para-verbal communication will be missed compared to meeting face to face. While use of teleconferencing will enable parties to infer meaning through voice, inflection, and tone, the nonverbal messages associated with visual communication will be missed. And picking up nonverbal and para-verbal messages will be impossible through written communication alone, such as through e-mails, texting, or online chats. As an additional or alternative discussion to this case, have students discuss the limits of communication and resolving conflict situations when the nonverbal and para-verbal communication channels are limited or unavailable as a result of using these alternative mechanisms for communicating.

PERSONAL GROWTH EXERCISE

During your next conversation with a friend or your spouse or significant other, observe the channels through which he or she is conveying feelings and meaning. Which channel was utilized most to convey the true meaning of the person's message? Which was utilized least?

TO LEARN MORE

The following books provide an in-depth study of interpersonal communications:

DeVito, Joseph A. *Communication: Concepts and Processes.* Englewood Cliffs, NJ: Prentice Hall, 1976.

Knapp, Mark L., and John A. Daly, eds. *Handbook of Interpersonal Communication*, 3rd ed. Thousand Oaks, CA: Sage Publications, 2002.

Richman, Virginia P., James C. McCroskey, and Mark L. Hickson, *Nonverbal Behavior in Interpersonal Relations*, 7th ed. Boston, MA: Allyn & Bacon, 2011.

Tague-Busler, Mary, and Tracey L. Smith. *The Key to Survival: Interpersonal Communication*, 3rd ed. Long Grove, IL: Waveland Press, Inc, 2006.

NOTES

1. *The Oxford Dictionary of Quotations*, 3rd ed. (New York: Oxford University Press, 1979), 735.

2. C. K. Ogden and I. A. Richards, *The Meaning of Meaning* (San Diego, CA: Harcourt Brace Jovanovich, 1923).

3. Fons Trompenaars, *Riding the Waves of Culture.* London: Nicholas Brealey Publishing, 1993, quoted in L. Axelrod and R. Johnson, *Turning Conflict into Profit: A Roadmap for Resolving Personal and Organizational Disputes* (Edmonton AB: University of Alberta Press, 2005), 124–25.

4. Geert Hofstede, *Culture's Consequences: Comparing Values, Behaviors, Institutions and Organizations Across Nations.* Thousand Oaks, CA: Sage Publications, 2001, quoted in www.geert-hofstede.com/hofstede_Mexico.shtml.

5. John Gray, *Men Are from Mars, Women Are from Venus: A Practical Guide for Improving Communication and Getting What You Want in Your Relationships* (New York: HarperCollins, 1992), 39.

LISTENING TO RESOLVE CONFLICT AND BUILD LASTING RELATIONSHIPS

PERFORMANCE COMPETENCIES

After you have finished reading this chapter, you will be able to

- List and describe three parts of a message and explain how to respond accurately to all three parts
- Describe the four levels of communication
- Communicate at all levels as needed when resolving conflict
- Paraphrase, produce empathic responses to diffuse anger, and build rapport when resolving conflicts

We will now study and learn how to hear all of what a person says and does. Hearing and accurately understanding all information others send to us is hard work. Fortunately, it is possible to hear all of a person when we understand the communication process we have invented for sending, receiving, and interpreting data. Knowing the process well and using the appropriate tools covered in this chapter will help us in our quest to understand others and to be understood. Only when our words and behaviors are communicated and heard accurately can we hope to avoid conflicts, resolve them, and build intimate relationships with others.

> All messages are composed of content, feelings, and relationship statements.

Let us begin our study by first recognizing that all messages are composed of three parts:

Part I   **Content:** Facts, data, information sent (written or spoken)

Part II   **Feelings:** Emotions and intentions felt by the communicator (usually sent nonverbally and para-verbally)

Part III   **Relationship:** Statement about the nature or quality of the relationship (the extent one values the relationship with whom he or she is communicating)

I like to listen. I have learned a great deal from listening carefully. Most people never listen.

Ernest Hemingway

Messages we send and receive may contain one or all three parts. Consider this message:

> Hey readers, I want you to come to my house for a party. Please, show up. I will give you directions later.

This message contains all three parts:

1. The **content part** is simple to detect: *The author is asking that you come to his party and is providing directions to his house (the directions will contain a great deal of content).*

2. The **feeling part** of the message is fairly obvious as well: *The author really wants you to come; he even wrote, "please."*

3. The **relationship part** of the message is unstated: *The author values your relationship enough to invite you to his party.*

We usually send content through the verbal channel. We generally send feelings and emotions through the nonverbal and para-verbal channels. We send relationship messages using all three channels. For example, you may tell your spouse or significant other you love her or him (verbal channel). You may say it using a sincere tone of voice (para-verbal channel). She or he may get the message that you value your relationship because you seek opportunities out of your busy schedule to spend time together (nonverbal/behavioral channel).

Many conflicts are created when we do not understand clearly or accurately the content of messages. Conflicts often result when people conclude that they are not valued. Most serious conflicts with relationships result when our content is contradicted by our behaviors, when what we say is contrary to what we do. A husband may verbally tell his wife that he loves her, but if he never wants to spend time with her, she may conclude just the opposite. Effective communicators attend to all three parts of the message as they seek to understand others and to be understood.

Sometimes we send very little content but a great deal of feelings. For example, the statement "You hurt me" contains only three words, but it conveys the deep feelings the sender wishes to express.

Active listeners respond first to the part of the message they think is most important to the sender. To be an active listener, you must probe, seek additional clarification, and do your best to understand the entire message. Active listening builds rapport quickly because listening affects relationships. People feel valued by those who hear and respond to the content and feelings of their statements.

> Conflicts often result when someone concludes that she or he is not valued.

FOUR LEVELS OF COMMUNICATION

We have discussed the three channels of communication (verbal, nonverbal, and para-verbal), the interpretive nature of language, and the three parts of a message (content, feelings, and a statement about the nature or quality of the relationship). Let us now examine how they are put into practice as we communicate within the four levels of communication. Here are the four levels and the tools used to exercise them:

Level I   **Not hearing:** We are inattentive for a variety of reasons.

   Tool used: None

Level II   **Hearing content:** We hear the facts, data, information, perceptions, and assumptions, both written and spoken (i.e., the literal message).

   Tool used: Paraphrase

Level III **Hearing feelings:** We hear and respond to the sender's emotions.

   Tool used: We send an empathic response; we acknowledge that we hear the sender's feelings.

Level IV **Therapeutic listening:** We help others gain insight into their patterns of thought and behavior.

   Tool used: About 80 percent of this level of listening combines paraphrasing and empathic responses; the other 20 percent takes formal study and practice in psychotherapy.

> The four levels of communication range from not hearing to therapeutic listening.

Most, if not all, of our communications fall in one or more of these four levels. Our behaviors, feelings, attitudes, and general reactions to others and the quality of our interpersonal relationships are shaped and influenced by the level of communication at which we operate. Each of the four levels produces both positive and negative consequences and is appropriate under certain circumstances. Resolving conflicts requires that we operate effectively at Levels II, III, and IV.

LEVEL I COMMUNICATION: NOT HEARING AND NOT LISTENING

We do not always hear or listen to what others say to us, and others do not always hear and listen to what we say to them. This happens for a variety of reasons. A primary reason is noise.

Two kinds of noise interfere with our hearing and listening to a message: environmental noise and internal noise. Communication is hindered greatly when either type of noise gets too loud. When you cannot hear the speaker, you are operating at Level I communication. Operating at this level can certainly cause conflict.

ENVIRONMENTAL NOISE

To listen to others, we must first be able to physically hear them. We have all had the experience of trying to talk to someone in a noisy place. People are generally aware of the level of environmental noise when they are surrounded by it. When we realize that the environment is interfering with our hearing, we may shout or move to a quieter place. We may decide to send messages using the nonverbal channel and create elaborate hand signals or other gestures to communicate our message.

The other kind of noise is not so obvious. We may be aware of our own internal noise, but the person with whom we are talking may not. Internal noise resides within our own mind and is also called *internal dialog* or *self-talk*. We all listen to our internal dialog. Many times the amount of self-talk and its volume interfere with our ability to hear and, thus, our ability to listen to what the other person is saying. We listen to our own thoughts as the other person talks. What turns on this internal dialogue and increases its volume? The most common reasons are the way our brains function, differing beliefs, indifference, special circumstances, and threats.

> Our internal dialogue may keep us from hearing others.

Our Brain

Our brain can think many times faster than we can speak, so we have a lot of idle mental energy when someone is talking to us. We may use this extra energy to think of other things. Our attention gets divided. We listen to both our inner thoughts and to the speaker. Or we may just daydream and think of totally unrelated things, like what to fix for supper or what to do this weekend.

Differing Beliefs

The amount of agreement or disagreement between what the speaker is saying and our own beliefs affects our ability and desire to listen. Listening to people spout their particular views on a subject that are totally opposite of our own can really get our internal dialogue going full blast. This is especially true when we care deeply about the topic or hold strong opinions about what the other person is saying. It is easier to listen to someone whose opinions are similar to our own. Listening to another's point of view when that view is causing us a conflict is tough to do. His or her opinion could differ greatly from ours on controversial issues such as politics and religion. Listening to our self-talk is a form of protection. It is a natural reaction to a threat.

Indifference

It is hard to listen to people talk about subjects that are of no interest to us. Listening to people we dislike or are indifferent to is also hard. Most of us can fake listening so speakers do not detect our indifference to them or to their subject. We nod, establish and maintain eye contact, and give attentive behaviors when we are not really listening. The speakers may be fooled into thinking we are listening to them. However, sometimes we only think they are fooled when they are not. If this happens often, we may be inviting conflict into our lives.

Special Circumstances

Our willingness to listen may be lowered or nonexistent under certain circumstances. We may become distracted when we are multitasking or when we are concentrating on our own thoughts. Or perhaps we are introverted and need to be alone to recharge our batteries. Under special circumstances, we may send obvious signs that we are not listening. We turn our attention to something or someone else. A common example is a man focused on reading the newspaper at the breakfast table who nods as his wife tells him something important but hears nothing. The supervisor may not be listening when she continually looks at the clock on the wall as her direct report tells her something important. We try to multitask by typing on our computer while carrying on a phone conversation. These situations have probably happened to all of us.

Sometimes we send obvious signals to others that we are not listening to them.

Reaction to a Threat

Any real or perceived threat will affect our ability and desire to listen. Ironically, this happens often when we are in a conflict, when we need to listen the most. When we realize that our position, opinions, or ideas are being challenged, we may take it personally and think the other person is putting us down. When this happens, we get angry or defensive and stop listening. For example, an employee may stop listening to the explanation his supervisor is giving him for a written warning for inappropriate work behavior because he feels threatened.

Someone who knows and cares about us may give us some constructive feedback on our behavior. We may not want to hear it because if we do, we might feel compelled to change. To many people, change is threatening. When we are threatened, our internal dialogue fires up and we begin to hear and perhaps rehearse in our minds what we will say when the speaker stops talking.

Managing Internal Noise

Can we stop internal noise altogether? Probably not, but we can reduce it. We are generally aware of our internal dialogue and when it begins to interfere. Luckily, we can turn down its volume and, to a degree, manage it. Listening with the intention to paraphrase the message back to the sender is an effective tool to use to reduce internal noise. How and when to use paraphrasing will be explained later in this chapter.

Internal noise volume can be lowered.

EXERCISE 6-1
A SAMPLE OF ME

To illustrate Level I communication and to be reminded how noise affects listening, complete the following exercise.

Time limit: Approximately three minutes

Instructions: Ask class members to form into pairs. Have each pair sit back to back. Both partners in the pair begin talking simultaneously and finish these statements with as much or as little detail as they see fit. When each pair of partners is finished, answer the discussion questions that follow.

1. The name I like to be called is . . .

2. I am here today because . . .

3. So far, I think this exercise is . . .

4. One of my favorite leisure time activities is . . .

5. An accomplishment that I am very proud of in my life is . . .

6. Others often comment that I am good at . . .

Discussion questions: As an entire group, answer the following questions:

1. What effect did the environmental noise have on you as a listener? As a speaker?

2. What effect did your internal noise have on you as a listener? As a speaker?

3. Are you sure you heard accurately what your partner said to you? If so, how do you know?

LEVEL II COMMUNICATION: HEARING CONTENT

Level II communication is about hearing and listening to the content part of a message. Content is the facts, data, information, or instructions we communicate. Sending content is a major reason we communicate with others. We need to listen to the content of what someone is saying to react appropriately. If a husband does not listen to his wife when she tells him to pick her up at 5 p.m., he could be in a tight spot when he does not show. We may overlook times when we are not heard or listened to, but if it happens regularly or if being ignored has serious consequences, we may conclude that we are not valued as a person. Conflict is often the result of such a conclusion.

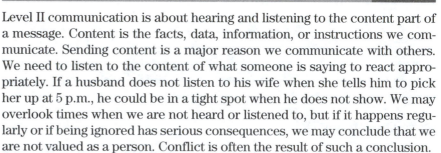

The two kinds of feedback are behavioral and verbal.

If your boss gives you an elaborate, complicated set of instructions she wants you to follow, how will she know that you indeed heard and understood them? Through feedback. The two kinds of feedback are behavioral and verbal.

BEHAVIORAL FEEDBACK

Your behavior—how you react and carry out your boss's instructions—provides feedback on your level of understanding the content of her message. However, behavioral feedback is inefficient. It informs us only after action is taken. When you carry out your boss's instructions as she intended, she concludes that you heard and understood them. When you do not carry out her instructions or make a mistake in carrying them out, she may conclude one of three things:

- You listened to her but did not understand what you heard and lacked the skill or knowledge to carry out her instructions.
- You listened and understood but lacked the motivation or desire to do what she asked.
- You did not hear or listen carefully enough to her.

Training is the fix for the first possibility. Changing motivation is the fix for the second possibility. More effective communication is the fix for the third.

Your boss may take precautions and alter the ways she communicates important or complicated messages to ensure that you understand the content of her message. She may send important messages in writing. Written memos are most appropriate when the message is complicated or long or when the outcome is important to the sender and/or receiver. Your boss may also invite your questions about the contents of the memo to ensure that her instructions are clear before you take action. Sometimes, however, misunderstandings can still occur. You may think you understand the contents of the memo when, in reality, you do not. If you think you understand your boss's memo, you will not ask questions for clarification. Why would you when you have no doubt?

To avoid miscommunication and misunderstanding and the mistakes they cause, we need a more efficient approach for giving feedback. We need to assess our level of understanding *before* we take action. Giving verbal feedback in the form of paraphrasing is the tool for accomplishing this.

VERBAL FEEDBACK: THE PARAPHRASE

A paraphrase is verbal feedback you give to the sender of a message *before* you take action. A paraphrase is a restatement in your own words of what you think the sender is saying in his or her message. A paraphrase will demonstrate to the sender how accurately you understand the contents of a message. After hearing the paraphrase, the sender can make corrections if needed. Dispatchers in emergency situations, such as firefighters, police, and 911 dispatchers, are trained to paraphrase their caller's statement to ensure they have the information correct before the caller hangs up. They also tape-record messages when possible.

> A paraphrase is a restatement in your own words of what you think the sender said.

A PARAPHRASE IS NOT PARROTING

A paraphrase is a restatement in your own words of someone's message. It is not a parroting of the message. Parroting is a verbatim restatement of the message. It demonstrates that you heard the message but not that you understood it. The difference between paraphrasing and parroting is best illustrated with the following joke:

> A wife buys her husband a parrot for his birthday. The husband hates the bird and is even developing an allergy to it. He wants to get rid of it but knows that his wife would be hurt if he did. So, he teaches the bird to say, "Here kitty, kitty."

The bird has the amazing ability to reproduce the sounds but obviously has no understanding of what it is saying.

WHEN TO USE THE PARAPHRASE TOOL

Paraphrasing is a communication tool. Like any tool it has a specific purpose and use. All tools have appropriate uses. A hammer is a tool; so is a toothbrush. When used for the right reasons, they are indispensable. You certainly would not try to drive a nail with a toothbrush or brush your teeth with a hammer. Extending that logic, knowing when to paraphrase and how to paraphrase is key. It is not appropriate to paraphrase when the message is short and obvious or mostly small talk. If you paraphrase everything people say to you, they will probably think you are strange and avoid you. Think how Lenny might react if he had the following encounter with a coworker:

> "Hey, Pete, good morning. How's it going?" Lenny asked as he entered the break room to get his morning coffee.

> "Let me see if I heard you correctly. You're saying it's a good morning and you are wondering how I am doing." Pete paraphrased.

If Pete continues to interact with others in this way, he will probably be the only one in the break room and may end up eating his lunch alone.

Remember, paraphrasing lets the sender know you have heard and understood the message. It is the appropriate tool to use when

- Understanding a message is important to you or important to the sender.
- The message is long and complicated.
- A misunderstanding could lead to a costly mistake.
- Your concentration begins to drift as someone is speaking to you.
- You want to turn down the volume on your internal dialogue.
- You are trying to resolve a conflict.

HOW TO BEGIN A PARAPHRASE

Paraphrasing is simple. You may start by saying something like

> "Let me see if I have this right. You are saying that . . ."

Or you may say it in the form of a question, such as

> "Are you saying that . . .?"

Then, restate in your own words what you think you heard.

In its purest form, paraphrasing is a restatement of what we as listeners think we have heard. We do not give our own views. We do not make a moral or value judgment and say whether we agree or disagree with what the sender has said. Our own opinions, ideas, and experiences with the subject can come later, after we demonstrate that we accurately comprehend the message. After all, how can we determine if we agree or disagree until we first comprehend the message? How can we be sure we comprehend the statement accurately without checking out our understanding of the message with the sender? In a practical sense, the only way we can be sure if we agree or disagree with what someone is saying is to first understand it accurately. This is what Stephen Covey is telling us to do when he says, "Seek first to understand, then to be understood."[1] Only after we understand the views of another person are we ready to evaluate those views.

> The only way to be sure if we agree or disagree with what someone is saying is to first understand it accurately.

WE ARE TAUGHT TO TALK MORE THAN TO LISTEN

Effective talking rather than effective listening is modeled for us on a grand scale. When was the last time one of your messages was paraphrased? How often does it happen? While listening to political debates, talk radio

PART II: Interpersonal Communication Skills for Resolving Conflict

programs, or those in-your-face TV talk shows, we rarely hear someone giving a paraphrase. We hear opinions, facts, and arguments, and we see conflicts arise as a result. But rarely do we hear any listening. Mostly we hear two or more people talking simultaneously. Who is listening? Unfortunately, our political leaders, teachers, and those who have the microphone teach us to talk, not to listen. Through example, we learn how to debate and argue. We are taught how to package our message and send it so it is a convincing one. We learn how to "spin" our views and how to discount and diffuse opposing views. We have become efficient talkers. As a result, talking skills have risen to ascendancy over listening skills.

Talking skills have risen to ascendancy over listening skills.

PARAPHRASING AFFECTS THE SENDER

A paraphrase not only informs the sender that you hear and understand her message. It also affects the sender's packaging of the message. When the sender knows the listener will paraphrase the message back, more care is given to the formation of the message. Usually the sender will be more concise and thoughtful in preparing what she will say. When the sender wants to send a long message, it is important that she stop talking occasionally to allow the listener the opportunity to give a paraphrase. When the message is important, it is advisable to ask for a paraphrase. The sender does not want to ask for a paraphrase too often, however. If she does, the listener may get the idea that the sender thinks he is too stupid to understand her.

TELLING OUR STORY

When resolving a conflict, those involved often want the opportunity to tell their side of the story. They have a story, and they want to tell it. They have an expectation that they will be given a chance to do so and that their story will be heard and understood accurately. Paraphrasing is the key to accomplishing this. As the story is told, the listener should occasionally stop the talker and paraphrase what he is hearing. Generally, the sender will want the listener to get the story correct and will gladly make any needed clarification and correction.

The more we practice paraphrasing, the better we get at it.

The more we practice paraphrasing, the better we get at it. A good way to practice paraphrasing is to complete the following exercise.

EXERCISE 6-2
LET ME PARAPHRASE

To illustrate Level II communication and to use paraphrasing, complete the following exercise.

Time limit: Approximately six minutes for each pair

Instructions: Ask class members to form into pairs. Have each pair sit face to face. Each partner takes a turn as speaker and listener.

Speaker: Pick any topic from the list below that you have opinions about and give a short summary of your opinions (no longer than three minutes) to your listening partner.

Listener: You are to listen with the expectation that when your speaker is finished, you will paraphrase to the speaker what you heard and understood the person to say about the topic. When the paraphrase is over and the speaker agrees that you have accurately paraphrased, switch roles.

Abortion/right to life

Voting reform

Gun ownership

Smoking cigarettes

Prayer in school

Trade unions

Pornography sales

Cloning animals

Victim's rights

Nuclear power generation

Legalization of marijuana

Others of your choosing

After the exercise, ask students to provide their answers to the following three questions:

What effect did the paraphrase have on the sender?

What effect did the paraphrase have on the listener?

What effect did the paraphrase have on the message?

TOOLS TO ADD TO YOUR CONFLICT SURVIVAL KIT

WHEN YOU ARE A MEDIATOR

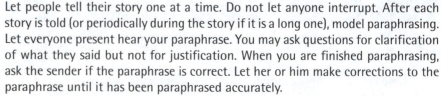

Let people tell their story one at a time. Do not let anyone interrupt. After each story is told (or periodically during the story if it is a long one), model paraphrasing. Let everyone present hear your paraphrase. You may ask questions for clarification of what they said but not for justification. When you are finished paraphrasing, ask the sender if the paraphrase is correct. Let her or him make corrections to the paraphrase until it has been paraphrased accurately.

Instead of paraphrasing the story, as the mediator, you may ask the other party to paraphrase the content of the speaker's story. Check the accuracy of the paraphrase with the sender before letting the other party tell his or her story.

Repeat this paraphrasing process as often as needed. The goal here is to demonstrate that each story was heard accurately. It is a good idea to remind everyone that an accurate paraphrase does not equal agreement.

Be sure that the conflicting parties demonstrate through paraphrasing that they heard and understood the other's point of view before they get their turn to tell their story. Be sure to stop people when they begin to tell their story without accurately paraphrasing the sender's story.

When You Are Negotiating a Conflict for Yourself

Listen to the sender's story with the expectation that when he or she is finished, you will paraphrase the message. It may be advisable to paraphrase periodically if the story is a long one or when your internal dialogue fires up and you begin to listen more to your own self-talk than to the speaker. As you listen, remind yourself of the following:

- Information is power and the more the other person talks, the more information the speaker provides.

- Listening is a powerful offense and not a passive tactic in resolving conflict.

- Listening to a person will change his or her point of view faster and more completely than talking to the person will.

- If you want others to listen to you, listen to them first.

Level III Communication: Hearing Feelings

Our feelings are one of the few things that belong exclusively to us. They are ours alone. They exist within each of us. We alone know our inner feelings. We may explain our feelings to other people and they may empathize, but they cannot feel what we are feeling. As nice as it sounds to hear, no one can "feel our pain." The only way someone can gain access to our feelings is through us. We have to communicate, and others have to listen.

Humans empathize. We have feelings and the ability to detect feelings in others. Effective communicators must hear feelings and emotions sent by the sender. This is especially true during conflict when feelings and emotions run high. Our emotions are often the most important part of the messages we send to others. We want our feelings heard by others. We define the quality of our relationships with others by their ability and desire to hear our feelings. We do not always expect others to do anything about our feelings, but we do expect that they want to hear them, particularly those with whom we have intimate relationships.

You must be able to hear feelings if you are to truly hear all of what a person is communicating. Whether one is depressed, angry, upset, hurt, worried, frightened, happy, content, or excited, we must become aware of it before we can react appropriately. Feelings are often sent subtly in the nonverbal and para-verbal channels and can be easily misinterpreted or missed altogether. If the listener does not hear feelings, the sender

> Effective communicators must hear feelings and emotions sent by the sender.

may conclude that the listener does not care about him or her or value their relationship. How do you react when your feelings are not heard or acknowledged?

To be an effective listener, you must hear feelings and demonstrate to senders that you heard their feelings. That does not mean you have to *do* anything about these feelings or that you have to agree with them. But you must have the ability to demonstrate to the sender of those feelings that you have heard them, whatever those feelings might be. We let the sender know we heard feelings by making empathic responses.

EMPATHIC RESPONSES

The listener gives an empathic response when he or she suspects that the sender has a feeling or emotion. It is not a complicated response. It is merely a statement or question of how the listener thinks the sender is feeling. Consider the following conversation between an employee, Susan, and her boss, David, as an illustration:

> "Susan," said David, "this new project will certainly test your skill at negotiating an agreement. This is a big contract and could be a real boost to our overall profits this year, and of course it will no doubt enhance your career."

> "I know," replied Susan. "It's the biggest responsibility I've had so far. I sure hope I can pull it off." Susan looked down and started to say something else but stopped and slowly turned away.

> "Wait a second," said David, sensing that Susan had more to say. "You know, I remember when I got my first shot at a deal this big; I was worried that I might fail. Are you worried about not doing well?"

> "Well…," replied Susan as she turned slowly to face David. "To tell you the truth, I'm petrified about it. I've been worried sick since last week when you told me I was chosen to negotiate the deal. What if I fail?"

> "I thought there was something going on," said David, as he looked her in the eyes. "You don't seem yourself and I thought you might be worried."

> "Thanks, David, for asking," said Susan as she let out a deep breath. "I feel better letting it out."

David sensed that Susan was worried, and he checked out his hunch. His empathic response, "Are you worried about not doing well?" was in the form of a question. David's hunch was correct.

Sometimes you might feel one way about a situation and the sender feels totally the opposite. As a listener, do not project your feelings onto someone else. Consider this example:

> Martin slowly closed the door to his boss's office as he walked out of it. He had a rather pensive look on his face, as if he were

deep in thought. He walked down the hall and decided to go to Stephen's office to talk about what just transpired. He opened Stephen's door and walked in.

"Hey, Martin," said Stephen, looking up from his desk. "You've been in the boss's office since you got here this morning. That's been over an hour. What's up?"

"Well," replied Martin as he took a deep breath, slowly pushing it out between his lips and making his cheeks puff out. "You know that promotion I put in for last month?" he said in a somber tone while clutching a memo he held in his right hand. "Well…I got it."

"WOW! That's great, man. Way to go. You know you deserve it. Congratulations." Stephen was obviously exited and happy for Martin. "When do you start?" he asked.

"The first of next month," replied Martin.

"That's totally great. I'm so happy for you! What a great opportunity. And think of the raise in pay. That should really help out with the baby coming and all. The boss really made the right call this time." Stephen came from behind his desk and patted Martin on the back.

"Yeah, I guess you're right. I should be happy about it," Martin said as he began to move toward the door. "Well…thanks, man; I'd better get back to work." Martin opened the door and left.

"Boy! That's great," thought Stephen. Martin really deserves it. He sat down in his chair and took a sip of his coffee. He smiled and reached for his computer mouse.

Stephen is genuinely happy for Martin. He said so and meant every word. He is happy for Martin because he would be happy if he got a promotion. Anyone would be happy with a big promotion, wouldn't he? But what is Martin feeling? What are his emotions? Does Martin seem happy about the promotion? Let us hear what Martin says when Stephen attends to the nonverbal and para-verbal messages and gives him an empathic response.

"Hey, Martin," said Stephen. "You've been in the boss's office since you got here this morning. That was over an hour ago. What's up?"

"Well," replied Martin as he took a deep breath, slowly pushing it out between his lips and making his cheeks puff out. "You know that promotion I put in for last month?" Martin sighed in a somber tone as he clutched a memo he held in his right hand. "Well…I got it."

"OK," replied Stephen as he paused to consider Martin's behavior. "Martin, you sure don't seem very excited or happy about the news. In fact, you look just the opposite. Is there something wrong?" Stephen got up from his desk to move closer to Martin.

"Well…to tell you the truth I'm…" Martin paused and looked away. "I…oh, I don't know, I guess I don't really feel good about the promotion. It's probably silly of me, but I'm not sure I can handle the new responsibilities. It's a big jump," Martin sighed and sat down. "And besides that, I'll have to relocate. I'll be moving to the Washington, D.C., office. I like D.C., but I will really miss all you guys here. We are a great team and this is a really great gig. Julie may not like it either. Moving away from her parents will be especially hard on her now that we're pregnant. I don't *even* want to tell her; she seems so content and happy here." Martin shifted in his chair. "So," said Martin as he looked squarely at Stephen, "what do you think?"

Stephen and Martin have very different feelings about the promotion. Stephen would be happy. Martin is not. In the first scenario, Stephen is projecting his feelings onto Martin. Stephen's feelings have nothing to do with Martin's feelings. If Stephen wants to find out Martin's feelings, an empathic response is the right tool. Did you notice how much Martin reveals to Stephen in the second scenario compared to the first scenario? An empathic response opens up, expands, and deepens conversations. Empathic responses give the sender permission to feel and to talk about his or her feelings with the listener. Senders often take this opportunity when it is given. Having a good listener to talk to offers a marvelous opportunity to gain insights into your thoughts and decisions.

> Empathic responses give the sender permission to feel and to talk about his or her feelings with the listener.

EMPATHIC RESPONSES REDUCE ANGER QUICKLY

Strong emotions are often present during times of conflict. Giving an empathic response has a positive effect on strong emotional reactions, especially anger. An empathic response reduces or eliminates anger faster than any other tactic or strategy you may use. Exactly why empathic responses reduce strong emotions has not been determined. Perhaps they ameliorate anger and other undesirable feelings because they validate the sender's internal experience. Senders appreciate that. An empathic response also gives senders permission to feel what they feel, free from evaluation or judgment. Empathy builds rapport and enhances relationships.

> An empathic response is the most powerful communication tool available.

Sending an empathic response is the most powerful communication tool available. It broadens and lengthens our interpersonal conversations. But because of its power, use it with discernment. Do not give an empathic response when you do not have time for lengthy conversations. Do not give an empathic response to another person when you really do not value the relationship or care to hear the feelings of others.

PHRASES DISGUISED AS EMPATHIC RESPONSES

Two examples:

> "I understand how you must feel"
> "I'm sorry . . ."

Many people think that saying "I understand how you must feel" is an empathic response. It is not. When the listener says, "I understand," he is reporting on how he as a listener feels, which has nothing to do with how the other person is feeling. Saying "I understand" is projecting or generalizing your feelings onto others. It is not an empathic response.

How can you accurately say you understand how another feels if you have not asked about her feelings? How can you know what the other person is feeling when you have never experienced what she is going through? For example, if you have never been through a divorce, how can you know what it feels like to get one? You can imagine feelings of anger, worry, and loneliness. You have felt those feelings before and may think that the other person might feel them, too, at this time. To be sure, you should ask how she feels and listen to what she tells you. Often a person will respond to the phrase "I understand" with, "Oh, no, you don't know how I feel. How could you?"

Likewise, saying "I'm sorry" is not an empathic response. Saying you feel sorry for someone may indeed be an appropriate response under certain circumstances. It is, however, another statement about how you feel internally. It does not check out the feelings of the other person.

Sometimes your empathic response may be wrong. You may say, "You seem worried," but the person is not worried. Instead, he feels angry. When this happens, the speaker will usually correct you and go on with the conversation. Conflicts arise when the listener tries to change the sender's feelings by saying, "Oh, don't feel that way," or when the listener discounts the feelings of the sender by saying something like, "You're way too sensitive. Lighten up!" Expressions such as these are evaluative and judgmental. They tend to be decoded as a putdown, and the reaction is usually defensive. They shorten and stifle conversations. The listener gets no new information and leaves the conversation with no more information than he came with.

> Sometimes your empathic response may be wrong.

Knowing the right time to give an empathic response is important. It is appropriate to give one

- When you have the time to listen to a lengthy conversation
- When you are negotiating or mediating a conflict
- When you truly value your relationship with the person

TOOLS TO ADD TO YOUR CONFLICT SURVIVAL KIT

WHEN YOU ARE A MEDIATOR

Listen for strong feelings among those involved. Provide empathic responses when those feelings start to manifest themselves in behavior, such as a face getting red, increases in speaking volume, and obvious agitation. Acknowledge that you hear the feelings of senders. You may make a statement about how you think they are feeling, or you may ask what they are feeling.

WHEN YOU ARE NEGOTIATING A CONFLICT FOR YOURSELF

Be aware of how your own feelings are affecting your ability to negotiate an agreement. Tell others how you feel. Do not wait for an empathic response from the other party. Provide empathic responses. This will lessen anger and other debilitating emotions.

EXERCISE 6-3
TELL ME HOW YOU THINK I'M FEELING

To illustrate Level III communication and giving empathic responses, complete the following exercise:

Time limit: Approximately six minutes for each pair

Instructions: Ask class members to form into pairs. Have each pair sit face to face. Each partners takes a turn as speaker and listener. The sender talks about something she or he is having difficulty with at this time, something that may be causing conflict in life. The listener listens for feelings. When the speaker is finished, the listener will try and determine how the speaker is feeling.

The listener will accomplish this by making statements to the sender like:

- You must feel...(listener fills in feeling word)

Or asking the following questions:

- Are you feeling...?
- How do you feel about this?

Listener: Do the following:

- Paraphrase the content of the message.
- Give empathic responses.

Listener: Do not

- Evaluate or label the sender's feelings as good or bad, right or wrong
- Discount or put down the sender's feelings
- Agree with or disagree with the sender's feelings
- Send any of your own feelings

Speaker will do the following:

- Correct the listener if the listener states the incorrect feeling

When this is accomplished, switch roles.

LEVEL IV COMMUNICATION: THERAPY

We are living organisms engaged in an active exchange with our environment. Each of us focuses on certain features of the environment, actively avoids some, and interprets others idiosyncratically in ways that are congruent with our own internal rules, views, and prejudices. Therapy is the type of listening that helps people gain insight into their patterns of thought and behavior. Mental health professionals, such as psychologists, use it in psychotherapy. One important purpose for this level of communication is to diagnose symptoms of mental disorders such as depression or anxiety. Once diagnosed, a treatment plan may then be prescribed. Therapy is not conflict resolution even if the communication skills used in doing both are identical. Therapy is a fairly long-term commitment between the patient and professional therapist. The relationships between therapists and their patients are intimate and private. Supervisors and mediators are not usually trained in psychotherapy or licensed to practice medicine. Their conflict negotiation conferences will, at best, lead to a satisfactory resolution of conflict. It will not lead to a diagnosis of symptoms or to a prescribed treatment plan.

We briefly describe this level of communication to point out that about 80 percent of it is composed of paraphrasing and empathic responses (Level II and Level III communication). The remaining 20 percent is composed of communication skills that apply to coaching, goal setting, counseling, supportive confrontation, treatment plan management, and even hypnosis. These skills are developed through years of practice, formal education, and training.

> Therapy is the type of listening that helps people gain insight into their patterns of thought and behavior.

PERFORMANCE CHECKLIST

- Only when our words and behaviors are communicated and heard accurately can we hope to avoid conflicts, resolve them, or build intimate relationships with others.

- All messages are composed of three parts: content, feelings, and a statement about the value of the relationship. We usually send content through the verbal channel, feelings and emotions through the nonverbal and para-verbal channels, and relationship messages through all three channels.

- Most, if not all, of our communications fall in one or more of four levels of communication.

- When you cannot hear the speaker, you are operating at Level I communication. Operating at this level can certainly cause conflict.

- Level II communication is about hearing and listening to the content part of a message. Content is the facts, data, information, or instructions we communicate.

- At Level II communication, the listener can use paraphrasing to let the sender know his or her message has been heard and understood.

- When resolving a conflict, those involved often want the opportunity to tell their side of the story. They have an expectation that they will be given a chance to do so and that their story will be heard and understood accurately.

- We communicate at Level III when we hear and respond to the feelings and emotions sent by those communicating to us. Strong emotions are often present during times of conflict. Giving an empathic response has a positive effect on strong emotional reactions, especially anger.

- Level IV communication is called therapy. Therapy is the type of listening that helps people gain insight into their patterns of thought and behavior. Hearing content and feelings is a big part of therapy.

- Communicating at Level IV requires expertise in communicating at Levels II and III. Supervisors and mediators will not be practicing therapy.

True/False

For each statement below, check true or false.

TRUE   FALSE

_____ _____ 1. Our most serious conflicts with relationships result when the content of our message is contradicted by our behaviors, when what we say is the opposite of what we do.

_____ _____ 2. We generally send feelings and emotions through the verbal and para-verbal channels.

_____ _____ 3. Therapeutic listening helps others gain insight into their patterns of thought and behavior.

_____ _____ 4. A paraphrase is a verbatim restatement of someone's message.

_____ _____ 5. It is not appropriate to paraphrase when the message is short and obvious or mostly small talk.

MULTIPLE CHOICE

Circle the letter next to the best answer for each question. On a separate sheet of paper, state why you chose that answer.

1. The three parts of a message are
   a. content, feelings, and relationship.
   b. content, feelings, and emotions.
   c. feelings, therapy, and paraphrasing.
   d. empathy, support, and rapport.
   e. none of the above.

2. Hearing feelings is communicating at which level of communication?
   a. Level I
   b. Level II
   c. Level III
   d. Level IV

3. An empathic response is
   a. the most powerful communication tool available.
   b. a paraphrase of feelings.
   c. therapy.
   d. saying, "I understand how you feel."
   e. a complicated response.

4. When you are sending an important message orally to another person, it is advisable to ask for
   a. clarification.
   b. a paraphrase.
   c. an empathic response.

d. written instructions.

e. all of the above.

5. It is appropriate to give an empathic response when

a. you are negotiating or mediating a conflict.

b. you truly value your relationship with the person.

c. you have the time to listen to a lengthy conversation.

d. all of the above.

1. In what situations would it be appropriate to paraphrase the content of someone's message?

2. What might happen if you were to project your feelings about a situation onto another person?

3. What are some things you could do to improve your paraphrasing and empathic responses?

4. Strong emotions are often present when you are in a conflict. What can you do if during a conflict resolution meeting, anger and frustration are building rapidly in the other person or in you?

One day, Joe is confronted by the following situations:

Scenario #1: Joe goes to the loading dock and sees Anton "Mr. Opportunity" Knox. He says "good morning" to Anton and asks how he is doing. Anton responds: "Man, not so good. My car was giving me fits again. I'm lucky I got to work at all, let alone a minute or two late. Not that anyone around here cares about my troubles. And, they upped the charges on my cell phone again. How am I supposed to pay for that?"

Scenario #2: Tamiko enters Joe's office. Joe asks, "How can I help you, Tamiko?" Tamiko appears nervous and shy. She says, "I need to talk with you about something." Joe responds, "Sure." Tamiko takes a few moments to collect her thoughts and then says, "Anton made some comments to me. Sally said I should talk with you about it. I'm not so sure I should. Anton probably didn't mean anything by it. I don't want to get anyone in trouble."

Scenario #3: Sally enters Joe's office later. She does not wait to be greeted and simply blurts out, "Joe, I'm really concerned about the way Fred is dealing with his staff. I think you have a serious problem on your hands. Has Tamiko talked with you? I can't believe Anton has been saying all those things. But does Fred care? No. He just lets things go on as they are. Joe, I really think you've got to do something about it."

Scenario #4: Joe sees Fred later. "Hey, Fred, is everything okay?" Fred responds, "Yeah, why?" Joe says, "Well, Tamiko and Sally were in my office. They say Anton has been saying some offensive things. Can you tell me what's going on?" Fred responds, as he ticks off points on his fingers, "Well, first of all, Sally needs to mind her own #!*# business. She's such a meddler. Second, if Tamiko has a problem, let her tell me instead of running off to Sally. Third, as far as I can tell, Anton has just been doing his job and minding his own business. Jeez, I can't believe they are making such a scene over a little joke."

Case Questions

In each situation, Joe is challenged to provide the appropriate response to show that he is listening. Consider each of these situations and, for each, discuss the following questions.

1. What messages is the individual giving through his or her words and actions?

2. What might Joe do or say to show that he is hearing content (Level II)?

3. What might Joe do or say to show that he is hearing feelings (Level III)?

4. What more can Joe do to encourage the other party to share more so that he can truly understand what the party is truly thinking and feeling?

Please be as specific as possible in your responses and provide concrete suggestions for how Joe might respond to each situation.

PERSONAL GROWTH EXERCISE

During your next conversation with a friend or your spouse or significant other, give an empathic response when you detect strong feelings being communicated. Note the reaction you get from the other person. Confirm whether your empathic response accurately captured what the other person was feeling. Keep giving empathic responses and paraphrases until the other person is convinced that you truly understand him or her. Afterward, consider how your conscious efforts to engage in these listening practices created greater rapport and intimacy in your relationship and communication with the other person.

TO LEARN MORE

Burley-Allen, Madelyn. *Listening: The Forgotten Skill: A Self-Teaching Guide*, 2nd ed. New York: John Wiley & Sons, 2000.

Carter, Kathryn, and Mick Presnell. *Interpretive Approaches to Interpersonal Communication*. Albany, NY: SUNY Press, 1994.

Cragan, John F., Chris R. Kasch, and David W. Wright. *Communication in Small Groups: Theory, Process, Skills*, 7th ed. Boston, MA: Wadsworth Cengage Learning, 2009.

NOTE

1. Stephen R. Covey, *Principle-Centered Leadership* (New York: Simon & Schuster, 1992), 111; and Stephen R. Covey, *The Seven Habits of Highly Effective People: Restoring the Character Ethic* (New York: Simon & Schuster, 1990), 235–260.

THE COMMUNICATION CONTINUA

PERFORMANCE COMPETENCIES

After you have finished reading this chapter, you will be able to

- List and describe the five response continua
- Give responses to others that build rapport and trust
- Help others solve problems and resolve conflicts

RESPONDING INTERPERSONALLY

Let us take a broad perspective on interpersonal communication by examining the supportive communication continua model. Conflict often arises out of our patterns of communication. Learning to use this model will provide a way to categorize messages that we give and receive. Knowing the type of message we are sending and receiving plays an important role in our ability to understand others and ourselves.

Many responses that we give and receive from others fall somewhere on these five communication continua. Recognizing where messages fall on the continua will provide a deeper insight into the patterns of communication in both written and spoken communication. Our ability to comprehend these patterns will enhance relationships with those with whom we communicate.

In the model in Exhibit 7-1, we have five continua or lines. Each continuum represents a type or category of response that we may either give to others or receive from others. The line also represents a range of responses within each of the categories. The extreme ends of the continua

> Many responses that we give and receive from others fall somewhere on these five communication continua.

The affairs of man are conducted by our own, man-made rules and according to man-made theories. Man's achievements rest upon the use of symbols.... [W]e must consider ourselves as a symbolic, semantic class of life, and those who rule the symbols, rule us.

Alfred Korzypski

EXHIBIT 7-1
The five response continua[1]

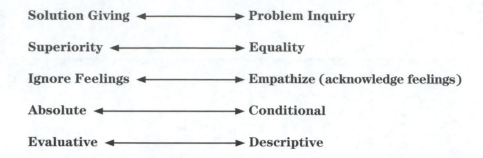

Solution Giving ◄─────────► Problem Inquiry

Superiority ◄─────────► Equality

Ignore Feelings ◄─────────► Empathize (acknowledge feelings)

Absolute ◄─────────► Conditional

Evaluative ◄─────────► Descriptive

Each line or continuum represents a type or category of response that we may either give to others or receive from others.

are examples of opposite comments or responses. Any particular response may fall at the extreme ends or somewhere along a continuum. We will examine each continuum separately.

THE FIRST CONTINUUM:
SOLUTION GIVING ◄─────► PROBLEM INQUIRY

Let us examine the *solution giving* end first. Here we give or receive solutions without any exploration or inquiry about what the problem might be. When you give someone a problem or ask for advice, you receive a solution. It is as simple as that. At this extreme end, the person responding does not ask any questions, he only gives solutions. We have all heard "pet solutions." These can be offered regardless of what the problem might be. Here are a few pet solutions:

"Don't worry about it."

"Sleep on it."

"Time heals all wounds."

"You made your bed, now lie in it."

"You'll get over it."

"Ignore it and it'll go away."

These are typically given as universal solutions.

In industry, female employees comment that their male coworkers are typically solution givers. Their male bosses and colleagues, they claim, do not listen to their problem before offering their own solution or volunteering to fix the problem for the female coworker. They find this annoying and wish men would stop doing it and try to listen to their problem without giving a solution. Their solution giving does not help, they say, and often comes across as a superior message from the male. Let us read an example of a supervisor giving a solution to one of his employees.

Female employees comment that their male coworkers are typically solution givers.

Darla goes to her supervisor with a problem:

"Say, Henry, have you got a moment?" Darla asks as she meets Henry in the hallway. "I have a problem I want to ask you about."

"Sure, Darla," replies Henry. "What's up?"

"It's about one of my employees," Darla begins. "It's Dave. He's come in late two days this week and I was…"

"Write him up, take disciplinary action today," Henry interrupts. "I'll cosign the disciplinary slip later. Right now I have a meeting." He turns and enters the CFO's office.

Darla, a bit stunned by Henry's remark, turns and walks away.

Darla took a problem to her boss, and he gave her a solution. How do you think this affected Darla? How would it affect you if your boss gave you a solution to a problem you were having without ever exploring any aspect of the problem with you? What if Darla was not looking for a solution? What if she just wanted to talk about the problem to gain some perspective on the situation? Darla may now feel trapped. Her boss just gave his solution and he fully expects her to implement it.

When you give a solution prematurely to a problem, three things can happen, two of which are undesirable:

1. *The solution given works.* When you approach your boss with a problem and he gives you his solution and it works, you will likely seek him out for a solution to your next problem. This may develop into a habit, and you become dependent on his problem-solving expertise. This is undesirable especially if he has a department full of dependent problem solvers. He will never be able to take a vacation.

2. *The solution given fails.* Another possibility is that the solution he gives you fails miserably, and the result makes your life a living hell. You may be angry with him, which is also undesirable.

3. *The solution given is ignored.* The third possibility is that you will just ignore his solution and seek advice from someone else or try to solve it yourself. Of the three possibilities, this is probably the most desirable. In Darla's situation, she may ignore her boss's solution, hopefully without upsetting the boss.

Let us now look at the *problem inquiry* end of the continuum. At this end, we ask open-ended questions such as the following:

- What's going on?
- Who is involved?
- How long has this problem been going on?
- What have you done so far?
- What have you thought about trying?

Open-ended questions such as these are probing questions. They tend to expand the conversation, open up our thoughts, and enrich our exploration of the problem. They help us identify symptoms and define the problem. Problem inquiry often leads to a better understanding of the problem and increases the number of possible solutions. A solution is the product of a problem-solving process, and problem inquiry is the foundation of effective problem-solving techniques. Solutions are considered only after a thorough examination of the problem has ended. Operating at the problem inquiry end of the continuum also affects motivation to carry out the

> Open-ended questions tend to expand the conversation, open up our thoughts, and enrich our exploration of the problem.

solution. It often helps others discover their own solution to their problems or conflicts. Generally, people are more motivated to carry out a solution they have participated in creating. A supervisor can teach her direct reports how to analyze their problems and conflicts by operating at the problem inquiry end of this continuum and empower them with a sound set of problem inquiry skills.

> Operating at the problem inquiry end affects motivation to carry out the solution.

Remember that one end of this continuum is not necessarily better than the other. Both extreme ends have consequences that may be positive or negative given the circumstances. Operating at the solution giving end would be appropriate, for example, when your direct report brings you a problem that only you have the expertise to solve. It would also be appropriate in a crisis situation that requires the implementation of an immediate solution and time does not allow you to help another gain insight into the problem.

TOOLS TO ADD TO YOUR CONFLICT SURVIVAL KIT

When someone brings you a problem, ask open-ended questions that probe into the symptoms of the problem.

THE SECOND CONTINUUM: SUPERIORITY ⟷ EQUALITY

Do you recognize those times when someone is talking down to you, when someone's responses are intended to let you know the person considers himself or herself to be in some way superior to you? The following phrases are good examples of messages from the *superiority* end of the continuum:

"I knew you couldn't do it."

"I told you so."

"I would never have made that mistake."

"Boy, are you that stupid and naïve?"

Generally, messages that start with the word *you* are from this end of the continuum:

"You really messed up."

"You have a problem."

"You always seem to make mistakes."

"You are too sensitive, I was just kidding."

Questions starting with the word *why* can also show a superior attitude:

"Why in the world did you do that?"

"Why can't you be more reasonable?"

Of course these are not really questions: They are statements disguised as questions.

Having to justify your action to another person can produce defensiveness and hard feelings. Superior statements such as these will often put you on the defensive. Sometimes you will get messages that make you feel that the sender is treating you like a child. For example, "I'm going to say this very carefully, very slowly, so that even *you* can understand it." Superior messages are intended to make us feel one down to the speaker.

Having to justify one's action to another person can produce defensiveness and hard feelings.

Let us now examine the *equality* end of this continuum. "We and us" are equality-type words. Examples of equality phrases include the following:

"We're in this together."

"We have a problem."

"We can work it out."

"We all make mistakes."

These statements send an equality message and are often regarded as being supportive by those who receive them.

The Third Continuum: Ignore Feelings ⟷ Empathize (Acknowledge Feelings)

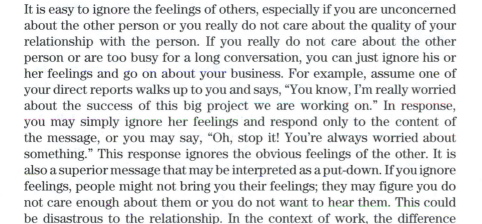

It is easy to ignore the feelings of others, especially if you are unconcerned about the other person or you really do not care about the quality of your relationship with the person. If you really do not care about the other person or are too busy for a long conversation, you can just ignore his or her feelings and go on about your business. For example, assume one of your direct reports walks up to you and says, "You know, I'm really worried about the success of this big project we are working on." In response, you may simply ignore her feelings and respond only to the content of the message, or you may say, "Oh, stop it! You're always worried about something." This response ignores the obvious feelings of the other. It is also a superior message that may be interpreted as a put-down. If you ignore feelings, people might not bring you their feelings; they may figure you do not care enough about them or you do not want to hear them. This could be disastrous to the relationship. In the context of work, the difference between the success and failure of a project could very well ride on the feelings people have about the project and their ability to talk to you about their feelings, regardless of what those feelings may be.

We have already learned about empathic responses in our reading about hearing and responding to feelings at Level III communication. When feeling messages are sent to you, you can acknowledge you heard them by giving an empathic response or by asking questions about the feelings of the other person. Acknowledging that you heard the feelings will affect the conversation. Empathic responses provide senders an opportunity to discuss their feelings with you if they choose. They usually expand the conversation as people open up and discuss their inner feelings. Empathic responses send the unspoken message that you care about the other person.

What are some absolute words that leave no room for variability, flexibility, or uncertainty regardless of the situation or circumstance? Here are a few examples:

Never

Always

Yes

No

Absolutely

I promise

> **Absolute words are used for effect and are rarely, if ever, accurate.**

Someone may use one of these words when describing your behavior. They are usually used for effect and are rarely, if ever, truly accurate. Statements such as "You never listen to me" or "You always make mistakes" are absolute statements. Are they really true? Does anyone *never* or *always* do anything? Usually not. These words are often exaggerations and extremes intended to get the other person's attention. The sender may also use these responses to convey strong feelings or emotions such as anger or frustration. Of course, they are also used when sending strong positive emotions such as love. "I will always love you" is nice to hear and say; it conveys a strong sentiment. But alas, in many relationships, *always* ends way too soon. Sometimes it is important and appropriate to use the words *yes* and *no*. Others often expect our *yes* to mean yes and our *no* to mean no. They count on us to be honest and forthright and want to be able to trust us. Yet, these are absolute words and you should use them only when you are determined and resolute in carrying out your yes or no. If you say, "Yes, I will be there for you," you had better deliver. If you say "yes" but do not mean it, others may conclude that you are untrustworthy or, worse, that you are a liar. The phrase *I promise* is also on the list of absolutes. Do not promise unless you are sure you can deliver on that promise. Breaking promises is a sure way to undermine your integrity and trust.

On the *conditional* end of the continuum are words and phrases such as

Maybe

Sometimes

That's not always the case

Perhaps

We'll see

I'm not sure

The following conversation between a boss and her direct report demonstrates an appropriate use of conditional words and phrases:

> "Hey, Theresa," shouts Ron as he approaches her in the break room. "I have a problem with the new inventory control software. I have an idea on how to change the software so it is more user-friendly. But, I'm not exactly sure the change will work."

"Well," responds Theresa, "let's hear your idea. I know this software is somewhat complicated. I have some experience with it, but I'm not sure of all the nuances and there are some programming aspects I don't totally understand. I'm still learning it myself, but I agree that it could provide better information with some changes. If you think your change will help, let's try it. It may not work, but it's worth a try."

"That's great, Theresa," Ron replies as he hands Theresa a memo. "I appreciate your being honest with me. Here are my ideas on the improvements. Let me know your thoughts."

When you are sure and confident about what you know, say so. If there are times when you are not sure about what to do, say so. Theresa is not sure about how to make the software better, and she lets Ron know this. Employees will respect your honesty and candor. Many situations and problems may have a variety of possible solutions or approaches to choose from, and in those cases, it is appropriate to respond conditionally. One's choice of one action over another is often a matter of preference or style. If you give absolute statements when they are not needed or for the sake of looking knowledgeable, problems could arise. When you operate at the absolute end predominately, your behavior may be interpreted as overbearing. Some may even think of you as a "know-it-all."

> When you are not sure and confident about what you know, say so.

THE FIFTH CONTINUUM: EVALUATIVE DESCRIPTIVE

Descriptive responses describe a situation or a set of data or observations. They do not evaluate the situation or data. For example, if you say that your boss holds a meeting every Monday at 9 a.m., you are being descriptive. If you say that your boss has too many meetings, you are being evaluative. A movie critic may give a movie a "thumbs down" to show dislike for it. If the movie's director wants to improve his moviemaking in the future, how useful are the critic's remarks? Not very, since all the critic said is that the movie is not good. Evaluative responses communicate only one's interpretation of events or data. Descriptive responses inform through specificity and are especially important when improvement is necessary.

Let us examine two responses that illustrate each end of the continuum. David just received the following memo from his boss:

Dave,

I just finished reading your 30-page report on your proposed changes to our production flow. This is an unsatisfactory report as written.

Please submit your revised report to me by the end of the week.

Thank you,
Roger

Dave's boss sent him an evaluative response. Dave now knows that his boss thinks his report is unsatisfactory, but he has no clue why, and even less of a clue of what needs to be revised. His boss did not provide any descriptive response. Dave is left to guess about what is wrong and what to change. Dave might guess incorrectly, make inappropriate changes, and turn in another inferior report. A conflict between Dave and his boss may arise if this happens.

Let us read the memo that contains descriptive responses from Dave's boss:

Dave,

I just finished reading your 30-page report on your proposed changes to our production flow. Before I send it forward, I want to give you my feedback.

On page 2, paragraph #3, page 5, paragraph #1, in several places on pages 13 through 20, and in Appendix I-A, you use acronyms that are unique to our company and not widely understood by outsiders. As this report will be read by outside investors, I think you need to explain the acronyms. Also, production data are missing from column #6 in the graph found on page 16.

Please submit your revised report to me by the end of the week.

Thank you,

Roger

This descriptive response from Roger provides Dave with important information he can use in revising the report. Dave can make the changes, improve his report, and learn that he must consider his audience when writing reports.

TIPS TO REMEMBER ABOUT THE FIVE CONTINUA OF RESPONSES

1. A mature communicator can move along the entire line of the continua when appropriate.

2. Being stuck at any one point on any one of the continua may inhibit effective communication, problem analysis, and problem solving.

3. Responding to others predominately at the left hand of the continua may endanger the quality of the relationship between you and the person with whom you are talking.

4. Responding only on the right side may be interpreted as passive. Others may see this as a weakness and try to take advantage of you.

5. Responding from the right side of the continua may build rapport quickly. Others sense your support and concern for them as a person, which enhances your relationship.

TOOLS TO ADD TO YOUR CONFLICT SURVIVAL KIT: THE FIVE CONTINUA OF RESPONSES

WHEN YOU ARE A MEDIATOR

When an individual responds predominately on the left side of the continua and this interferes with the process, set an example. Give responses from the right side of the continua. Your modeling responses from the right side may motivate the individual to do likewise.

WHEN YOU ARE NEGOTIATING A CONFLICT FOR YOURSELF

Be cognizant of how your responses are affecting the other person and the negotiation process. Operate along all areas of each continuum. In most cases, it is advisable to operate more to the right end of the continua than the left end.

EXERCISE 7-1
PATTERNS OF RESPONSES

To chart your pattern of responses, complete the following exercise.

The pattern of responses we give and receive defines the quality of our interpersonal relationships. It is important to study our communication patterns to make necessary adjustments that may improve our relationships with others. Try the following exercise.

Over seven days, plot the responses you receive from others and you give to others on the following five continua of responses. Use an uppercase "X" to identify responses that you receive from others. Use an uppercase "O" to identify responses that you give to others so you can tell them apart.

For example, when you receive a solution from someone, you will place an uppercase "X" at the solution giving end of the first continuum. If you give a solution, you will place an uppercase "O" at the solution giving end of that continuum. If you give a superior response, place an "O" at the superior end of the second continuum. If you receive an equality response, place an "X" at the equality end on that continuum and so forth. (See the following example.)

The Five Response Continua

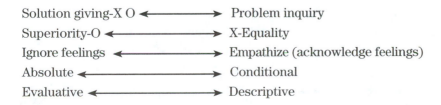

Solution giving-X O ⟵⟶ Problem inquiry
Superiority-O ⟵⟶ X-Equality
Ignore feelings ⟵⟶ Empathize (acknowledge feelings)
Absolute ⟵⟶ Conditional
Evaluative ⟵⟶ Descriptive

> The pattern of responses we give and receive defines the quality of our interpersonal relationships.

Study the distribution of responses you have plotted. Reflect on the effect the responses had on you as a receiver and think about the reaction of those to whom you gave your responses. After reflecting on the placement of responses, you may see a need to adjust the distribution. For example, if you continually receive responses from your boss that fall on the left end of the continua, you may desire that she send responses from the right end. You can influence her to do so by operating on the right end of the continua yourself as you respond to her. Perhaps she will follow your example. If you predominately operate at one end, simply adjust your responses to the other end of the continua.

PERFORMANCE CHECKLIST

- Many responses that we give and get from others fall somewhere on the five communication continua. Recognizing where messages fall on the communication continua will provide a deeper insight into the patterns of communication in both written and spoken communication.

- Solution Giving ◄——► Problem Inquiry:
  - Conflict often arises out of our patterns of communication. Our ability to comprehend patterns of communication enhances our relationships. A supervisor who gives *solutions* may negatively affect the decision-making ability of his employees.
  - Engaging in *problem inquiry* often helps others discover their own solution to their problem or conflicts. Problem inquiry uses open-ended questions to expand the conversation, open up our thoughts, and enrich our exploration of problems; they help us gain insight into our problems.

- Superiority ◄——► Equality:
  - People generally respond negatively to *superior* messages. They produce defensiveness and hard feelings.
  - *Equality* messages have the opposite effect. Those who receive them often regard them as being supportive.

- Ignore Feelings ◄——► Empathize (acknowledge feelings):
  - *Ignoring feelings* can cause conflict and damage relationships.
  - *Empathic* responses provide senders an opportunity to discuss their feelings if they choose. These responses usually expand the conversation as people open up and discuss their inner feelings. They send the unspoken message that you care about others.

- Absolute ◄——► Conditional:
  - *Absolute* responses are seldom accurate. They leave no room for variability, flexibility, or uncertainty.
  - *Conditional* responses are appropriate to give when you are unsure about how to respond to another person or when there are a variety of possible solutions or approaches from which to choose.

- Evaluative ◄——► Descriptive:
  - *Evaluative* responses communicate only one's interpretation of events or data.
  - *Descriptive* responses inform through specificity and are especially important when improvement is necessary.

- An effective communicator can respond anywhere along the five communication continua.

- Responding from one end of the continua is not necessarily better than responding from the other end. Both ends of the continua have consequences that may be positive or negative given the circumstances.

For each statement below, check true or false.

TRUE   FALSE

_____ _____ 1. Descriptive responses describe a situation or a set of data or observations and do not evaluate the situation or data.

_____ _____ 2. Absolute responses are seldom accurate.

_____ _____ 3. Descriptive responses communicate only one's interpretation of events or data.

_____ _____ 4. An effective communicator has the ability to respond anywhere along the five communication continua.

_____ _____ 5. Female employees comment that their male coworkers are typically solution givers.

Circle the letter next to the best answer for each question. On a separate sheet of paper, state why you chose that answer.

1. Saying, "You'll get over it" is an example of a
   a. solution.
   b. description.
   c. conditional response.
   d. paraphrase.

2. Asking "How long has this problem been going on?" is an example of a(n)
   a. conditional inquiry.
   b. problem inquiry.
   c. superior message.
   d. equality message.

3. Descriptive responses
   a. create defensiveness in the hearer.
   b. are evaluative.
   c. inform through specificity.
   d. are *not* important unless improvement is necessary.

4. A supervisor who gives solutions may
   a. negatively affect the decision-making ability of employees.
   b. encourage dependency.
   c. have a difficult time taking a vacation from work.
   d. all of the above.

5. Absolute responses are
   a. seldom accurate.
   b. usually accurate.
   c. conditionally stated.
   d. open for interpretation.
   e. none of the above.

DISCUSSION QUESTIONS

1. When you are mediating a conflict between two of your direct reports and one of them is sending superior-type responses, how would you handle the situation?

2. This chapter noted that female employees report that their male coworkers tend to offer solutions without much problem inquiry. Do you think this is an accurate observation? Explain your point of view.

3. Think back to a time when you were really upset as a customer and called a customer representative in the company to complain. How was your complaint handled? What did the person say or do to help you? Where did the representative's responses fall on the five continua?

CASE: THE RIGHT RESPONSE

Joe recently had a heated argument with Tina Tumultuous that ended badly. Tina accused Joe of treating her unfairly when he disciplined her for her offensive and rude interactions with customers. At the time, Tina had just returned from a three-day suspension for such conduct. After Tina threatened to file a lawsuit, Joe yelled at her and told her to get out of his office. Feeling badly about this, Joe again asked Tina into his office and apologized for being angry and frustrated with her. Tina accepted the apology. Joe then invited Tina to discuss the situation with him in a calmer manner.

To have a successful encounter this time, Joe must engage in the appropriate communication responses.

Case Questions

For each of the situations that follow, answer these two questions:

1. What is the appropriate response (or responses) on the communication continua that Joe should engage?

2. What might Joe say or what actions might he take to use the response you selected on the continua?

Situation #1:
Tina shares that she has recently divorced and is having problems with her older son, who is experiencing legal trouble. Though she has not shared these personal concerns before, she wants Joe to understand what these personal issues are, which are affecting her ability to perform her job.

Response (or responses) on the continua:

Joe might say or do the following:

Situation #2:
Despite Tina's personal struggles, Joe needs to reinforce that Tina's behavior with customers is unacceptable. He wants her to understand that the three-day suspension was justified because her inappropriate behaviors with customers continue to occur and, if anything, appear to be getting worse.

Response (or responses) on the continua:

Joe might say or do the following:

Situation #3:
Tina tries to explain why she has behaved the way she has lately.

Response (or responses) on the continua:

Joe might say or do the following:

Situation #4:
Tina requests that the recent disciplinary action be removed from her personnel file. Joe must tell her that he cannot do this and why.

Response (or responses) on the continua:

Joe might say or do the following:

Situation #5:
Tina asks Joe about ways that she can perform her job better. She asks for specific performance deficits and how these deficits may be overcome.

Response (or responses) on the continua:

Joe might say or do the following:

PERSONAL GROWTH EXERCISE

Over a seven-day period, plot the responses you receive from others and that you give to others on the five continua of responses. Use an uppercase "X" to identify responses that you receive from others. Use an uppercase "O" to identify responses that you give to others so you can tell them apart.

TO LEARN MORE

DeVito, Joseph A. *The Interpersonal Communication Book*, 12th ed. Boston: Allyn & Bacon, 2008.

Lumsden, Gay, Donald Lumsden, and Carolyn Wiethoff. *Communicating in Groups and Teams: Sharing Leadership*, 5th ed. Boston: Wadsworth, 2010.

Stewart, John. *Bridges Not Walls: A Book About Interpersonal Communication*, 11th ed. New York: McGraw-Hill Higher Education, 2011.

NOTE

1. Adapted from Jack Gibb, *Trust: A New Vision of Human Relationships for Business, Education, Family, and Personal Living*, 2nd ed. (North Hollywood, CA: Newcastle Publishing Company, Inc., 1991).

PART III

PREPARING TO RESOLVE CONFLICTS

If you know the enemy and know yourself, you need not fear the result of a hundred battles.

Sun Tzu

ARE YOU CAPABLE?

PERFORMANCE COMPETENCIES

After you have finished reading this chapter, you will be able to

- List criteria used to determine one's readiness to resolve a conflict
- Use ego maturity to develop a conflict resolution strategy
- Determine your and the other party's personal "conflict capability"

Are you personally capable of resolving a conflict through negotiation or mediation? Are you emotionally ready or in the mood to address conflict? What level of formal training have you received in conflict negotiation or mediation? Do you possess the appropriate skill set and level of experience to engage in negotiation or mediation? Are you mature enough to handle the negotiation process where uncertainty and ambiguity are often present? Can you communicate effectively? Are there some types of conflicts you typically avoid? Are there certain types of people with whom you are unwilling or unable to negotiate? Answering these questions will assist you in assessing your level of capability (and the level of others) to resolve conflicts through negotiation and mediation.

ASSESSING YOUR CAPABILITY

Know your personal capability prior to engaging in a conflict resolution process.

You should know your personal capability prior to engaging in a conflict resolution process. Assessing and knowing your capability will influence this process and your negotiation or mediation strategy. Your strategy will in turn influence the quality of the solution to any conflict. It is, therefore, important to consider your capability to resolve conflict as you plan your overall strategy.

It takes at least two people to negotiate.

Cliff Goodwin

It is also important to calculate the capability of the other person involved in your conflict. It may not be possible to directly ask these questions of the person with whom you are about to negotiate. In this case, you may be able only to assess indirectly the other person's capability as the negotiation process progresses. For example

- The other person may tell you during the negotiation that she has taught conflict resolution in the law school at the local university for ten years. If this should happen, it is safe to assume that this person has skill in negotiation. Knowing this will influence your strategy.
- You might correctly assume that a used car salesperson has more experience and training than you do in negotiating the sale price of a car. The assumption that he or she has a greater level of capability in this area of negotiation should be used to help you prepare to negotiate and design your strategy.
- On the other hand, you may come to learn something about the other person that reduces his capability or willingness to negotiate. He may have an overwhelming problem that will make negotiating with him highly unlikely or impossible. For example, you may be negotiating with someone who is an alcoholic and skilled in manipulating others to get his way.

You can calculate your degree of capability and the degree of capability of others involved in a conflict by completing the questionnaire in Exhibit 8-1.

You may come to learn something about the other person that explains his or her capability or willingness to negotiate.

You can calculate your degree of capability and the degree of capability of others involved in a conflict.

EXHIBIT 8-1
Conflict capability questionnaire

Purposes

- To determine a numerical value on your overall capability for resolving conflict
- To determine the difference in overall capability between two parties involved in a conflict

Uses

- To determine when you should negotiate your own conflict or use the services of a mediator
- To determine the best strategy for managing the mediation process

Instructions

When negotiating your own conflict
- Circle the number that best describes your personal assessment of each of the seven factors.
- Circle the number that best describes your perceived assessment of the seven factors for the other party with whom you are having conflict.
- Complete this questionnaire before you choose to negotiate your own conflict.

When mediating a conflict between two parties
- Have each party complete the questionnaire to calculate their personal quotient prior to the first mediation meeting.

EXHIBIT 8–1
Conflict capability questionnaire
Continued

Factor	1	2	3	Score for self or for Party A	Perceived score for other party or for Party B
1. Experience in resolving conflict	Little or no experience	Some experience	Great deal of experience		
2. Amount of formal training in resolving conflict	Little or no training	Some training	Great deal of formal training		
3. Attitude towards conflict in general	All conflicts are bad and best avoided	Conflict is difficult, but possible to resolve	Conflicts are sometimes unavoidable and can be resolved		
4. Current mood over this conflict	Angry, defensive, and holding a grudge	Only moderately angry and defensive	Calm and rational over this conflict		
5. Level of willingness to confront this conflict	Little or no willingness	Somewhat willing	Highly willing		
6. Level of willingness to resolve this conflict	Little or no willingness	Somewhat willing	Highly willing		
7. Level of personal responsibility for resolving this conflict	I take no share of the responsibility for resolving this conflict	I take some share of the responsibility for resolving this conflict	I take my share of the responsibility for resolving this conflict		

Scoring the questionnaire

Total score for self: _____

Interpreting the scores:

Total score for other party: _____

High score: 17 to 21 points
Medium score: 12 to 16 points
Low score: 7 to 11 points

WHEN NEGOTIATING YOUR OWN CONFLICT

Prior to negotiating your own conflict, calculate your self-score and your best guess of the score for the other party:

- If your self-score is in the high range (17 points or higher), you are most likely capable of negotiating an effective resolution to your conflict.
- If your self-score is in the medium range (12 points to 16 points), you will probably be able to negotiate a satisfactory solution to your conflict. It would be to your benefit to raise your capability through self-development and study of negotiation strategies prior to attempting to negotiate. When the conflict is a serious one or very important, hire a professional mediator.
- If your self-score is in the low range (11 points or lower), you should consider hiring the services of a professional mediator or seek the advice of someone you perceive to have a high level of capability.
- If your total perceived score for the other party is 9 points different from your own personal score (higher or lower), consider hiring a professional mediator.

WHEN THE SUPERVISOR ACTS AS A NEGOTIATOR

Conflicts arise over a variety of human behavior issues that occur at work. Employees may break established rules or have disagreements and conflicts with other employees or with their supervisor. Mistakes, errors in judgment, disciplinary action, or the results of a performance appraisal may be common sources of conflict between employees and supervisors. Effective supervisors must be skilled negotiators.

> Effective supervisors must be skilled negotiators.

Supervisors may also have to negotiate with other supervisors or managers. Allocation of resources, new initiatives, and changes in operations or policy are sources of conflict. Supervisors may need to negotiate with upper management or with union officials when their interests or the interests of their department or employees are threatened.

Upper management generally expects that conflict be resolved at the lowest level in the management hierarchy. Therefore, resolving conflict usually starts with supervisors. How well supervisors negotiate a conflict can have serious ramifications for them and their organization. Poorly negotiated conflicts can result in turnover of good employees, low productivity, lower quality of work, low motivation and morale, union grievances, and lawsuits.

> Resolving conflict usually starts with the supervisor.

To illustrate how the conflict capability questionnaire can be used to assist a supervisor to negotiate a conflict, consider the following situation:

Laura was socializing too much with other employees, overstaying her coffee breaks, and too often making personal telephone calls. Her supervisor, Michelle, was inclined to be tolerant of this behavior until she noticed that Laura's socializing was negatively affecting the productivity of others.

Michelle was not always confident in her ability to resolve conflicts. She had practically no positive experiences with resolving conflict. This was true both at home and at work. Upon the recommendation of her supervisor, she completed an in-service training course in conflict management. All employees had the opportunity to attend the course, but the training was voluntary. Only a small percentage of employees volunteered.

Michelle was glad she took the course. She had already used some of what she learned at home to resolve a long-running conflict with her husband. Michelle was motivated to use her new skills in this situation at work.

Prior to confronting Laura, Michelle prepared her strategy. First she took out her notes from the course on conflict and reviewed the handouts on strategy. There were several strategies from which to choose. The one she picked to follow was appropriate for work-related conflicts. It was one of her favorite strategies because it was simple and straightforward. The handout contained the following strategy:

Step 1: Determine the seriousness of this conflict. Is it a routine daily event requiring only that you monitor the situation, is it an evolving conflict requiring some form of intervention, or is the conflict deeper requiring more direct confrontation to resolve? Can it be ignored? If not, move to Step 2.

Step 2: Complete the conflict capability questionnaire on yourself and on the other party involved in the conflict. If you score in the low range (11 points or lower), ask for assistance from your supervisor or human resources specialist. Do not attempt to negotiate this conflict before seeking advice.

Consider the attributes of the employee with whom you will negotiate. What is your perception of his or her capability to resolve conflicts? How similar is his or her capability to yours? If the employee scores in the low range, involve your supervisor or human resources specialist.

Step 3: Check all your facts, perceptions, and assumptions for accuracy that pertain to this conflict.

Step 4: Conduct a meeting with the other person. Begin the meeting by letting the other employee know why you are having the meeting. As the meeting unfolds, remember to use the communication tools taught in this course.

Michelle followed the strategy. She assessed the seriousness of the conflict and her feelings about it. She did not think it was serious yet, and she was not angry with Laura. However, she did not want Laura to continue engaging in her behavior. Michelle then completed a quick self-analysis on herself and on Laura using the questionnaire. They both scored in the medium range. Michelle was not sure of Laura's experience with conflict but knew that she too had completed the conflict training. She thought this was good because they could use their new skills together as they worked through the process. Michelle next made sure that her observations of Laura's work behaviors were accurate. She then considered Laura's past record as an employee. Being Laura's supervisor for nearly a year, Michelle knew her pretty well and believed that Laura was dependable and conscientious. She also thought that Laura would take responsibility for her behavior and be willing to confront and resolve the conflict in a mature manner. Michelle decided to confront Laura in a supportive way and asked Laura to come to her office.

Michelle began the meeting with a careful explanation of the reason for their meeting. She stated her observations and concerns quickly and was careful not to show any hostility. Michelle explained to Laura how her recent behavior was affecting her coworkers. Laura was defensive at first but became less so when Michelle gave her a chance to explain and defend her actions. Michelle paraphrased Laura's comments and gave a few empathic responses. Michelle and Laura used their newly learned skills in conflict negotiation.

Michelle's assessment of Laura proved to be accurate. The discussion ended with a positive resolution of the conflict. Both parties were satisfied with the process and the outcome. In a couple days, Michelle was pleased with the way Laura had curtailed her socializing. She was also pleased with the strategy she used.

It is advisable for supervisors to take the conflict capability questionnaire to assess their own capability before negotiating a conflict. The higher the score is, the greater the capability. Low-scoring supervisors must work independently or in conjunction with their employer to raise their capability. They should take classes at their local college or attend in-service training seminars when offered by their employer, just as Michelle did.

WHEN THE SUPERVISOR ACTS AS A MEDIATOR

The skills to negotiate are similar to the skills required to mediate. Mediation, however, requires that the supervisor help negotiate a resolution of conflicts between employees. Conflict may arise over differences of opinions, job duties, working schedules, and personalities. Potentially serious conflicts like charges of sexual harassment can be ameliorated and even resolved by supervisors proficient at mediating conflicts.

Let us examine the following strategy for mediating a conflict between two employees and how the questionnaire can help the process.

Step 1: Determine the seriousness of this conflict. Is it a routine daily event requiring only that you monitor the situation, is it an evolving conflict requiring some form of intervention, or is the conflict deeper requiring more direct confrontation to resolve? Can it be ignored? If not, move to Step 2.

Step 2: As mediator, complete the conflict capability questionnaire on the employees involved. Base your scores on your experience with the employees, their track records as employees, and on any training or experience with negotiating conflicts that you know they possess. Do not disclose your scores to anyone. Calculate the score for each employee and calculate the difference in scores between the parties.

Step 3: After calculating each employee's capability score, review the following suggestions.

When both parties' scores are in the high range, the following is likely:

- The mediator can focus on interest-based negotiation.

- Both parties will likely be calm, willing to talk, cooperate, compromise, and collaborate.

- A general description of the mediation process needs to be communicated, but the process may be open and flexible and not bound to strictly enforced guidelines or rules.

When both parties' scores are in the low range, the following outcomes are likely:

- An inexperienced mediator will need the help of an experienced mediator to manage the meeting between the parties.

- The parties may react defensively and aggressively, verbally attack, or have outbursts of anger.

- The parties will engage in positional bargaining.

- Trust in the other party, the mediator, and the mediation process in general will be low.

- The mediation process should be highly structured with established ground rules. For example, establish the rule that all parties get to speak their mind and tell their side of the story without interruption. These ground rules will need to be communicated to each party and strictly enforced by the mediator.

- The parties may not take responsibility for their part in the conflict and may thus blame the other.

- The parties may try to avoid mediation or disrupt the process using dirty tricks.

- The parties may have to be separated from one another during the process. The mediator separates the conflicting parties into two locations and engages in a process of shuttle diplomacy, by which he delivers messages back and forth between the parties. This process is also referred to as "caucusing."

When one party's score is 9 points different from the other party's score (higher or lower), the mediator may choose to do the following:

- Level the playing field somewhat for the less capable party without playing favorites or doing more than is warranted to assist him or her. For example, do not let the less capable party agree too quickly to a resolution that will undermine or jeopardize his or her interests. Help the party identify and communicate his or her interests to the other. Take time to explain how the mediation process works and what the party can expect as the process unfolds. Help him or her listen to the point of view and interests of the other person to gain understanding. It may be necessary to paraphrase back to the party what the other is saying.

- Do not let the less capable party dominate the discussion. Do not let him or her intimidate or threaten the other party. If the party engages in these tactics or "dirty tricks," ask him or her to stop. If those tactics continue, call off the mediation.

- Talk to the less capable party about not using dirty tricks. Explain that using dirty tricks will not help anyone get what he or she wants. Help the party identify strategies to use to improve his or her overall capability to resolve conflicts.

IMPROVING YOUR CAPABILITY

You should consider seven factors as you assess your overall capability to resolve conflicts. One factor may influence your capability more than another, but each one is important. Whatever your capability score is now, you may decide to improve it. Let us examine some ways you can improve in each of the seven factors.

FACTOR 1: EXPERIENCE IN RESOLVING CONFLICT

Experience is a great teacher, and the more experience you have with negotiation, the better off you will be. There is an old saying that you can't beat a man at his own game. A used car salesperson is just such a person. He has more experience at selling cars and negotiating the selling price than the average car buyer. He has a game (to sell cars) and experience in playing it. He also possesses more information about the car's worth and value than the average buyer. You may never achieve his level of experience, but you can increase your experience indirectly through preparation. Preparing to negotiate requires that you complete two activities: do your homework and rehearse.

> Preparing to negotiate requires that you complete two activities: do your homework and rehearse.

Do Your Homework

Your homework should consist of gathering facts and details pertinent to the conflict or issue being negotiated. You must gather information because information is power. The more power you have, the better. If you are buying a car, learn as much about the car as possible. For example, find out what other dealerships are charging for the same or similar car. What is its resale value? What do current owners have to say about the quality of the car? If it is a used car, find out its maintenance history. Ask for the name of the previous owner and contact that person. Ask any questions you feel are relevant. Know your budget and decide how much you can spend on a car.

In preparing to negotiate, you must know your *best alternative to a negotiated agreement* (BATNA). In general terms, your BATNA is the point at which no agreement is better than any agreement you can achieve through negotiation. This concept is discussed in greater depth in Chapter 11. Your BATNA is an excellent criterion for analyzing the quality and desirability of any negotiated agreement. For example

> You have negotiated the price of a car you desire from a dealer-ship for $20,000. You have the deal locked up and all you have to do is sign the purchase agreement. But, before you sign, you decide to shop around a little to see if you can beat the price. The $20,000 is your BATNA for any further negotiations. If you can negotiate a better price for the identical vehicle at another dealership, your negotiation will have paid off in your favor. Negotiating to pay more than $20,000 to another dealer for the identical car is obviously undesirable.

During negotiations, keep your BATNA private. Remember that the reason you are negotiating is to beat your BATNA. If you were to reveal it to the car salesperson, for example, he may only match the price of his competitor and your time and effort spent negotiating a better deal would be in vain.

Let us consider a more subtle use of your BATNA:

> Patel's employer has offered him a 3 percent annual increase, an across-the-board amount that everyone at his level in the organization will receive. But, Patel desires a higher raise. He feels strongly that he deserves a 5 percent raise. To negotiate a higher raise, he worked to improve his BATNA. Over the past six months, he networked and interviewed to get a new job. Three days ago he was offered a new job with a starting salary that is 5 percent higher than his current one. His new job offer is his BATNA for negotiating the 5 percent increase he seeks from his current employer. Without revealing his true BATNA, he can inform his employer that he has an attractive offer from another company. He further states that he really wants to stay and will do so for a 6 percent rise in salary. His employer may or may not make a counteroffer. But Patel has an excellent BATNA if his employer declines on any raise higher than the original offer of 3 percent.

Remember, going to court to resolve a conflict is not a desirable BATNA in most conflicts. Litigation is expensive and contentious and seldom results in a win/win solution for the parties involved. If you think going to court is your BATNA, work hard and creatively to develop a better one.

Going to court to resolve a conflict is not a desirable BATNA.

Practice and Rehearse

Practice and rehearse mock negotiations with others through role-playing prior to doing it for real. Play the buyer and ask a friend to play the role of the salesperson, or vice versa. It is best to pick someone to role-play who has more experience than you. For example, go to several dealerships and negotiate with the salesperson at each before making a final decision regarding a car purchase.

FACTOR 2: AMOUNT OF FORMAL TRAINING IN RESOLVING CONFLICT

Increase your knowledge base. Reading on conflict resolution will help you increase your knowledge in negotiating resolutions to conflict. You may also get on the Web and research the topic. Take a course in conflict resolution at your local community college or university. If you do not have the time to do these things, hire the expertise. Professional negotiators, mediators, and lawyers are excellent resources. Do your homework on selecting the right person. There are many so-called professionals who unfortunately lack experience or training.

Mediators, lawyers, and other professionals may have mediation experience you lack.

FACTOR 3: ATTITUDE TOWARD CONFLICT IN GENERAL

The overall attitude you have about conflict will influence your behavior when dealing with it. Therefore, it is important that you think about your attitude in two ways. First, consider the factors that shape and influence your attitude. Attitudes are learned and influenced by our experiences, society, media, teachers, leaders, family, and friends. Examine what you are learning from these sources. Second, because our attitudes are learned, they can be changed as long as we are open to new experiences and influences. The great antecedent to change is doubt. As long as there is a doubt in our minds about the truth of our beliefs, change is possible. Those who are convinced they know all there is to know about a subject will not and perhaps cannot learn anything new about it. They are captives of their present knowledge. The freedom to choose a new attitude is difficult and, over time, nearly impossible. If you desire to change your attitudes about change, do things that challenge your perceptions. Seeking out diverse opinions of others and listening to those opinions with an open mind are useful approaches. Listen for understanding. Do not fear change and overcome your resistance to change through personal study. Be a lifelong learner and experiment. Read books about conflict, take a college course, or attend a workshop. As you learn new things, challenge the correctness of your attitudes.

Those who are convinced they know all there is to know about a subject will not and perhaps cannot learn anything new about it.

FACTOR 4: CURRENT MOOD OVER CURRENT CONFLICT

Do not negotiate or attempt to resolve a conflict when you are in an agitated state of mind or mood. Strong emotions like anger, frustration, hurt, fear, or worry interfere with your ability to think and reason. Strong negative emotions are natural when the conflict is serious. Instead of ignoring your feelings, try to manage them. Before attempting to negotiate, settle down. Use proven methods for reducing your emotions. If you are using the services of a professional mediator, ask her to meet privately (caucus) with you and tell her how you are feeling. When you are negotiating your own conflict and you start to lose your temper at any time during the process of negotiation, take a break. Excuse yourself and leave the room. Put some time and space between you and the other person. Do not just walk away, however. Let the other person know you are interested in negotiating an agreement, but you need time to collect your thoughts and emotions. When you negotiate in an agitated state, you are vulnerable and will likely be disappointed in the outcome.

FACTOR 5: LEVEL OF WILLINGNESS TO CONFRONT THIS CONFLICT

Complete a SWOT analysis.

Completing an analysis of your personal strengths, weaknesses, opportunities, and threats (SWOT) can help increase your willingness to confront a conflict. This analysis is an organized way to assess the level of your personal resources in four areas. The following are examples of what you might find in your SWOT analysis.

Strengths

- You have some formal training in resolving conflict.
- Others have volunteered to help you.

Weaknesses

- As a result of your busy schedule, you do not have the time to invest in resolving the conflict.
- You really dislike confronting conflict and will avoid it most of the time if possible.

Opportunities

- Resolving this conflict will lead to resolving others.
- You will gain respect from your peers.

Threats

- The other party is belligerent and hostile toward conflict. For example, you may be having a conflict with your supervisor who brings vengeance on anyone who confronts him, who "kills the messenger," as it were.
- To resolve your conflict you may need to spend money you do not have.

After the SWOT analysis is completed, you must identify specific objectives or steps you can take to exploit your strengths, minimize your weaknesses, open doors to opportunities, and remove or cope with threats.

FACTOR 6: LEVEL OF WILLINGNESS TO RESOLVE THIS CONFLICT

If you desire to increase your willingness to resolve a particular conflict, it is advisable to complete a cost/benefit analysis of the conflict. Take out a sheet of paper. On one half, list all the costs associated with the conflict. The costs may be tangible, intangible, or both. For example, if your conflict is over an unpaid debt, the lost money is tangible. A conflict over how decisions are made with your boss that frustrates you has intangible costs such as lowering your overall attitude toward work. If your attitude lowers your productivity, there may be tangible effects as well. On the other half of the page, list the benefits you will gain from resolving the conflict. The analysis will help you document the costs of the conflict and the benefits you might get from resolving it. You may also seek the input of others when creating your lists. If the cost is more than you wish to pay, you may be willing to resolve it. If the benefit is too small compared to the amount of work needed to resolve the conflict, you may choose to avoid the conflict.

FACTOR 7: LEVEL OF PERSONAL RESPONSIBILITY FOR RESOLVING CONFLICT

The level of responsibility one is willing to take for the circumstances in his or her life (including its conflicts) is indicative of overall ego maturity. Those who are unwilling to take any responsibility for their actions or behaviors and for circumstances they cause are at a low level of maturity. Resolving conflicts with someone who takes little or no responsibility, however, is difficult and often frustrating. Such an individual can also be easily manipulated and controlled by those who possess a higher level of maturity.

Increasing our level of maturity is a developmental task. How a person develops to higher levels of maturity is not totally understood. Jane Loevinger, a researcher and theorist in ego developments, provides some insight when she writes, "The only way to understand development consists in conceptualizing it as a sequence of structural changes, often stimulated by the interaction of an organism with its environment."[1]

> The level of responsibility one is willing to take is indicative of his or her level of overall ego maturity.

EGO MATURITY

Based on Loevinger's ego maturity research, Dr. Stephen Earnest has developed four categories of ego maturity.[2] Using these four levels, Earnest provides an intuitively appealing conceptualization of how people at each level see the world generally and how they deal with conflict specifically.

OPPORTUNIST LEVEL

Description: This is the lowest of the four levels of maturity. A person at this level

- Views nearly all conflicts as win/lose.
- Views any gain for the other side as a loss to himself whether it is or not and will engage in distortion to gain an advantage. For example, he will say that the other side is getting more than he is out of a negotiated settlement whether or not that is true.
- Cannot be counted on for insight, honesty, or acceptance of responsibility.
- Will usually use manipulation to get his way.
- Blames his problems on anyone or on anything other than on his own decisions and actions.
- Views work as onerous and often has an employment file filled with reprimands.
- Fantasizes cause-and-effect relationships where little or none exists. For example, he may say that the other person made him do this or that thing.

To this person, being wrong equals getting caught. A win/win negotiation strategy is usually not attainable with this level of maturity. An opportunist-level employee will strive for immediate advantage and view any gain by another party as a loss for himself.

Managing Conflicts Involving Opportunist-Level Employees

Having to supervise this level of employee is challenging. When a supervisor has a conflict over work-related behavior, such as poor productivity, she must take immediate action. Behavior modification techniques that use reinforcement strategies are useful in changing this person's behavior. Punitive action for rule breaking is usually needed.

A supervisor must enforce company rules according to the company's established disciplinary procedure to the letter. Any deviation or mistake will be exploited by the opportunistic employee. The supervisor must be sure of all the facts involved in the conflict, however minor they may appear to be, before taking disciplinary action. When confronting the opportunistic employee, the supervisor must arrange to have another supervisor or manager as a witness to the proceedings. It is important to remember that the opportunistic employee will be difficult to hold to any agreement and can be expected to wiggle out of any resolution if given the smallest space. Therefore, any resolution must be in writing and clearly worded to alleviate ambiguity. Everyone involved should sign it. If the employee does not change his behavior, proceed through each step in the disciplinary procedure to termination.

> When confronting the opportunistic employee, the supervisor must arrange to have another supervisor or manager as a witness to the proceedings.

RULES LEVEL

Description: People at the rules level of maturity are conformists. They

- Are motivated by clearly defined rules and will follow them
- Are usually polite and concerned about fairness
- Wish to avoid any unpleasantness
- Frame problems simplistically in relationship to cause and effect
- Often engage in stereotypical thinking
- Identify with their group (being wrong equals breaking the established rules or norms of their group)

Managing Conflicts Involving Rules-Level Employees

Negotiating or mediating with people at this level may appear easy. They value harmony and belonging above all else. People at this developmental level have little insight into their own or anyone else's motivation. Be alert for simplistic cause-and-effect assumptions. Help them construct more accurate and complete cause-and-effect models of a situation, models that provide a richer and more accurate picture of the actual situation. The more they understand the conflict, the better the chances are for resolving it.

When a supervisor is at this level of maturity, she may look the other way when rules are broken or when work performance is inappropriate to avoid conflicts in the false hope of maintaining harmony and to please everyone. Employees may take advantage of this supervisor, especially those at the opportunist level. During negotiations, she may rush the process to regain harmony and may overlook serious breaches in performance.

> A rules-level supervisor may look the other way when rules are broken.

The supervisor attempting to resolve a conflict with a rules-level employee will need to spend time explaining all the reasons why the conflict exists. She must explain the issues clearly, allow for two-way dialogue, and encourage questions. Rules-level employees' lack of insight and eagerness to conform may produce initial acceptance of a resolution that is not really workable. As a result, the supervisor must not rush to a resolution. Allowing a few days to let things cool off and to think about proposed outcomes or having others evaluate proposed outcomes is advisable.

> The supervisor attempting to resolve a conflict with a rules-level employee will need to spend time explaining all the reasons why the conflict exists.

SELF-AWARE LEVEL

Description: People at the self-aware level have insight and some mastery of problem solving that enables them to engage in any type of conflict resolution. They

- Are generally competent in resolving conflict
- May be critical of others, particularly those of lower developmental levels or lesser achievement, which can interfere in resolving conflicts
- May have trouble with long-range planning and with comprehending complex causation

- Strive to achieve the one best solution even when finding one is highly improbable
- Have insight and understanding of their own motivation, which makes true empathy for others possible
- Are typically ambivalent about feedback
- May be reluctant to seek feedback about their behavior from others or even uncomfortable when given feedback they have solicited
- Aspire to achieve a well-solved problem

Managing Conflicts Involving Self-Aware–Level Employees

When negotiating with a person at this level of maturity, engage in careful analysis of the conflict. They may have some difficulty accepting a different definition of the problem at hand. Bring all salient points up for discussion. Make sure their questions are satisfactorily answered. Brainstorm a list of as many solutions as possible and do not rush to closure. They will not usually see their part in the creation of a conflict without some help. Help them by thoroughly examining the dynamics of the conflict and explore their part in creating and maintaining that dynamic. They need patience and reassurance that there is more than one cause for a conflict and more than one possible solution. Be careful to limit their criticism of others. Encourage them to empathize with the other party.

This is the first level of maturity at which you can realistically expect workable, long-lasting resolutions.

> The self-aware level is the first level of maturity at which you can expect workable, long-lasting resolutions.

GOAL LEVEL

Description: People at this level generally possess insight into their own motivation as well as the motivation of others. They

- Engage in goal setting and problem solving
- Are fully capable of collaboration and finding a win/win solution
- May at times have trouble with people of different professional backgrounds
- Will be somewhat faster than the self-aware–level person in the process of defining the problem as well as in finding solutions
- Will take ownership of a particular problem statement
- May have trouble reframing or defining problems in different ways

Managing Conflicts Involving Goal-Level Employees

Having to negotiate with a goal-level employee or mediate a conflict between two parties who are at this level of maturity is relatively easy to do. Interest-based negotiation is probable. The most difficult task for the mediator will be slowing the process enough so that more creative definitions and resolutions can emerge. This is particularly true if the cultures or backgrounds of the participants happen to be different.

Two goal-level people can hope to achieve a win/win resolution to their conflict. One task will be to control the speed of the process so that neither person in the conflict feels left out or slighted. Another task will be to ensure that both participants are careful about how they define the problem, for there will be a tendency on the part of both to think that there is only one correct definition of the problem. When a goal-level person negotiates with a self-aware person, he or she must ensure that the self-aware person feels safe enough and has time enough to ensure that proper insight is available. While negotiating with a self-aware person will be much easier than with less mature participants, the goal-level person should still use caution.

When two goal-level people negotiate, each individual's training teaches him or her a perspective on framing problems that may be different from the way another discipline frames problems. The difference between an engineer and an accountant is a good example. They may have trouble seeing their part in the genesis and perpetuation of conflicts because their own professional perspective may blind them. However, if they can transcend these differences, good long-term resolution to a conflict and strong buy-in are possible.

> Two goal-level people can hope to achieve a win/win resolution to their conflict.

TOOLS TO ADD TO YOUR CONFLICT SURVIVAL KIT

WHEN YOU ARE A MEDIATOR

Complete the conflict capability questionnaire (Exhibit 8-1) on each party in preparation for the mediation meeting. Recognize that the results are your perception of the party's capability score and may not be accurate. As the meeting progresses, pay attention to each party's behavior and adjust your score, mediation techniques, and goals as needed.

WHEN YOU ARE NEGOTIATING A CONFLICT FOR YOURSELF

Complete the conflict capability questionnaire (Exhibit 8-1) on yourself. Ask for feedback from others if you are unsure of your score on any factor. Study each of the seven factors in the questionnaire and use the ideas provided in this chapter to improve your score on any one factor or overall score.

Identify your own level of ego maturity as defined in this chapter. Work to increase your personal maturity level. This can be done in a variety of ways but realize, first and foremost, that your personal maturity is your responsibility. Your maturity may need development if

- You are having conflicts you cannot seem to resolve because others refuse to see things your way.

- You believe that you are a victim of circumstances or that people are constantly taking advantage of you.

- You continue to make the same mistakes over and over.

- Assessing your personal capability will influence your negotiation or mediation strategy, and your strategy will influence the quality of the solution to any conflict. To assess your capability, complete the conflict capability questionnaire presented in this chapter.

- Prior to negotiating your own conflict, calculate your personal score and your best guess of the score for the other party. The higher the score you receive on the questionnaire, the higher the capability.

- Low-scoring supervisors must work independently or in conjunction with their employer to raise their capability. There are many ways to improve your conflict capability score, such as

  - Knowing your *best alternative to a negotiated agreement* (BATNA)
  - Researching conflict resolution strategies
  - Taking a conflict resolution course
  - Rehearsing mock negotiations prior to negotiating for real
  - Dealing with strong emotions before negotiating
  - Completing cost/benefit and SWOT analyses
  - Taking responsibility for your behaviors and the consequences they bring
  - Continually developing your ego maturity

- Upper management expects that conflict be resolved at the lowest level in the management hierarchy. Resolving conflict usually starts with the supervisor.

- How well the supervisor negotiates a conflict can have serious ramifications to him or her and to the organization, including turnover of good employees, low productivity, lower quality of work, low motivation and morale, union grievances, and lawsuits.

- Individuals exhibit one of four levels of ego maturity, which require different conflict management strategies:

  - *Opportunist-level* individuals are the least mature and are generally not capable of negotiating win/win outcomes.
  - *Rules-level* individuals are conformists who are motivated by rules and will follow them.
  - *Self-aware–level* individuals are capable of problem solving, having insight into their motivations, and empathizing with others.
  - *Goal-level* individuals are the most mature. They have insight into their and others' motivations. They engage in goal setting and problem solving and are capable of collaboration.

Test Yourself

True/False

For each statement below, check true or false.

TRUE   FALSE

_____ _____   1. If your self-score on the conflict capability questionnaire is in the high range (17 points or higher), you are most likely capable of negotiating an effective resolution to your conflict.

_____ _____ 2. When both party's conflict capability questionnaire scores are in the low range, the parties may react defensively and aggressively, verbally attack, or have outbursts of anger.

_____ _____ 3. Opportunist-level employees will strive for immediate advantage and view any gain by another party as a loss for themselves.

_____ _____ 4. When confronting the opportunist-level employee, the supervisor must arrange to have another supervisor or manager as a witness to the proceedings.

_____ _____ 5. A person at the opportunist level views nearly all conflicts as win/win.

MULTIPLE CHOICE

Circle the letter next to the best answer for each question. On a separate sheet of paper, state why you chose that answer.

1. If your self score on the conflict capability questionnaire is 17 points or higher you are
   a. most likely capable of negotiating an effective resolution to your conflict.
   b. unskilled in negotiation.
   c. a highly skilled mediator.
   d. free of serious conflicts.

2. If your total perceived score for the other party is 9 points different from your own personal score (higher or lower), consider
   a. negotiating your own conflict.
   b. hiring a professional mediator.
   c. taking a course on conflict resolution.
   d. negotiating a win/win agreement.

3. Upper management generally expects that conflicts be resolved
   a. by the company's lawyers.
   b. by a human resource manager.
   c. at the lowest level in the management hierarchy.
   d. by a professional mediator.

4. During a conflict negotiation, you can expect a goal-level employee to
   a. often engage in stereotypical thinking.
   b. use manipulation to get his way.
   c. blame his problems on anyone or on anything other than on his own decisions and actions.
   d. engage in goal setting and problem solving.

5. During conflict negotiation, you can expect an opportunist-level employee to
   a. view any gain for the other side as a loss to herself whether it is or not.
   b. seek a win/win resolution.
   c. avoid any unpleasantness.
   d. be generally competent in resolving conflict.

1. What are some of the factors that influenced your personal rating for each of the seven factors on the conflict capability questionnaire?

2. Explain thoroughly how you negotiate with a person at each of the maturity levels:
    Opportunist level
    Rules level
    Self-aware level
    Goal level

3. As a supervisor, explain thoroughly how you would mediate a conflict with two employees who are at these maturity levels:

    Both employees are at the opportunist level.
    Both employees are at the goal level.
    One employee is at the opportunist level and another at the goal level.

CASE: ASSESSING CONFLICT CAPABILITY

Joe was intrigued to learn about the conflict capability questionnaire in his Managing Conflict class, so he decided to assess both his own capability for addressing conflict and the capability to address conflict of his colleagues at More Power, including his boss, peers, and direct reports.

Case Questions

Review the role profiles for Joe and other employees at More Power to see how Joe might rate himself and others.

1. Based on your educated guess for each employee, what would you say is his or her conflict capability? Is the employee an opportunistic, rules-, self-aware–, or goal-level individual?

2. What are the potential conflicts you might anticipate in More Power's work environment? Think in terms of paired relationships (e.g., Joe and Jim, Joe and Tina, Sally and Fred, Fred and Anton, Joe and Kim). Based on how you scored and identified the individuals involved in each paired relationship, what will be the best approach to addressing the potential conflict, given the conflict capability of each individual? Discuss as many paired relationships as possible.

ALTERNATIVE PROCEDURE FOR ONLINE LEARNING FORMATS

Break the class into pairs, trios, or larger groups (no more than five students is recommended) and assign each group a specific paired relationship (e.g., Joe and Jim, Joe and Tina, Sally and Fred, Fred and Anton, Joe and Kim). Have them discuss their paired relationship off-line and respond to the questions above. Have each group then post its collective response for all class members to view. Be sure to establish a firm deadline for posting responses. (An alternative to assigning groups is to assign specific paired relationships to individual students.)

Once all responses have been posted, have each student post critiques of at least two of the groups' (or individual students') responses regarding specific paired relationships *other than the paired relationship to which they were initially assigned.* With respect to each critique, have them identify what they agree and disagree with regarding the initial group's response, and why. Be sure to establish a firm deadline for posting responses.

1. Assess your own capability to resolve conflicts by completing the conflict capability questionnaire presented in this chapter. How accurate do you think the questionnaire was in assessing your capability? Explain your answer.

2. Complete an analysis of your personal SWOT analysis to assess your willingness to confront a conflict.

The following resources provide additional information regarding maturity development and human interaction.

Covey, Stephen R. *Principle-Centered Leadership.* New York: Simon & Schuster, 1992.

Gordon, Thomas. *Group-Centered Leadership.* Boston: Houghton Mifflin, 1955.

Loevinger, Jane. *Ego Development: Conceptions and Theories.* San Francisco: Jossey-Bass, 1980.

Putney, Snell, and Gail Putney. *The Adjusted American.* New York: Harper, 1964.

Rogers, Carl. *On Becoming a Person.* Boston: Houghton Mifflin, 1963.

1. Jane Loevinger, *Ego Development: Conceptions and Theories* (San Francisco: Jossey-Bass, 1980), 51.

2. Stephen Earnest, unpublished lecture delivered at Indiana University-Purdue University, Indianapolis (IUPUI), November 25, 1999. The authors gratefully acknowledge Stephen Earnest, Ph.D., organization development consultant and associate faculty for the Purdue School of Engineering and Technology, IUPUI, and the IUPUI School of Continuing Studies for the use of the information gained from this lecture.

OPENING THE DOORS TO CONFLICT RESOLUTION

PERFORMANCE COMPETENCIES

After you have finished reading this chapter, you will be able to

- Identify problem ownership
- Explain the six steps involved in the conflict resolution through supportive confrontation strategy
- Organize your conflict resolution rehearsal
- Describe I-messages and you-messages
- Describe two goals to accomplish when meeting to confront a conflict
- Describe the characteristic differences between a conversation and a sell-job

CONFLICT RESOLUTION THROUGH SUPPORTIVE CONFRONTATION

In every conflict, some need is not being met. Someone is bothered, frustrated, or disturbed about the behavior of another person or group of people. Conflicts arise when we are bothered by a circumstance or event that is the result of others' behavior or action. For example:

- Dave has to work the weekend in order to get a last-minute project finished because his supervisor, Maria, is a poor planner.
- A retail corporation plans to build one of its superstores near your small town, and you are the leader of a community group that opposes the idea.

The easiest, most tempting and the least creative response to conflict within an organization is to pretend it does not exist.

Lyle Schaller

- A neighbor keeps a junk car in his backyard that you see from your new deck.
- Kathy is a spendthrift who is burying her family under a mountain of consumer debt.
- An office manager calls a meeting of her entire staff of twelve people to complain that staff members are making too many personal telephone calls and that it should stop. There are only two offenders, and the staff knows who they are.
- Lester has a small refrigerator in his office where he keeps bottled water. His coworker Samir is helping himself to Lester's supply without asking.

These behaviors or situations are caused by others' actions that may certainly cause conflict. Obviously, some are more serious than others, but each situation can cause distress and, if left unresolved, lead to more serious conflicts. While different strategies may help resolve these conflicts before they escalate, the most useful ones depend on our ability to communicate our problem. An effective strategy for doing this is called *conflict resolution through supportive confrontation*. This strategy is useful in resolving conflicts involving two people or groups of people. It involves six steps:

Step 1: Identify problem ownership using your "window on behavior"

Step 2: Research and reflect

Step 3: Select an alternative to follow using the "three alternatives rule"

Step 4: Rehearse

Step 5: Meet to resolve the conflict

Step 6: Follow through and follow up

Let us use the first situation from the list above involving Dave's overtime problem with his supervisor, Maria, to illustrate the use of this strategy:

Dave has to work the weekend in order to get a last-minute project finished because his supervisor, Maria, is a poor planner.

Dave is really angry because he has to work this weekend. He had planned to spend the weekend with his family at their favorite state park. Now he has to work. His wife is going to be upset when he tells her; the kids have been looking forward to this weekend.

This is the third time in the past two months that his boss has scheduled him to work the weekend. This last-minute overtime fattens his paycheck, but he values time with his family more than the extra money. Overtime is mandatory and Dave knows he cannot refuse it.

Dave suspects that the cause of the problem is Maria's inability to plan ahead. He watches her constantly putting out fires. This last-minute overtime could be avoided.

Dave is fed up and wants to do something about it. Maria doesn't seem to realize how upset and angry he is.

"What should I do? I need a plan," Dave thinks to himself.

This is a potentially dangerous conflict in that it involves his boss. Maria's behavior and the quality of the resolution will have short- and long-term effects on their working relationship. Let us look at a typical plan that Dave might use and study the particular characteristics of each step.

STEP 1: IDENTIFY PROBLEM OWNERSHIP USING YOUR "WINDOW ON BEHAVIOR"

The first step is to identify problem ownership. Dave must answer the question, "Who owns the problem?" Deciding who owns the problem is important because it influences the remaining steps in the strategy.

Problem ownership can easily be determined.[1] Imagine that you are looking out the window onto the world outside. Further, imagine that there is a line running across the window from one side to the other near the middle of the window. Through the window, you observe behaviors, events, or situations. Those that are above the line are acceptable to you and do not bother you. However, the behaviors, events and situations below the line are unacceptable to you, and, thus, you have a problem with them. The farther away the behavior is from the line the more certain you are about your label of the behavior or event.

In Dave's situation, he owns the problem because he is the one bothered by Maria's behavior of scheduling overtime. He is upset that he must work the last-minute overtime on the weekends. As owner of the problem, Dave has the responsibility to inform Maria. He should not assume that Maria knows he is having a problem with her overtime scheduling.

Looking into a Mirror

It is also useful to think of the window as a mirror when determining if your own behavior is causing you a problem. As you look into the mirror again, imagine a line running across the mirror, like the sash in the window example. All your behaviors above the line are acceptable to you, and those below the line are unacceptable. When your unacceptable behavior causes you a problem, you own it. For example, if you smoke cigarettes and it bothers you to the extent that you want to quit, you own the problem. You must seek out ways to resolve the conflict. Others might agree that you should quit and encourage you, but remember it is not their problem.

Your unacceptable behavior may be unacceptable to another person as well. In that case you both own the problem. For example, smoking cigarettes may be unacceptable to the smoker and also unacceptable to the spouse who has a problem with breathing the secondhand smoke. People must work together to find a resolution when they own the same problem.

The responsibility to confront is born by the owner of the problem.

STEP 2: RESEARCH AND REFLECT

Before Dave confronts Maria, he must do some important homework. First, he needs to conduct some organized research on the situation. He must check out his facts and test his assumptions and perceptions. He must answer questions that add clarity to what he assumes about the problem. Good questions for him to investigate include the following:

- Is the problem real or only imagined?
- Is Maria's behavior really causing the problem as he thinks it is?
- What are the underlying reasons for the problem behavior?
- What is motivating his supervisor to behave this way?
- What are his assumptions and are they true?
- What, perhaps, does he not know about the problem?
- Is his supervisor aware of how her actions and decisions are affecting others?

Some of these questions can be answered prior to confronting Maria, and some can be answered only during his face-to-face meeting that comes in Step 5 of the strategy.

The second subpart in this step is to engage in self-reflection. Through self-reflection, we give ourselves the opportunity to reason critically. We analyze our own thought process. As we reflect, we are opening our minds and hearts to the possibility of gaining insight into our personal mental processes and reasoning, which helps us determine whether a behavior is acceptable or unacceptable. Dave will find it helpful to ask questions like these and to reflect on his answers:

> Through self-reflection, we give ourselves the opportunity to reason critically.

- What attitudes, beliefs, and views do I have that might be influencing my reaction to this problem? What are my reasons for labeling this particular behavior or situation as unacceptable? What are the tangible effects of the problem? For example, a loss of income due to a conflict is a tangible loss.
- What is my emotional state of mind regarding this conflict? Am I angry, worried, hurt, confused, or disappointed? And what are the real underlying reasons for these feelings?
- What responsibility do I have in this conflict? Am I doing anything to contribute to this conflict?
- What is(are) my desired outcome(s) and how will I know when I have it(them)?

The importance of conducting effective self-reflection cannot be understated. Self-reflection at its best leads us to critical reasoning. Critical reasoning is an important antecedent to change. Ironically, we are not routinely taught the art of self-reflection. To complete effective self-reflection takes practice, and sometimes it requires the help of others. It is best to ask for help from someone with expertise in doing self-reflection, such as a professional counselor or therapist. Even those adept at self-reflection seek the help of professionals when the conflict is a serious one. A trusted colleague, loved one, or close friend can also help you engage in self-refection.

> Critical reasoning is an important antecedent to change.

The *three alternatives rule* is simple. It states that when someone's behavior or a situation causes you a problem, there are basically three things you can do about it:

1. *Change your attitude.* Psychologically move the behavior from the unacceptable area of your window into the acceptable area so it no longer is a problem and you can just ignore it.

2. *Change your environment.* Make changes to your physical environment or remove yourself from it.

3. *Confront the person about his or her behavior.* Make the other person aware that you have a problem with his or her behavior. Attempt to persuade the other person to change the behavior and then lend support and help if needed.

Dave must pick one of the three alternatives.

Change Your Attitude

If Dave chooses the first alternative, implementation is straightforward. He will simply change his attitude. He may convince himself, for example, that his family needs the overtime pay from the weekends he works. What was once unacceptable now becomes acceptable.

Change Your Environment

If Dave chooses the second alternative, he will need to decide exactly what environmental changes to make, plan the change, and manage the implementation of the plan. He may, for example, choose to transfer to another department.

Confront the Person about His or Her Behavior

There are times when changing our attitudes or environment is inappropriate and not the best or legal thing to do. For example, when an employee is breaking a workplace safety rule that may cause serious injury or death to him or others, changing our attitude, overlooking the behavior, or simply changing the rule may increase the risk of harm. Perhaps we could change the environment in some way so his behavior is no longer a safety risk.

If doing this is too costly or takes too long, we must instead choose the third alternative. We must confront the person about his behavior with the goal of motivating him to stop breaking the rule. Sometimes management will use the company's established disciplinary procedure as a tool for change. The disciplinary procedure is the supervisor's way of motivating the offender to change his inappropriate behavior. A disciplinary procedure is a timed, sequenced series of steps imposed on the employee, usually by a supervisor. The procedure is based on behavior modification theory and becomes more punitive for the employee as he progresses through the steps. The first step is usually a verbal warning, and the last step is usually termination.

Returning to Dave's problem, he decides that he cannot ignore the problem or change his environment by asking for a transfer. He does, however, often fantasize about his boss leaving. He has half-seriously considered sending Maria's resume to a corporate headhunter in hopes that she will be hired away by one of his employer's competitors. However fortunate Maria's leaving would be, Dave does not realistically believe that she would choose to leave the company. So, he chooses the third alternative and decides to confront Maria in hopes that she will change her behavior.

Of the three alternatives, the third is the most difficult one to accomplish. This is because it directly involves another person's behavior.

STEP 4: REHEARSE

Before you confront the person who is creating a problem for you, you should rehearse. Ask a friend to role-play with you. Play yourself and ask your friend to play the person you will confront. Make your rehearsal as real as possible. Rehearse the meeting several different ways; mix it up. In one scenario, have your rehearsal friend act defensive, angry, and obstinate. In another scenario, ask him or her to act calm, cooperative, and compliant.

> Make your rehearsal as real as possible.

The more serious the conflict is, the more the need for rehearsal. Rehearsing will benefit you in two ways. The first benefit is obvious: You can practice talking and practice listening. You can improve and refine these skills. The second benefit is more subtle and perhaps more important. Through rehearsal, you will gain the opportunity to experience any emotional reaction you might have to what the other person does and says. Rehearse until your emotions no longer dictate your behavior. Learn to manage your emotions in this specific context. Once you have experienced undesirable emotions, they are more readily anticipated, comprehended, and managed. Having already experienced the emotions in rehearsal will lessen their power over you when you have the real meeting.

> The more serious the conflict is, the more need for rehearsal.

Dave asks one of his close friends to rehearse with him. His friend is not an employee of the company.

STEP 5: MEET TO RESOLVE THE CONFLICT

Schedule a mutually convenient time and place to meet with the person whose behavior is causing you a problem or conflict. Dave asks Maria for a meeting, and she schedules it for later that day.

Dave has two goals to accomplish during this meeting. The first goal is to make Maria aware of his problem within a supportive atmosphere. The second goal is to engage in the appropriate conflict resolution process to resolve the problem.

The First Goal: Make the Other Person Aware of Your Problem within a Supportive Atmosphere

As owner of the problem, do not assume that the other person is aware of the problem. Dave must tell Maria. If he does not tell her, he is asking her to read his mind or to interpret his nonverbal behaviors. Since mind reading is difficult and the nature of nonverbal behavior is quite ambiguous

As owner of the problem, do not assume that the other person is aware of the problem.

and open to multiple interpretations, Dave's message may not be correctly interpreted and his problem may grow.

Many people dread confrontation and avoid it, choosing instead to cope with the problem as best they can for as long as possible. They do not want to confront the other person for good reason. They may not know how to tell the other person. They may think the other person will react defensively, feel attacked, and make a scene. These are reasonable fears, but confrontation is easier and less risky when you build and maintain a "supportive atmosphere" as you meet to disclose your problem. Within this atmosphere, confrontation is not a hostile action, nor is it something to dread.

A supportive atmosphere fosters an openness in which actions and words are nonjudgmental. You build this atmosphere using supportive confrontation tools. Reach into your Conflict Survival Kit and grab your paraphrasing and empathic response tools. They will be needed as the meeting progresses. Use them early and often. Active listening is an important characteristic of a supportive atmosphere, and the more listening, the more supportive the confrontation becomes. One of the best ways to encourage the other person to listen to you is to listen to her. Model the behavior you desire from her. This may be the first time she realizes you have a problem with her behavior. Encourage questions and answer them thoughtfully and thoroughly. Remember that at this step the goal is to communicate the problem using supportive confrontation and *not* to recommend solutions.

The more listening, the more supportive the atmosphere becomes.

The following tips will help you accomplish the goal of creating and maintaining a supportive atmosphere:

Tip 1: Engage in conversation and not a "sell-job." Conversations are integral to creating a supportive atmosphere. A conversation is an open discussion that does not have an agenda or an intended outcome or goal. The outcome of a conversation is therefore unknown and open to possibilities. The outcome of the conversation is determined or created out of or by the conversation itself. It is the result of a conversation.

A sell-job is the opposite of a conversation. It is a persuasive speech that has an intended outcome, an agenda. The agenda for a sell-job is usually to have the listener change his mind, buy something, or agree to something. Many people are more skillful at giving sell-jobs than they are at having conversations. This is mainly because we give and receive more sell-jobs than we do conversations. Sell-jobs tend to reduce possibilities, and conversations tend to expand them. Think about your encounters with others over the past week. How many of them were conversations and how many were sell-jobs?

Sell-jobs tend to reduce possibilities, and conversations tend to expand them.

There is nothing inherently wrong with sell-jobs. This is generally how conflicts are negotiated and deals struck. When we have a conflict, our agenda is to make it stop. We want to sell other people on the idea that it is in their best interest to resolve the conflict. We may also wish to sell them on the efficacy of our solution. As we attempt to resolve conflicts, we naturally engage in selling our ideas, positions, or solutions. Likewise, when we negotiate the price of something we wish to buy or sell, we generally have an agenda to get the best deal possible.

It is rare for conversations to occur during conflict negotiation. To sell is the nature of conflict. Unfortunately, sell-jobs have a serious downside. If the other party is not buying what we are selling, we may get angry, impatient, or frustrated. This can cause negotiations to break down. Our agenda may

PART III: Preparing to Resolve Conflicts

be founded on false hopes and improbable expectations. We may try to sell something unrealistic and far-fetched. We may also have a hidden agenda.

Hidden agendas are primary obstacles to supportive atmospheres. They are used to manipulate others without their knowledge. We may omit information, allowing other people to assume something that is not true, or in the worst case, outright lie to them to get what we want. Keeping a hidden agenda is duplicitous. When we get caught, we will more than likely create a human relations conflict in addition to our original conflict. When people discover or suspect a hidden agenda, they question the other party's veracity and likely resist efforts to negotiate. Do not keep hidden agendas. Let the other party know what you want, and he or she may agree to help you get it.

Conversations are needed to resolve serious conflicts. A negotiation is like the beautiful waltz. The waltz has an agenda; it is made up of required steps and movements performed around a predictable musical score. But a waltz is also like a conversation. It is open to unique and different interpretations and to countless possibilities even when partners have waltzed together many times. For the dancers, each waltz they dance together is a singular negotiation.

Tip 2: Eliminate anger. Anger is the enemy to any negotiation because it will destroy any supportive atmosphere. Do not allow yourself to get angry during the negotiation meeting. Unfortunately, this is easier said than done, because anger is often a reaction to conflict. It can be controlled, however. As mentioned previously, rehearsal helps us work through our emotions. It also helps to remember that we own our anger and, therefore, others do not "make" us angry. We make ourselves angry. A person may do something that makes us angry, but anger, like any other emotion, is our responsibility. We own it. We can be truly thankful for this. Think of it: Who else do you want to control your emotions? When negotiating a conflict, do not relinquish control of your emotions to anyone else. Do not let others make you angry. When you do, you diminish your power to reason. You can lose a large portion of your freedom of choice and thus become more vulnerable to manipulation.

Everyone recognizes a put-down. They are usually used to fix blame; impugn character; and communicate judgment, ridicule, criticism, or shame. Put-downs are used to create anger in others. Do not be manipulated by put-downs from another person, especially during negotiations. When negotiating a conflict, think of anger as a two-edged sword—one that usually does more harm than good. Think of yourself as a martial artist of emotions. When a person slings a put-down your way, see it coming and maneuver so that it does not touch you or get into your mind through any of your senses. Practice is needed to thwart these intended blows because some opponents are extremely skillful in the art of put-downs, and these people will test you the most. Do not let your opponent gain the upper hand by making you angry. With anger comes defeat. Any athlete will tell you this.

Keep your wits about you; they are needed as the negotiation unfolds. If you do not succumb to anger, your opponent will notice and perhaps become angry herself. When this happens, she has diminished reasoning power. She is the one who is vulnerable and exposed.

In some cases, we hide our anger, which over time can grow out of control. Our anger is often the motivator for hurting others with whom we have conflicts, and we become obsessed with the goal of hurting the other

> It is rare for conversations to occur during conflict negotiation.

> A negotiation is like the beautiful waltz.

> Put-downs are used to create anger in others.

> When you are angry, you diminish your reasoning power and are therefore vulnerable and exposed.

person. In the worst case, getting even and hurting others becomes our hidden agenda.

Tip 3: Send I-messages, not you-messages. A great tool to put in your Conflict Survival Kit is the I-message. Use it to describe your reaction to a problem you are having. Also, use it when you wish to influence other people to change their behavior. An I-message is an honest statement in that it discloses to the other person how you genuinely feel. I-messages are much less apt to provoke resistance, anger, or resentment because they place the ownership of the feeling squarely with the one having it. One of the best features about this tool is that it describes rather than evaluates.

People often send their evaluations of things rather than their descriptions. They do so usually by sending you-messages. For example, they say, "You have a pretty face," an evaluative remark, rather than saying, "I like your face," a descriptive remark. You-messages are a primary tool used for sending both compliments and insults. "You have a pretty face" and "You are intelligent" are complimentary you-messages, and they are certainly nice to receive. Often, however, you-messages are used to insult or accuse. When used for this purpose, they only exacerbate a conflict or even cause it. For example, if a supervisor says to his employee, "You are lazy," the employee would most likely feel insulted and get defensive. If the supervisor sent instead a descriptive I-message like, "I am concerned about your productivity," he may indeed get a very different reaction from the employee. In actuality, the supervisor's descriptive I-message is probably more indicative of what he is really thinking, feeling, and wanting to say. Ironically, many people find it more difficult to communicate descriptive I-messages than evaluative you-messages.

> Many people find it more difficult to communicate descriptive I-messages than evaluative you-messages.

Dave might send to Maria an I-message like, "I am concerned about this last-minute overtime" and choose not to send a you-message like, "You don't know how to schedule." His I-message simply describes how the over-time affects him. His you-message sends his negative evaluation of Maria.

The use of you-messages is indicative of low-level maturity. A person of low-level maturity will put the responsibility for his behavior or situation onto someone else rather than owning his behavior and taking responsibility for it. He communicates his level of maturity with his overuse of you-messages, often blaming others for making him do this or that thing. For example, you might hear a low-level maturity person say, "You made me angry" or "It's your fault I was late for work and got fired." By using you-messages, he dodges his responsibility for his behavior and diffuses his part in a conflict. Maximize the use of I-messages and minimize the use of you-messages.

Using the Tools

Let us review how Dave uses these tools as he confronts his supervisor, Maria:

> "Maria, I want to thank you for taking the time to meet with me. I really appreciate this opportunity to discuss a problem I am having."

> "That's OK, Dave, what's the problem?" Maria asks.

"Well, I don't want to sound like I'm whining, but my problem is with this weekend overtime I've been working lately. I've had to work three Saturdays in the last five weeks. Also, being told on Thursday that I will work on Saturday is a bit late and really interferes with plans I've made for the weekend. For example, I was just informed today that I have to work this coming Saturday and Sunday. I have plans to go to the park with my wife and kids on Saturday. They are really looking forward to going, and I am really concerned how they will take this news. I know they'll be upset. I know we've been busy lately and going through some major production changes, but I want to let you know how this overtime is affecting me."

Maria listens without interrupting, takes a sip of her coffee, leans back in her chair, and says, "I'm glad you're telling me about this, Dave. I've been concerned how you are taking this overtime business. And, you are not the only one to express concern. Others have come to me as well. I have been trying to figure out a way to resolve the problem but quite frankly, I'm stumped."

Dave effectively introduced the problem and gave his reactions to his problem using I-messages. He was happy to have rehearsed the meeting because he anticipated Maria's reaction. Maria listened to Dave nonjudgmentally, owned her own feelings, and used I-messages of her own. Dave and Maria must actively listen to each other throughout this step in order to maintain the supportive atmosphere they have created.

Dave and Maria are now ready to work on the second goal in this step of the strategy. They must resolve the conflict.

The Second Goal: Engage in Conflict Resolution

After hearing Dave's problem, Maria has a choice to make. She can choose to change her behavior or not to change it. If she chooses to stop giving him last-minute overtime, the conflict has been resolved, preserving their relationship. If she chooses to continue causing Dave a problem, it can be reasonably assumed that her reason is not due to the lack of communication. Her reasons may be motivational: She simply does not want to change or cannot change because of forces beyond her control. It could also be skill based: She may not know what changes to make or how to make them. If the overtime problem is due to a lack of planning skills, for example, Maria will need to improve these skills, no matter how motivated she is to change.

Maria chooses to make a change but is unsure about what to do. Let us see what happens:

"Well, Maria," says Dave, after a moment of thinking. "I'm not exactly sure what to do either. For now I'd like to suggest a couple of solutions. Take me off the work schedule for Saturday because I have made plans with my family that I do not want to cancel. And second, let me know a week in advance when I will work on the weekend."

Maria stands up and begins to pace. After a moment, she says, "Okay, I will find someone else to work this Saturday, but I must ask that you work Sunday." She pauses for a second and then goes on. "About telling you sooner, I don't know how I can. I mean, I find out about it myself only moments before I announce it, and it's never been a week in advance. I just don't know what to do. I will think about this and get back to you later." Maria looks at the clock and gathers up some papers. "I've got to go now to another meeting. I hope you understand." Dave nods and their meeting ends.

Dave is pleased with how Maria reacted to his confronting the conflict. She seemed genuinely concerned about his problem and glad that he brought it to her attention. She listened and asked for his input. Dave is satisfied with the solution to his problem even though it is only a partial solution. He is very pleased not to have to work Saturday. However, Maria did not agree to give any advanced notice of weekend work. Dave senses her frustration about not knowing how to handle the last-minute overtime. He decides to change his attitude about it and not get so frustrated and angry. He decides to allow her time to find an appropriate solution to this last-minute overtime problem.

STEP 6: FOLLOW THROUGH AND FOLLOW UP

The sixth and final step in our conflict resolution through supportive confrontation strategy is to follow through and follow up. Be sure to implement the solution and periodically evaluate how well the solution is working. Maria must do what she agreed to do and remove Dave's name from the overtime list for Saturday.

Sometimes a solution will work in the short term only to fail over the long term. Continuously monitor the solution for any unintended consequences. A solution can sometimes create unforeseen problems and conflicts for other people or the organization. For example, Maria will have to be careful as she selects someone to replace Dave on Saturday. She does not want to create a similar conflict for someone else. If she chooses not to require anyone to work overtime on Saturday, she must be sure that the company is not harmed.

TOOLS TO ADD TO YOUR CONFLICT SURVIVAL KIT

WHEN YOU ARE A MEDIATOR

Introduce the parties to the conflict resolution through supportive confrontation strategy and help them work through each step. Help them identify problem ownership using the window on behavior diagram. Help the parties choose a course of action using the three alternatives rule. Ask both parties to use I-messages.

WHEN YOU ARE NEGOTIATING A CONFLICT FOR YOURSELF

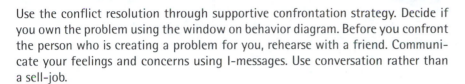

Use the conflict resolution through supportive confrontation strategy. Decide if you own the problem using the window on behavior diagram. Before you confront the person who is creating a problem for you, rehearse with a friend. Communicate your feelings and concerns using I-messages. Use conversation rather than a sell-job.

PERFORMANCE CHECKLIST

- Conflicts arise when we are bothered by a circumstance or event that is the result of another person's behavior or action. The best strategies for addressing the conflicts that affect us depend on our ability to communicate our problem. An effective strategy for doing this is called conflict resolution through supportive confrontation. This involves the following steps:

  1. Identify problem ownership using your window on behavior. The farther away the behavior or event is from the sash, the more certain you are about your label of the behavior or event. Your unacceptable behavior may be unacceptable to another person as well. The responsibility to confront the problem is borne by the owner of the problem.

  2. Research and reflect. Ask and answer questions that add clarity to what you assume about the problem. Through self-reflection, we give ourselves the opportunity to reason critically and open our minds and hearts to the possibility of gaining insight into our personal mental processes and reasoning, which helps us determine whether a behavior is acceptable or unacceptable.

  3. Select an alternative to follow, using the three alternatives rule. The three alternatives rule states that there are basically three things you can do about a problem. You can:

     a. Change your attitude

     b. Change your environment

     c. Confront the person about his or her behavior

  4 Rehearse. Before you confront the person who is creating a problem for you, rehearse with someone who can help you practice talking and listening about the problem and provide the opportunity to experience any emotional reaction you might have to what the other person does and says.

  5. Meet to resolve the conflict.

     - The first goal is to make the other person aware of the problem within a supportive atmosphere. Three tips to follow when meeting to resolve a conflict follow:

     Tip 1. Engage in conversation and not a sell-job.

     Tip 2. Eliminate anger.

     Tip 3. Send I-messages, not you-messages.

     - The second goal is to engage in conflict resolution.

  6. Follow through and follow up. Sometimes a solution will work in the short term only to fail over the long term. Continuously monitor the solution for any unintended consequences. A solution can sometimes create unforeseen problems and conflicts for other people or the organization.

True/False

For each statement below, check true or false.

TRUE   FALSE

_____   _____ 1. Resolving conflicts starts with identifying problem ownership.

_____   _____ 2. Critical reasoning is an important antecedent to change.

_____   _____ 3. A supportive atmosphere fosters an openness in which actions and words are nonjudgmental.

_____   _____ 4. Sell-jobs tend to increase possibilities and conversations tend to expand them.

_____   _____ 5. Hidden agendas eliminate obstacles to supportive atmospheres as they attempt to manipulate the other person.

MULTIPLE CHOICE

Circle the letter next to the best answer for each question. On a separate sheet of paper, state why you chose that answer.

1. The first step to resolving a conflict is to
   a. confront the problem openly.
   b. identify problem ownership.
   c. use I-messages to let others know you are upset.
   d. sell the other person on the idea that he or she is causing you a problem.

2. Which of the following statements *best* describes how to determine problem ownership?
   a. Whoever is bothered by someone's behavior or by a situation owns the problem.
   b. If someone tells you that you are bothering him, then you own the problem.
   c. Whoever causes a problem owns the problem.
   d. When someone denies that he or she has a problem, he or she owns it.

3. Self-reflection leads to which of the following?
   a. Problem ownership
   b. Critical reasoning
   c. Supportive confrontation
   d. Open conversation
   e. None of the above

4. Which of the following is *not* a part of the three alternatives rule?
   a. Change your attitude.
   b. Change your environment.
   c. Confront the person about his or her behavior.
   d. Ignore the problem.

5. Which statement best describes an I-message?

    a. It is an evaluative statement.

    b. It is an honest statement that discloses how you genuinely feel.

    c. It is likely to provoke resistance and anger.

    d. It is used to send specific solutions to others.

    e. None of the above.

DISCUSSION QUESTIONS

1. How can you make someone realize that his or her behavior is causing you a problem?

2. What would you do if you told someone that his or her behavior was a problem for you and the person reacted as though he or she really did not care?

3. What would you do to help someone engage in reflection?

4. Discuss how you generally show your anger to a significant other person in your life.

5. Discuss your experiences with conversations and sell-jobs in your daily life.

CASE: ENGAGING IN SUPPORTIVE CONFRONTATION

Joe has noticed some distance growing between himself and Kim Kahn, assistant manager for Tools and Hardware. Joe must interact with Kim on a frequent basis, since Joe's team performs many functions that service Kim's tool and hardware areas. Joe appreciates that Kim is an expert in the tool and hardware business. Yet, when Joe attempts to talk with Kim and learn more about the business, he feels that Kim is dismissive and even a little irritated. At times, Joe feels as though Kim is deliberately trying to make him feel stupid.

Joe is also concerned with the way Kim interacts with employees. Kim is clearly not a people person. This would not bother Joe so much, except that Kim is often very gruff with Joe's staff as well, causing them to feel confused and hurt. Joe is not certain if Kim intends to be so gruff or if that is simply Kim's nature.

Finally, Joe has become irritated with some less-than-subtle comments Kim has made during management meetings. Kim likes to talk in sarcastic terms about the way "supervisors these days" like to "coddle" their employees and "do all that touchy-feely stuff." Kim says, "It's too much education and not enough hard work. That's what the problem is." Although Joe is not the only manager who has or is pursuing a college education, Joe has the distinct impression that Kim is referring to him.

Joe decides to talk to Jim Talent about his concerns. Jim is not very sympathetic. Jim challenges Joe to solve the problem on his own by talking with Kim directly. "And do it quickly," Jim says. "I've got a big project that I want the two of you to work on together."

Case Questions

Part A.

Using the supportive confrontation model, analyze Joe's situation involving his relationship with Kim and discuss the following:

1. What are the problems, and who owns them based on the window on behavior?

2. What research and reflection should Joe do to test his assumptions and perceptions? What are the facts? Does Joe have legitimate reasons to feel as he does? What more should he seek to understand about Kim before attempting to address the situation?

3. Should Joe seek to (a) change his attitude, (b) change his environment, or (c) confront Kim regarding Kim's behavior? Defend your choice.

Part B.

After you have analyzed the situation, walk through in class as a whole or in small groups the process you would go through as Joe to rehearse, meet to resolve, and follow through and follow up with Kim.

Alternative procedure:

Role-play this scenario. Break the group into pairs and have one individual in each pair play the role of Joe and the other play the role of Kim. In class as a whole, discuss the following:

4. Is rehearsal a useful tool? How or how not?
5. What tools are necessary to confront Kim in this scenario? If you role-played, what worked well? What did not work well?
6. What sort of follow through and follow up will be necessary in this scenario?

ALTERNATIVE PROCEDURE FOR ONLINE LEARNING FORMATS

To role-play the scenario as discussed for the alternative procedure above, consider the following process:

Step 1: Form pairs and have each pair engage off-line in the role-play activities outlined above. Unless video conferencing is available, students should be encouraged to meet to engage in the role-play in person or to engage in the role-play via telephone. Role-playing through e-mail or online chat formats is discouraged.

Step 2: Either have each pair prepare and post a joint report on their experience in role-playing this assignment by responding to the questions above, or have each student prepare such a report individually. After all students have posted their reports, students may also post additional comments in response to other students' reports. Continue an online conversation on these experiences as time and interest allow.

PERSONAL GROWTH EXERCISE

Think about your encounters with others over the past week. How many of them were conversations and how many were sell-jobs? Engage in as many conversations as defined in this chapter as you can and avoid engaging in sell-jobs.

TO LEARN MORE

In the following book, rehearsal is called *scenario planning*. Reading about scenario planning will help you understand how rehearsal affects our emotions:

Senge, Peter, Art Kleiner, Charlotte Roberts, Richard Ross, and Bryan Smith. *The Fifth Discipline Fieldbook: Strategies and Tools for Building a Learning Organization.* New York: Doubleday, 1994.

NOTE

1. Thomas Gordon, *Leader Effectiveness Training: Proven Skills for Leading Today's Business into Tomorrow*, rev. ed. (New York: Berkley Publishing Group, 2001), 29–38.

APPLICATION AND PRACTICE

It is not the ship so much as the skilled sailing that assures the prosperous voyage.

George William Curtis

10

THE BUILDING BLOCKS OF COLLABORATION

PERFORMANCE COMPETENCIES

After you have finished reading this chapter, you will be able to

▪ Describe the basic model for engaging someone in a collaborative discussion

▪ Describe the essential steps for collaborating with someone with whom you are experiencing conflict

▪ Apply the model to a conflict situation in your life and work

There are times when it is necessary to encourage collaboration with another individual, yet you anticipate resistance. Perhaps you need something from someone who is unprepared to respond to your needs. Perhaps you are experiencing smoldering conflicts with someone and want to mend things so you can continue with an otherwise productive relationship. Perhaps there is a perceived incompatibility of interests, and you want to explore whether reconciliation is possible.

If you have decided that collaborating with another individual is appropriate for your situation rather than avoiding, competing, or taking some other approach, a basic model can help you encourage collaboration and, if the other party is receptive, pursue a collaborative solution.

Alone we can do so little; together we can do so much.
Helen Keller

ANALYZE THE SITUATION REQUIRING COLLABORATION

Your decision to pursue collaboration assumes you have identified a situation requiring it. You have done some analysis and concluded that you have a strong interest in working with the other party to achieve an outcome that is mutually beneficial. If your interests are different—for example, you want to avoid conflict altogether or you are competitive and want to win at all costs—then collaboration is not for you. The Thomas-Kilmann Conflict Mode Indicator can provide additional insight to determine whether collaboration or some other approach is appropriate under the circumstances.

Before approaching the other party, analyze what you hope to achieve by collaborating and, to the extent possible, how the other party views the situation. For example:

- What are the issues involved?
- What are your needs and interests? What are the other party's?
- What are your goals for collaborating? What goals does the other party have for which collaborating will prove beneficial?
- How are your needs, interests, and goals compatible with the other party's? How will you "sell" collaboration as a means for addressing these interests?
- How are your needs, interests, and goals incompatible? What reservations might the other party have about collaborating? How will you overcome potential barriers?
- What principles and values are at stake? Are there differing principles and values that neither of you would be willing to compromise?

As you evaluate these questions, you may not have all the information you need, particularly relating to the other party's perspective. How will you acquire this information? While the answers may be clear to you, the other party may see things completely differently. How will you gain insight into this perspective, demonstrate that you understand and appreciate the other party's concerns, and work through differing viewpoints to achieve a mutually satisfactory result?

Your analysis may also include a history review. If you have developed a trusting relationship with the other party in the past, your ability to encourage collaboration will be greater than if previous interactions were negative. To what extent will history affect your ability to collaborate? How much time and effort will be required to deal with the baggage of past encounters before you can begin any meaningful dialogue? Can you afford to expend this effort? You must engage in an honest assessment of these questions, be prepared to acknowledge these issues, and demonstrate a willingness to mend fences before any true engagement can occur.

The value of this "homework" cannot be overstated. Many individuals tend to proceed headlong into their conflicts and give this formative assessment stage short shrift. Dispense with the notion that you must quickly "get into it" without some forethought about what you are doing and why you are doing it. Before taking any action, sit down and think about it.

Before seeking to collaborate, sit down and think about the situation. Figure out what you hope to accomplish and why the other party should want to collaborate.

Once you have determined a basic plan, you must convince the other party that collaboration is in your mutual interests. Just as in planning, you cannot usually jump right into a collaborative discussion and expect the other party to be receptive. A little tact is required.

At the outset, remember to use I-statements. People who invite confrontation tend to approach the individual with whom they are having conflict in a way that will put the burden of the problem squarely on the other party's shoulder:

- "You did this."
- "Your actions caused this problem."
- "You don't understand."

There is no better way to quickly close the door on collaboration. I-statements will garner more support:

- "I would like to discuss this with you."
- "I feel upset when we have these disagreements."
- "I know you are frustrated about this situation too."
- "I want to work this out with you."

You might also consider "we" statements to demonstrate that you own the problem together:

- "We both have responsibility for what has occurred."
- "We both care deeply about having a successful project."
- "We probably have more in common than we realize regarding how to resolve this issue."

When you are prepared to engage in a discussion, be clear at the outset about the purpose of meeting:

- "I'd like to discuss a concern I'm having about our working relationship."
- "I'd like to talk through the difficulties we've been having working together on the Grafton project."

Then, arrange the appropriate time to meet. If you approach the other party prepared to discuss it at that moment, ask:

- "Can we talk about this now?"
- "Is this a good time to discuss this matter?"

It may be preferable instead to arrange a time to meet in advance. This will give the other party time to think through the situation and prepare:

- "Could we meet tomorrow at 10:30 to discuss this?"
- "Would later today work for you?"

When you meet, start by expressing your appreciation for agreeing to meet. Realize that the other party may not have come to the decision to meet easily and may feel as tense and uncertain about the matter as you. Acknowledge this upfront:

- "I realize this has been difficult for you."
- "I know we haven't seen eye to eye on this matter, so I appreciate your willingness to talk about it."
- "I think it's fair to say this has been a challenge for both of us."

If you are discussing a project for which there has been resistance or you anticipate further resistance, acknowledge this:

- "I know you're really busy right now."
- "I realize how complex this assignment has been for you."
- "I can understand why you've been reluctant to talk about this; so have I."
- "I know things have been pretty stressful around here lately."

EXPRESS YOUR CONCERNS

As you proceed with the substance of your meeting, state the situation as you see it in the most objective terms possible. For example:

Professor to student: You received another failing grade on a quiz. When I offered to help you after you failed the last quiz, I didn't hear from you. In class, I've observed that you do not participate in class discussions, which might help you understand the material better. Instead, I see you staring down at your notebook while I'm lecturing. You have also avoided my attempts to talk with you.

Manager to employee: Over the past few weeks, I've tried to give you additional assignments such as the Zuminsky project. I've indicated to you that these assignments are important and that you will need to give them priority. But you have resisted new assignments, claiming your current projects require your complete focus.

Any conflict involves emotions and contrasting personalities. At this early stage, however, stick with articulating your understanding of what the conflict entails based on concrete, objective facts and observations. While underlying emotional and personality issues should not be minimized, the key is to present a balanced picture of the situation that is as free as possible from your particular slant or bias. This will help reduce the other party's natural instinct to become defensive as he or she sees that you are not attempting to make it personal or place blame.

After you have articulated the situation as you see it, you may wish to emphasize your concern by noting the tangible impacts the situation is having on you, on your relationship, on other team members, on your

> When encouraging someone to collaborate, use I-statements, express appreciation for his or her willingness to discuss the situation, and acknowledge legitimate concerns.

> After you have articulated the situation in objective terms, note the tangible impacts the situation is having on you, on your relationship with the other person, on achieving business goals, or other considerations.

ability to achieve business goals, or any other relevant consideration. This will help you illustrate the gravity of your concern from your perspective, further reinforcing your need to have the other person give attention to the matter and engage in conversation with you.

> **Professor to student:** Obviously, if you don't improve on the next test, your overall grade will be affected. And when you don't come to me for help, I feel that either you don't care about understanding the material or you are afraid to ask for help. When you keep your head down in class, I'm concerned that you are not paying attention.

> **Manager to employee:** When you don't take on your fair share of the work assignments, it creates a workflow problem. When you resist my attempts to give you additional assignments, I feel you are not respecting my authority and that perhaps you don't trust me. Your claim that you have to work on other projects besides Zuminsky also suggests that you are having difficulty prioritizing your work.

Before moving on, seek to arrive at a general agreement about what the problem is. Ask, "Does this accurately state the problem as you see it?" If the other party sees it differently, invite her or him to state the conflict in similar objective terms. One method for encouraging this input is to use language that demonstrates that you are open to a different interpretation of what has happened and to having your point of view challenged:

- "If you see things differently, I'd like to hear your point of view."
- "I could be mistaken; if so, tell me how."
- "I'm open to other possibilities here. Is there something I need to know or don't understand?"

Just as you would expect the other party to disagree with your perspective, you may be challenged with what he or she says and how he or she defines the problem. Resist the temptation to react. Listen. And, even if you do not agree with the other party's view of the situation, demonstrate your empathy:

- "If I were in your position, I might feel the same way."
- "I can understand how you might feel this way because . . ."

Keep working on defining the problem until you have arrived at a reasonably agreeable interpretation. This need not be an exhaustive discussion; greater clarity will come later as you work through the issues.

Finally, it is time to explore whether the other party shares your interest in collaborating. Express a few basic options that you believe might solve the problem and meet the needs of both parties. Do not insist on any option, but merely present them as possibilities for exploration.

Then express your interest in knowing any options for resolution the other party might suggest. The key point is to ask, in some way, "Are you interested in discussing this further?"

TOOLS TO ADD TO YOUR CONFLICT SURVIVAL KIT

One useful tool when attempting to engage in a collaborative discussion is "scripting" in which the individual prepares, either mentally or in writing, the "script" he or she will use before approaching the other individual. Think of a situation in which you need to encourage collaboration. Focusing only on the three steps above, think through the situation and prepare a script using the suggestions and examples in these sections as your model.

Before approaching the individual, find a trusted colleague or friend and rehearse your script. Ask for his or her input on suggestions for improvement. Do not overdo it so that you sound rehearsed. Do not recite your script verbatim when you meet with the individual with whom you want to collaborate. In fact, instead of writing a script verbatim, write short bullet points that you can use as a guide. The goal of this exercise is to give you confidence in approaching the other individual while appearing natural and sincere.

Once you have rehearsed and refined your script, you are ready to approach the other individual to encourage collaboration.

LISTEN AND SEEK TO UNDERSTAND

If you have been successful thus far in engaging the other party in a collaborative process, your task now is to listen. You need to allow the individual to open up about his or her views and feelings about the situation without passing judgment, arguing, or responding defensively. To do this most effectively, you must listen for content and for feelings.

LISTENING FOR CONTENT

When listening at this level, you are focused on the facts, data, and information regarding the sender's message. You are not concerned about understanding underlying feelings and emotions. The goal is simply to grasp and to demonstrate to the other person that you understand the factual information being conveyed. To show your understanding, you can respond with a paraphrase:

- "If I understand you correctly, you are saying that . . ."
- "Are you saying that . . .?"

Some paraphrasing may be as simple as repeating back the same or nearly the same words that were said:

Speaker: I'm tired and hungry.
Listener: You are tired and hungry.

Speaker: I want to discuss this later.

Listener: You want to discuss this at another time.

With this form of paraphrase, you are simply showing the other person that you hear her or him. Be careful that you use this technique sparingly or you may come across as mocking. A more common paraphrase technique is to rephrase what was said in your own words:

Speaker: The Smith project has gotten out of hand. No one knows what is going on anymore, and everyone is expecting me to fix it.

Listener: You are saying that you are frustrated with the Smith project and how no one seems to have a handle on it. Everyone seems to be looking to you to make things better.

If the message is important, the sender will usually let you know if you have received it correctly. You might even consider ending your paraphrase with a question, such as "is that correct?" or "did I state that correctly?" This gives the other person the opportunity to correct you until he or she is assured that you fully understand.

LISTENING FOR FEELINGS

While listening for content is vitally important, listening for feelings provides the opportunity to demonstrate your concern for the underlying feelings and emotions the individual is attempting to convey about the situation. As the sender conveys facts and data, her deeper concerns are how she feels about the facts and data and the emotions they are creating. Where you have paraphrased to show content understanding, you will want to go a little deeper at this level and give empathic responses. One way to do this is to make statements that reflect an understanding of both the content of the other person's message and her feelings about the content:

> Individuals do not merely communicate facts and data. They communicate underlying thoughts and feelings about the facts and data. Listen for both.

Student: You keep talking and talking and don't ever slow down. I can't keep up and my notes get all garbled. Then I worry that I'll screw up on the test because I will miss the key points.

Professor: You are saying that I'm covering too much material and that you feel frustrated and confused. You are worried about failing when it's my fast talking that is really to blame.

Employee: Things are pretty stressful right now. I can't believe you want me to take on the Zuminsky project. Do you realize how involved that project is? I'm not sure I can handle it right now. And I hate not having time to do it right.

Manager: You feel that if I give you this additional project right now, you will be overloaded and concerned that the project will not be done well. This bothers you greatly. You take pride in your work.

It is important to note that empathic responses involve more statements than questions. The problem with questions is that they often involve probing:

"*What* happened next?"

"*When* did that occur?"

"*Why* do you feel that way?"

"*How* does that work?"

While it may seem that you are being supportive by trying to elicit information, such questions are often received as intrusive. Further, when you ask such questions, you are guiding the other person down a particular path that you believe the conversation should go. You are thus projecting your own "spin" on the story when the goal is to allow the individual to tell the story as she has experienced it. If you ask questions, ask them for clarification or elaboration or to assist the other person in continuing on the same thought pattern. In particular, ask questions that will help the individual open up more regarding feelings and emotions:

- "Can you tell me more about why that concerned you?"
- "How did that make you feel when I made that statement?"
- "Having time to complete a project is really important to you. Can you help me understand how I have not allowed you sufficient time?"
- "Has this been a value you have held for a long time?"

When an individual feels that you are truly listening, establishing rapport is more likely and the individual may naturally open up. The individual will work with you to clarify any misunderstandings to be sure you have clearly received the message. As you have listened, you have begun to identify what the important issues are as the other person perceives them. You have put yourself in her shoes for the moment. You have also allowed her to vent her emotions, feelings, and frustrations surrounding the situation. If you have truly been empathetic, she will become convinced that you have grasped the situation as she sees it.

Similarly, you should be afforded the same opportunity to express your view of the situation without judgment. You should expect to have the same opportunity to openly share your views and to be received with the same level of openness and consideration as you afforded the other party. Be careful to play by the same rules. Do not personalize your issues and feelings by making accusations, placing blame, or engaging in other behaviors that create defensiveness and resistance. Just as you have been careful to listen without reacting, do nothing to cause the other party to stop listening or build up defenses. Rather, focus your discussion on objective facts, opinions, and experiences that are the basis for feeling as you do. Finally, give the individual the benefit of the doubt; let her know that you realize she intended no harm and that she was not in the position to understand how you would feel:

- "I know you didn't realize how your [comment, behavior, actions] made me feel."
- "I realize you were distracted and busy at the time."

- "I know you didn't realize your decision would have this result."
- "You may not have had all the information you needed before deciding to assign that project to me."

This process of listening and understanding should lead to a deeper understanding of the issues and feelings involved. If you have done this effectively and allowed for plenty of opportunity to share your views, both parties should be open to collaboration.

TOOLS TO ADD TO YOUR CONFLICT SURVIVAL KIT

Empathic listening requires practice. Before you are required to use these skills to address a conflict situation, try empathic listening in a less threatening environment. For example, consider asking questions on a topic the other person will want to talk about, such as the following:

- What is a value or belief you hold dear? Why is that value or belief so important to you? How has that value or belief shaped you and guided your life?

- What is your greatest passion in life? If you had all the freedom in the world, what would you do to feed that passion? How did that passion come to be? Why is this passion so important to you?

- What is most important to you in a relationship? To what kinds of individuals do you feel closest? What are the characteristics and values that are important to you in the other person? What do you give to such relationships? What do you want in return?

As you engage a person in such a discussion, commit yourself to the following:

- Be silent and listen.

- Give appropriate signals that you are listening (nod of head, eye contact, and an occasional "uh-huh").

- Make the conversation about the other party. Seek first to understand his or her thoughts. Refrain from interjecting your own opinions, judgments, or assumptions.

- Make appropriate paraphrasing statements or empathic responses that show you understand.

- Ask questions only for clarification. This will help the individual clarify or elaborate on his or her statements or continue on a thought.

- Summarize at the end. Ask if you have fully understood what he or she said. Keep working to summarize until the individual is convinced you understand.

- Thank the person for being open and sharing.

Spend at least fifteen minutes on this activity. Ideally, find someone with whom you can switch roles and give the other person the opportunity to practice empathic listening. This will also give you the opportunity to have the experience of someone listening to you. Share with each other how this experience made you feel. Did you feel you were being truly listened to and understood? Did the other individual interject his or her own judgments or assumptions? Was the exercise difficult or awkward? How might you improve your listening for the next time?

Try the exercise again with someone else. Practice listening and you will improve your skills.

DEFINE THE PROBLEM

Through the process of listening and understanding, you and the other party should have a firm grasp of what each hopes to achieve through collaboration, as well as the needs, interests, and goals you have in common and that are in conflict. Such thoughtful consideration of each other's views should then lead to a clear definition of the problem for which collaboration is necessary. Yet defining the problem can be tricky.

When defining the problem, many people often confuse solutions with problems, or they disguise the solution as the problem. Consider this example:

> A supervisor calls a meeting with his direct reports fifteen minutes before the end of the shift and says, "I've asked you to come to this meeting because we have a problem; someone has to work about four hours overtime tonight."

The supervisor has actually presented a solution (someone must work four hours overtime) and not the problem. Just what is the problem? Did a last-minute order arrive? Is the crew stressed with too much work to do in too little time? Is the need for overtime a one-time concern or is there a larger systemic issue the supervisor is ignoring? The actual problem has not been defined, and any discussion will likely be about how to implement his solution and not to define the real problem.

The supervisor might instead say:

> We have a last-minute order that must be shipped before midnight tonight. How might we solve this problem?

Here, discussion is open to addressing the possible solutions to a defined problem. The need for someone to work four hours of overtime is just one possible solution.

As you collaborate, be sure that your discussion focuses on creating a problem statement on which you both can agree. Be careful not to impose a solution as a guise for the problem. This will only frustrate the other party and close off meaningful, open discussion centered on achieving a mutually beneficial resolution. The following are examples of problems and problem statements:

> **Problem:** Lu is upset with Jovan because he always needs to leave early to pick up his children from soccer practice. Lu thus has to stay late to clean up their workstation and complete last-minute projects on her own. Jovan is upset with Lu because he comes in early to set up the workstation on his own. Lu always comes in late after her

morning water aerobics workout. As a result of these resentments, they no longer work well together.

Problem statement: How can Jovan and Lu overcome their resentments toward each other so that work can be done and their personal and work needs can be met?

Problem: Mustafa, the managing partner of a law firm, wants Glenda, a legal secretary, to reorganize the entire shelving system in the law firm library. There are just too many books and not enough shelves. Books are piling up everywhere, and the law firm partners can't find their reference material when they need it. Glenda is overworked with legal briefs and filings. Organizing the library is insignificant compared to these duties. Mustafa could always order Glenda to do it, even if she has to stay late a few nights. Yet Glenda works hard as it is, and Mustafa doesn't want to create any hard feelings.

Problem statement: How can Mustafa enable Glenda to tackle the law library reorganization without sacrificing more important duties or requiring her to stay late?

> When defining the problem, be careful that you are not imposing a solution instead.

Note that in each case, the problem statements focus on meeting the interests of the parties involved and do not impose solutions. Though Jovan and Lu may perceive each other as the problem, the problem statement acknowledges the underlying resentments that are at the root of the problem and recognizes the legitimate concerns of both. Mustafa could impose a solution on Glenda over whom he has authority. Instead, the problem statement focuses on attempting to meet his and the law firm's needs while also accommodating Glenda's work and personal needs.

You must devote adequate time and care to address the underlying issues at the root of the problem and then to craft an appropriate statement that defines the problem in a way that both parties agree will address their needs, interests, and goals. These efforts will benefit your collaborative efforts and increase the likelihood of realizing concrete, workable solutions.

BRAINSTORM AND EXPLORE POSSIBLE SOLUTIONS

When you have defined the problem correctly, it is time to solve it. This involves three phases: (1) brainstorming, (2) evaluation, and (3) refinement.

BRAINSTORMING

Brainstorming involves an open, nonjudgmental process focused on generating as many ideas as possible. When brainstorming, keep these pointers in mind:

- Discuss with the other party all possible options that may solve, in whole or in part, the problem or problems you have identified.
- Be as open, honest, and creative as possible.

- Remember the schoolteacher's admonition that "there is no such thing as a dumb idea." There is also no such thing as a crazy idea.
- Do not pass judgment on any option presented. Do not evaluate, criticize, or ridicule. Criticism of any kind can "chill" a party from bringing up some of the wildest ideas that may also be the best ideas. To enforce this, consider invoking a "no criticism rule" or a "no laughter rule."
- Even if you think the other party has suggested something silly or stupid, refrain from commenting and write it down. Write all comments down so that you can evaluate them later.

During this formative stage, it is important to remember that you are trying to expand the possible solutions. You are creating possibilities. Therefore, it is critical that you do nothing that will hinder this creative process.

EVALUATION

Once you have exhausted the brainstorming process, it is time to assess the validity and viability of the options on your list. Both parties should be prepared to constructively challenge any option about which they are uncertain.

As you engage in this exploration, be open about any reservations in terms of costs or burdens you or others may incur or about questions of fairness, equity, consistency, and similar considerations. If the other party likes an option that you question, ask him to defend why he feels the option is workable. Has he considered any inconvenience, cost, or inequity it may create? On what principle or theory does he rely to make his claim that the option is feasible or equitable? Is there an objective basis for selecting the option, or does the option lack a clear rationale? Of course, you should also be prepared to defend any options that you like but the other party questions.

With respect to your evaluation of any option, the option should at a minimum

- Meet the legitimate needs, interests, and goals of both parties
- Resolve or help resolve the conflict
- Be specific, achievable, and realistic
- Help preserve or enhance the relationship between the parties

REFINEMENT

The process of evaluation involves "pruning." As you work through the list of possible options, you will identify many that will not work to the satisfaction of either party and can therefore be eliminated. The list can then be narrowed down to a shorter list of potential options, which will require deeper review.

If you have come this far and found common ground, you will have honed in on one or two solid solutions that will meet your criteria. In the process, each party will likely have found room for compromise, rethinking positions, and conceding less crucial issues in favor of issues that truly matter. In the course of exploring options, new options may have been created or hybrid options formed from original proposals that more satisfactorily meet each party's needs. This process has the tendency to generate creative options that could only have been discovered through thorough discussion. However, to realize such outcomes, recognize that time, effort, and patience are crucial. Too many collaborations fail for want of these. Do not give up too quickly.

COMMIT TO A SOLUTION

As you analyze the remaining option or two that may form the basis for agreement, you must test them thoroughly. Each party should ask probing questions of themselves and each other to determine if they could truly live with the proposed outcome. For example:

- "How will this result in a change in [a specific behavior, a performance expectation, morale, teamwork, efficiency, productivity]?"
- "What will be the impacts of this on [you, me, your team, my team, our organization, other constituencies]?"
- "What will be the costs to you for pursuing this outcome [e.g., additional costs, more work, added processes and procedures, loss of control]?"
- "What are the benefits [e.g., increased efficiency and productivity, improved morale, additional support from others, more flexibility, reduced stress]? Do the benefits outweigh the costs?"
- "Who else do we need to consult before agreeing to this?"
- "What if we don't agree to this? Would we be better or worse off?"
- "Are there any alternatives that would be better at this time?"
- "Is there anything about this proposal that makes you uncomfortable?"

You cannot ask too many questions to be sure all issues have been addressed to your satisfaction.

Once you have arrived at a workable solution, summarize it to be sure you have correctly captured all aspects of your discussion. Write it down, especially if the agreement is complex or involves multiple layers of conditions and obligations that must be satisfied. Be specific. For example, in a collaborative discussion between a manager and an employee concerning the possibility of a change in work duties as an opportunity for job growth, the outcome might look like this (whether written as a formal document or simply jotted down in notes to the conversation):

> Camille agrees to allow Lebron, on a trial basis, to perform the following duties: 1. _____; 2. _____; 3 _____.
> Lebron will perform these duties for a period of three months, which will be a trial period to determine his capability for performing them. At the same time, Lebron agrees that his level of performance of his current duties will not diminish. Camille agrees to give support to Lebron as he attempts to perform these duties, such as on-the-job training and coaching. However, if

> To be sure you can live with the agreement, ask probing questions such as whether the agreement will achieve the outcomes intended, preserve or enhance relationships, and be acceptable to others who will be affected by it.

work demands require, Lebron understands he may be pulled off these new duties to focus solely on his current duties. If the potential for an increase in pay or promotion is involved, Camille and Lebron further specify the manner in which they will evaluate this process based on existing standards and policies.

In a discussion in which a manager has asked an employee to take on a major, long-term, time-sensitive project, the outcome might look like this:

Tony and Peyton agree to revise the deadlines on other, less crucial projects to allow Peyton time to focus on completing the project in question. Peyton will review with Tony projects that have a low priority with the possibility of reassigning such projects to other staff or eliminating them. Tony and Peyton will meet on a weekly basis to discuss the progress of the project to consider whether Peyton can again assume other projects or whether further balancing of his workload will be necessary. Peyton will express at any time when he honestly feels overloaded or frustrated with his ability to complete the project or to take on additional assignments. If necessary, Tony will explore the possibility of eliciting the help of other employees to assist Peyton with completing the project.

As noted from these examples, it is important to be clear about the duties and obligations each party has agreed to, as well as time frames, deadlines, performance expectations, next steps, and standards for evaluation.

It is possible that the parties will not come to complete agreement on all aspects of their collaborative discussion. Regarding unresolved issues, the parties can agree that despite some acknowledged reservations, they will proceed with the current agreement. Unresolved issues can be noted in the summary of the discussion with the understanding that the parties will revisit them at a later date, which should also be specified.

IMPLEMENT AND MONITOR THE AGREEMENT

The next step to collaboration is simple: Do what you have agreed to do. Of course, this can often be where the process breaks down. To remedy this, the parties should commit to a process of monitoring. As part of their agreement, they might agree to periodic meetings to review their progress. Between a manager and an employee, this is especially important. The employee can report progress to date on what has been accomplished. The manager can in turn provide feedback and confirm her commitments upon a demonstration that the employee has met his obligations. Along the way, the parties may find that fulfilling the agreement is not as simple as initially contemplated. Perhaps it is taking longer to fulfill the obligations because they are more complex than initially thought or other demands have prevented timely completion. Monitoring provides the opportunity to renegotiate terms that are more realistic and achievable.

The monitoring process also affords the opportunity for the parties to express any dissatisfaction with the agreement. Either party may indicate that it is simply not workable now that it has been tried. This dissatisfaction could involve the entire agreement or just a small aspect. If the problem involves an aspect of the agreement, modifications and new agreements may be easily achieved and implemented. If it involves the complete agreement, then it is back to step one. This may happen for one of three reasons:

- Insufficient time was taken to fully define the problem and articulate each party's interests.
- All possible options were not fully explored.
- One or both parties did not truly wish to collaborate and had other interests that did not become evident until the agreement was implemented.

Except for the final reason, nothing has been lost through collaboration. Engaging in collaboration involves a learning process and requires time. If the parties truly want to collaborate, time is their ally. The willingness to start over is a testament to the value the parties place in the relationship over realizing speedy, yet often unproductive, outcomes.

> If your agreement is not working out as planned, revisit the steps in the process and renegotiate. If you and the other party are truly committed to the process, time is your ally.

FOSTER THE RELATIONSHIP

The parties should view their collaboration as an opportunity to enhance the relationship. Usually, a collaborative engagement does not end with the resolution of a single issue but is only one incident within a larger context, such as the ongoing relationship a manager enjoys with the employees he or she supervises or with other managers, customers, and other business constituencies. Taking time to evaluate the success of the collaboration may prove useful. As you contemplate future collaborations, ask the following questions:

- What worked well?
- Where is improvement needed?
- What further skills and competencies should you develop to improve as a collaborative partner?
- What aspects of your relationship require further refinement?

Do not simply reflect on these questions alone; ask the other party for his or her thoughts and suggestions. If the initial collaboration was successful, both parties will welcome the opportunity to collaborate again.

PERFORMANCE CHECKLIST

- Before pursuing collaboration, decide whether the situation warrants it and, if so, analyze the issues, concerns, and interests involved and how you will approach the other party to encourage collaboration.

- When inviting someone to collaborate, acknowledge the individual's concerns about collaborating, show empathy, and state your desire to achieve a mutually satisfactory resolution.

- Share your concerns in the most objective terms possible and help the other party understand the tangible impacts these concerns have on you, your relationship, or other considerations.

- When beginning the collaboration, encourage the other party to discuss his or her view of the situation, including both facts and underlying emotions, and listen empathetically before attempting to share your own views.

- Come to agreement about defining the problem requiring collaboration, being careful not to impose a solution in the guise of a problem.

- When problem solving, brainstorm as many options as possible that may solve the problem without criticizing or evaluating the suggestions offered, then narrow down the list to select the best option that may solve the problem.

- Test the proposed solution against relevant criteria to ensure you can commit to it, ask probing questions to determine its impacts on you and others, and develop a strategy for implementing the solution.

- Implement the agreement and have a process in place for monitoring its progress and modifying or renegotiating aspects of the agreement as needed.

- Evaluate the success of your collaboration, using it as a springboard for future collaborations and fostering an ongoing, positive relationship.

TEST YOURSELF

True/False

For each statement below, check true or false.

TRUE   FALSE

_____ _____ 1. A good example of a clarifying question designed to encourage the speaker to open up about her feelings is "when did that occur?"

_____ _____ 2. During the implementation and monitoring phase of an agreement, the parties will generally not need to start over with the collaborative process even if they did not define the problem as thoroughly as they should have.

_____ _____ 3. Before attempting to collaborate with someone, you must first analyze the situation and decide whether collaboration is in your best interests.

_____ _____ 4. You must be careful about using I-statements because they tend to cause defensiveness in the other party.

_____ _____ 5. An effective problem statement acknowledges the interests and concerns of both parties without imposing a specific solution.

MULTIPLE CHOICE

Circle the letter next to the best answer for each question. On a separate sheet of paper, state why you chose that answer.

1. Which of the following questions is *least* likely to help an individual open up about a situation that concerns him and clarify his feelings?

   a. Can you tell me more about how that made you feel?

   b. Why do you feel that way?

c. How did that situation make you feel?

d. Can you give me an example of how the situation made you feel?

2. The process of brainstorming involves *all but one* of the following activities:

a. recording the options generated.

b. generating as many possible options that may solve the problem identified.

c. evaluating the options identified by the parties.

d. affirming that no idea is too crazy or too dumb.

3. Henry said, "I have to work late every night this week. I hate this." Which of the following statements is *not* an effective paraphrase of Henry's statement?

a. "You're complaining about working late every night."

b. "You hate working late every night this week."

c. "Working late every night bothers you. You don't like it."

d. "You have to work late every night this week. You hate that."

4. In some cases, after implementing and monitoring an agreement for a while, the parties may realize that it is necessary to start from the beginning with the collaborative process because

a. they did not properly define the problem, so they must come to an agreement on what the true problem is.

b. the agreement overall seems to be working out, but a few aspects of the agreement are troublesome.

c. they did not fully explore all possible options that might resolve the problem, and the option they selected is not working.

d. a and c, but not b

e. a and b, but not c

f. b and c, but not a

g. all the above

5. The first step in the collaboration model outlined in this chapter is to analyze the situation. You would do this for all the following reasons *except* to

a. determine whether collaboration is warranted.

b. determine to the extent possible what the other party's interests are.

c. assess your goals for collaborating.

d. prepare an argument to persuade the other party to agree with you.

DISCUSSION QUESTIONS

1. Discuss in groups the many situations and circumstances in which seeking to engage in a collaborative discussion would be beneficial to you as a supervisor and to the individuals with whom you are attempting to collaborate. You will probably find there are more opportunities to engage in such discussions than you realize.

2. Some believe that in our society we are not good listeners. In what ways have you observed this to be true? Give some examples in society or from your personal experience that support or refute this assertion. How can we become better listeners?

3. What should be the manager's goal in encouraging collaboration among those he or she manages? When is engaging in a collaborative discussion counterproductive to accomplishing organizational goals?

OBJECTIVE

To practice engaging in a collaborative discussion by applying the building blocks of collaboration to a work situation.

PROBLEM

Joe must assign a project to a couple of employees. The project involves assessing and realigning the process for ordering and retrieving purchased items from the warehouse to ensure that they are delivered in a timely manner to the customer service desk for pickup. There have been a lot of complaints about long customer wait times.

Joe has been avoiding assigning the project because he believes the assignment will be met with resistance. The project will be challenging and time consuming. It will also require two employees, which could double the amount of resistance he will receive.

Joe believes that Fred Staid and Sally Ambitious would be the ideal candidates to assign to the project. Fred has an analytical mind and methodical approach to addressing problems. He would probably have a lot of great ideas about how to improve warehouse efficiency and would take a deliberate, step-by-step approach. Sally is one of Joe's most energetic employees. She is the team leader in the warehouse, and it would not surprise Joe if she eventually moved to a sales or management position. Sally has good instincts about how to improve processes and has, in fact, implemented many of them already. She is a go-getter and would be a good balance with Fred's more methodical approach.

Joe anticipates the following resistance:

1. Both Fred and Sally may suggest that the customer service function is not their area of responsibility. Indeed, there is a vacancy for the position of team leader of the customer service desk, so they may argue that Joe should do the project himself, assign a couple of team members in the customer service desk to do it, or wait until a team leader has been hired. Yet, Joe and Jim Talent believe all functions are interrelated and that cross training is important. They also do not believe that any of the customer service employees possess the qualifications or drive to take on this project.

2. Joe has some reservations about whether Fred and Sally will work well together. Though generally cordial to each other, they do not spend a lot of time working together. Joe thinks they would be a good team because of their unique work qualities that are needed for the project. However, he is concerned that their personalities may clash.

3. Joe is concerned that either Fred or Sally or both will be annoyed by his continued overtures to encourage them to collaborate. Joe has suggested that they work together on other projects in the past but was rebuffed. Joe has been patient, but this project is too important to let go. Joe is concerned that if he is too insistent, either or both individuals will be more emphatic in their refusal to work together. Then, they will build up resentment toward Joe, putting at risk a relatively good working relationship Joe currently enjoys with them.

4. Fred may express resistance because the problem does not appear to involve delivery and the loading dock, while it does involve the warehouse, which is Sally's area of responsibility. Because of this, Fred may also think that he is not qualified to address customer service issues. Fred is also a little set in his ways and seems to focus only on the delivery function to the exclusion of any concern about other functions.

5. Though Sally is energetic, she may express resistance because she does not have the time to devote to it because of all the changes and new procedures she is trying to implement in the warehouse. She may also be resentful about the project, feeling perhaps that she is being faulted for the long wait times between the warehouse and the customer service desk. However, Joe believes that the problem is more systemic than anything Sally could have corrected through her efforts alone.

6. Sally may feel threatened by Fred's involvement in addressing warehouse issues. She may see this as an intrusion into her "turf."

Joe must approach Fred and Sally individually and encourage them to accept the assignment and work together to accomplish the task.

PROCEDURE

There are two options for selecting players for this role-play: (1) Three students volunteer to play Joe, Fred, and Sally or (2) all students pair up in groups of two.

Option 1: If the first option is selected, the students who volunteered will role-play two scenes: (1) Joe engaging in collaboration with Fred and (2) Joe engaging in collaboration with Sally. Allow approximately ten minutes for each scene. All other students will observe the role-plays and critique whether the efforts to collaborate were successful.

Option 2: If the second option is selected, each pair of students should role-play the two scenes, as follows: (1) the first student plays Joe and the second student plays Fred and (2) the second student plays Joe and the first student plays Sally. Allow approximately ten minutes for each scene. After all students have finished their role-plays, the class will reform and discuss whether they succeeded and what challenges they faced in encouraging collaboration.

With either option, players should be encouraged to fully assume the personality of the character selected. They may also be creative in adding additional facts and information regarding Joe's need for collaboration and Fred's and Sally's resistance to it, provided the facts and information are consistent with the scenario and the role profiles. Though the players role-playing Fred and Sally should not be unduly obstinate, they should not willingly collaborate either unless a truly workable plan for collaboration can be achieved.

Additional role-play option: To extend the role-play, consider a third role-play scenario. In this option, assume Joe has been successful in encouraging one of the two individuals to work with the other, but unsuccessful in encouraging the other individual. In this scenario, leave Joe out of the scenario and have the student role-playing Sally approach Fred to encourage collaboration, or vice versa. Whoever role-plays the individual being approached should continue to offer resistance, at least initially, depending on how effective the collaborative party is in his or her approach.

Case Questions

In class, discuss the following:

1. How successful was Joe in applying the building blocks of collaboration?

2. How successful was Joe in his attempts to encourage Fred and Sally to collaborate with him and accept the assignment?

3. What aspects of the collaborative discussion went smoothly? What aspects were more difficult?

4. What creative ways did you come up with to overcome barriers to collaboration?

5. If the third role-play option was used, address the preceding questions from the perspective of Sally or Fred.

Step 1: Form pairs and have each pair engage off-line in the role-play activities outlined above. Students will likely need to engage in the Option 2 process for role-playing or the alternative third option in which they role-play a scenario involving a conversation between Sally and Fred. Also, unless video conferencing is available, students should be encouraged to meet to engage in the role-play in person or to engage in the role-play via telephone. Role-playing through email or online chat formats is discouraged.

Step 2: Either have each pair prepare and post a joint report on their experience in role-playing this assignment and responding to the questions above or have each student prepare such a report individually. After all students have posted their reports, you may also have students post additional comments in response to other students' reports. Continue an online conversation on these experiences as time and interest allow.

PERSONAL GROWTH EXERCISE

Find an opportunity to engage in a collaborative process to resolve a conflict in your organization. Seek to collaborate with your boss, a peer, or someone you manage. After you have completed the process, whether or not you were successful, seek to engage the other party in a discussion of what occurred and what more you can do to improve the chances for a successful collaboration in the future. Ask questions, such as the following:

- How did this process foster or hinder our relationship?
- What could I have done to listen more effectively to you and understand your concerns?
- What can we do next time that will improve the chances of a successful collaboration?
- What do you need to know from me that will help you more effectively collaborate with me in the future?
- If you don't wish to collaborate with me, why not? Have I done something to offend you?
- Do you think that a collaborative outcome is possible in this instance? Why or why not?

TO LEARN MORE

The following resources provide additional information regarding collaborative problem-solving models for resolving conflict:

Levine, Stewart. *Getting to Resolution: Turning Conflict into Collaboration*. San Francisco: Berrett-Koehler Publishers, 1998.

Masters, Marick F., and Robert R. Albright. *The Complete Guide to Conflict Resolution in the Workplace*. New York: American Management Association, 2002.

Patterson, Kerry, Joseph Grenny, Ron McMillan, and Al Switzler. *Crucial Conversations: Tools for Talking When Stakes are High*. New York: McGraw-Hill, 2002.

Stone, Douglas, Bruce Patton, and Sheila Heen. *Difficult Conversations: How to Discuss What Matters Most*. New York: Viking, 1999.

Tjosvold, Dean. *Learning to Manage Conflict: Getting People to Work Together Productively*. New York: Lexington Books, 1993.

INTEGRATIVE NEGOTIATION: NEGOTIATING AS PARTNERS

PERFORMANCE COMPETENCIES

After you have finished reading this chapter, you will be able to

- Describe the process of engaging in an integrative, or interest-based, negotiation

- Plan for a negotiation to ensure the best possible outcome

- Apply the appropriate strategies and techniques to conduct such a negotiation

Integrative negotiation involves problem solving in which the parties work side by side in an attempt to achieve outcomes that are mutually beneficial to all. It is distinct from *distributive* negotiation, wherein parties engage in face-to-face confrontation with one another to achieve maximum gains for themselves.

Integrative negotiation is also referred to as *interest-based negotiation*. The classic blueprint for this method is *Getting to Yes: Negotiating Agreement Without Giving In* by Roger Fisher, William Ury, and Bruce Patton.[1] These authors and others associated with the Harvard Negotiation Project have provided a wealth of research and practical knowledge to this field and have authored numerous other titles related to integrative negotiation, including *Getting Past No: Negotiating Your Way from Confrontation to Cooperation*,[2] by Ury, and *Getting Ready to Negotiate: A Step-by-Step Guide to Preparing for Any Negotiation*,[3] by Fisher and Danny Ertel.

The discussion that follows relies primarily on these resources to outline the basic framework for principled, interest-based negotiations and provides managers with the fundamentals for engaging in meaningful and productive negotiations with employees, customers, and others with whom they regularly interact.

You see things; and you say "Why?" But I dream things that never were; and I say, "Why not?"

George Bernard Shaw

The Limits of Traditional Negotiations

Another term for distributive negotiation is *zero-sum*, which refers to the concept that any gain for one party is achieved at the expense of the other. When parties enter into such negotiations, they bargain from fixed positions. Each party has an optimum position to which he aspires. In the sale of a house, for example, the seller aspires to sell his house for $200,000, while the buyer aspires to purchase it for $180,000. These are their target points, which, if achieved by either party, would leave that party feeling he has received the optimum bargain. Since the parties are usually at variance with regard to these target points, neither is likely to realize them. Therefore, the parties also have fixed positions beyond which there is no deal. For example, the seller might accept $185,000 and the buyer might pay $190,000. These are the parties' resistance points, and the space in between where they will realize a sale, in this case $5,000, is their settlement range.

Negotiating in this way may be acceptable, even expected, when price is the only variable, when the stakes are low, or when the parties are engaged in a one-time deal and are unlikely to interact again. In such contexts, parties are primarily motivated by a desire to achieve maximum gains for themselves with less concern about fostering an ongoing relationship. The parties, therefore, resort to tactics designed to get the other party to agree to a resolution that is as close to their target point as possible. These tactics include the following:

- Touting how reasonable and fair one's offer is while criticizing the other side's offer as extreme

- Setting arbitrary deadlines to push the other party into settling quickly

- Applying psychological pressure to cause a party to feel guilty

- Playing to a party's sympathies to accept concessions

- Threatening adverse consequences such as lawsuits, delay, or taking one's business elsewhere to goad the other party into settling

Distributive negotiation assumes an adversarial relationship wherein the parties work against each other, which results in rewarding behaviors that break down trust. The parties become stubborn, take extreme positions, concede little and demand much, engage in deceptive practices, and issue threats and ultimatums. For parties who are interdependent, wanting and needing a positive ongoing relationship to achieve optimum gains, distributive negotiation will not help them.

The Promise of Integrative Negotiation

Integrative negotiation recognizes that the wisest, most efficient, and most durable agreements depend on open communication among cooperative, trusting parties who explore opportunities for mutual gains while preserving, or improving upon, their relationship. In *Getting Ready to Negotiate:*

> The most durable agreements depend on open communication among cooperative parties who explore opportunities for mutual gains while preserving, or improving upon, their relationship.

A Step-by-Step Guide to Preparing for Any Negotiation, Roger Fisher and Danny Ertel outline seven elements that are essential to successful negotiations wherein mutual gains can be achieved: alternatives, interests, options, legitimacy, communication, relationship, and commitment.[4] Each element is integral to the complete process of analyzing, preparing for, and conducting the negotiation.

TOOLS TO ADD TO YOUR CONFLICT SURVIVAL KIT

Successful negotiations start with good preparation. As you examine the elements of a successful negotiation, think about a negotiation currently confronting you. Are you in the market for a new car or to buy a house? Are you contemplating a new job opportunity and want to negotiate a fair salary? Do you need to negotiate with employees or your boss regarding work issues? Are there issues at home, in your neighborhood, or in the community requiring negotiation?

The Conflict Survival Kit for this chapter provides tools designed to assist you in the preparation process. Following the discussion of each element are "Thought Starters" related to the element. (See Exhibit 11-1.) Use them to help you think through your goals for the negotiation. They will help equip you for success as you engage in negotiations.

EXHIBIT 11-1
Thought starter: Issue and parties

Before proceeding further, provide the following information regarding the conflict or negotiation you are currently addressing:

Issue
(Provide a succinct statement of the central issue or problem you need to negotiate, as you understand it.)

Parties	
Party (or parties) with whom I need to negotiate:	Others who may need to be consulted regarding any proposed agreement: (Include those who have decision-making authority regarding any agreement reached, or who will be expected to implement the agreement or otherwise be affected by the agreement.)

ALTERNATIVES

Effective negotiators know what they hope to achieve in an agreement and when any proposed agreement will result in less than the minimum they are willing to accept.

Although integrative negotiation is more effective than adversarial bargaining in bringing about a workable agreement, its faithful use does not guarantee agreement—nor should it. As much as the integrative negotiation process is useful in realizing a wise and productive agreement, it is also useful in ferreting out a bad one. The parties who are most effective at integrative bargaining enter negotiations with a clear idea of what they hope to achieve in an agreement and when any proposed agreement will result in less than the minimum they are willing to accept. They know their walk-away point or, in other words, their *best alternative to a negotiated agreement*, or BATNA.

The point of negotiation is to realize an agreement that benefits you. If not agreeing will actually achieve a better result than agreeing would, it is better to walk away than to settle. Knowing your BATNA, as well as the other party's, is central to effective bargaining. Having a good BATNA relative to the other party is key to having power. It is the basis by which you can persuade the other party to accept a particular agreement because other proposals are not worthy of your consideration, and a result otherwise will prove less advantageous to the other party. Conversely, having a weak BATNA relative to the other party provides knowledge about when to agree to a proposal because it meets or exceeds your BATNA and when to walk away because agreement would be less advantageous.

In *Getting Past No*, William Ury suggests having three proposals in mind relative to your BATNA when entering a negotiation:[5]

- To what do you *aspire*? What would genuinely satisfy your interests and enough of the other party's interests that would make agreement possible?
- What would make you *content*? What would satisfy your basic interests?
- What could you *live with*? What would you accept, even if barely, because it is better than your BATNA?

To illustrate these positions, consider an individual pursuing employment opportunities:

The individual *aspires* to a salary of $60,000 with good health benefits; retirement benefits; and other perks such as flexible hours, generous paid leave, paid parking, and tuition reimbursement to pursue an MBA. Though he would like to travel some, he does not wish to be away from family for weeks on end. Advancement opportunities within two years are also important.

He *would be content with* a salary in the range of $53,000 to $60,000 with full health and retirement benefits. If advancement opportunities within two years cannot be guaranteed, a job that provides solid experience and the possibility of advancement within a reasonable time would be acceptable. The perks are negotiable depending on the benefits package the company offers. If full tuition reimbursement is not possible, some financial assistance would be helpful. His feelings on travel remain the same.

He *will live with* $53,000. Any less would be a deal breaker, regardless of other considerations. So would the absence of reasonable health and retirement benefits. His feelings on travel are also nonnegotiable. As long as the job provides good work experience, he will accept limited perks, no tuition reimbursement, and the absence of viable advancement opportunities. He can always find a better job elsewhere after two years and will probably do so.

With this analysis, the individual has the power of knowing what an acceptable agreement will look like once it is presented. Without this, he will flounder in negotiations, having no basis to recognize whether any proposed agreement truly meets needs and interests. Indeed, he does not have a good idea of what needs and interests are. Even when negotiations do not result in agreement, there is power in knowing when to walk away rather than accept an agreement that compromises personal values (Exhibit 11-2).

EXHIBIT 11-2
Thought starter: Assessing your BATNA and theirs

Regarding the negotiation for which you are preparing, complete the following:

My BATNA
Consider both tangible (money, status, things, etc.) and intangible (love, relationships, respect, etc.) outcomes you hope to achieve and complete the following statements:
As a result of this negotiation, I aspire to realize the following outcome:
I would be content if I achieved the following outcome:
If I absolutely had to, I could live with the following outcome: (Note: Anything beyond this point will not satisfy my needs and interests, and I will be better off—or at least no worse off—with no agreement.)

The other party's BATNA
If I were the other party, I would want:
If I were the other party, I would accept no less than:

INTERESTS

In traditional bargaining, parties take positions, such as insisting on a certain dollar amount, holding firm on a term or condition in a contract, or demanding that another party perform or cease from performing a particular action. While these considerations remain relevant to the integrative negotiation process, a focus on interests involves an examination of why a party takes the position he does, including the motives, emotions, needs, goals, fears, and desires underlying the position. What do the parties really want? What problem are they trying to solve? It is important to know what your true interests are and to discern the interests of the other party in order to get at the heart of the problem, search for common ground, and move beyond entrenched positions.

> With traditional bargaining, parties take positions. Integrative negotiation examines the motives, needs, goals, fears, and desires underlying their positions.

Consider this example:

A manager insists that an employee must do a particular assignment and must complete it by a certain time and in a certain way. The employee responds that she cannot do the assignment or will not be able to do it according to the manager's time frame and specifications.

If further exploration is not done to understand their respective positions, each party might assume the other is being unreasonable. Since the manager has authority, he could simply compel the employee to do the assignment as requested. Doing so may ensure compliance but will undermine goodwill. Instead, he can explore the employee's underlying interests for resisting the assignment. To get at this, Fisher, Ury, and Patton suggest asking problem-solving questions such as these:[6]

- *Why?* Why is each party taking its position?

   By looking at what he knows about the employee, the manager can analyze what reservations the employee might have in accepting an assignment at this time. Why does the employee feel so strongly about the issue to the point of refusing the manager's instructions? What are her worries and concerns?

- *Why not?* Why is the proposal not acceptable?

   The manager can analyze the barriers that prevent the employee from accepting the assignment. The employee mentioned concerns about the time frames and specifications imposed by the manager; could these considerations have a bearing on her resistance? The manager can ask what specifically is holding the employee back from agreeing. He can also practice empathy and consider how he might feel under similar circumstances.

Probing in this way will reveal a deeper understanding of the problem through the employee's lens:

The employee says she wants to meet the manager's request but is swamped with other assignments at the moment. She also does not believe she has the experience to accomplish the task in the manner requested. However, she further believes she has a more efficient process for completing the assignment if the manager is open to hearing about it.

Through the same process, the manager can help the employee understand his own interests:

The manager indicates that he is on a tight time frame, is worried about meeting business objectives for the month, and needs his team to put in a little extra effort for the organization to remain viable. He believes his way, though not the only way, has at least been tested and will likely result in meeting the time frame that concerns him. While open to new methods, now is not the time.

Notice that the parties have multiple interests impacting their ability to reach a resolution. The parties must identify these interests and seek to address each one. It might be helpful to list them:

Employee	Supervisor
Too much work to do	Time pressures
Lack of training and experience	Financial pressures; business survival
Need for autonomy	No time to train or consider new ideas
Manager isn't open to my suggestions	Needs work done quickly and correctly the first time

Through this exploration, the parties can build a framework from which to engage in deeper dialogue about interests. For example, the employee may need to elaborate on the specific projects she has that are affecting her ability to take on additional assignments. The manager might provide more information about the company's financial pressures and examples of how he is asking other employees to step up during this time of crisis. As they do so, they must be explicit in further defining their interests and concerns. The parties should also avoid turning their exploration into a gripe session about the past and instead frame their interests as needs, goals, and aspirations necessary for realizing a better future. Lastly, Fisher, Ury, and Patton stress, "[b]e hard on the problem, soft on the people" by being firm in attacking the problem while remaining supportive of the other party.[7] Exhibits 11-3 and 11-4 outline processes to guide parties in a negotiation to identify their and others' interests.

EXHIBIT 11–3
Tip: Getting "unstuck"

At times, parties have difficulty getting beyond making positional statements and need help getting "unstuck." To do this, help the individual reframe the position as a statement of interests. Positional statements usually reflect basic human needs, such as a need for respect, appreciation, friendship, security, attention, help, understanding, money, and/or status. Ask the individual to elaborate on what these needs are. What does he or she want as an outcome of the negotiation? What particular fear, doubt, or anxiety causes him or her to hold to the position? Once this is done, you can help the individual articulate the position as an interest statement:

EXHIBIT 11-3
Tip: Getting "unstuck"
Continued

Someone who says...	May actually be saying...
"I can't do that."	"I need more training." "I don't have time." "I have to leave early today."
"I won't stay late today."	"I have a sick kid at home." "It's my wedding anniversary." "I've worked overtime for the past two weeks, and I'm tired."
"You must do this for me."	"I need your help. I can't do it alone." "We're experiencing a time crunch right now." "We're all stressed, but we need to pull together on this one."
"I refuse to accept a penny less."	"I'm experiencing financial difficulties and can't afford to work here anymore." "I feel I've demonstrated that my work warrants a higher pay rate. I want respect."
"I'm going to quit if things don't change."	"I don't feel...appreciated, safe, respected, etc." "I want more challenging work." "I need a boss who is more supportive and caring."

Regarding the negotiation for which you are preparing, complete the following:

EXHIBIT 11-4
Thought starter: Identifying interests

My interests are:
(Be as specific as possible, focusing on the underlying needs, goals, motivations, and other factors that explain why you are pursuing a negotiated agreement. Why is the matter so important to you?)
The other party's interests are:
(Remember that the other party may be making positional statements. How can you reframe these statements to identify the underlying interests that are motivating the other party to take the positions he or she does?)

EXHIBIT 11–4
Thought starter: Identifying
interests
Continued

We have the following interests in common:

The following interests appear to be incompatible:

(Note: *Appear* is the key word as discussion may reveal ways that these may be reconciled. In what ways do you think these interests may be reconciled?)

OPTIONS

With traditional bargaining, the parties enter negotiations taking narrow positions and, therefore, operate under the assumption that there are only one or two possible solutions. Integrative negotiation involves exploring multiple options that may solve the problem. This involves creativity and openness.

Fisher, Ury, and Patton suggest that the parties "separate inventing from deciding" by delaying decision making until all options have been invented, put on the table for consideration, and evaluated.[8] The parties can engage in standard problem-solving activities of defining the problem, brainstorming options that may solve the problem, and evaluating the options to narrow down to the best possible options. For an option to be given serious consideration in this process, it must be tested against the actual problems confronting the parties with a goal of reaching a mutually beneficial agreement. In other words, it is not enough to simply identify *good* options. The parties must select the *best* options that will help them realize *mutual gains*.

To illustrate this process, consider an example from a labor/management dispute.

> Exploring options involves not simply finding good options, but also selecting the best options that will help the parties realize mutual gains.

IDENTIFYING THE PROBLEM

A manufacturing company is concerned about remaining competitive in the market and particularly about the growing trend among its competitors to move most or all of their operations overseas where labor costs are lower. It is concerned about keeping prices for its products competitive when its competitors may eventually be able to lower their prices due to lowered production costs over time.

The union is also concerned about this growing threat. It worries about the prospect of layoffs and the impact competition may have on depressing wages, reducing annual pay increase percentage rates, and placing more of a burden on union members to cover the cost of some benefits.

BRAINSTORMING AND EVALUATING

The process of evaluating options will help the parties realize they have a number of shared interests. Clearly, both parties share an interest in remaining profitable and competitive while avoiding moving operations overseas. Through the process of brainstorming and evaluating, some options they might consider include the following:

- Form management/labor teams to address how they can realign job duties and assignments to ensure the existing labor pool is fully used.
- Offer early retirement plans with appropriate incentives.
- Implement total or partial hiring freezes for areas that can be covered adequately through realignment.
- Bring in new employees with a new set of expectations regarding pay and benefits while "grandfathering" existing employees.
- Offer reduced work schedules for interested employees.
- Restrict or eliminate overtime.
- Eliminate costly fringe benefits that are not widely used.
- Sell off operations for which it would be more cost-effective to outsource or move overseas, and arrange appropriate reassignments and training for individuals in affected positions.

SELECTING THE BEST OPTION

From a list of good options, the parties must hone in on the best options for mutual gain. They may find that many options can be easily reconciled. Fisher, Ury, and Patton use the term *dovetailing* in which the parties' exploration of options reveals differences in interests that may be mutually satisfied without causing either party difficulty.[9] Such an approach is possible especially when the cost to one party is low while the benefit to the other is high. For example, the parties have

Different interests: The union's vital interest is security and the standard of living of its members, and management's vital interest is profitability and, hence, survival. If the options presented to avoid moving overseas will maintain both of these interests, neither party has cause to object.

Different values placed on time: Perhaps the company is contemplating selling off some of its less profitable operations or moving them overseas. It wants to do this soon. The union wants to delay this to allow for retraining of displaced workers as well as attrition through early retirement to create openings for displaced workers.

Management might agree to delay these changes for a short time if the union will cease resisting these inevitable moves and cooperate in helping retrain displaced workers quickly.

Different forecasts: Management's view on what constitutes true financial viability to avoid a move overseas probably differs widely from labor's view. Management may want a quick turnaround while labor may want more time. Perhaps the parties can agree to take discussions about moving operations overseas off the table for incremental periods (six months, a year, two years) if certain levels of profit can be achieved through internal realignments and related efforts supported by the union.

Differences in aversion to risk: Management may have a low tolerance for loss and, therefore, a greater incentive to move operations overseas. Labor may be more risk averse with respect to moving because it does not perceive the immediate impact of financial losses on union members. While management's risk is high, perhaps labor can be persuaded to accept lower annual pay increases, slight increases in the cost of benefits to offset costs, and reduced work schedules and elimination of overtime. When profits turn around and management's risks are lessened, these matters can be addressed to labor's benefit.

An amicable resolution is more achievable through this process than through positional bargaining, which often leaves the parties entrenched. Yet there remains the matter of selecting the option, or options, that will achieve the best and most mutually desirable outcome and committing to it. Ultimately, the decision goes back to consideration of each party's BATNA. While parties do not generally reveal the full extent of their BATNAs, an open exploration of their respective interests and options provides clarity regarding the point at which each party is prepared to walk away and a basis for evaluating options against it.

For both labor and management, their respective BATNAs will likely hinge on the cost or benefit of financial considerations such as the amount of the annual pay increase percentage (if any), the amount of overtime available, the cost of benefits and how they will be paid, and similar issues.

The union will have to decide at what point the options still on the table affect its members' pocketbooks so greatly that it is better to risk the prospect of a move overseas and the loss of jobs. At this point, the union, figuring it has no more to lose, may strike and perhaps initiate a campaign highlighting the company's unwillingness to bargain fairly at the cost of American jobs.

Management will have to decide at what point the cost of maintaining an American workforce is no longer financially viable or productive and that it is better to risk labor's wrath in favor of benefiting its customers and shareholders in the long term.

Factored into evaluating their BATNAs are less tangible considerations such as the long-standing relationship and goodwill between the parties, the company's reputation as an American company supporting American jobs, and labor's pride in working and supporting its members and the company during tough economic times.

When all is said and done, it is up to each party to decide whether any proposed option meets or exceeds the point at which it is better to walk away.

Use Exhibit 11-5 to examine your interests and those of the other party to identify potentially mutual interests.

Regarding the negotiation for which you are preparing, complete the following:

EXHIBIT 11-5
Thought starter: Exploring options

My interests	The other party's interests	Possible options that may satisfy both our interests
Interest 1:		
Interest 2:		
Interest 3:		

Add additional interests, as needed. (Note: This is a preliminary list of possible options. You will likely expand this list as you explore with the other party all possible options that will achieve mutual gains.)

LEGITIMACY

As they evaluate options for resolution, the parties will need to agree on the criteria they will use to assess whether an option adequately meets their needs. Such discussions are essential when the parties are negotiating outcomes based on the merits as opposed to using pressure tactics or a superior ability to persuade or manipulate. Having independent standards for considering the validity of the options proposed, based on objective criteria, removes the guessing game from the negotiation process because it produces reliable, consistent outcomes based on principles.

Use independent standards to determine the validity of proposed options. This removes the guessing game and results in reliable, consistent outcomes based on principles.

The options you consider must first be based on fair standards.[10] These standards will generally be based on situations similar to the one you are facing. Some of the measures parties use to determine this question include the following:

- Traditional cost-benefit analyses
- Review of previous decisions under similar circumstances (or *precedents*)
- Legal precedent from courts or regulatory agencies within the relevant jurisdiction
- Company policies
- Employment laws
- Standard contract terms and principles
- Industry practice and standards
- Relevant guides for pricing and quality measures
- Consultation with experts and neutral third parties

The level of sophistication of the measure used will depend on the level of complexity of the issue. For example, consider the employee requests in Exhibit 11-6.

EXHIBIT 11-6
Considering employee requests

Request:	Objective standards for considering the request:
Leave time	Company policy regarding leave, and consideration of: • The employee's position, including exempt or nonexempt status • Current earned leave available • Type of leave requested (e.g., sick, vacation, funeral, family or medical leave under FMLA)
Work schedule modification	• Company policy, if any, regarding work schedule modifications • Company practice for modifying work schedules for other employees in similar classifications and circumstances • Balancing the employee's true needs for the modification against current work demands
Change in work duties	Analysis of: • What are the employee's duties now? • What does his job description state? • What are others in his position doing? • What are the standards for promotion or job enrichment for employees in his position and level of experience? • Is advancing him to assume new duties fair to others who may be more qualified or have seniority? • Is holding him back fair compared to what has been done for others?

The options you consider should also be based on fair procedures.[11] How are differences settled? If the negotiation does not result in an amicable resolution, how will the relationship be governed, and by whom? The parties must identify appropriate procedures for resolving their issues or recognize what procedures exist by which a resolution may be imposed if an amicable agreement is not reached. For example:

- Company progressive discipline procedures guide the process by which a supervisor must proceed if an amicable resolution to a performance or conduct issue is not reached.
- Company grievance procedures, external agencies, and the courts guide the manager and the organization as to whether disciplinary action taken against an employee is fair.
- In contract negotiations, basic contract principles help define what performance is, whether the contract has adequate consideration, and what constitutes a breach.
- In interpersonal relationships, parties recognize norms of appropriate behavior and the consequences for not behaving appropriately (e.g., disputing children run to Mom; spouses form subtle processes for arriving at agreements).

As the parties enter their negotiation, they should determine as early as possible the criteria by which they will evaluate whether a proposal is fair, as well as the procedures for resolving disagreements. As they continue to negotiate, they can then openly discuss what a fair and reasonable agreement would look like for any particular issue, based on the criteria they have outlined. Having the appropriate principles from which to judge a proposal also helps the parties resist pressure to settle for terms that are less than favorable and discern when a proposal amounts to manipulation and when it is well intentioned and reasonable.

Use Exhibit 11-7 to identify standards for evaluating proposals in a negotiation.

Regarding the negotiation for which you are preparing, complete the following:

EXHIBIT 11-7
Thought starter: Standards for evaluating proposals

The following standards will help us evaluate whether any proposed agreement is fair and reasonable:
(List any relevant standards that apply, including precedent, practice, policies, procedures, regulations, third-party experts, quality standards, and price comparisons.)

We can most effectively and fairly conduct our negotiation discussions, including resolving any disagreements, by using the following process or procedure:

(Note: It is important that you discuss these standards up front with the other party and come to agreement on the standards and procedures you will use before proceeding with substantive discussions.)

COMMUNICATION AND RELATIONSHIP

> Integrative negotiations are based on clear communication and improving, or at least not harming, the parties' relationship.

A successful negotiation is one in which the agreement reached is based on clear communication and improves, or at least does not harm, the parties' relationship.

A significant cause for breakdown in negotiations is the tendency for parties to confuse relationship issues with substantive issues. They point fingers at each other; label each other's behavior as the cause of the problem; and take other actions that create, rather than eliminate, barriers and defensiveness.

Parties stuck in this situation struggle with distinguishing between the *content* of their negotiation and the *process* for negotiating. Discussion to this point has focused on the content of the negotiation. That is, it is *what* the parties have met to talk about. Elements involving communication and relationship relate to *how* the parties address the content of their negotiation.

Generally, it is essential in an interest-based negotiation to address process issues first. The parties should inquire of each other how they are communicating, whether they are being understood, whether they are doing anything in the course of negotiation that is offending the other party, and so forth. Failure to do so may doom the negotiation altogether. All the talk in the world about interests, options, and alternatives is ineffective if the parties cannot communicate effectively or have a contentious relationship. Conversely, once the parties have adequately addressed their process issues, they can more confidently step back into the negotiation to engage in meaningful dialogue involving the content issues that represent the reason for meeting to negotiate in the first place.

Many "people problems" are due either to problems with perceptions, problems involving emotions, or problems in communicating.

PROBLEMS WITH PERCEPTIONS

Often disputes arise because the parties perceive each other and each other's positions as unreasonable, and themselves and their positions as inherently reasonable. Yet the truth often lies somewhere in between. Fisher, Ury, and Patton offer these suggestions for addressing perception problems:[12]

■ ***Seek to view the situation from the other party's point of view.*** While you need not agree with the other party's view, practicing empathy will provide you a better picture of his or her true feelings and a basis from which to work toward agreement. You may even be persuaded to modify your view based on consideration of the other party's views that have merit.

Jack has been disciplined for attendance infractions. He believes he is being judged unfairly given his supervisor's lax treatment of other employees for similar infractions. Juanita, his supervisor, believes she has given Jack all the breaks and worries that other employees will start complaining or, worse, will file a discrimination suit. Nonetheless, she listens to Jack's concerns about the issue.

Jack points out to Juanita various attendance infractions by other employees of which Juanita was unaware and had unwittingly rewarded. From this standpoint, Juanita can appreciate why Jack believes he is being treated unfairly. She then assures Jack that she will at least examine these abuses by others and that she intends to treat each attendance issue consistently.

■ ***Don't blame the other party for the problem, label his or her behavior, or act in other ways that create defensiveness.*** Parties in conflict tend to make statements that reflect a view that the other party is totally accountable while they are free from any responsibility. Such statements automatically create defensiveness in others, who often lash back with similar counterproductive statements.

A company relies on a vendor to deliver certain products on time. The vendor's delays create back orders and anger the company's customers. The company's former manager tended to make accusatory statements to the vendor, such as, "Your delivery service is consistently lousy" (labeling) or "I'm losing customers in droves because of you" (blaming). This angered the vendor's salesperson, who believed that the company had not managed customer expectations regarding back orders for a quality product that was selling off the shelves. He said defensively, "I think your poor customer service practices are to blame."

Sensing the cause of this communication breakdown, the company's new manager encourages the vendor's salesperson to engage with him in an objective review of past performance—both the company's and the vendor's—and avoids labels and judgments. In exchange, the vendor's salesperson responds more professionally.

■ ***Encourage open discussion of perceptions.*** The parties should be honest about their true intentions in pursuing the negotiation and frank about how they perceive the other's intentions.

Their discussion should involve an open expression of concerns about each other's views and positions and how those positions affect their ability to enter an agreement. Each party may then be able to identify what issues are truly important or bothersome to the other party and what issues are less important.

Indira believes that her employer is paying her substantially below market given her current level of experience and contribution to the company. Alec, her manager, cannot possibly pay more in view of concessions already given and the fact that Indira's salary is actually above market.

Indira says the company has consistently undervalued her contribution and has added more responsibility without acknowledging the impact these increased burdens have had on her work and personal life. A pay increase would at least mollify these concerns, making her feel that taking on these added pressures was worth something. Alec has thus discerned that while fair pay is important to Indira, more appreciation and perhaps assistance in balancing work/life issues would mean more to her at the present time.

- ***Ensure that the other party has a stake in the outcome by encouraging his or her participation in the process for achieving resolution.*** In the employment context, employees become frustrated when they think that they have no control over decisions affecting them. Their perceptions about what the employer is truly willing to do for them and consequently their reasons for taking hard bargaining positions are often an outcome of this lack of empowerment.

Chan wants to be assigned more challenging work. He believes that he has proven himself capable, but Constance, his boss, seems to be blind to his true abilities. However, Constance believes that Chan needs more time on the job because he has made significant errors on less challenging projects.

Chan continually complains about the lack of challenging assignments and slows down his production in the belief that nothing else he can do will get his supervisor's attention. When Constance meets with Chan to address his attitude and decline in performance, Chan expresses the feeling that decisions over who does what assignment seem to be totally within Constance's control, so there is no point in putting in extra effort.

In this instance, the employee's behaviors are keeping him from realizing the outcome he wants to achieve. Yet, if his concerns are correct, the supervisor must attempt to involve the employee more so that he has greater ownership in the solution:

Constance addresses performance issues that have been holding Chan back, outlines specific steps he can take to be ready for more challenging assignments, and promises training and other support necessary to prepare him. In response, Chan shows a greater willingness to negotiate a plan for realizing his goals, including changing his attitude and returning to prior levels of production.

PROBLEMS INVOLVING EMOTIONS

In traditional bargaining, parties take hard stances. The more adversarial the relationship, the more rigid these stances become. The physical demeanor and body language of skilled bargainers, such as lawyers or business associates, often reflect this rigidity. It leaves the impression that emotions and feelings about the issues do not matter. In integrative negotiation, emotions are a central aspect of the negotiation process, and meeting emotional needs is as important as meeting other needs when searching for workable solutions.

To appropriately deal with emotions, Fisher, Ury, and Patton suggest that you[13]

- Recognize that both parties have emotions that are central to the problem and that may affect the outcome of the dispute.
- Acknowledge your fears, worries, and concerns and encourage the other party to do the same. Doing so will allow you to unburden yourselves of pent-up emotions and focus more clearly on the problem after the air has cleared.
- Allow the party to give full voice to his or her emotions, being careful to withhold judgment, refrain from reacting to accusations, and ensure that the party has fully vented before attempting to respond.
- When necessary, set ground rules about how to appropriately express emotions, such as a rule that only one person can express anger at a time or an agreement that the parties will take periodic breaks to cool off.
- Use symbolic gestures, such as a handshake, a supportive touch or embrace, eating together, or the offer of an apology, to defuse a tense situation, show understanding, or call a truce.

In *Beyond Reason: Using Emotions as You Negotiate*, Fisher and Daniel Shapiro note five core concerns that generally underlie the emotions parties are feeling and expressing: appreciation, affiliation, autonomy, status, and role.[14] They suggest dealing with these concerns—how they have been ignored and how they can be addressed—rather than ignoring or dealing directly with the emotions themselves.[15]

PROBLEMS IN COMMUNICATING

Problems in communicating and how to address them are discussed in Chapters 5 through 7 of this text. The key is to communicate through empathic listening—showing that you have grasped not only the content of the party's message, but also the emotions, logic, and reasons underlying the message—before attempting to articulate your own message. Listen to the feelings and not just the words.

WORK AS PARTNERS, NOT AS ADVERSARIES

Fisher, Ury, and Patton suggest a shift in orientation from face-to-face confrontation to side-by-side cooperation.[16] This might be done literally, if necessary, by encouraging the parties to sit on the same side of the table to look squarely at the problem facing them rather across the table at each other. This has the effect of making the parties realize they are working together to confront a common problem, rather than to view each other as the problem. Exhibit 11-8 focuses on how parties in a negotiation view the issues before them.

EXHIBIT 11–8
Thought starter: Our relationship

Regarding the negotiation for which you are preparing, complete the following:

In our conflict, we appear to view the following situation differently:	
I view the situation this way:	**The other party views the situation this way:**
We may view this situation differently because:	
(Consider any problems with emotions, perceptions, or communication in your relationship that may be causing the disagreement.)	
These concerns can be addressed in the following manner:	
(What strategies can you use to improve your relationship and overcome any problems with communication, emotions, or perceptions? What barriers are preventing you from working together and how can you address these barriers?)	

PART IV: Application and Practice

COMMITMENT

As the parties define interests, explore options, and weigh alternatives, they must also discuss what each party will be expected to do once agreement is reached. These expectations must be clearly defined, as they will have a bearing on whether the parties are comfortable with the options considered and whether they will ultimately embrace the agreement. Establishing commitments should occur throughout the negotiation process and not just at the end when it is time to memorialize the parties' understandings. The parties should engage in full and open discussion of all issues before locking themselves into firm commitments.

> Parties should discuss and establish commitments throughout the negotiation process and not just at the end when it is time to memorialize the agreement.

The parties should discuss process commitments first. This will provide clarity to the parties for making decisions on substantive matters later. For example:

- How will each agreed-upon option be implemented?
- What are the time frames, goals, and expectations for each option?
- Through which measures will parties know goals and expectations have been accomplished?

The parties should discuss their commitments to substantive issues at the end of the negotiation process rather than in bits and pieces along the way. Substantive issues include matters such as

- What will one party pay the other and in what amount?
- What will a party do in the future or refrain from doing?
- What will one party do for another?

Substantive matters tend to be considered independently from one another. When parties agree too early to accept a change in behavior or to provide a particular benefit, it may affect their ability to make other commitments later. While commitments can always be renegotiated, the process of reevaluating prior commitments is time consuming and inefficient. Piecemeal agreements tend to also lock parties into commitments that they are reluctant to change at the risk of losing face or appearing soft or indecisive.

Overall, commitments in the agreement, whether written or verbal, should

- Be clear about what issues have been resolved, what product (e.g., term, conditions, dollar amounts, and performance) is expected, and who is responsible for each aspect of the agreement.
- Be realistic and achievable. The parties must believe, for both practical and emotional reasons, that they can honor and perform the agreement.
- Include, as appropriate, time frames and benchmarks toward completion and procedures for reviewing progress.

- Take into account the impacts on others who have authority for approving the agreement or who will be expected to implement the agreement. Such parties should be consulted and their input considered prior to finalizing the agreement.
- Involve consideration of how the parties will deal with obstacles to implementation, including processes for revisiting the agreement and renegotiating terms when necessary.

Exhibits 11-9 and 11-10 address preparing and assessing an agreement.

EXHIBIT 11-9
Thought starter: Commitments

Regarding the negotiation for which you are preparing, complete the following:

A successful agreement will include the following:
(Include the terms, conditions, and interests that must be met, time frames, roles, expectations of each party, etc.)

EXHIBIT 11-10
Agreement checklist

At the conclusion of negotiations, before final agreement, ask the following questions:

Does the agreement:	Yes	No
Satisfy my interests?		
Satisfy the other party's interests?		
Meet or exceed my BATNA?		
Meet or exceed the other party's BATNA (as I understand it)?		
Incorporate options that allow us to achieve mutual gains?		
Include terms that are based on standards and procedures appropriate to the organizational and/or interpersonal context involved? (Have we identified these standards and used them as the basis for agreement?)		

198   **PART IV: Application and Practice**

EXHIBIT 11-10
Agreement checklist
Continued

Does the agreement:	Yes	No
Provide appropriate time frames and benchmarks for fulfilling each term? With respect to each term, is it: 		

	Yes	No
Specific		
Measurable		
Achievable		
Realistic		
Time-specific		

(Check "yes" if all items above are checked "yes"; check "no" if any single item above is checked "no") ⟶

Does the agreement:	Yes	No
Indicate who is responsible for carrying out each specific term?		
Include a process for monitoring progress and renegotiating issues if necessary?		
Take into consideration others who need to be consulted or who will be affected? (Have these parties been consulted?)		
Maintain or improve our relationship? Does the agreement address and attempt to resolve:		

	Yes	No
Problems involving emotions		
Problems with perceptions		
Problems in communicating		

(Check "yes" if all items above are checked "yes"; check "no" if any single item above is checked "no") ⟶

Does the agreement:	Yes	No
Have my full support and the full support of the other party so that we will follow through on our commitments?		

If you cannot answer each question in the affirmative, one of two alternatives must be considered:

1. You should continue to work with the other party until a mutually satisfactory agreement can be achieved; or

2. You have reached a point where further discussion is not productive and agreement is not possible at this time. Such an outcome

may have occurred because there is no agreement that will satisfy one or both party's BATNA. It may also be the result of concerns regarding your relationship that have not been adequately addressed. In either case, you and the other party will need to consider how you will proceed at this point without an agreement.

PERFORMANCE CHECKLIST

- Integrative negotiation provides parties the opportunity to explore their mutual interests in achieving resolution of their conflict or negotiation so they may realize mutual gains. A successful agreement achieved through integrative negotiation

    - Takes into account the parties' *best alternative to a negotiated agreement*, or BATNA, which the parties use to gauge when a proposed agreement is better or worse than realizing no agreement at all.

    - Involves an exploration of the parties' *interests*, how they are compatible or incompatible, and how all interests may be met to achieve a mutually satisfactory agreement.

    - Involves an exploration of all possible *options* that may satisfy the parties' interests and the selection of the best options that will help the parties realize mutual gains.

    - Has *legitimacy*, in that the agreement and the process through which it was reached are based on external, objective standards that are defensible and acceptable to the parties.

    - Is based on clear *communication*, ensuring that significant communication barriers that may affect the agreement have been addressed and resolved.

    - Attempts to preserve, if not improve upon, the *relationship* between the parties and respects the interests of others who may be affected by the agreement.

    - Must have the full *commitment* of the parties to follow through on the agreement, including clearly defined expectations, measures of accountability, and mechanisms for implementing and monitoring the agreement and reevaluating it along the way.

TEST YOURSELF

True/False

For each statement below, check true or false.

TRUE   FALSE

_____   _____   1. If you don't have a good BATNA, you shouldn't bother to negotiate.

_____   _____   2. *Dovetailing* means eliminating from consideration all options except those that can be easily reconciled by the parties.

_____   _____   3. The BATNA is a powerful tool because it educates the negotiator regarding his or her desired outcome and the strength of his or her bargaining position.

_____   _____   4. Relying on precedent means that the parties consider how situations similar to their own were resolved to determine how they will proceed.

_____   _____   5. When an employee negotiates with his or her manager about how a Performance Improvement Plan (PIP) should be structured, they should keep in mind the company's policy regarding PIPs and how the company typically implements them.

Circle the letter next to the best answer for each question. On a separate sheet of paper, state why you chose that answer.

1. In salary negotiations, Ezra wants $68,195 in salary but will accept no less than $63,725. The employer believes that a fair salary for the position is $59,185 but is willing to pay up to $65,950. The settlement range is

   a. $2,245.
   b. $2,225.
   c. $4,470.
   d. settlement is not possible in this scenario.

2. The BATNA is useful to a negotiator for all the following reasons, *except* that it

   a. helps the negotiator gauge whether a proposed offer will meet or exceed his or her needs and interests.
   b. helps the negotiator decide whether pursuing negotiations is worth it.
   c. helps the negotiator assess his or her capability in using tactical maneuvers to outwit his or her opponent.
   d. informs the negotiator regarding the point at which it is better to not agree than to accept a proposal that does not satisfy his or her BATNA.

3. All of the following are examples of positional statements, *except*

   a. "I'm not going to work overtime tonight."
   b. "Your expectations about completing this work tonight are unacceptable."
   c. "I need you to understand the time constraints and pressures I'm under right now."
   d. "I'm going to file a grievance if you require me to work overtime tonight."

4. To encourage a party with whom you are negotiating to accept your proposal, the *least effective* approach is to

   a. consider the difficulties she may face in persuading others she must answer to or who may be responsible for implementing the agreement and find ways to help her make the proposal attractive to them.
   b. agree to concede issues that are less important to you but that are of vital importance to her.
   c. "dovetail" common interests, showing how your and her interests can be reconciled.
   d. make clear to her the actions you will be forced to take if she does not agree to the proposal.

5. Jeff is being placed on a Performance Improvement Plan (PIP). He is negotiating with his supervisor, Margo, the terms of this plan, such as specific tasks and expectations he must fulfill and timelines for completion. To determine whether these terms are fair and reasonable, they should consider all of the following criteria, *except*

   a. company policies concerning performance improvement plans.
   b. performance standards for Jeff's position.
   c. measures used for PIPs in the past for employees in Jeff's position.
   d. current performance indicators for above-average performers in Jeff's position.

1. Think about a negotiation or conflict situation that you must soon address. When thinking about how to engage in integrative negotiations, what are the greatest challenges you think you will face? Discuss these challenges in small groups or as a class and how you may overcome these challenges to experience success.

2. Many negotiations appear to lend themselves to only distributive, fixed-pie outcomes. For example, when buying a house or a car, negotiations often seem limited to discussions of price alone. What other situations do you think offer limited fixed-pie outcomes? Thinking a little deeper, what are some underlying needs and interests involved with these situations that can be explored? How can you convert these situations into discussions about satisfying mutual interests and achieving mutual gains?

CASE: NEGOTIATIONS FOR LIFE

OBJECTIVE

To practice integrative negotiation.

PROBLEM

Scenario 1

Joe has been working a lot of hours lately. Not only does he need a break, but he also worries that his studies are suffering. Midterm exams are coming up, and Joe has a research paper due. There never seems to be enough time to study on the weekends, particularly since he works on Saturdays. And it is tiring to come home at night after a long day of work or after night classes. With June pregnant and working full time, Joe worries about not being at home to help with household duties. He feels he has not been as involved as he needs to be in looking after their daughter, Betsy.

Adding to his frustrations, there have been problems at the customer service desk. Not only is he dealing with difficult employees like Tina Tumultuous, but the team leader position for the customer service desk is still vacant. At the same time that he is advertising to fill the position and conducting interviews, he is working two jobs—his own and the vacant position. Jim Talent has been after him to fill the position.

Jim has also been talking to all the managers about improving customer service. The level of service has suffered in recent months, which translates into reduced revenues. Usually patient, Jim has been pushing lately to turn things around. He does not dictate the precise hours his assistant managers must work, but the expectation is that, for now, they will put in extra time. Although Jim has honored Joe's need to leave work early on various days to attend class, Joe is sensing growing impatience.

Now does not seem like the time to ask Jim for a reduction in work hours—say, from sixty-five hours to fifty—at least for the next month so he can catch up on studies and deal with his family situation. But he must nonetheless ask.

Scenario 2

Joe and Kim Khan have worked out their differences—sort of (see Case in Chapter 9). While Kim no longer takes pot shots at Joe for his lack of experience, Kim and Joe have clearly different perspectives on how to perform their jobs, serve customers, and treat employees. Jim Talent continues to encourage

Joe to work with Kim to address their relationship issues. This will be particularly important because Joe and Kim will need to present a united front in an upcoming negotiation they'll be having with representatives from Do or Dye Tools (see Case in Chapter 12).

Among the recent issues that have created concerns are the following:

1. ***Store policy regarding returns.*** The standard store policy is a 30-day "no questions asked" policy. After 30 days, store policy is generally to give store credit. Kim routinely promises customers who purchase tools full money-back guarantees, regardless of how much time has passed. Customers then refer to Kim's representations when they come to the customer service desk that Joe manages, making claims for money back for tools returned beyond 30 days. Kim thinks that Joe and his team do not understand the need to work around company policy at times in the interest of "putting the customer first." Joe and Kim must come to agreement on what "putting the customer first" and honoring store policy mean, and whether these two concepts are compatible or mutually exclusive.

2. ***Philosophical disagreement over "handshake" deals.*** Kim tends to make informal handshake deals with vendors. Kim did this with Do or Dye Tool's former representative, Axel Rod, regarding the sale of its Super-Deluxe 15-90 Power-Matic Reversible Drill/Screwdriver set and accompanying package sets of drill bits and screwdriver heads (see Case in Chapter 12). This deal has angered Vic Vendor, Do or Dye's current representative, and could result in Do or Dye severing its business relationship with More Power. Although Kim may have rational reasons for doing this, Joe believes that such actions reflect poor business practice. Before meeting with Do or Dye, Joe and Kim must agree on how they will represent More Power and the level of formality or informality that is appropriate when negotiating.

3. ***Treatment of employees.*** Kim's actions create a "spillover" effect on Joe's customer service desk team because they must manage the customer service issues that Kim's actions generate. When Kim's actions appear to run contrary to store service policy, some of Joe's employees have attempted to address any misunderstandings with Kim directly. Kim's response has been gruff, dismissive, and defensive. Kim makes clear that these actions will continue in the interest of serving customers without apology for the impacts on Joe's team. Kim clearly has little tolerance for what appear to be arbitrary procedures that interfere with good customer service. Joe's employees complain about Kim's gruff manner and express concerns about being caught between a rock and a hard place: They will either get in trouble for running afoul of store policy by honoring Kim's representations to customers or incur the wrath of Khan and customers by holding customers to store policy despite Kim's representations to the contrary. Joe and Kim must come to agreement about how to work with Joe's employees, how to avoid situations that put employees in this bind, and how to serve customers in a consistent manner.

PROCEDURE

Choose either Scenario 1 or Scenario 2 to role-play. Break the class into three teams. One team will assume the role of Joe. One team will assume the role of Jim (Scenario 1) or Kim (Scenario 2) respectively. The third team will serve as observers. Joe's team and Jim's/Kim's team should each select a member who will role-play a negotiation in front of the class.

Before the role-play, have each team spend twenty minutes analyzing the problem. Each team should go through roughly the same analysis to prepare for the negotiation, considering the seven elements of a successful negotiation from both Joe's perspective and Jim's or Kim's perspective. Each team should then decide on the negotiation strategy it should take and coach the selected representative accordingly. The team of observers should consider the problem from both parties' perspectives. The teams may use the tools in this chapter to analyze the situation and prepare for the negotiation.

After twenty minutes, have the selected representatives engage in an integrative negotiation in front of the class. The negotiation should last no more than ten minutes. The selected representatives must take their roles seriously, given what they know about Joe and Jim or Kim from the profiles and scenario described. Neither party should arbitrarily agree to anything unless he or she believes that it genuinely serves his or her interests.

Case Questions

1. After the role-play, have the selected representatives for Joe and Jim (Scenario 1) or Kim (Scenario 2) first discuss how engaging in the integrative negotiation made them feel. Did they feel successful? What challenges did they face?

2. The members from each of the two teams representing Joe and Jim/Kim should discuss how the outcome of the negotiation compared to what they hoped to achieve during preparation discussions. Was the result positive, or was it disappointing? What worked well? What did not work well?

3. The members of the observing team should discuss the overall effectiveness of the parties' attempt at integrative negotiation. Were the parties effective in applying the seven elements? Despite the outcome and whether or not agreement was reached, did the parties engage in integrative negotiation strategies, or did negotiations become distributive and adversarial? What caused them to be one way or the other? Did they work toward achieving mutual gains?

ALTERNATIVE PROCEDURE FOR ONLINE LEARNING FORMATS

Choose either Scenario 1 or Scenario 2 to role-play. Assign students to pairs. One student will assume the role of Joe. The other student will assume the role of Jim (Scenario 1) or Kim (Scenario 2) respectively. Have students role-play the scenario off-line. Preferably, the students should meet in person to engage in the role-play or, if that is not possible, conduct the role-play via appropriate videoconferencing capability. At worst, they may conduct the negotiation via telephone call or other audio-conferencing capability. Students should not negotiate this role-play via e-mail or other text-only methods.

Have students complete their role-play exercise by a specified time period. Then, have pairs jointly prepare written responses to the questions and post them on the class Web-based learning environment by a specified time period. Alternatively, create an online forum discussion group, chat room, or other synchronous or asynchronous environment for students to engage in online conversations concerning their experiences in conducting the role-play and their responses to the questions.

PERSONAL GROWTH EXERCISE

Look for an opportunity to engage in an integrative negotiation with someone at work or in your personal life. If you are unfamiliar with the integrative negotiation process or more accustomed to adversarial negotiation, you might initially choose situations for which the stakes are not particularly high, then work up to negotiating for outcomes that are more important to you.

Some examples of low-stakes negotiations follow:

- Purchase of a small consumer good, such as a toaster, a lawn mower, or a suit or dress.
- Requesting opportunities at work, such as new assignments, a training opportunity, or a modified work schedule.
- Talking with your neighbor about who will mow the fence line or shovel the sidewalks after a large snowstorm.
- Negotiating project and paper deadlines, opportunities for extra credit, and ways to improve a grade with your professor.
- Discussing what color to paint the living room or where to plant a shrub with your spouse or significant other.

Some examples of higher stakes negotiations follow:

- Purchase of a new car or a house, or working with a contractor to build a house.

- Negotiating salary; requesting changes in job status, title, or classification; or asking to be promoted.
- Negotiating with your neighbor regarding a barking dog or noisy children, the accumulation of broken down cars and junk along the property line, or disputes over the location of the property line.

The Harvard Negotiation Project is a research project at Harvard University and is part of the Program on Negotiation at Harvard Law School. Information regarding the Program on Negotiation and resources to assist conflict management practitioners is available at

PON Clearinghouse
800-258-4406
www.pon.org

The Program on Negotiation (PON)
Harvard Law School
513 Pound Hall
Cambridge, MA 02138
617-495-1684
www.pon.harvard.edu

1. Roger Fisher, William Ury, and Bruce Patton, *Getting to Yes: Negotiating Agreement Without Giving In*, 2nd ed. (New York: Penguin Books, 1991).

2. William Ury, *Getting Past No: Negotiating Your Way from Confrontation to Cooperation*, revised ed. (New York: Bantam Books, 1993).

3. Roger Fisher and Danny Ertel, *Getting Ready to Negotiate: A Step-by-Step Guide to Preparing for Any Negotiation* (New York: Penguin Books, 1995).

4. Ibid., 5–7.

5. Ury, *Getting Past No*, 25–26.

6. Fisher, Ury, and Patton, *Getting to Yes*, 44.

7. Ibid., 54–55.

8. Ibid., 60–63.

9. Ibid., 73–76.

10. Ibid., 85–86.

11. Ibid., 86–87.

12. Ibid., 22–29.

13. Ibid., 29–32.

14. Roger Fisher and Daniel Shapiro, *Beyond Reason: Using Emotions as You Negotiate* (New York: Viking, 2005), 15–21.

15. Ibid., 3–14.

16. Fisher, Ury, and Patton, *Getting to Yes*, 11.

OVERCOMING BARRIERS TO INTEGRATIVE NEGOTIATION

PERFORMANCE COMPETENCIES

After you have finished reading this chapter, you will be able to

- Describe the common barriers to reaching agreement through integrative negotiation, including

  - Impasse
  - The refusal to negotiate
  - Positional or hard bargainers

- Develop and practice strategies for overcoming these barriers

If everyone had the same idea about how to negotiate and resolve conflict, negotiations would be far less challenging. And far less interesting! Yet many barriers can get in the way of realizing cooperative, integrative outcomes:

- Despite the parties' best intentions to reach an amicable resolution, they reach an impasse where it appears their needs and interests cannot be reconciled.
- A party will not negotiate either because he does not perceive the existence of a conflict or he has a power advantage.
- A party does not see the value of integrative negotiation, either because she does not know about its advantages or does not care to engage in cooperative processes. She resorts instead to positional (or hard) bargaining strategies, including in the worst case "dirty tricks."

In any negotiation, there is no guarantee regarding the disposition, competence, or integrity of the individual with whom you must negotiate. But integrative negotiation remains the appropriate tool, whether the other

If you run into a wall, don't turn around and give up. Figure out how to climb it, go through it, or work around it.

Michael Jordan

party is difficult to work with or congenial. You must remain steadfast to the principles of integrative negotiation and attempt to bring the other party to your side. This chapter discusses approaches for overcoming barriers to integrative negotiation.

WHEN THE PARTIES ARE AT IMPASSE

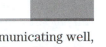

A negotiation can go along smoothly. The parties are communicating well, they are trying to understand and address each other's needs and interests, and they appear to be hammering out an agreement inch by inch. Then, everything comes to a halt.

- Max finds a term or condition for agreement to be unacceptable and sees no way of resolving the issue. He feels he is giving up too much and receiving too little.
- Loretta becomes angry about something Duane did or said, and she does not see the value of continuing the discussion.
- In a mediation involving custody of their children, Rita feels that her ex-husband has not truly heard or understood her concerns, nor is he attempting to do so, and she doubts he ever will.

The parties have come to an impasse when one or both parties believe they cannot take another step toward achieving resolution. Their reasons for not proceeding may be deliberate, such as a means for gaining tactical advantage, or more sincere, based on an honest assessment that a party cannot in good faith continue negotiations without compromising some fundamental principle. In many situations, such as when the parties' interests are truly incompatible, they do not desire a better relationship, or the status quo is acceptable, an impasse spells the end of the negotiation process. So be it.

Yet, where the parties are fundamentally committed to their relationship and to achieving a mutually satisfactory outcome, breaking off negotiations in the face of impasse would be a shame. For these situations, impasse signals a genuine concern by one or both parties that a need or interest is not being addressed. It often occurs at a point in negotiations when a party's deepest interests are at stake, and the party is communicating that the process should slow down or halt until these issues can be addressed to his satisfaction. Rather than marking the end of meaningful negotiations, impasse can present the breakthrough point at which a genuine discussion of needs and interests can take place and a genuine, durable resolution can be achieved.

Impasse should not be confused with a failure to bargain, a lack of good faith, or a form of obstinacy or manipulation. While a party may become entrenched in a particular position, critical of the other party or the options proposed, or dissatisfied with the negotiation process, such actions should not be interpreted as tactical maneuvers traditionally associated with positional bargaining. Nor should expressions of distress, doubt, or displeasure be viewed as tactics aimed at pressing an advantage. Rather, an individual at impasse has genuine reasons for holding to a position, questioning the viability of proposals offered, or doubting the other party or the process. As long as a party has remained at the table and demonstrated good faith, the party is entitled to the benefit of the doubt that he or she is dealing with genuine impasse.

> Impasse often occurs at the point at which a party's deepest interests are at stake, and he or she wants to slow down the negotiation process or halt it until these interests can be addressed.

> Impasse can present a breakthrough point leading to genuine discussion. It should not be confused with a failure to bargain, a lack of good faith, obstinacy, or manipulation.

When at impasse, time and attention must be devoted to exploring the party's reservations for resolving the dispute. Why is he or she struggling? What interests or needs have been ignored or threatened? Does the other party have concerns about your relationship that should be shared with you? An individual may be reluctant to proceed for a myriad of reasons. You must help the party diagnose these reasons and attempt to address them in a way that bridges the gap between the interests of both parties and that will help the other party feel successful. In *Getting Past No: Negotiating Your Way from Confrontation to Cooperation*, William Ury refers to this as "building a golden bridge."[1] He notes that the tendency in negotiations is to push the other party toward agreement when frustrated with his resistance. Yet this serves only to increase resistance. Ury advises instead "to *draw* them in the direction you want them to move....You need to reframe their position as an advance toward a better solution."[2]

> You must help the party diagnose the reasons for impasse and attempt to address those reasons in a way that bridges the gap between the interests of both parties.

COMMON CAUSES OF IMPASSE AND WHAT TO DO ABOUT THEM

The following are examples of some standard reasons for impasse and suggestions for responding to them. While reaching agreement is never guaranteed, note how these responses help bridge the gap and bring the other party closer to an integrative agreement.

Reason: A party's needs and interests have not been met or have not been met at the appropriate level of depth.

A manager agrees to a pay increase, flexible scheduling, and other benefits to encourage a top performer to stay. The employee feels the manager has ignored her need for affiliation, respect, and more challenging assignments but has not felt comfortable expressing these concerns.

Tools for responding: Do not assume that an individual has only tangible interests at stake. Addressing such interests satisfies needs at a superficial level but fails to meet needs at a deeper heart level. Negotiations may be at impasse because you have not taken the time to explore these deeper interests, and the party is waiting to see whether you will. If you sense that dissatisfaction remains after offering the more obvious options for resolution, ask the individual what more you can do to make resolution possible.

Reason: A party has made bottom-line commitments and does not want to lose face.

A union representative has promised union members he would accept nothing less than a 4 percent annual pay increase, but management is offering only 3 percent with a modest reduction in the cost of health care premiums.

Tools for responding: It is never wise to negotiate yourself into a corner. When a party has done this, his chief interest is finding a way to accept new agreements while preserving his dignity. You must help him reframe the issue in a way that makes the outcome look far better than his initial position. You can do some number crunching for the union official, for example, to show how the agreement provides both the short-term benefit of increased pay and reduced health care costs and the long-term benefit of job security since the lower rate helps the company remain viable. Another response is to show how circumstances have changed, requiring a different paradigm for agreement. For example, perhaps new financial projections demonstrate that the larger percentage increase requested by the union is not feasible.

Reason: The parties have not come to an agreement on defining the problem or are not defining the problem at the appropriate level of generality or specificity.

> Jean, a manager, engages in a philosophical argument with another manager about the meaning of teamwork when the issue involves how their teams are not supporting each other.

> An employee, Mavis, manages to sidetrack the manager over the finer points of her attendance record while the manager's intent in meeting is to discuss the employee's poor attitude and work ethic.

Tools for responding: In the heat of discussions, it is easy to get sidetracked into details that are not wholly relevant. One reason for this may be that insufficient time was spent to clearly define the problem in the first place. When this happens, encourage the other party to revisit with you the purpose of the negotiations and the precise problem you have asked him or her to solve with you. For example, you may need to encourage the party to narrow down the discussion to the issues that require attention:

> Jean, I'm not sure we'll ever agree on the precise meaning of *teamwork*. I think we can come to agreement on how our staff members are, or are not, assisting one another. Let's get a handle on that problem and see what we can do about it.

Or to broaden the focus:

> Mavis, this is not a discussion about attendance per se. There are bigger issues to discuss—mainly, your attitude and work ethic. Attendance is just one small aspect of this problem. Let me try to illustrate for you again what I mean.

Reason: The parties are "stuck" on two proposals, one each advocated by the parties. Neither is satisfied with the other's proposal.

> At an advertising agency, a problem has developed concerning a group of graphic artists who take excessive smoking breaks in front of the building. It is causing morale problems with other staff and is offensive to customers. The manager for these employees argues that smoking breaks are essential because it fosters their creativity to step away from the confines of their work

spaces in order to gain new perspectives. He suggests requiring them to smoke at least thirty feet away from the building entrance. The other manager wants to crack down on smoking breaks in front of the building entirely because the graphic artists who take them are too visible and distracting to his department members, who are not allowed to take such breaks. He suggests writing a policy prohibiting such practices.

Tools for responding: Sometimes, the parties argue over solutions before they have clearly defined the problem. They should come to realize how locking into a few narrow, self-serving solutions does not serve this goal. They should revisit the problem and their overall goal in seeking resolution. They can then brainstorm the full range of possible solutions to identify a third alternative that will satisfy all parties.

After such deliberations, a possible solution for the smokers might look like this:

The parties agree to develop a smoking shelter just outside the loading dock in the back of the building. They agree that a restrictive policy should not be written, but smokers are reminded to be discreet when taking smoking breaks to avoid distracting coworkers or offending customers. All staff is reminded to respect one another's personal choices and privacy.

Reason: A party does not wish to take responsibility for a proposed agreement.

In a discussion between a manager and an employee regarding establishing new performance standards, the employee balks at many of the manager's suggestions and offers none of his own.

Tools for responding: A party may not wish to take ownership of a proposed agreement. He may behave this way due to fear, a lack of motivation, or a feeling that his input is not valued. If you are formulating ideas, ask how the other party would solve a particular problem, draft a particular sentence, or go about accomplishing a particular task. If you have contributed the bulk of the proposals, step back and ask the party to offer constructive criticism. What does he like? What would he add or take away? If you sense the person has reservations because he feels you are imposing an agreement on him rather than inviting his participation, seek to identify why he feels that way. Ask if there is anything you have done that causes him to question your input or doubt that the agreement is fair. If so, apologize and return to a relationship of mutual problem solving.

Reason: A party does not believe that a proposed agreement is reasonable or achievable.

An employee hesitates about the time frames, processes, and resources proposed for completing a project and thinks the terms are unfair.

Tools for responding: When impasse involves basic factual information, the best response is to explore the data, facts, and other specifics from which the terms for agreement were derived. If a party does not feel the terms are reasonable or achievable, ask her to provide specific examples of terms she finds objectionable and to explain why she feels this way. Conversely, be prepared to offer information supporting why you believe such terms should be acceptable. Perhaps you have not spent sufficient time discussing the standards by which to judge a fair agreement. Revisit these standards and assess whether the terms you have discussed are aligned with them.

Reason: A party is fixed on his position and does not see the potential for integrative bargaining.

> A contractor wants two lump-sum payments for his services, half before work begins and the other half after work is completed, and is not interested in considering alternative payment methods.

> A customer haggles over the price of a car, wanting to drive the price down, and ignores the sales representative's attempts to offer a better, albeit more expensive, deal with incentives, add-ons, and reasonable financing that may better suit the customer's needs.

Tools for responding: Some individuals are not interested in or knowledgeable about integrative approaches to problem solving. Your opportunity to change this mind-set may be limited. But if time allows, the issues are important, and you value the relationship, it may be time well spent. When a party is fixed on a position, you must spend time on reframing these positions into interests. Ask questions focused on why the individual is taking the position. Suggest reasons why such a position may not be in the best interests of either party, including the consequences for not agreeing and the benefits if you do.

Reason: A party feels overwhelmed.

> A party feels he is being asked to consider too much too fast.

> A party becomes emotional during the course of discussions.

Tools for responding: The best remedy for feeling overwhelmed is to take a deep breath. Negotiations are seldom so crucial that time cannot be taken to step away to think about the situation. This could mean a fifteen-minute break, a lunch break, or a day or a week away to consider what has transpired and how to proceed next. Pressure tactics should not be used to force a party to come to a quick agreement. For reasons of her own, a party may feel incapable of reaching an agreement or proceeding further at the moment. She needs space. Afterwards, she can return to the negotiations refreshed and with new perspectives.

Reason: A party is inordinately fearful or worried.

> A party cannot ultimately bring himself to accepting an agreement that on its face appears reasonable and that both parties have hammered out together. He deliberates excessively

over the finer points. Is he giving up too much? Is he being tricked into something? Just as it appears that agreement is close, he says he needs a day or two to think about it.

Tools for responding: Despite your best efforts to establish trust and work out an agreement that has clear benefits, no amount of time or deliberation will calm the inordinately fearful or worried. While remaining supportive, help the party do a reality check. On one hand, help him visualize a world without an agreement. Will that world be better or worse than the new world you are creating? The agreement will likely create a better world. Otherwise, why would the party continue to negotiate since he is working against his BATNA? On the other hand, ask him to consider the worst that could happen. Perhaps he thinks you will betray him. Perhaps he feels inadequate in some way. Reaffirm the trust you have built in your relationship and how unlikely such doomsday scenarios are.

Reason: A party is concerned that negotiations lack objectivity.

> In a dispute between the owner of a small business and a contractor concerning payment for computer support services, the manager of the business becomes confused about all the proposals offered by the contractor to resolve the dispute and is not sure she can trust his representations.

Tools for responding: If negotiations are complex or if they drag on, the issues can become muddled. Other times, despite the best intentions of one party, the other party is not certain she can fully trust the facts, data, and representations presented. It is time to step back and seek a more objective viewpoint. On their own, the parties can revisit the standards on which an objective and fair agreement should be gauged. However, if they are struggling with this question, they can ask a neutral third party to help them establish objective standards. In formal settings, this may be a mediator or arbitrator. In the work setting, this may be another manager, the boss of the two employees in dispute, or a representative from human resources. If technical issues are involved, the appropriate expert may be required.

When the Other Party Won't Play

What if a party refuses to negotiate? This can be extremely frustrating, especially when you have an ongoing relationship with the individual and must rely on him or her to have your needs met. It is especially troublesome when the other party has more power than you and uses that power to ignore you.

One such scenario involves the party who does not recognize that a conflict or need to negotiate exists. There is no conflict in his mind because he has not been made aware of a situation causing conflict:

> Jerry's boss, Elaine, is lousy at delegation. Jerry has become increasingly frustrated with the way she has passively

dismissed his suggestions for improving work processes and requests to take on more challenging assignments. At the same time, she complains about how overburdened she is with her workload and how only she can take on certain tasks, such as writing business proposals and meeting with important clients. Jerry is beginning to think that he made a mistake in accepting the job, which he now believes was misrepresented to him. Yet, he has not said anything to Elaine.

A second scenario involves a party who is fully aware that a situation exists, but the situation is troublesome *only to the other party*. Conflict involves a perceived incompatibility of needs. To this individual, the situation does not create any such incompatibility, regardless of the other party's feelings about the situation:

> Since she began work at Hairbrushes Unlimited, Daphne has been taking on more and more responsibility in her position as customer service representative. Over time, she has proven herself to be a top performer, selling hairbrushes over the phone and responding to customer complaints. Although her boss, Martin, has occasionally commended her performance, she has not seen this appreciation in any tangible way. For a few months, she has complained to Martin about how she believes she is entitled to additional compensation for her efforts and to pay bonuses. She also claims she was unfairly passed over for a promotion to Customer Service Manager. Martin tells her not only that he cannot but that he will not do anything to help her. He says he has his reasons for giving the manager position to someone else, but he is not at liberty to say more. At one point, she asks Martin, "You just don't care, do you?" Martin does not respond.

A third scenario involves a party who is fully aware that conflict exists but uses his power to refuse to negotiate or if negotiations have begun to negotiate further. The refusal to negotiate is, thus, a tactic—a power play:

> Bob owns a small delicatessen. Emily is the local sales representative for a large national bakery that supplies most of the bread products for his shop. Bob has become increasingly irritated with the way Emily "nickels and dimes" every order. Emily also recently announced a significant price increase on her company's products, effective in two weeks. Bob fears he may have to raise his prices to account for these increases and sales tactics. Although initial discussions with Emily were cordial, Emily eventually tells Bob "take it or leave it." Although the bakery has competitors in town whose prices are more reasonable, Bob does not believe that their quality is as good or their delivery service as efficient. He also does not have the resources to wage a legal battle. Emily, of course, knows this.

CREATING AWARENESS

Parties may not negotiate because they do not realize negotiations matter. Such a response (or nonresponse) is often due to ignorance. Other times, a party may not negotiate when he believes this choice is his best bargaining position based on a perception of having greater power. In either case, your job is to educate the party as to why he should want to negotiate and why doing so will lead to an outcome that is better for both of you than any outcome he could achieve alone. Ury suggests, "Use power to educate."[3] Questions to consider include the following:

> Parties may not negotiate because they don't realize that negotiation matters, or they believe they have a power advantage and don't need to negotiate.

1. *Is the other party aware of your concerns?* Take the time to carefully lay out your concern with the other party and the impact the failure to address the concern is having on you. Then request the opportunity to discuss the situation at length.

   Jerry arranges a meeting to discuss the need for Elaine to delegate meaningful assignments to him and why this is important. He gives her the benefit of the doubt that she did not realize his concern earlier.

2. *Is the party aware of the benefits of negotiation?* Think through all the advantages *to the other party* that make negotiation more attractive than not negotiating.

   Jerry has the chance to sell himself to Elaine and demonstrate why delegation will help Elaine with her workload, expand the opportunities the firm has to reach new clients, and improve the impact and reputation of the firm.

   Bob could explain to Emily that negotiating with him is far better than losing business, which is likely to happen if he is forced to raise prices due to her tactics and the bakery's price increases.

3. *Is the party concerned about your ongoing relationship?* Take a careful look at your relationship with the other party. Ask pointed questions about whether enjoying a positive and productive future together is important to the other party. Has the party considered the costs and consequences to the relationship if the matter is not resolved?

   Jerry may quit his job.

   Daphne may file a lawsuit if she believes she is being treated unfairly.

   Bob may take his business elsewhere.

   In all cases, relationships will be strained. Do such considerations concern the other party?

4. *Does the other party have all the facts?* The more you can show a command of the facts and why these facts have a bearing on decisions you are likely to make if matters do not get resolved, the more likely the other party will listen. It also helps the party make

more informed choices regarding how to proceed in negotiations with you.

Daphne stops complaining and assembles a list showing how she has outperformed her colleagues, including how she has met or exceeded sales quotas and how these successes qualify her for bonuses. She makes a second list showing how her qualifications match or exceed the qualifications of the individual who got the management job. She shares this information with Martin and requests a pay raise and strong consideration for the next opportunity for promotion.

Bob researches the bakery's competitors' prices. He talks with other customers of the bakery to see if they share his concerns and would consider a collective response to Emily and the bakery. He does profit-and-loss projections to show Emily how a price increase will result in a loss of business for both of them.

5. *Is there a communication gap?* As much as you may not like to acknowledge it, one reason the other party is not negotiating may be due to communications problems you have created. What behaviors are causing the other party to not take you seriously? Take a step back to assess how you are contributing to the problem. Ask those to whom you are close to give their honest assessment. Better yet, ask the other party.

Upon careful reflection, Jerry realizes he has not been assertive in expressing his needs. When he does express his concerns, Elaine confirms that she was unaware of them. She also states that while she wants to give him more opportunity, she does not believe he is ready to take on certain assignments. Jerry asks what he can do to improve his performance so that he can be ready.

Daphne asks Martin why she has been passed over for the manager position. Martin indicates that she has been a little too "pushy" with him and her coworkers. While her assertive nature is an asset when dealing with customers, being a manager requires sensitivity. Daphne asks how she can "tone it down."

STRENGTHENING YOUR NEGOTIATION POSITION

In positional bargaining, an imbalance of power between the parties is generally used by the stronger party to take as large a piece of the pie as possible. In integrative bargaining, with which fostering relationships is important, a power advantage is not necessarily an asset for one party or a liability for the other. While the stronger party may use his power as leverage, he will do so sparingly as he realizes the costs to the relationship and future outcomes if he uses a heavy hand.

> You *can* strengthen your negotiation position.

The key for the weaker party in these circumstances is to find ways to strengthen his power in the negotiations. Fisher, Ury, and Patton suggest developing one's BATNA:[4]

1. *Know your BATNA and theirs.* By knowing all the facts, examining the strengths you bring to the table, identifying what each of you values and needs in the relationship, and understanding your weaknesses and liabilities, you will have a better picture of your negotiating power. Further, as you probe into what the other party needs and values, what her interests are, and where she is vulnerable, you put yourself in a better position to know the likelihood that she will work with you to achieve agreement. You will also have a firmer understanding of what the other party's alternatives are to negotiating with you, as well as the alternatives you are prepared to face if matters do not proceed as you would like. Your BATNA is your gauge against which to evaluate whether the other party's offer is better or worse than no deal at all.

2. *Strengthen your BATNA.* Developing your BATNA also means finding ways to increase it. Before engaging in negotiations, ask, "What would make my position even stronger?" Based on your answer, you may or may not feel fully prepared to enter the negotiation. You may first need to take measures to make a stronger BATNA a reality. Consider these examples:

   Jerry can increase his BATNA by exploring the duties and responsibilities of his position in his field. He can identify the relative ease or difficulty he would have in finding a similar position if he were to quit. He could go as far as obtaining a job offer. This will show Elaine that he is a valuable commodity and is serious about his career choices if she is unwilling to give him a career opportunity. In a less drastic move, if he can show how he has added value by increasing profits or cutting costs, he can make the case that these benefits would be missed if he were to leave. He could also cultivate a potential client and offer him up to Elaine on the condition that he is allowed to develop the relationship.

   Daphne could also go through the effort of establishing her value in the job market. If she can make a case that she is entitled to pay bonuses or to promotion based on law or company policy, she can argue, without threatening, that she has a case for legal action.

   Bob could begin discussions with one or more of the bakery's competitors. If a competitor can address his concerns about price, quality, or delivery, he would eliminate the need for doing business with the bakery. Bob could also pursue other customers of the bakery to band together in a united front against unreasonable sales tactics and price increases. If the bakery's pricing practices are unethical, he could suggest to Emily that he may need to contact the local Better Business Bureau. If Bob is concerned with Emily's sales tactics, he could suggest that he may need to contact the larger corporation to see if these practices are in keeping with the organization's standard customer service practices.

When using your strengthened BATNA as leverage, do not threaten the other party with what you will do. This will cause the party to become defensive. Instead, warn him or her about what may happen if agreement is not reached. For instance, Bob should not say to Emily, "I'm taking my business elsewhere." He might say instead, "If these sales practices and price structures do not change, I'm not sure I'll be able to afford doing business with you anymore."

Further, to sell your improved BATNA, it must be something of true value to the other party. For instance, if Martin believes he can make a solid case that his decision not to promote Daphne is sound, he will not be persuaded by her arguments. On the other hand, what a party values need not always be something as high stakes as the resignation of an employee, a threatened lawsuit, or the loss of business.

In addition to her regular duties, Jerry has been fulfilling various secretarial duties in the absence of a secretary who has been on maternity leave. Perhaps Elaine cannot afford the loss of these skills right now.

Emily is in the running for an incentive award. The sales Emily realizes from Bob's delicatessen may mean the difference between winning a trip to Hawaii and staying home.

3. *Defuse or weaken their BATNA.* Instead of increasing the strength of your position, you may be able to weaken the strength of theirs. A classic, yet simple, example is the response a customer service representative might give a customer threatening to complain to the boss or the corporate consumer hotline:

"Please do call my boss. I want to know if I am not handling this situation correctly. Here's the toll-free number for our hotline."

Strengthening your BATNA generally weakens the other party's BATNA. Emily, for instance, may feel her bakery is the only game in town. If Bob manages to find a comparable competitor, Emily will feel less secure. But a party could also suggest additional measures that could have a larger impact than the other party bargained. Bob's attempt to instigate a larger-scale community response from other businesses, for example, would impact the bakery's community relations with the town. The greater the loss a party perceives, the more prepared he or she will be to listen.

When the Other Party Won't Play by the Same Rules

If you encounter any of the situations discussed previously, you may be dealing with a hard bargainer. When dealing with such individuals, do not confuse their demeanor and personality with bargaining style.

While some hard bargainers may be difficult to work with, many can be pleasant and friendly. Rather, hard bargainers are characterized by the extent to which they view negotiations as offering only fixed-pie outcomes and engage in positional bargaining tactics accordingly. While many of these tactics reflect a party's legitimate attempts to advocate for her or his interests, not all tactics are legitimate and are aptly called "dirty tricks."

In considering how to respond to hard bargainers, realize that their use of such tactics does not mean your negotiation will be unsuccessful, nor does it mean you cannot persuade them to consider alternatives that are mutually advantageous.

> Having to negotiate with a hard bargainer does not mean you cannot achieve a satisfactory agreement.

To respond effectively to hard bargainers:

1. *Do not play their game.* Hard bargainers may seek to engage you in personal attacks, critical assessments of your proposals, take-it-or-leave-it proposals, and pressure tactics. The more contentious they become, the more tempted you will be to respond in kind. Recognize that doing so will only perpetuate a cycle of unproductive negotiations. Your attempts to play the same game will not only limit what the other party will realize from the negotiation, but what you will realize as well. You must remain calm, hold to principled negotiation strategies, and seek to bring the other party to your side.

2. *Use tactics as opportunities to focus on the problem.* The hard bargainer may engage in any number of tactics that the integrative negotiator would never consider. The natural instinct when confronted with them is to push back and defend against them. Instead, Fisher, Ury, and Patton recommend sidestepping the party's attacks and deflecting them against the problem.[5] They suggest a few strategies:[6]

   (1) Turn a personal attack . . .

   Employee: You obviously don't care about the well-being of your employees. If you did, you would give me the day off tomorrow. You gave Betsy a day off yesterday. That's blatantly discriminatory.

   . . . into an attack on the problem.

   Manager: I share your concern about the well-being of our employees. If there is a health concern I should know about, please let me know. I also care about treating everyone fairly. As for Betsy, she had some earned time she could use. You have used up your earned time for the year. Let's talk about how we can avoid this situation in the future.

   (2) Turn an aggressive posture . . .

   Employee: I want a 5 percent increase this year. I've earned it. I know it's in the budget. If I don't get it, I will be out of here within the year.

. . . into a focus on underlying interests, . . .

Manager: You realize the standard increase for most employees is 3.5 percent? Can you tell me more about why you feel 5 percent is warranted in your case?

. . . an exploration of options, . . .

What if I am unable to give you 5 percent? What will you do? Is that all that matters to you, or are there other things we can do to improve your feelings about working here?

. . . and a discussion about objective standards.

If I gave you a pay increase that is inconsistent with our pay and performance guidelines, how would I justify that to others who received less for similar performance?

(3) Turn an attack of your ideas . . .

Union Representative: Your proposal to work four days and be off Fridays won't fly. It's a nonstarter.

. . . into an invitation for constructive criticism, . . .

Labor Relations Manager: I would be interested in knowing what the union's concerns are about the proposal.

. . . and request their advice.

We're trying to cut production and labor costs during the summer months. As you know, there's always a downturn in the summer. If you were in our position, what would you do to avoid layoffs?

Then incorporate their concerns into a new proposal.

You say some employees may be willing to take Fridays off, and that you also want to avoid layoffs. What if we first see if there are enough employees willing to take Fridays off to offset the need for layoffs? If not, let's get back together to see if there's an equitable way to share the burden so that no one is laid off. How does that sound?

Fisher, Ury, and Patton note that an important tool for deflecting attacks is asking questions rather than making statements. Questions open up the possibility for finding answers, whereas statements generate resistance.[7]

3. *Discuss consequences if they do not agree (and positive benefits if they do).* Despite his bluster, a hard bargainer does not want to walk away empty-handed. Yet he must do a reality check if he insists on holding to fixed positions. If you know your BATNA and have a sense of his, you should have some idea of the answers to these questions:[8]

   ▪ What will happen if we do not reach an agreement? What will you do?
   ▪ What do you think I will do? What would you do if you were in my position?
   ▪ What will happen if you do [file a lawsuit, quit your job, disregard my directions, etc.]? Is that something you want?

   The individual should be brought to an understanding of a world without an agreement. These questions may clarify the need to work more collaboratively with you. Conversely, you can paint a picture of a positive world if agreement is reached.

4. *Call them on their use of tactics and negotiate the rules of the game.*[9] When you have identified the tactic being used, point it out to the party. For example, if they arranged the meeting place and you believe they deliberately arranged the seating so the sun is in your eyes, ask, "Do you mind if I close the shades?" You may need to be even more direct and let them know that you see what they are doing. For instance, if they keep you from taking a break, say humorously, "Guys, you must have bladders the size of a whale. Not me. Let's take a break. Where's the bathroom?" If the tactic is a more serious one, such as a pressure tactic, respond more seriously:

   "No, sorry, I don't buy it. There is nothing in this proposal that can't wait a day or two. When you're ready to sit down and talk through these issues in a more constructive, relaxed way, give me a call."

   If the tactics continue and are affecting your ability to engage in meaningful negotiations, you may need to stop negotiating the substance of the issue and negotiate, or renegotiate, the process for negotiating. If you have been concerned about the use of these tactics for some time, such as repeated delays, calls to consult a higher authority, or the good guy–bad guy routine, let the other party know what you have observed, how it concerns you, and how you would like to discuss a better approach to conducting negotiations. Review the principles on which a mutually agreeable resolution should be based, including the need for mutual respect and objective and fair standards. Tell them what you would prefer: "Either get the authority you need to authorize an agreement or bring the appropriate individual with you." Remember that a failure on their part to negotiate honestly does not justify a wavering of principles on your part. Regardless of their stance, insist on principled negotiations.

5. *Learn how to respond to "dirty tricks."* Some common dirty tricks and suggestions for responding to them are provided in Exhibit 12-1.

EXHIBIT 12-1
Questionable tactics and
"dirty tricks" and strategies
for responding to them

Tactic	Description	How to respond
Good guy–bad guy routine	One member of a negotiating team is reasonable and supportive to you. The other is argumentative, disruptive, and critical. The goal is to get you to open up about your interests, while pressuring you to make concessions.	• Insist that any position or demand the other party takes is based on objective standards. • State you will negotiate with one or the other party, but not both. • Hold the good guy accountable for the bad guy's behavior: "I assume he speaks for both of you." • Call them on the tactic and refuse to negotiate further until the tone changes. • Get your own bad guy to level the playing field.
Need to consult a higher authority (not at the table)	An agreement appears to close, but the other party indicates he must consult a higher authority. If authority limits were not stated up front, this ploy is unethical. The goal is to wheedle more concessions from you, and perhaps restart negotiations after consulting this alleged authority.	• Be clear up front about authority limits. Insist either that the person with ultimate authority be present during negotiations or easily accessible. • Set a short time limit when the agreement must be reached. Hold the other party to it. • Call the party on it. Note the cost to your time, your trust, and the relationship. • Make clear that no further concessions will be forthcoming.
Take-it-or-leave-it offers and arbitrary deadlines	A party makes a declarative statement that no further concessions will be made and that you must either accept or the offer will soon be off the table. Often accompanied by a deadline to pressure you into acceptance.	• Ignore it. If negotiations continue, you have called his bluff. Help the party find a face-saving way to retreat from the demand. • Treat the statement as an aspiration, then encourage further discussion: "I understand the pressure you are under, but I think you can appreciate that agreement at this point is not possible unless it makes sense to both of us."

EXHIBIT 12-1
Questionable tactics and
"dirty tricks" and strategies
for responding to them
Continued

Tactic	Description	How to respond
		• Test the basis for such finality. Why these terms? What pressures dictate such a time frame? Revisit objective standards and inquire how this stance compares. • If the party persists and your BATNA has not been fulfilled, call off negotiations.
"One more thing" (after the deal seems to be made)	The party brings up issues late in the process or makes escalating demands after it appears agreement has been reached. The goal is to get more concessions from you on the assumption you will not back out after such an investment of time and effort.	• Anticipate the potential for this to occur. Seek assurances that escalation will not occur, nor will you agree to further terms once agreement has been reached. • Call the other party on it and revisit principles for a fair agreement, noting the impact on your trust. Ask whether the party truly wants to renegotiate the entire agreement based on these new, often miniscule demands. • Consider your BATNA and walk away if necessary.
Extreme demands	The party makes a demand that is either at the extreme end of the anticipated negotiation range or beyond it. Often such demands are made as initial offers. The goal is often to overstate what the party expects to achieve to ultimately reach an outcome that is still more favorable to him.	• Do your research. Understand the standards by which a fair and objective agreement should be based. • Know your BATNA so you can recognize when demand is unreasonable. • Create alternatives to increase your power. Use these alternatives (such as another interested party) to encourage the other party to be more reasonable. • Walk away. If he is serious about negotiating, he will reconsider his position.

PART IV: Application and Practice

EXHIBIT 12-1
Questionable tactics and
"dirty tricks" and strategies
for responding to them
Continued

Tactic	Description	How to respond
Delays	The party either states explicitly that he needs more time to decide, or he passively does not respond to your offer. While the reason for delay may be legitimate, it is often done to unnerve you, particularly if you need an answer soon. It is also done to test your urgency or to buy time to gain more information about you.	• Inquire about the party's concerns that necessitate delay. Ask how you can facilitate a quicker response. • Know your BATNA to determine if you can afford delay. If not, do what you can to remove obstacles causing delay. • If your BATNA is strong, indicate that you have alternatives if the delay becomes unreasonable. • Negotiate the length and timing of the delay. Indicate that if delay continues after that point, you will exercise your alternatives. Be prepared to exercise these options if further delay occurs.
Splitting the difference	As the parties get closer to a particular sum or other term, a party suggests splitting the difference. While this strategy may appear reasonable, a party often suggests it because the result is more favorable to him than to you.	• Unless the split truly seems reasonable, do not accept it. Knowing your BATNA will help you determine this. • State how splitting the difference is not fair to you. Revisit the standards for an objective agreement. • Suggest that if you split the difference, you find a split that distributes the burden and obligations more evenly.

PERFORMANCE CHECKLIST

■ One significant barrier to achieving an agreement occurs when a party who may be genuinely interested in engaging in an integrative negotiation process is experiencing an impasse that is preventing him or her from moving forward at the moment.

■ Another barrier occurs when a party perceives he or she has a superior bargaining position and does not wish to bargain cooperatively or is simply not knowledgeable about the process or benefits of integrative negotiation.

■ A third barrier occurs when a party takes a hard bargaining position and, in the worst case, engages in "dirty tricks."

- If you value integrative negotiation and view it as the best means for achieving positive and durable agreements, you must not grow weary in the face of such barriers.

- The use of negotiation tactics, whether legitimate bargaining techniques or true dirty tricks, should not deter you from holding to negotiating based on principles of fairness, cooperation, and trust.

- The key to dealing with barriers is to understand them and why a party is putting up barriers, learn strategies for responding to barriers, and gain proficiency in using these strategies to bring the other party to your side.

TEST YOURSELF

True/False

For each statement below, check true or false.

TRUE   FALSE

_____ _____ 1. When someone is at impasse, he or she is usually unwilling to negotiate.

_____ _____ 2. Parties often refuse to negotiate because of a perceived superior bargaining position over the other party.

_____ _____ 3. One reason that a party is at impasse may be because you have not fully addressed the party's deepest concerns about the negotiation.

_____ _____ 4. Seeking the help of a trusted third party to examine the terms of your proposed agreement can help provide an objective viewpoint regarding its fairness.

_____ _____ 5. One approach for responding to a hard bargainer is to insist that you agree on appropriate standards of fairness before proceeding further with negotiations.

MULTIPLE CHOICE

Circle the letter next to the best answer for each question. On a separate sheet of paper, state why you chose that answer.

1. Of these statements, the one that *most closely describes* impasse is that a party is
   a. unwilling to negotiate.
   b. not likely to reach an agreement.
   c. unwilling to discuss the issues.
   d. not ready to agree at the moment.

2. Examples of genuine impasse, as distinct from hard-bargaining tactics, include all the following *except*
   a. the parties have different ideas of the best proposal that will resolve the problem.
   b. a party is concerned about the time frames for implementing a proposed agreement.
   c. a party is holding out to get the best possible outcome for himself.
   d. a party wants to call off negotiations to have time to think about a proposal made.

3. As negotiations draw to a close, a party becomes concerned about the fairness or objectivity of the negotiation process. Your *least effective* response would be to
   a. revisit the standards on which a fair agreement should be based.
   b. question the other party's motives for challenging the objectivity of the process at this late date.

c. consider the assistance of a neutral third party to help establish objective standards.

d. explore any issues of trust affecting the party's ability to accept the standards you propose.

4. When a party refuses to negotiate with you, the *least effective* method for encouraging her to negotiate is to

a. increase your negotiating power by improving your BATNA.

b. appeal to the party's sense of fair play.

c. sell the benefits that negotiating will have on improving your relationship.

d. know the facts and use them to show what may happen if an amicable resolution is not reached.

5. Of the following examples, the *least questionable* negotiating tactic is

a. a party says he needs time to think about a proposal and promises to get back to you early the next day.

b. a party tells you that an agreement must be reached today or he cannot guarantee the settlement amount agreed to will be available tomorrow.

c. as negotiations appear to have concluded, a party apologizes and says he neglected to mention a particular item and would like to discuss it.

d. a party says, as you appear to be close to agreement, "Why don't we split the difference?"

DISCUSSION QUESTIONS

1. Think of a difficult negotiation you must soon address. What barriers do you perceive in achieving an integrative resolution? In small groups, share your concerns about this negotiation, talk about the barriers, and come up with strategies to overcome them.

2. As a manager, what would you say are the most common barriers to integrative solutions that you face when negotiating with employees? Identify these barriers and discuss general strategies you can use to address them.

3. What personal misgivings do you have about responding to barriers to integrative negotiation? Do you believe that bringing the other party to your side, despite the reservations or gambits he or she is using, is achievable? Are you tempted to engage in the same hard bargaining tactics and strategies as the other party? Discuss the challenges to maintaining the spirit of integrative negotiation when confronted with these barriers. What can you do to hold to principled negotiations in the face of these challenges?

CASE: OVERCOMING BARRIERS

OBJECTIVE

To understand how barriers to integrative negotiation can occur and to practice responding to such barriers.

PROBLEM

Vic Vendor, new sales representative for Do or Dye Tools, is uncomfortable with the way More Power has been selling its tools. For months, he has been saying to Kim Khan, assistant manager for tools, that the former Do or Dye representative, Axel Rod, let More Power "get away with murder" regarding pricing, return of defective products, placement of tools on its shelves, and various "deals" More Power has offered its customers concerning the sale of Do or Dye tools.

Do or Dye's biggest seller is the Super-Deluxe 15-90 Power-Matic Reversible Drill/Screwdriver set. This product is Do or Dye's premiere item and generally beats out all competitors in terms of quality. Do or Dye has advertised this product as "the only product you'll ever need for all your drill and screwdriver requirements."

The 15-90 retails for $159.95. There are also 27 different drill bits and 21 screwdriver heads available for the 15-90. The total package of drill bits and screwdriver heads sells for $59.95. If a consumer wants only drill bits, the complete package of 27 bits sells for $39.95. Similarly, the complete package of 21 screwdriver heads (straight and Phillips) sells for $29.95. Do or Dye also sells combination packs of bits and heads based on size, including "small to medium projects," "large projects," and "heavy duty projects." Each of these packs consists of nine drill bits and seven screwdriver heads and is priced at $34.95. Do or Dye does not sell bits and heads separately.

More Power is generally pleased with how the 15-90 sells. But its price is often out of range for many customers. More Power likes to give customers options. Therefore, it places the 15-90 low on the shelf and places other less-expensive, lower-quality sets higher up on the shelves. Its rationale is that the truly dedicated "weekend warrior" or professional will look for the 15-90. Meanwhile, there are plenty of other good drills and electric screwdrivers to select from, in a broad range of quality and prices. Using similar logic, More Power places Do or Dye's bit/head combination packs on lower shelves near the 15-90. But it also has numerous other bits and heads to select from, many of which are sold separately rather than in combination packs.

Vic Vendor learned early on that his predecessor, Axel Rod, allowed this practice. Apparently, Kim Khan made the argument that as a locally operated store serving a single community, More Power should not have to worry about shelf placement and the marketing of Do or Dye's products in the way Do or Dye expects larger retail chains to market them. Kim further argued that More Power customers are turned off by the limited options concerning Do or Dye's combination packs. To get around this, Kim often persuaded customers to purchase the 15-90 at Do or Dye's recommended price by encouraging them to buy off-brand bits and heads. Axel Rod looked the other way. But not Vic Vendor.

Vic Vendor is furious. He upset with the low placement of these products on the shelves. Moreover, the sale of the 15-90 and the combination packs are part of a broader marketing strategy. While the 15-90 is a quality tool, the bits and heads are even more valuable. They are made of a special patented alloy. Do or Dye sells them in combination packs, rather than singly, to increase the demand for them in the market. Do or Dye does not want its bits and heads to be confused with any other brand on the market or to have consumers view them as "ordinary." Selling them in combination packs is a means of protecting their unique qualities and value in the market. Vic Vendor believes that allowing even one exception in which customers are encouraged to buy off-brand bits and heads to be used with the 15-90 will have an adverse impact on the overall profitability of the 15-90 and the combination packs.

Vic finally tells Kim to either honor Do or Dye's expectations for the sale of the 15-90 and combination packs or it would discontinue its relationship with More Power. More Power is generally pleased with all of Do or Dye's tools, not just the 15-90. Although it sells other brands, the loss of Do or Dye's business would significantly impact More Power's bottom line. On the other hand, More Power has been frustrated with Do or Dye's practice concerning the 15-90 and has always been concerned about its less than generous limited warranties, its return policy for defective tools, and service to customers after the sale. In all these areas, More Power has received complaints from customers that suggest that all Do or Dye cares about is "making a buck."

Realizing this is an important issue, Kim informs Jim Talent about Vic's ultimatum. Talent directs Kim and Joe to negotiate with Vic. Kim arranges a meeting with Vic. At the meeting, Vic brings a fellow sales representative, Sue Ply, with him.

PROCEDURE

Break up the class into teams of four. In each team, the members should assume the roles of (1) Joe Newcomer, (2) Kim Khan, (3) Vic Vendor, and (4) Sue Ply, respectively. Divide each group again into teams of two, representing More Power and Do or Dye Tools, respectively.

Based on the factual situation presented and what the class knows about More Power and the characters from the profiles, have the two teams within each group negotiate the situation. More Power's overall goal is to maintain its relationship with Do or Dye, provided it can do so based on sound principles, such as the need to remain profitable while serving its customers' needs and keeping their trust. On the other hand, whereas the

More Power team is encouraged to attempt integrative negotiation, Do or Dye's goal is to get satisfaction on its demands, even if that requires engaging in hard bargaining and creating barriers to More Power's attempts at integrative negotiation. However, it must keep in mind its overall interest in remaining profitable.

Prior to engaging in negotiations, each team should spend approximately ten minutes strategizing how it will approach the negotiation. Each team should conduct an analysis of its interests, options, and alternatives. Each team should also identify its BATNA or best alternative to a negotiated agreement. The Do or Dye team should also create ways it can deliberately present barriers to resolution. More Power should anticipate these possible barriers and be prepared to respond to them. Both teams are encouraged to create additional facts, provided they are consistent with the overall factual scenario presented.

Have the teams engage in the negotiation process for twenty minutes. The More Power team wins if it holds firm to using integrative negotiation strategies throughout and loses if it reverts to hard bargaining in response to the Do or Dye team's actions. The Do or Dye team wins if it maintains its hard-bargaining position but loses if holding to such a position results in an outcome that is less than its BATNA.

Following this process, write the outcome that each foursome achieved on a flipchart or whiteboard. This includes both outcomes in which mutual gains were and were not achieved.

Case Questions

In class, discuss the following:

1. What difficulties did the parties face when confronted with barriers to integrative negotiation?

2. How did these barriers impact the negotiation process?

3. What worked well with respect to responding to such barriers? What did not work well?

ALTERNATIVE PROCEDURE FOR ONLINE LEARNING FORMATS

Assign students to groups of four and have them role-play off-line. While meeting in person may be preferable, this role-play may be accomplished via telephone, teleconferencing, or video-conferencing because negotiating this way replicates many long-distance business negotiations. Specify a time period by which students should complete their role-play assignments and post responses to the questions above in the appropriate online class learning environment. If telephone, teleconferencing, or videoconferencing is used, have students also respond to the following question: What was different about negotiating this business issue via long-distance methods instead of in person?

PERSONAL GROWTH EXERCISE

Think about a negotiation in which you are currently engaged. Are you considering buying or selling a house or large consumer good? Are you in negotiations with your boss or organization regarding work assignments, flexible scheduling, salary, growth opportunities, or other work-related issues? Are you in ongoing negotiations with a teenage son or daughter or other family member about boundaries and expectations? Pick something that is real and that is challenging to you.

Now, consider how effective you felt the last time you negotiated with this individual or the last time you negotiated a similar issue. What barriers are preventing you from engaging in an integrative negotiation process with this person? Look back at this chapter and consider the various barriers discussed. Is the other party dealing with a genuine impasse? Is he or she refusing to negotiate with you? Is he or she a hard bargainer or playing dirty tricks? Whatever the situation, evaluate the barrier, return to the negotiation, and apply the specific strategy that may help you overcome the barrier to achieve a positive outcome. Even if the outcome is not successful for you, learn what you can from the experience for the next time you negotiate.

To Learn More

In addition to *Getting to Yes* by Fisher, Ury, and Patton and *Getting Past No* by Ury (see Chapter 11), the following resources also provide insights on the use of negotiation tactics:

Cohen, Herb. *You Can Negotiate Anything: How to Get What You Want.* New York: Carol Publishing Group, 1994. (Originally published, 1980)

Cohen, Herb. *Negotiate This! By Caring, But Not T-H-A-T Much.* New York: Warner Books, 2003.

Dawson, Roger. *Secrets of Power Negotiating: Inside Secrets from a Master Negotiator*, 3rd ed. Pompton Plains, NJ: Career Press, 2011.

Karrass, Chester L. *Give and Take: The Complete Guide to Negotiating Strategies and Tactics*, revised ed. New York: Harper Business Publishers, 1995.

Karrass, Chester L. *The Negotiating Game: How to Get What You Want*, revised ed. New York: Harper Business Publishers, 1992.

Lum, Grande. *The Negotiation Fieldbook: Simple Strategies to Help You Negotiate Everything*, 2nd ed. New York: McGraw-Hill, 2011.

Mulhotra, Deepak, and Max H. Bazerman. *Negotiation Genius: How to Overcome Obstacles and Achieve Brilliant Results at the Bargaining Table and Beyond.* New York: Bantam Dell, 2007.

Nierenberg, Gerald I., and Henry H. Calero. *The New Art of Negotiating: How to Close Any Deal.* Garden City Park, NY: Square One Publishers, 2009.

Shell, G. Richard. *Bargaining for Advantage: Negotiation Strategies for Reasonable People*, 2nd ed. New York: Penguin Books, 2006.

Notes

1. William Ury, *Getting Past No: Negotiating Your Way from Confrontation to Cooperation* (New York: Bantam Books, 1993), 105–29.

2. Ibid., 109.

3. Ibid., 130–56.

4. Roger Fisher, William Ury, and Bruce Patton, *Getting to Yes: Negotiating Agreement Without Giving In*, 2nd ed. (New York: Penguin Books, 1991), 97–106.

5. Ibid., 108.

6. Ibid., 108–12.

7. Ibid., 111.

8. Ury, *Getting Past No*, 134–36.

9. Ibid., 98–102.

MEDIATING CONFLICTS BETWEEN PARTIES

PERFORMANCE COMPETENCIES

After you have finished reading this chapter, you will be able to

- Describe the purpose and role of the manager in mediating disputes between parties

- Describe the basic structure, elements, and strategies involved with mediating conflicts between parties

- Apply what you have learned in order to help parties resolve workplace conflicts

Mediation involves the intervention of a third party who acts as a facilitator to assist the parties to achieve resolution of their issues. The mediator is a neutral, unbiased, and impartial party focused on aiding the parties to achieve an outcome on their terms. In the ideal setting, the mediator is not directly associated with the organization or the parties in dispute since such detachment will better ensure neutrality and impartiality. Yet, more often than not in the workplace, it is the manager who will be called upon to intervene to help parties for whom she has direct responsibility to settle their disputes. The manager is challenged to step out of her traditional decision-making role and facilitate a mediation process that is fair, objective, and balanced.

You guys are both saying the same thing. The only reason you're arguing is because you're using different words.

S. I. Hayakawa

THE CONTEXT FOR WORKPLACE MEDIATION
VS. OTHER CONTEXTS

Internal mediators have the advantage of being more familiar with the organization, the parties and the issues compared to external mediators, but may also be too "close" to the issues and be perceived as biased.

The field of mediation has evolved over time to the point at which the opportunity to pursue mediation to resolve disputes and facilitate negotiated settlements exists in a wide array of endeavors. In addition to the workplace, mediation is used to assist with disputes involving neighbors; communities; schools; domestic relations; litigation; regulatory matters before municipal, state, and federal agencies; real estate and landlord/tenant issues; consumer grievances; environmental issues; victim/offender reconciliation; international affairs; labor relations; and numerous other contexts.

Although this chapter focuses on the important role the manager or other professional can take to mediate workplace disputes as part of everyday work activities, it is instructive to compare and contrast this context with the broader context of mediation in business, law, or other areas. For the purposes of this discussion, we refer to those who mediate workplace conflict within the organization as "informal" or "internal" mediators and those who mediate conflict as "professional" mediators who are not generally employed full time by the organization they serve as "formal" or "external" mediators.

RELATIONSHIP TO THE ORGANIZATION

The advantages to having informal mediators are their accessibility to be called upon at a moment's notice to mediate; the low cost in utilizing their mediation services, which generally form part of their regular duties; and their knowledge and familiarity with the institution, the parties, and the issues at hand. This knowledge and familiarity can also be a disadvantage as the individual called to mediate may be too "close" to the issues and therefore be perceived as biased by one or both parties. Further, as someone employed within the institution, the potential for undue influence on the mediator by someone higher in authority, whether overt or subtle, could compromise the mediator's ability to objectively mediate a dispute.

Use of an external mediator eliminates such concerns. This may be beneficial when the issues are highly sensitive and confidential. For example, external mediators may be preferable for disputes involving high-level executives on matters for which there is great concern about confidentiality or for which undue pressure could be placed on an internal mediator to address. In addition, some highly complex issues, such as financial and accounting issues or matters involving highly technical information, may require an external mediator with specialized expertise. External mediators generally assess fees for their services. An internal mediator may, therefore, be preferable because he or she can devote more time and attention to working with the parties, such as beforehand when conducting individual preliminary meetings and other pre-mediation activities or during mediation to delve more deeply into issues.

RELATIONSHIP TO THE PARTIES

In formal mediation settings, such as mediations facilitated through the court system, there is an expectation that mediators ensure that they are not biased or prejudiced toward any party in the mediation or have any biases or prejudices with respect to the issues involved that would unduly sway them in their facilitation of the mediation. The mediator is generally expected to decline the mediation under such circumstances as well as situations in which the mediator has a prior relationship with a party or prior knowledge of the issues that would affect his ability to be impartial. However, if the mediator believes such considerations would not affect his ability to mediate in a neutral, impartial manner, he must at a minimum disclose the information to the parties. Upon disclosure, if a party does not believe the mediator can remain impartial, the mediator should then withdraw.

With use of formal mediators within judicial and government regulatory systems, well-defined rules and procedures provide guidance to parties and mediators on how to proceed in these situations. Guidance is less clear in informal settings in which the informal mediator could be, for example, the manager of two employees in dispute, their peer, or a human resources professional who may also have responsibility for advising management on employee discipline and performance issues. Some practical considerations may help the organization navigate these waters.

First, the context for internal mediation is quite different from that for external mediation. Internal workplace mediation is especially effective for preventing escalation of conflict before such matters lead to legal action such as the filing of a lawsuit in court or a complaint before a state or federal agency. Unresolved workplace conflicts also directly impact the achievement of business goals. Organizational leaders, therefore, have incentive and the authority to step in to correct matters. Mediation offers a more supportive means for addressing interpersonal conflict than more coercive means such as progressive discipline. In this context, mediation is an organizational tool provided for the benefit of managers and employees, but the same ethical considerations as in the judicial context are not as applicable.

Second, the organization can develop appropriate procedures to minimize, if not fully eliminate, concerns about bias and related factors involving use of internal mediators. For instance, when a manager is concerned about the undue influence she may have on two employees working through their conflict, she might ask another manager to mediate who is more removed and not as knowledgeable about the employees or the history of their conflict. A manager can also withdraw and find a replacement when he believes he can remain impartial but one or both parties believe otherwise. The organization can also develop internal third party mediators with specific responsibilities for resolving workplace disputes and who are removed from the operational functions where manager/employee conflicts arise. Examples include internal mediators from the organization's HR, equity, or organizational diversity offices.

Finally, an individual manager's ability or desire to completely guarantee the absence of bias or related concerns may simply not exist in many circumstances. The manager has the authority to call his employees into a meeting to discuss workplace challenges, including conflicts in their working relationship. Because such matters affect business goals, he may not be able to fully ensure that the conversations occurring during mediation can be kept confidential. Still, the skills and tools discussed in this chapter are effective for processes other than mediation wherein a manager is attempting to facilitate open and supportive communication and relationship building among employees. If you find yourself in a situation in which facilitating such a process for employees may be beneficial, but you are concerned about the unattended message you are sending by calling the process "mediation," simply offer to convene the employees in a meeting to talk through their issues without putting a name to the process.

APPROACHES TO MEDIATION

Mediators can adopt a number of approaches for their mediation practice. The most prominent ones follow.

Evaluative. Mediation is often thought of as a process whereby the mediator facilitates communication between the parties, leaving decision making in the hands of the parties. An evaluative mediator is more involved than mediators in other contexts in offering possible solutions for resolution and in offering insights on the merits of the parties' positions, arguments, and proposals.

Facilitative. Facilitative mediation is more focused on supporting the process of communication and decision making between the parties and less involved (and often completely uninvolved) in evaluating the merits of the issues. A facilitative mediator actively engages in reflective listening skills and other communication processes designed to ensure each party is fully heard and fully understands the other party's views and positions (whether or not they agree). The model discussed in this chapter is facilitative.

Transformative. While transformative mediation is also concerned with facilitating an effective communication process, it has a broader focus in supporting the parties' ongoing relationship. Popularized by Robert Baruch Bush and Joseph P. Folger in *The Promise of Mediation: The Transformative Approach to Conflict*, such processes seek to give more personal power to each party in the relationship and how they will resolve their differences and to encourage each party to give recognition and understanding to the other party's perspective. In contrast to evaluative and facilitative approaches, wherein the goal is to assist the parties to reach an agreement on current issues, transformative mediation goes beyond immediate concerns to help parties increase their understanding of and improve their ongoing relationship. Often, in a transformative process, this is considered the primary goal that is necessary to accomplish before the parties can meaningfully work on reaching agreement on substantive issues.

In formal mediations involving long-arm business transactions, settlement negotiations to avoid litigation or other legal, judicial, or administrative matters, it is generally not expected or expedient to delve into deeper relationship issues. Such mediations are inherently transactional and limited to reaching agreement on the specific issues at hand. Depending on the nature of the dispute and style of the mediator, mediation processes in these contexts are generally evaluative or facilitative. Similarly, in the workplace, while a pleasant by-product may be to have coworkers understand the deeper roots of their conflict, it is not an expectation. A facilitative process is probably best in most circumstances to ensure that the employees in dispute are heard and have the opportunity to reach agreement in furtherance of business goals. On the other hand, because internal mediators are perhaps more accessible and have fewer time and cost constraints than external mediators, they may have more opportunities to help parties work through deeper relationship issues.

PROCEDURAL DIFFERENCES

In formal mediations initiated through legal processes, parties are generally represented by attorneys. While attorneys support mediation as a means for realizing the best possible outcome for their clients in lieu of litigation, they are often guarded with respect to how much information their clients should divulge during mediation. They take care not to reveal too much about their legal strategy in the event mediation is unsuccessful and litigation is necessary.

To protect these interests, formal mediation processes use caucuses. In a caucus, the mediator separates the parties and meets privately with each. This usually begins after the parties initially meet to deliver opening statements. The mediator thereafter shuttles between the parties, gradually hammering out a resolution as she conveys to each side new proposals suggested by the other side.

Caucuses are used in these situations to allow the parties, aided by their attorneys, to engage in open discussion with the mediator about matters that are confidential or that may ultimately form part of their trial strategy should the case not settle. In the workplace, the practice of caucusing is not as applicable because the issues do not involve pending litigation, the parties speak for themselves, and the matters discussed are not strictly confidential. The parties are generally discussing work-related matters that depend on the candid sharing of information. Except for limited circumstances in which holding separate meetings is warranted (addressed later in this chapter), the parties remain in the same room and observe and hear every aspect of the mediation and the positions and arguments offered by each party.

WHEN/WHEN NOT TO MEDIATE WORKPLACE DISPUTES

Mediation is a powerful tool to empower individuals to resolve disputes on their own terms. The most effective mediation processes occur when the manager can truly detach herself from the decision-making process and be content with whatever outcome the parties decide. Mediation is especially appropriate when the manager genuinely wants the parties to make their own decisions regarding the outcome of their dispute but believes the parties could use a little help with their communication and decision-making processes. As noted previously, business considerations may prevent the manager from fully removing her decision-making hat. Nonetheless, if she believes mediation would benefit the parties, she must seek to facilitate the fairest, most objective mediation process possible.

Mediation is most helpful to parties who

- are mature
- have sufficient trust in one another, in the process, and in the manager to meet and discuss their situation
- are willing to work together at problem solving
- believe that mutually satisfactory outcomes are possible

A number of workplace issues lend themselves to mediation, including matters involving

> The manager should not mediate disputes where she or he cannot remain neutral or emotionally detached.

- work assignments
- workflow, operational issues, and processes
- interpersonal communication difficulties
- personality clashes
- differences in culture, work styles, and values

The following situations would be inappropriate for mediation under any circumstance:

- progressive discipline and grievance processes
- complaints and investigations of criminal or civil wrongdoing, discrimination, harassment, and workplace violence
- ethical breaches
- performance issues wherein one or both parties are clearly misbehaving and corrective action is required
- situations involving a party's personal, emotional, medical, or psychological concerns that must be held in confidence

SETTING THE STAGE FOR MEDIATION

Once you have identified a situation that is appropriate for intervention, the first task is convincing the parties that mediation would benefit them. The conflict you have identified is likely one in which the parties have experienced frustration in trying to resolve it on their own. Depending on the level of frustration, bringing the parties to the table may be difficult. If the parties are simply having difficulty communicating but are otherwise maintaining a level of trust and cooperation, they may be more amenable to the process. But if deeper emotions are at play, your task will be more challenging. To begin, approach each party individually and invite his or her participation:[1]

Scenario involving Mike and Charlie
Mike, I've observed your interaction with Charlie lately regarding the Landmark project and was wondering if I could help the two of you sort through the problem. I think we can

all agree that proceeding in the way you have been will lead only to more frustration and time wasted. What if the three of us meet tomorrow morning to walk through the project step by step so I can help you identify a resolution you both can live with?

Scenario involving Joelle and Caitlin

Joelle, you have come to my office a number of times in the past few weeks exasperated by the way you feel Caitlin has been treating you. Caitlin has expressed similar concerns. I know you both mean well and want to realize a more positive working relationship. I feel at this point that sitting down to discuss the issues face to face would be beneficial. Perhaps I can help you work through this matter in a way that is acceptable to both of you. What do you say?

In these illustrations, the manager is supportive rather than condemning. The manager identifies the precise situation causing the conflict and explains why meeting to discuss the matter will be beneficial. He frames the statement as an invitation, rather than a command, leaving the choice to meet up to the party. He is also clear that the process will empower the parties to resolve the dispute on their terms.

> To encourage mediation, explain why meeting will benefit the parties. Make an invitation, rather than a command, leaving the choice to meet up to the parties.

Of course, a positive invitation does not guarantee acceptance. The manager should not accept initial rejections but should persevere by responding to the parties' reservations. Common causes of resistance and possible responses include the following:

A belief that there is nothing to mediate.

Mike:	There's nothing to discuss. Nothing Charlie can say will convince me that his approach will work.
Manager response:	Both you and Charlie feel very strongly about your views. But I would hate to think that we have overlooked some possibilities that might solve the problem. If I were in your position, I would also like to know if my way wouldn't work before more time is invested. Besides, even if you are right, what do you have to lose by spending a little time to discuss the situation?

Personal considerations regarding the other party.

Joelle:	I don't trust Caitlin. I don't see how meeting to talk about it will help.
Manager response:	Perhaps you are right. One thing is for sure, though, and that is that things won't improve if we continue on the course we are on. Part of the reason for meeting is so that we can talk about these feelings and how they have affected your relationship. If things don't change, at least we tried, and it can't hurt to take the time to find out.

Reservations about the process.

Charlie:	How can I be sure I'll be heard? Mike likes to talk and talk and I can never get a word in edgewise.
Manager response:	I'll be there and it's my job to be sure each of you has full opportunity to say your piece. It's also my job to help each of you understand the other party's point of view. I won't let Mike gang up on you.
Caitlin:	Joelle makes me nervous.
Manager response:	I understand. I'll be there to help you through the process. I'll help you get your message across so that you'll be understood.

Here, the manager encourages open dialogue and offers the hope that the process will benefit the parties. The message is that it is "worth a try" and that attempting to mediate is better than maintaining the status quo. The manager also shares a little about his role, which is to ensure openness, full and complete dialogue, and fairness. While not an advocate for either party, he is their "voice" when needed to ensure the party is heard and understood, and that no party takes undue advantage.

THE MEDIATION ENVIRONMENT

To ensure a productive process, the manager should take care to create an environment that will encourage the parties to feel safe, comfortable, and as free from extraneous stressors as possible. Some factors to consider include timing, location, and seating arrangements.

TIME OF DAY, WORK SCHEDULES, AND SESSION LENGTH

Schedule the session when the parties' energy level and ability to focus are strongest. For most individuals, this will be morning, but the time will vary depending on the parties' work schedules and preferences. Identify a time and date that you and the parties will feel the least pressure from other work demands. Do not permit outside distractions such as unexpected visitors or phone calls. Ninety minutes is generally sufficient time to talk through the issues and, if the parties engage in meaningful dialogue, achieve a breakthrough that will lead to resolution. If more time is needed, plan for breaks to allow parties time to stretch, refresh, and refocus. If the issues are complex, scheduling multiple sessions may be necessary.

LOCATION

Find a location that is removed from the office or where team members congregate. This ensures privacy and conveys a message of neutrality where neither party enjoys "home court advantage."

As the mediator, it is important to minimize the overt message of authority that your position as manager conveys. Find a location that is physically removed from your office or areas where team members work or congregate. This will help preserve the parties' privacy. It also conveys a message of neutrality where neither party enjoys "home court advantage."

The space selected should have all the creature comforts. Though the room need not be large, it should not be so cramped that the parties feel boxed in or cornered. Chairs should be comfortable. The room should be well lighted. If there is a window, be sure to draw the shades to reduce outside distractions and glare from the sun. Provide water or other non-alcoholic beverage of choice.

TABLE AND SEATING

There is no clear consensus regarding the best table and seating formation to use to facilitate a productive mediation. You must decide for yourself what approach is most comfortable and will foster collaboration. Some considerations are provided in Exhibit 13-1.

BEGINNING THE MEDIATION AND GROUND RULES

When the parties arrive for the session, begin by creating a friendly, nonthreatening, and comfortable tone. Start with small talk. Talk about commonalities if they exist, such as their families and children, similar hobbies, sports, favorite foods or restaurants, or a movie they saw or book they read. Find ways to engage them in non-consequential topics for which they have common interests. It could be the basis for finding common ground later concerning topics that do matter.

When you are ready to begin the formal process, set the stage with some introductory items, such as the following:

1. *Show appreciation for their willingness to meet to discuss their issues and to take responsibility for the situation.* Acknowledge your understanding of how difficult it may be for them to meet together and discuss their conflict.

2. *Explain the purpose of the meeting and your role in the process.* Specifically, you will facilitate discussion about their conflict and, you hope, help them arrive at a mutually satisfactory resolution. Acknowledge that although you are their manager, your intent is to be neutral and leave the process of deciding outcomes to them. However, to the extent that your manager role may affect outcomes, be up front about this. For example, you may interject from time to time how certain options and outcomes proposed may affect you as their manager or others in the organization. At the same time, encourage them to be open with you if they think at any time that your managerial role is impacting your ability to act impartially.

3. *Explain how the process will proceed and how you will interact with them.* Specifically, each party will present a statement reflecting her or his understanding of the problem. After initial statements, you will help the parties narrow down the problem and identify specific interests and needs that are at stake.

EXHIBIT 13-1
Table and seating configurations

Diagram	Configuration	Effect
Party A □ Mediator Party B	Square or rectangular Parties sit across from each other and mediator sits in between.	Establishes mediator as clear neutral. If issues are heated or contentious, promotes increased security and prevents either party from getting too close or appearing menacing or threatening. However, may reduce intimacy. Also may send message that negotiation process involves hard and inflexible bargaining.
Party A □ Party B Mediator	Square or rectangular Parties sit at 90-degree angles.	Increases communication and intimacy somewhat. Allows mediator to look and speak to both parties at the same time. May create stress if issues are heated or contentious or one or both parties are uncomfortable sitting near each other.
Party A ○ Party B Mediator	Oval or round Parties and mediator sit more or less equidistant from each other around table.	Reduces perception that parties are taking "sides." Sends message that the process is open and collaborative. Increases intimacy. Reduces formality, which may not necessarily be beneficial if mediator wants to maintain neutrality and avoid perception that he or she is their "buddy."
Party A Party B Mediator	No table Parties sit next to one another. Mediator faces them.	Increases informality and intimacy. Encourages parties to view process as working side-by-side to solve a common problem, rather than face-to-face and perceive each other as the problem. Makes parties more vulnerable, which may create problem if issues are heated or contentious.

To the greatest extent possible, you will allow the parties to engage in open dialogue without interruption. However, you may intervene to ask clarifying questions, keep them focused on the issues at hand, and take other measures to help them hone in on the problem and explore options. The goal is to arrive at a resolution that will be mutually satisfying and will help them maintain and preserve a positive working relationship.

4. *Establish ground rules.* You can either suggest a few ground rules and ask the parties if they would like to add additional rules or have them identify ground rules first and suggest others they may want to consider. Some standard rules include

- Be open and honest and have an open mind toward each other and about solving the problem.

- Each party will have the opportunity to speak and believe that he or she has been heard.

- When one party is speaking, the other party will listen without interruption, argument, or reaction.

- Feelings and opinions will be supported by specific facts and behaviors.

- If anyone begins to feel angry or upset, we will take a break to allow time to cool off and calm down.

- All discussions are confidential, except as agreed to by the parties. (Note: If absolute confidentiality cannot be assured because other parties will need to know or policy will not permit it, these parameters must be outlined up front.)

- The mediator will take notes which will not be shared with anyone outside the meeting.

Indicate that these rules serve as the basis for proceeding throughout the session. Record these on a flipchart or whiteboard so they will be visible throughout the session, and obtain the parties' commitment to abide by them. When necessary during the session, remind the parties of the rules when they are not being followed.

THE MEDIATION PROCESS

The process of mediating is like sifting ever-finer grains through a sieve. It involves uncovering the underlying issues driving the dispute and bringing the parties to increasing levels of understanding and agreement. If successful, through a process of continual refinement, the parties will achieve a realistic, durable agreement addressing all issues. The process is illustrated in Exhibit 13-2.

> The mediation process can be like unpeeling the layers of an onion or sifting ever-finer grains through a sieve.

1. STORYTELLING

As you begin discussions, allow each party the time to openly discuss his or her situation and perception of the problem. This is their chance to tell their stories. It is their time to uncover facts and issues underlying the problem;

EXHIBIT 13–2
The mediation process

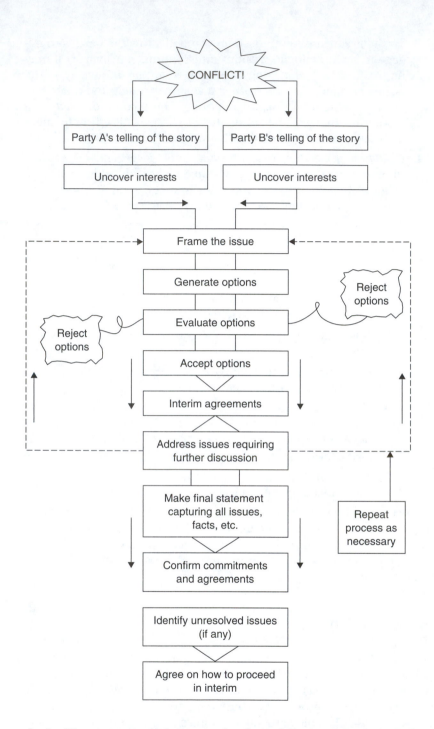

deal with assumptions that may cloud an objective appraisal of the situation; and identify the specific interests, needs, and wants they hope to have met as a result of meeting.

While one party tells her story, be cognizant of the other party's behavior. If he becomes reactive or interrupts, remind him of the ground rules and encourage him that he will have his chance to respond. Be aware of body language. Rolling of the eyes, grunts and sighs, slumping in the chair, or other behaviors can communicate more loudly than words that the individual is not listening. Remind the party that these actions are a form of interruption and that his undivided attention is expected. If necessary, write down your observations of these behaviors to discuss with the offending party later.

While a party is speaking, do not sit idly by. The party has agreed to mediation to receive help in communicating her message. It is your job to pull out the underlying interests and needs that a party is expressing through her positional statements, emotional outbursts, and possibly incoherent ramblings. It is also the mediator's job to help each party articulate her or his story in a way that will be clearly understood by the other party.

To help uncover a party's story, use open-ended questions. These questions serve different purposes to help the party clarify his statements, dig deeper into the reasons for feeling as he does, and identify needs and desired outcomes. Examples follow:

- How do you feel about that?
- What would you like [the other party] to understand about that?
- What would be the impact of proceeding that way?
- How would you like to respond to [the other party] regarding _____?
- Would you like to share more about that?
- How would that be accomplished?
- If I understand you correctly, you said _____ [paraphrase]. What corrections, if any, would you make to what I just said?
- Can you give me some examples of that?
- What is frustrating you about [the other party's position, statement, viewpoint]?

2. UNCOVER INTERESTS

The goal of storytelling is to arrive at a complete understanding of each party's view of the situation so that the problems affecting the relationship can be clearly defined. For example:

Charlie and Mike
Charlie's story: I need more flexibility to make last-minute changes to the marketing brochure before production. We are paid for our creativity and to produce a quality brochure that will sell our clients' products. We'll lose clients if we can't handle their demands and produce flawless marketing products.

Mike's story: Last-minute changes frustrate the production staff and are very costly. The client doesn't pay for these changes; we do. If we don't get a handle on costs, we'll have to pass these extra costs on to our clients. But then, we'll lose our competitive advantage and our clients will look elsewhere.

Joelle and Caitlin
Joelle's story: Caitlin is constantly in my area looking over my shoulder and asking about my progress in completing the spreadsheets. It's distracting. The spreadsheets are just one part of my job. I've got a lot to do.

Caitlin's story: Joelle knows I need those spreadsheets so I can prepare my report by the end of the month. I don't know what the holdup is. I'm sorry if she thinks I'm distracting her, but I've offered to help and she yells at me.

Through storytelling the parties' underlying interests are naturally generated.

Write these down. For example:

Charlie and Mike		Joelle and Caitlin	
Charlie's interests	Mike's interests	Joelle's interests	Caitlin's interests
Flexibility	Burden on production staff	Autonomy to do work	Time pressure to complete report
Creativity	Avoid additional costs to company	Freedom from distractions	Desire for more control over task that affects her work
Responsive to client demands	Avoid charging clients more	Feeling trusted instead of micromanaged	Feeling appreciated rather than ignored

3. FRAME THE ISSUE

If you have helped the parties tell their stories and uncover their interests, you should be able to articulate the problem in a way that captures both parties' concerns.

If you have helped the parties tell their stories and uncover their interests with appropriate facilitation and inquiry, you should be able to articulate the problem in a way that captures both parties' concerns. To do this, frame the issue in the form of a question that the parties must work together to solve:

Charlie and Mike
Framing the issue: How can we produce quality marketing products that will satisfy clients' fluctuating demands and allow for last-minute changes yet avoid passing additional costs on to our clients or incurring these costs ourselves?

Joelle and Caitlin
Framing the issue: How can Joelle complete the spreadsheets in a timely manner without Caitlin's interference or offer to help so that Caitlin can have what she needs to prepare her report?

This process may, in fact, lead to more than one issue:

Joelle and Caitlin
Framing a secondary issue: What can Joelle and Caitlin do to improve their working relationship and collaborate to ensure timely completion of the reports?

Once the problem has been framed, ensure that the parties agree that it adequately captures the situation. If not, have the parties continue to articulate their views and work at defining the problem until they are satisfied.

4. GENERATE OPTIONS

After identifying the problem through framing, the parties generate suggestions, possibilities, ideas, and proposals that may solve the problem. As the mediator, you can enhance this exploration by guiding the parties through brainstorming activities. The most viable options will address the interests and needs of both parties.

Charlie and Mike

Charlie: Perhaps a member of the production team should join me when working with clients to communicate realistic expectations regarding changes, deadlines, and schedules. I also need to learn more about the financial end of our business, so I won't make promises I can't keep.

Mike: We could establish a schedule of additional costs that clients may incur. Charlie could provide this to clients during initial negotiations. We can then work more closely with Charlie to ensure against the need for last-minute changes.

Joelle and Caitlin

Joelle: Perhaps I could allow Caitlin to help me prepare the spreadsheets. But I'll need to train her first on the computer program we use. I may also need Caitlin's help to reduce other distractions in the office when I need to focus on the spreadsheets. I suppose I could also give Caitlin a weekly update on my progress.

Caitlin: I'll try to be more patient. Perhaps we can break down the project so that Joelle can provide the spreadsheets to me bit by bit instead of all at once. Since Joelle prefers doing the spreadsheets on her own, perhaps we can agree on a "drop dead" date and I'll intervene only after that date.

5. EVALUATE OPTIONS

After sufficient time is given to generating possible options, the parties evaluate the options for consideration for final agreement. While this may occur naturally through discussion, be sure as the mediator that all options are given fair consideration.

Charlie and Mike

Charlie: I don't want to be too rigid about the potential costs for last-minute changes. I don't want my creativity to be hampered, and I don't want to scare off the client.

Mike: I don't think our production team should be involved in initial negotiation meetings with the client. We don't have the time and we don't want to interfere with the negotiation process.

Joelle and Caitlin

Joelle: The spreadsheets can't be done in bits and pieces, but must be submitted all at once. I don't like the idea of a "drop dead" date because that just gives Caitlin permission to "nag" me.

Caitlin: I don't have the time to assist Joelle with the spreadsheets, so I don't want to be trained.

6. REJECT OPTIONS, ACCEPT OTHERS, AND FORM INTERIM AGREEMENTS

As the parties evaluate options, they will reject some and accept others. Accepted options will, of course, resolve some aspects of the problem and provide the basis for interim agreements.

Charlie and Mike

Rejected options: No rigid price schedules. The production team will not be involved in initial negotiation meetings with clients.

Accepted options, interim agreements: Mike will work closely with Charlie, but not the clients, to be sure he has the information he needs to negotiate reasonable agreements that build in potential additional costs for last-minute changes.

Joelle and Caitlin

Rejected options: Joelle will not train Caitlin to do the spreadsheets. There will be no "drop dead" date when Caitlin will inquire about the spreadsheets.

Accepted options, interim agreements: During the monthly time crunch when spreadsheets are due, Caitlin will assist Joelle with assignments other than doing the spreadsheets so that Joelle can focus on completing that task.

7. ADDRESS ISSUES REQUIRING FURTHER DISCUSSION

As some aspects of the problem have been addressed, the parties can now focus on the remaining issues.

Charlie and Mike

For further discussion: A method for anticipating potential costs for last-minute changes that can be built into contracts and that is fair yet remains competitive.

Joelle and Caitlin

For further discussion: A way Caitlin can assist Joelle that is supportive and does not cause Joelle to feel she is being micromanaged or pressured. An improved working relationship.

As the mediator, encourage the parties to engage in the same option generation and exploration process as before. How often the parties will need to repeat this process will depend on the complexity of the issues and their ability and willingness to work through the issues in the initial stages. Repeating the process may not be necessary for many situations, while other situations may require a number of rounds. If discouragement should set in at this point, celebrate the parties' success in achieving interim agreements on other issues as a hopeful sign that they will ultimately achieve a lasting agreement on all issues.

> If discouragement sets in, celebrate the parties' success in achieving interim agreements as a hopeful sign that they will ultimately achieve lasting agreement on all issues.

8. MAKE FINAL STATEMENT CAPTURING ALL RELEVANT FACTS AND ISSUES

As the parties get closer to reaching a final agreement, they must become as specific as possible about framing the issues so that all concerns and interests are captured and may be fully addressed. This process of refinement facilitated by the mediator should continue to bring out additional facts, ideas, interests, and proposals from which the parties can formulate a statement that will provide a solid basis for final agreement.

> The process of refinement will bring out additional facts, ideas, interests, and proposals from which the parties can formulate a statement that will provide a solid basis for final agreement.

Charlie and Mike

Final statement: We need to identify the most common types of changes that our clients generally want, establish appropriate prices for them, and figure out how to build them into the negotiated price for our contracts. We need to then agree on a method for responding to last-minute changes between us without troubling our client further.

Joelle and Caitlin

Final statement: We need to look at Joelle's workload during the time crunch when spreadsheets are due and identify specific tasks that Caitlin can do. To avoid feeling pressured, we need to communicate more directly with one another about Joelle's progress on the spreadsheet and well before it is due. If progress is delayed, Caitlin needs to be prepared to jump in and assist with Joelle's other assignments.

9. CONFIRM COMMITMENTS AND AGREEMENT

Through this process of continual refinement, the parties now have a firm basis from which to form an agreement. This is in essence an action plan with specific goals to be achieved and expectations to be met. As the parties discuss this, encourage them to be as specific as possible regarding the commitments they are making.

Instead of:	Say:
"Joelle will complete the spreadsheets in time for Caitlin to do her report."	"Joelle will complete the spreadsheets by the fifteenth of each month so that Caitlin can prepare the report by the end of the month."
"Mike will provide costs for various items that Charlie will negotiate with clients."	"Mike will provide costs for x, y, and z, which will be part of the negotiated price for all client contracts."
"Caitlin will help Joelle with a few tasks during crunch time."	"Caitlin will help Joelle with filing, answering phones, and receiving customers when Joelle needs time to focus on the spreadsheets."

You should work with the parties through all aspects of the agreement, ensuring that each task, assignment, or obligation is specific, realistic, and achievable. Give careful attention to identifying the times and dates for completion of each item, as well as an understanding of what *complete* means. Specify how you and the parties will monitor progress on the agreement and how and when you will follow up to ensure that items have been completed. You must also come to an understanding of how and when you will reconvene to discuss unsettled issues.

For each item, summarize your understanding of the agreement. Paraphrase what you understood the parties to have said and agreed to, and allow them to offer critiques, suggest changes, or talk through the particulars until they are satisfied that the item meets their approval. The time taken for this process is important, as agreements can fail for lack of attention to the finer points. Take careful notes on the details of the agreement.

In the work setting, a final agreement need not be a formalized, legalistic document. Indeed, if the issues are not complex and the number of commitments few, a written document in any form may not be necessary. Nonetheless, you may prefer to follow up the discussion with a memorandum detailing the basic issues addressed and agreements reached. In doing this, submit a draft memorandum and ask each party to review it and suggest revisions before making the memorandum final. This ensures that the parties have had complete input on the agreement up to the final draft and that you have not misunderstood or misrepresented any aspect of it.

Assuming the mediation has been thorough and thoughtful, the parties now have a roadmap to guide their actions and relationship, as well as direction on how they will handle bumps along the way. Although the agreement involves a commitment between the parties, you must recognize that you retain a commitment to them. As a mediator, you have helped the parties determine for themselves the best course for effective collaboration and a positive working relationship; now you must remain accessible as their manager. You must remain as a support, when needed, to guide them based on new understandings and commitments.

10. IDENTIFY UNRESOLVED ISSUES (IF ANY) AND AGREE ON HOW TO PROCEED IN THE INTERIM

There is no guarantee, of course, that the mediation process will end as smoothly as suggested by our examples. There is no standard formula for bringing the parties to agreement. While the parties may resolve less significant issues, they may come to an impasse on larger issues. In some cases, the whole discussion may unravel for want of achieving a final resolution. However, in many situations, it may be possible to proceed with a less-than-perfect agreement and adjourn to revisit tougher issues later.

In this case, before concluding the mediation session, be sure that the parties can agree to a process for revisiting these issues, including how they intend to cooperate pending resolution of them and how and when the parties will reconvene to discuss these issues in greater depth. It is important to keep the parties on task regarding these matters and not simply let them remain unresolved indefinitely through inattention.

HOLDING SEPARATE MEETINGS

The purpose of mediation is to encourage the parties to share information and work collaboratively at problem solving. As noted previously, holding separate meetings with individual parties, or caucusing, can interfere with this goal and is not advised for most workplace mediation settings. However, there are a few limited circumstances in which holding brief separate meetings may support the process of open communication and problem solving:

> Holding separate meetings with parties can interfere with the goal of encouraging parties to share information and work collaboratively at problem solving, but may be warranted in limited circumstances.

- To discuss how to manage confidential information. In private, the manager can discuss with the party how he will share with the other party issues related to the confidential information without divulging its confidential aspects. For example, they can strategize how to communicate why the party's performance has declined recently without divulging a health condition or personal issue affecting performance.
- To help someone calm down, vent privately, or reassess how his negative or hostile behaviors are affecting his ability to negotiate objectively. A private conversation may be necessary to avoid embarrassing the party by calling out his inappropriate behaviors in front of the other party.
- To discuss the validity and feasibility of proposals made. For example, if a party becomes obstinate concerning a reasonable proposal made by the other party, the manager can encourage the party to evaluate the proposal seriously before dismissing it.
- To tone down the rancor of an overly aggressive party and build up the confidence of a less assertive party.
- To help a party express feelings and thoughts that she is unable to express in the joint session. The manager can help the party find a way to sort through and articulate these issues when the parties reconvene.

- Upon the request of a party. The manager should grant such a request, unless she perceives that the party is using it to avoid the other party or is attempting to manipulate her.
- To confer with a co-mediator. It may be necessary to call for a short break so co-mediators may check in and strategize, particularly if they perceive they are at an impasse.

PERFORMANCE CHECKLIST

- Workplace mediation generally follows a facilitative model in which the mediator facilitates the process of communication and decision making between the parties but does not get involved in evaluating the merits of the parties' positions, arguments, or proposals.

- A manager may choose to mediate a conflict between employees when he or she wants to help them through the process of conflict resolution but wants to encourage them to achieve a resolution on their terms.

- When you have identified a situation that is appropriate for mediation, offer to meet with the parties to talk through their issues.

- In preparing to mediate, establish the appropriate mediation environment, including meeting space; time of day; and other circumstances that are conducive to private, open, and honest discussion.

- Begin the mediation by explaining the process through which the parties will discuss their issues, including ground rules.

- The initial phase of mediation involves helping the parties define and discuss the problem, including framing an appropriate problem statement that captures both parties' concerns.

- The core of the mediation process involves leading the parties through a process of framing the issues, exploring and evaluating options, selecting options for interim agreements, and repeating the process until all significant issues have been addressed and a final agreement reached.

- To conclude the mediation, help the parties commit to an agreement and establish measures for following through on their commitments.

TEST YOURSELF

True/False

For each statement below, check true or false.

TRUE   FALSE

_____ _____ 1. The best place to conduct mediation for two employees you manage is in your office.

_____ _____ 2. Mediation is not recommended for situations in which progressive discipline is being considered or implemented.

_____ _____ 3. Before proceeding with trying to resolve problems between the parties, it is important to frame the parties' issues so that both parties agree on what the problems are.

_____ _____ 4. Caucusing is generally recommended for a manager mediating a dispute between two employees.

_____ _____ 5. The best table and seating arrangement for promoting a mind-set of side-by-side problem-solving, as opposed to an adversarial mind-set, is a rectangular table with the parties sitting at 90-degrees from each other.

Circle the letter next to the best answer for each question. On a separate sheet of paper, state why you chose that answer.

1. In a mediation, use of a rectangular table with the parties seated across from one another and the mediator in between is *best* when

   a. as the mediator, you are trying to encourage intimacy in the relationship.

   b. you are unable to find an oval or round table.

   c. discussions are heated or contentious.

   d. as the mediator, you want to be able to look at both parties at the same time.

2. It would be inappropriate for a manager to attempt mediation under the following circumstances *except* when

   a. one employee has threatened another.

   b. one employee in the proposed mediation blames the manager for an unrelated negative performance evaluation.

   c. two employees are pointing fingers at each other for an alleged misappropriation of cash from the cash register.

   d. two employees are angry at each other about a work assignment that is not going well.

3. The *most effective* method of framing an issue is to

   a. write a detailed list of each party's interests and concerns and use the list as a basis for problem solving.

   b. ask the parties to write down their understanding of the issue and see if they match. If not, try again until there is general agreement.

   c. frame the issue in the form of a question that captures both parties' concerns.

   d. as the mediator, summarize the issue, as you understand it.

4. Although caucusing should be used sparingly when mediating a dispute between employees, it can be helpful in the following situations *except* when a party

   a. wants the manager to persuade the other party to agree to a particular resolution.

   b. has a private matter to discuss with the manager.

   c. is getting overly excited and angry and needs to calm down.

   d. needs the manager's help expressing a viewpoint or feeling to the other party.

5. When the parties are brainstorming, they are *most likely*

   a. telling their stories.

   b. trying to define the problem in a way that is agreeable to both.

   c. generating options that may address the issue.

   d. finalizing their agreement.

1. What are the benefits of a third-party intervention by a manager among the employees he or she manages? What are the drawbacks?

2. Describe specific conflict situations in your work or that you might anticipate when you become a manager, and discuss how you might intervene to help the parties resolve their issues. In small groups, address the specific challenges you may face in attempting third-party intervention and help one another identify strategies for overcoming them.

3. How would your ability to successfully engage in mediation with employees be affected by concerns either party has in trusting you? Is it possible to reestablish this trust so that you can intervene? How would you go about doing this?

CASE: MEDIATING A DISPUTE

OBJECTIVE

To practice mediating a dispute between two employees in the role of manager.

PROBLEM

Joe Newcomer assigned a major project to Fred Staid and Sally Ambitious. The project involves assessing and realigning the process for ordering and retrieving purchased items from the warehouse to ensure that they are delivered in a timely manner to the customer service desk for pick up. The problem has been vexing Joe for weeks, exacerbated by the vacancy of the team leader position for the customer service desk. Joe was stretched thin and was not able to focus on the problem the way he would like. He felt confident that Fred and Sally could manage the assignment and would provide the ideal mix to creatively and carefully improve this process.

Joe selected Fred because he has an analytical mind. He thought Fred would have a lot of good ideas about how to improve warehouse efficiency. Fred also takes a deliberate, methodical approach to addressing problems. Joe selected Sally for her energy. In contrast to Fred, Sally tends to operate from good instincts about how to improve processes. Many of these instincts have led to the successful implementation of processes that have greatly improved efficiency in the warehouse. She is a go-getter and would be a good balance with Fred's more methodical approach.

Convincing Fred and Sally to work together was not an easy task. Although they generally get along with one another, they had not worked closely together until this project. It would be the first real test of their relationship. Having learned from Professor Justice a process for encouraging collaboration, Joe spent time individually with Fred and Sally convincing them that working together would produce positive results for them and the organization. In doing this, Joe had to address each party's concerns regarding the additional workload this project created, reservations each had about his or her ability and role in taking on the assignment, and personal perceptions each had about the other and his or her working style. Slowly, Joe was able to persuade them to take on the challenge.

This working arrangement worked great—for about five minutes! It was not long before Fred and Sally were griping about every little thing. Sally kept jumping in to address problems, and Fred kept telling her to hold on and take some time to think things through. Further, it became evident that Fred and Sally had completely different ways of communicating and working. There were also evident differences in culture and values.

After a week, Fred and Sally each approached Joe separately and begged to be removed from the assignment. Joe decided to set up a meeting to talk with both of them about the project and their difficulties in communicating.

PROCEDURE

Two options are available for selecting players for this role-play: (1) three students volunteer to play Joe, Fred, and Sally, respectively or (2) all students form groups of three and divide the roles of Joe, Fred, and Sally within each group.

If the first option is selected, the students who volunteered will role-play a scene in which Joe attempts to mediate the dispute between Fred and Sally. Prior to doing this, divide the class into three groups and have each group assume one of the three roles. Each group should coach the selected student on how the character should behave during the mediation as suggested by the scenario and the role profiles. Group members should also discuss strategies about how each character would approach the mediation. The groups should take no more than ten minutes to do this. The selected students should then role-play the scenario in front of the class. All other students will observe the role-plays and critique whether the efforts to mediate were successful. Allow approximately fifteen minutes for this process.

If the second option is selected, each group of three students should role-play the mediation. Allow approximately ten minutes for each student to prepare for the meeting, and approximately fifteen minutes for the mediation process. After all students have finished their role-plays, the class will reform and discuss the challenges they faced when engaging in the mediation process and whether their efforts were successful.

With either option, additional facts may be created, provided they are consistent with the scenario and role profiles. Further, to set the stage and help the players get a sense of how each party is behaving and reacting to one another, Fred and Sally should engage in appropriate griping, complaining, and arguing for a couple of minutes. Joe should then attempt to engage them in a mediation process based on the process outlined in this chapter. All characters should play their characters sincerely and should be neither unquestioningly agreeable nor arbitrarily disagreeable. Rather, they should agree only to solutions based on principles consistent with their characters. Also, Joe's goal should be to convince them to achieve an outcome on their terms and try to avoid imposing his own suggestions for resolution.

Case Questions

In class, discuss the following:

1. How successful was Joe in facilitating a process for mediating the dispute without imposing his own outcome on the parties? (Note: Whether a successful outcome was achieved in this exercise is less important than how the process of mediation was used to bring the parties together to discuss the problem, identify interests, explore options for resolution, and work toward resolution.)

2. What went well in the mediation process?

3. What challenges did Joe face in attempting mediation?

ALTERNATIVE PROCEDURE FOR ONLINE LEARNING FORMATS

Option 1: If appropriate videoconferencing capability is available, select three students to engage in the role-play online as outlined for the first option above, with all other students observing. Alternatively, select three students to role-play the scenario, create a video, and post it online for all students to view. Then, have students respond to the questions above and post them within a specified time period. After all students have posted their reports, students may post additional comments in response to other students' reports. Continue an online conversation on these experiences as time and interest allow.

Option 2:
a. Step 1: Form trios and have each trio engage off-line in the role-play as outlined for the second option above. Unless video conferencing is available, students should be encouraged to meet to engage in the role-play in person. Role-playing through e-mail or online chat formats is discouraged.

b. Step 2: Either have each trio prepare and post a joint report on its experience in role-playing this assignment, responding to the questions above, or have each student prepare such a report individually. After all students have posted their reports, students may post additional comments in response to other students' reports. Continue an online conversation on these experiences as time and interest allow.

PERSONAL GROWTH EXERCISE

Study mediation and how mediations are conducted in various situations. The more you observe how mediations are conducted and learn about the process of mediation, the better prepared you will be to conduct mediation among the employees you manage. Here are some suggestions:

- Read books and articles on mediation. The references in this and other chapters in the book provide an excellent start. Also, check the Internet for sources on mediation and read articles that interest you.
- Read the newspaper and popular news magazines and look for examples of mediation in the news. For example, read the international section to study examples of attempts at mediation in the Israeli/Palestinian conflict, in the Middle East, or elsewhere in the world. Read the local section for examples of community conflicts. Read the business section and find examples of mediations involving mergers and acquisitions, bankruptcy settlements, environmental protection, contract and personal liability lawsuits, employment discrimination, and management/labor disputes.
- Talk to lawyers, professional mediator associations, community and religious leaders, advocacy groups, and others, and ask about how they go about resolving disputes and how they utilize mediators.
- Talk with the human resources and labor relations departments within your organization and ask about the processes and methods they use to resolve conflicts between two or more employees. In particular, if you don't already know, ask how they can assist you if and when you need to intervene in conflicts among employees you manage.
- Talk with marriage and family counselors, social workers, and others involved in helping couples, families, and others resolve conflicts in their relationships. You can also talk with mediators specifically trained to mediate family and domestic issues.
- Sign up for continuing studies courses involving conflict resolution. Many of these courses include components on mediating disputes.

TO LEARN MORE

The following organizations and associations provide online resources regarding mediation and related alternative dispute resolution (ADR) processes:

American Bar Association, Section of Dispute Resolution (www.abanet.org/dispute)
Association for Conflict Resolution (www.acrnet.org)
Institute for the Study of Conflict Transformation, Inc. (www.transformativemediation.org)
Mediate.com (www.mediate.com)
Mediation Training Institute International (www.mediationworks.com)
National Association for Community Mediation (www.nafcm.org)

The following resources provide additional information on mediation in various contexts:

Beer, Jennifer E., and Eileen Stief. *The Mediator's Handbook*. Gabriola Island, BC, Canada: New Society Publishers, 1997.

Bush, Robert A., and Joseph P. Folger. *The Promise of Mediation: The Transformative Approach to Conflict*, rev. ed. San Francisco: Jossey-Bass, 2005.

Coltri, Laurie S. *Alternative Dispute Resolution: A Conflict Diagnosis Approach*, 2nd ed. Boston: Prentice Hall, 2010.

Dana, Daniel. *Conflict Resolution: Mediation Tools for Everyday Worklife*. New York: McGraw-Hill, 2001.

Friedman, Gary, and Jack Himmelstein. *Challenging Conflict: Mediation Through Understanding*. Chicago: ABA Publishing, 2008.

Mayer, Bernard. *The Dynamics of Conflict Resolution: A Practitioner's Guide*. San Francisco: Jossey-Bass, 2000.

Moore, Christopher W. *The Mediation Process: Practical Strategies for Resolving Conflict*, 3rd ed. San Francisco: Jossey-Bass, 2003.

Phillips, Barbara A. *The Mediation Field Guide: Transcending Litigation and Resolving Conflicts in Your Business or Organization*. San Francisco: Jossey-Bass, 2001.

Slaikeu, Karl A. *When Push Comes to Shove*. San Francisco: Jossey-Bass, 1996.

NOTE

1. To illustrate the mediation process, two scenarios are described throughout this chapter. These scenarios involve (1) Mike and Charlie and (2) Joelle and Caitlin.

DECISION-MAKING CHOICES FOR THE MANAGER

PERFORMANCE COMPETENCIES

After you have finished reading this chapter, you will be able to

- Describe the various decision-making processes a manager may choose to resolve conflict among parties, including
  - Joint decision making
  - Consultative decision making
  - Directive decision making
- Apply these processes, as warranted, to resolve conflict situations

While we may want to empower employees to resolve their own conflicts, there are times when you must exert more direct influence. A number of decision-making processes can assist you. The process you choose will depend on the amount of input you give employees in the decision.

THE ROLE OF PARTICIPATIVE MANAGEMENT IN ADDRESSING CONFLICT

Participative management practices allow employees to have a say in decisions that affect them. Through effective use of such practices, the possibility for a high-quality decision is enhanced because the process uses the knowledge and problem-solving abilities of many rather than a few or only one. Implementing a group decision is easier because individuals are more motivated to implement it when they played a part in formulating it. Participative management also helps the manager develop employees' decision-making and problem-solving skills.

> Individuals are more likely to buy into the decision and implement it when they played a part in formulating it.

If officers desire to have control over their commands, they must remain habitually with them, industriously attend to their instruction and comfort, and in battle lead them well.

Stonewall Jackson

Participative management is not appropriate for all situations. The decision-making process you use depends on the degree of influence you wish to share with those you manage. Options include the following:

1. *Directive decision making:* Make the decision on your own with little or no input or participation from others.

2. *Consultative decision making:* Make the decision on your own after inviting input from others and seriously considering their suggestions and ideas.

3. *Joint decision making:* Share equally in the decision-making process with no greater input or influence over the decision than any other participant.

4. *Delegation:* Give authority and responsibility for decision making to others while specifying the degree to which you require them to consult you and seek your prior approval before they make and implement a final decision.

In choosing the procedure to use, several variables are relevant:[1]

- How important is the decision to overall operations? Is the manager highly visible in the organization, so that a poor decision will reflect badly on him or her? What impact will the decision have on performance and the course of operations? Can a poor decision be easily or quickly corrected, or are the consequences more serious?

- How important is acceptance of the decision from those affected by it or expected to implement it? Will the decision be readily accepted because of its routine nature, the level of trust between manager and employees, or the organizational context in which the decision is framed? Or will the decision be met with resistance if others are not permitted to engage in the decision-making process?

- What role does time play in the decision? Is a decision required so quickly that engaging others in discussion is not feasible, or is there more time to render a decision based on the informed input of many?

- Do employees share the manager's and the organization's values and goals? If brought into a decision-making process, will they engage in a collaborative process that is consistent with these aspirations, or will they resist?

Let us examine the joint, consultative, and directive decision-making processes and how they can assist the manager to resolve conflict among employees and teams.[2]

JOINT DECISION MAKING

Joint decision-making procedures are used when the manager wishes to retain some control over the decision yet share the process with those affected by it. In contrast to directive and consultative decision-making procedures whereby the manager retains greater control over determining the outcome, the manager utilizing joint decision making is a partner in, rather than an overseer of, the decision-making process. The manager shares a voice that is equal and not superior to all other participants.

A manager will use joint decision-making processes when he or she genuinely wants or needs the buy-in of others to implement a decision. The manager must believe that those involved in decision making are mature individuals who share his or her goals and values and that their input will provide a creative and effective decision. Joint decision making is most appropriate when there is sufficient time to work through the issues and when the decision will have a significant impact on the group.

> Use joint decision-making processes when there is sufficient time to work through the issues and the decision will have a significant impact on the group.

Joint decision making is best suited for situations involving potential or actual conflicts about work processes, deadlines, assignments, policies, and related issues affecting group or team functions. It works well when significant change that affects a group of individuals over time is contemplated.

JOINT DECISION MAKING IN ACTION

Consider these examples of joint decision making:

1. Two employees working for a direct mail order catalog department have been discussing for days how best to change their process for handling specialty orders. Such orders have been piling up, and current practices are no longer efficient. The manager has a sense of the best way to change the process but wants to ensure that the process chosen will best serve the interests of the two employees who have direct responsibility for this area.

2. To encourage cross-training and professional development, the manager is planning to institute a number of changes to work assignments, which would involve a significant realignment of duties among the work group. Anticipating resistance, the manager engages in joint decision making so the group members can decide on the best way to realign duties while facilitating their professional development.

3. Many of the work unit's exempt staff take an inordinate number of breaks during which the employees smoke or are otherwise absent from their workstations. They argue they can do this because they are not paid on an hourly basis and that longer breaks compensate for all the time they are required to work during evenings and weekends. Some of the unit's nonexempt employees have been complaining because of the perceived inequity this practice creates. They can take only prescribed fifteen-minute breaks because they are paid on an hourly basis. The manager decides some parameters must be set regarding permissible breaks. Recognizing the impact such a change will have on some dearly held practices, he brings exempt and nonexempt staff together to set parameters that will address all legitimate concerns.

ACHIEVING CONSENSUS

One common method for engaging in joint decision making is through consensus decision making. In general terms, *consensus* is an agreement among all members of a group or stakeholders. However, when working to achieve consensus, the group must decide the extent to which unanimous agreement is required before they can move forward with a decision.

If the group believes that every individual must agree before it can proceed, group members must recognize that such an approach takes time and may result in not reaching a decision at all. When this occurs, the decision by default is to revert back to the status quo. If time is on your side, working toward absolute consensus may not be a problem. But insisting on absolute consensus may prove counterproductive when a quick decision is needed.

A more practical approach is modified consensus decision making in which the group seeks but does not require agreement among all members. In this context, the views of those individuals who do not agree with an otherwise mutually agreed-upon decision are noted, and every attempt is made to address their concerns and interests. However, modified consensus does not require absolute conformity to a particular decision or anticipate that every member will see eye to eye with every other member before a decision is reached. It does mean that every member has had the opportunity to have his or her concerns heard; understood; evaluated; and, when possible, accommodated before a final decision is agreed upon.

While formal processes are available for developing consensus, many of the day-to-day concerns that a manager faces can be tackled through less formal means. A basic process for doing this involves the following steps.

> *Consensus* is an agreement among all members of a group or *stakeholders*.

> With modified consensus, every member has the opportunity to have his or her concerns heard; understood; evaluated; and, when possible, accommodated before a final decision is agreed upon.

1. COMMUNICATE THE PROBLEM TO THE GROUP AND AGREE ON A PROBLEM STATEMENT

Present the problem, as you understand it. Then, allow open discussion among the group to create a problem statement. In working to define the problem, identify the tangible effects of the problem on the work unit, working relationships, customer service, organizational effectiveness, or other concerns. Review and analyze relevant data to assist in forming the problem statement.

Formulating a Problem Statement

Effective problem statements are often phrased in the form of a question that points to the precise problem to be solved. For example:

> How can we improve collaboration among our teams to meet customer needs?

Often, however, more specificity is required. For example, rather than a statement that says, "how can we improve customer service," an analysis of data and a discussion of results desired will lead to a more definite articulation:

> How can we improve the level of collaboration and communication among the retail, delivery, and service teams so that (1) sale-to-delivery time is reduced by 30 percent; (2) turnaround time for responding to complaints is reduced from 48 to 24 hours; and (3) overall customer satisfaction, as reflected in customer satisfaction surveys, improves from "below average" to "above average"?

Further, many problems involve interests that the parties may perceive to be incompatible. The problem statement must acknowledge the need to address all interests. For example:

> **First party's interests:** How can our call center staff make credible promises of a 24-hour turnaround time to respond to customer service and repair needs...

> **Second party's interests:** ...while ensuring that our service staff does not become backlogged and has ample time to diagnose and fix the problems correctly the first time?

2. ALLOW EVERYONE AN OPPORTUNITY TO EXPRESS HIS OR HER VIEWS

As you work to craft a serviceable problem statement, encourage the open sharing of how members in the group perceive the problem and how the problem is affecting them or their work. This should be done in a nonjudgmental atmosphere, ensuring that each participant can give full ventilation of his or her feelings about the problem. Every attempt must be made to ensure that each individual can agree to the problem statement before proceeding to solve it.

3. BRAINSTORM SOLUTIONS

Once the problem statement is formed, have the group engage in standard problem-solving processes to brainstorm possible solutions to the problem, create options for resolution, evaluate alternatives, and narrow down to the best options that may solve the problem. Exhibit 14-1, Group Brainstorming Techniques, provides suggestions for ways to encourage open, nonjudgmental idea generation. Additional resources on group process techniques are provided in the "To Learn More" section at the end of this chapter.

4. NARROW DOWN THE LIST OF PROPOSED SOLUTIONS

Through problem solving, the group will likely come up with a number of options that all agree are not as feasible or attractive as others. These can be ruled out quickly with little argument. For each option still under consideration, have the group further brainstorm to refine the option, add

When facilitating any brainstorming activity, keep in mind a few basic ground rules:

- Use a flipchart or whiteboard to record ideas.
- Remind participants that no idea is off limits.
- Generate as many ideas as possible that will address the problem.
- Suspend all evaluation, judgment, or criticism while creating a list of ideas.
- Record all ideas verbatim.
- Combine ideas to create new ideas.

Groups can use a number of brainstorming techniques to maximize creativity and encourage openness and participation:

EXHIBIT 14–1
Group brainstorming techniques

Technique	Description	Advantages/ Disadvantages
Full group discussion	Facilitator leads the group through an open discussion to identify all possible ideas that will address the problem, strategy, task, or issue identified. The facilitator writes all ideas on a flipchart for further discussion.	Effective when the group is cooperative and trusting. Less effective if members are afraid or cautious about sharing ideas in front of others. Ideas generated may come only from those comfortable with speaking in front of the group.
Round robin	Facilitator hands out index cards and asks members to write down their ideas that will address the problem or issue identified. Each member shares his or her ideas one at a time, and the facilitator writes the responses on a flipchart for further discussion. Continue round robin until all ideas are recorded.	Encourages members to seek their own counsel when generating ideas rather than be influenced by the input of others. Addresses the problem of individuals who dominate. On the other hand, reduces the possibility of synergy where one member's contribution feeds on another's.
Anonymous idea generation	Facilitator hands out index cards and asks each member to write down his or her ideas that will address the problem, task, or issue identified. Group members turn in their cards and facilitator writes responses in random order on the flipchart for further discussion.	Eliminates fear of being associated with an idea, which could be especially important when someone in authority is present. Encourages openness and candor. However, if clarification or elaboration is needed, the individual who offered the idea cannot be consulted.

EXHIBIT 14–1
Group brainstorming techniques
Continued

Technique	Description	Advantages/ Disadvantages
Group rotation	Where multiple issues must be addressed, or a single issue can be segmented, the facilitator writes down on separate pieces of flipchart paper these multiple issues or segments. The group is divided into teams. Each team is given a period of time to generate ideas that will address the issue. The teams rotate until each team has had a chance to address all issues or segments.	Maximizes idea generation. Gives each member a chance to consider each issue. This technique is especially helpful when a complex issue or multiple issues must be addressed in a limited time. Also allows subsequent teams to refine or elaborate on ideas recorded by prior teams. Could lead to an excessive amount of data that must be sifted through.
Rotation among individual contributors	Rather than have the group tackle multiple issues or segments of an issue, the facilitator has each issue or segment written on a separate piece of $8\frac{1}{2}$ x 11 paper. A separate issue is given to each member who records two or three ideas that will address the issue. After each round, the sheets are passed until each individual has had a chance to respond to all issues.	Like group rotation, encourages maximum idea generation and expounding upon ideas recorded by prior contributors. Has the added benefit of encouraging participation of individuals who would not otherwise contribute in a group setting. Could also lead to an excessive amount of data to be sifted through, yet may be beneficial for complex issues involving large groups.
Individual team idea generation	Facilitator divides the group into teams. If there is a single issue, each team generates ideas that may address the issue. If there are multiple issues, each team is assigned a separate issue to address.	Where a single issue is discussed, encourages creativity since each team may offer a different perspective on the problem. If teams are assigned different issues, this maximizes idea generation, but limits the number of members who can contribute.

to it, and consider how the option will solve the problem identified. It may be helpful to test each proposed solution by completing an impact statement examining the positive and negative effects the solution may have on group members and the organization if the solution is implemented.

Ultimately, the solution chosen must meet three criteria:

1. It must solve the problem. Look back at the problem statement and the information, data, and desired results that went into forming the problem statement to ensure that the solution is on target with the problem to be solved.

2. It must meet the needs of those involved with implementing the solution. Are the parties most intimately affected by the solution satisfied that it will meet their needs? Or do they believe the problem will continue or even escalate?

3. It must not become the problem or create a new problem for someone else or the organization. Effective solutions are generally simple, elegantly stated, and intended to improve efficiency. The solution should not be overly complex or involve multiple steps. It must address the problem squarely and not incorporate tangential matters that may frustrate implementation. The solution should not create new responsibilities or burdens for others or the organization, unless there are sound business reasons for doing so. If the proposed solution may cause such impacts, you may be creating new problems.

5. SELECT A SOLUTION

After the most viable options have been identified, have the group select the option it believes will best address the problem. If several options remain, one approach is to take a vote to see which option the group prefers. This could be done informally by asking for a show of hands of those who support Option 1, Option 2, and so forth. This could also be done privately by asking each member to write his or her choice on a slip of paper and then tabulating the results.

Note, however, that voting can be tricky. Many groups opt not to engage in a voting procedure because it contradicts the notion of consensus. Other groups decide that when they vote only a super majority, such as 66 percent or 75 percent, will prevail, rather than a simple majority of 51 percent. For an informal process, voting may be appropriate only to narrow down to the few most promising options, while true consensus may be reserved for arriving at the ultimate decision.

Once the group appears to have reached agreement over a single option, poll each member to ensure there is agreement. For example, ask each member:

"Can you live with this decision?"

"Will you support this decision within the group?"

"Will you support this decision outside the group?"

Alternatively, instead of polling, you could ask the group as a whole:

"Is there anyone who could not support this decision?"

"Is there anyone who has any reservations about this decision?"

If any disagreements remain, endeavor to address these concerns by asking what would need to change for individuals who disagree to support the decision and what specific modifications they would suggest to make the decision acceptable. Once modifications have been proposed and discussed, ask the group again whether it can support these changes and ask those who disagreed initially whether these modifications would sufficiently address their concerns. Ultimately, the group will need to proceed with a decision while finding a constructive and supportive way to work with dissenters.

Working with Dissenters

When working with a group to achieve consensus, you may have members who will not readily agree with the group regarding the best solution. A true consensus process contemplates this possibility and requires that so-called "dissenters" are respected and that their concerns are addressed before moving forward.

Sarah McKearnan and David Fairman suggest three reasons why individuals generally do not agree to a group decision: (1) The decision does not meet their needs, (2) they have unrealistic aspirations regarding what can be achieved through consensus, or (3) they perceive a specific risk they will be taking by agreeing and are seeking contingent agreements to protect against that risk.[3] They identify three strategies to address these concerns:[4]

1. "Create more joint gains." Explore trade-offs one party may be willing to make in exchange for concessions by others. Look beyond the agreement at issues that the parties have not yet considered and which may be mutually advantageous.

2. "Use fair standards to divide joint gains." Look back at the overall goals, values, standards, and agreements the parties understood when they began the process to ensure that what parties are seeking remains consistent with these parameters.

3. "Use dispute resolution procedures to handle impasse and the strong emotions that come with it." This can be accomplished by encouraging members to consider the consequences for agreeing or not agreeing, reframing positions into interests, refocusing the parties on the overall purpose and goals of the meeting, encouraging empathic listening, referring back to ground rules when disruptive behavior occurs, and intervening directly in disputes to diffuse anger and strong emotions.

Ultimately, the group must move forward with a decision. How much the group works with a dissenter will depend on the nature of the issue and members' interest in moving forward without his or her full support. The consensus process presents a number of choices:

■ The dissenter can agree to "stand down." He states for the record that he does not agree with the decision. However, he will not get in the way of its implementation and will abide by its terms in the interest of group conformity and common goals. In these instances, the issue involved is likely not so crucial to him that he cannot cooperate with the decision.

- The group can continue to work with the dissenter until absolute consensus is achieved. If the dissenter's viewpoint is close to the group's viewpoint, and time allows, the group may decide to continue with the discussion until these viewpoints are reconciled. The group may also decide to continue the discussion because the dissenter, such as the manager, is essential for implementation and proceeding without her agreement is not realistic.
- The group can suspend any decision either indefinitely or until a time that the group can reconvene. This may give the dissenter and individual group members time to discuss the matter informally without the pressure of a formal meeting or arbitrary deadlines to see if a mutually agreeable decision is yet possible.
- The group can override the dissenter and implement the decision. If the group believes it is being "held hostage," it may decide that proceeding without the dissenter's support is in the group's best interests. Any resistance to implementation by the dissenter should be addressed through other conflict resolution methods.

6. DEVELOP AN IMPLEMENTATION STRATEGY

If all are in agreement about the solution, it is time to implement the decision. Have the group clarify and organize the timed sequence of steps or objectives needed for implementing the solution.

7. EVALUATE

As you proceed with implementation, reevaluate the symptoms that led to the problem statement. Provide group members continuous feedback regarding their progress on implementing the solution. Use project management techniques to ensure that implementation remains on course with what the group agreed to and that efforts are truly in line with resolving the problem. If aspects of the solution do not seem to be working, do not be afraid to revisit the solution strategy and make modifications. In some cases, it may be necessary to revisit the initial problem statement to ensure that the group correctly diagnosed the problem in the first place.

8. CELEBRATE WHEN THE PROBLEM IS SOLVED

When the group has successfully resolved the problem, recognize its efforts. Use the victory as a means for celebrating the team and reinforcing the need in the future for using consensus decision-making processes to address problems as they arise.

Management Tip: Neutral–Facilitated Consensus–Building Processes

You may have good intentions as a manager to facilitate a consensus decision-making process but find it challenging not to exert your authority and sway the group to adopt a particular option. Further, even if you can act in a neutral fashion, the perception that you will wield your authority may lead employees to doubt the open nature of the process.

When time and resources permit or the gravity of the situation requires, you might consider the assistance of an outside facilitator or another manager with no direct authority over the parties. This option will ensure a fair process and help avoid any perception that you will exert undue influence. A skilled facilitator is experienced at ensuring that all parties are heard and that no party is allowed to dominate or unduly persuade another.

CONSULTATIVE DECISION MAKING

A manager uses consultative decision-making processes when he chooses to be the ultimate decision maker but wishes to invite input from others. This means that the manager has not fully formed a decision and is genuinely open to the suggestions of others to make the most informed decision possible. A manager who acts otherwise—seeking input when in fact the decision is made—engages in directive decision making under the guise of consultation and risks losing his employees' trust. In consultative decision making, participants must believe that their viewpoints have been considered and that they have played a role in the decision-making process, even when the ultimate decision made does not fully embody their input.

> In consultative decision making, participants must believe that their viewpoints were considered and they played a role in the process, even if the decision made does not fully embody their input.

Consultative decision making is best suited for situations in which the manager's authority to make the decision is clearly recognized. Employees in a hierarchical, top-down management structure may expect to be consulted on important decisions, but they realize their manager will most often make the final decision. For these organizations, this is often the most efficient and time-saving method for decision making.

CONSULTATIVE DECISION MAKING IN ACTION

Consider these examples of consultative decision making:

1. A work group has attempted to resolve an issue through joint problem solving but has made little progress. The manager sets a deadline by which a decision must be made and communicates clearly that if the group is unable to resolve the issue through consensus, she will take the sense of the group and make the best decision possible as informed by group input.

2. A few employees are engaged in strong disagreement about various work processes and the next steps to take. All employees have sound ideas, yet each has a slightly different twist on the best way to proceed. They call upon the manager to decide. He engages them

in discussion to hear their ideas. He weighs their thoughts, seeks to reconcile differences, and renders a decision he believes will best satisfy their concerns and serve the interests of the organization.

3. Each of two employees has been engaged in a subtle game of running to the manager and blaming the other for the problems they are experiencing in completing a large project. The manager brings them together to discuss the situation. She stresses that they must put aside any personal issues for the time being and must refocus in order to complete the project on time. She asks each to tell her about their progress to date, next steps, and the time frames they envision for completion. After considering their input, she delineates a step-by-step process, establishes interim and final dates for completion, and assigns specific tasks.

VARYING LEVELS OF PARTICIPATION AND INPUT IN CONSULTATIVE DECISIONS

1. MORE PARTICIPATION AND INPUT

At one level, the manager retains control over the decision but seeks to approximate consensus by rendering a decision that incorporates the group's collective wisdom as closely and genuinely as possible. Accordingly, the manager uses some of the same process techniques as consensus decision making:[5]

- She asks the group to engage in problem solving to help her make a decision that will meet the needs and desires of the group.
- She considers the viewpoints of those who express contrary opinions and attempts to reconcile differences.
- When a general consensus appears to have formed, she summarizes her understanding of what the group has recommended. For example, she might say, "If I'm understanding you correctly, you agree that we must do x." The group can then evaluate whether the manager has adequately captured the consensus or whether further refinements are necessary.

At this point, the process deviates from standard consensus decision making as the manager moves toward making the decision on his or her own. At the same time, the manager weighs the input of the group before acting:

- She informs the group of the decision she is inclined to make that is both acceptable to her and that appears most consistent with the general will of the group.
- She explains the basis for the decision, including how she believes it satisfies the interests expressed or why she believes the decision is sound even though it may not fulfill all interests.
- She asks each member if he or she can support the decision. In general, if the group has been fully engaged in the process, the members

will agree to support the decision, even if some individuals' needs have not been fully addressed.

- Upon gaining support of all or most group members, she implements the decision.

2. LESS PARTICIPATION AND INPUT

One danger of engaging in a process that invites extensive input and participation from the group is that the group may arrive at decisions that the manager is not comfortable implementing. If this is a possibility, the manager may choose instead to engage in a consultative process wherein there is no expectation or guarantee among the group that the manager will ultimately implement a decision based on group consensus. Accordingly, the manager engages in the following process:[6]

- He brings employees together to ask for their informed input on how they believe he should proceed on a particular issue. At the outset, he either has a distinct view of the direction he thinks he should take or he has only some general ideas but no clear direction.
  - If he has a distinct view, he tells the group what it is. He may even state that he is not sure the group will be able to sway him to take a different direction, but he would like the group to challenge him to ensure that the decision is sound or to convince him that it is not.
  - If he has only a general idea but no clear direction, he shares his thoughts and asks employees to come up with some recommendations on how they believe he should proceed.
- He leads the group through a process to generate ideas and alternatives and arrive at a number of possible options. However, unlike consensus methods, wherein the group narrows down alternatives to select the most promising ones, the manager selects those alternatives he prefers and rejects all others.
- He asks employees to evaluate the remaining alternatives. After listening to their concerns, he expresses which alternative he prefers and asks them what particular concerns they have about the alternative. If he remains unsure about certain aspects of the alternative, he asks if employees have any ideas about how the alternative might be improved.
- He allows the group to continue to offer refinements to his proposed decision until he is satisfied he has arrived at the best decision possible.
- He implements the decision with the understanding that the decision may or may not be the preferred decision of all group members.

HOW MUCH PARTICIPATION AND INPUT SHOULD A MANAGER ALLOW?

As you engage in consultative processes, you must decide how much time and effort you are willing to spend to test and retest the decision you are considering against the group's judgment. As illustrated in

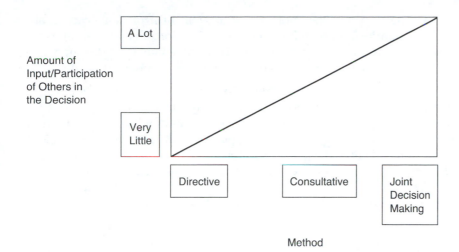

Exhibit 14-2, you will find that your efforts will blend with other methods discussed in this chapter (directive and joint decision making) based on the amount of participation and input you allow among group members.

The more participation and input you allow, the more you blend consultative methods with consensus decision-making methods. The less participation and input you allow, the more you blend consultative methods with directive methods.

The amount of participation and input you allow will be influenced by factors such as the following:

- The importance of making a quick decision
- The level of agreement or discord you experience from the group on the issue
- The amount of group buy-in you need to successfully implement the decision
- The group's comfort level with managerial decision making without full participation and input of employees

DIRECTIVE DECISION MAKING

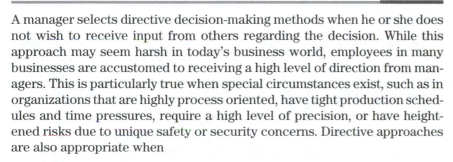

A manager selects directive decision-making methods when he or she does not wish to receive input from others regarding the decision. While this approach may seem harsh in today's business world, employees in many businesses are accustomed to receiving a high level of direction from managers. This is particularly true when special circumstances exist, such as in organizations that are highly process oriented, have tight production schedules and time pressures, require a high level of precision, or have heightened risks due to unique safety or security concerns. Directive approaches are also appropriate when

- Employees lack the maturity or competence in their jobs to be given much leeway

- The decision does not require a great deal of deliberation, and subordinates are indifferent to the direction the manager takes
- Conflicts must be settled quickly, involve immature disputants, or are unlikely to be resolved without the exertion of authority

With directive decision making, the high level of participation used in consultative or joint decision making is absent. The manager does not seek input regarding the parties' preferred alternatives for resolution. While the manager may seek information from the parties before making a decision and allow the parties to present facts and argument in support of their positions, he or she will evaluate the information received from the standpoint of an arbitrator. The manager will use his or her authority to direct the parties in a course of action rather than engage them in a collaborative process.

> In directive decision making, managers use their authority to direct others in a course of action rather than engage them in a collaborative process.

DIRECTIVE DECISION MAKING IN ACTION

Consider these examples of directive decision making:

1. Two parties are arguing intensely and disrupting the work environment. The manager steps in and states that they must end their argument immediately and get back to work or face discipline.

2. A team does not seem to be any closer to resolving an issue regarding work processes, and its project is now hopelessly delayed. The manager has lost his patience with the ongoing debate and steps in. Other than asking focused questions to clarify his understanding of the problem, he affords little leeway for discussion or debate. He then instructs each party what to do.

3. Gladys has reported an incident of inappropriate, offensive language used by her coworker, Kim. Kim denies this and says that Gladys has been extremely rude and cold toward her, which Gladys denies. The manager has observed a negative relationship between the employees but has not observed any offensive language or overtly rude behavior. She must decide between two diametrically opposed reports on what has occurred before taking corrective action. She meets separately with the parties, asks directed questions to determine what has occurred, and uses her best judgment to decide upon the action she will take.

THE IMPORTANCE OF FAIRNESS AND CONSISTENCY

Directive decision-making processes must be equitable and serve the best interests of the parties, the manager, and the organization. To ensure this:

- Ask questions focused on obtaining facts and concrete information—who, what, when, where, why, and how. You must use effective inquiry and investigative skills and seek to understand what occurred, how and why it occurred, who was involved or witnessed it, and when and where it occurred.

- Encourage the parties to be concrete and objective. They should support their assertions, feelings, and thoughts with facts and information that will explain why they feel or think as they do. If they provide input concerning their preferred options for resolution, they should identify the objective criteria, such as a particular policy, practice, procedure, or standard of fairness that would justify such options.

- Consider the parties' credibility, demeanor, motives, and prejudices. You must be astute in understanding the messages and intentions underlying the issue and the parties' words and actions. Can you trust what a party is saying? Do tone of voice, body language, and demeanor suggest that a party is hiding something? Is a party being manipulative, or does the party have a reason to embellish a story? Is one party fearful and the other aggressive? What is the parties' history? Is their behavior consistent with past incidents or unique to this incident?

- Check for biases that may unduly influence your decision. Has a party "pushed your buttons" in the past? Reflect on any emotions, biases, or other concerns that may affect your ability to render an objective decision. Consider a second opinion from another manager to ensure the decision is consistent with what others would do under similar circumstances. Further, be sure your decision is supported by relevant policies and procedures governing the situation.

- When all relevant information has been gathered, weigh it to arrive at a balanced decision. Consider outcomes that will best serve the interests of the parties but that are also acceptable to you and the organization. If win/win is not possible, seek an outcome that is efficient and will do the greatest good and cause the least harm. Consider outcomes that hold the most promise for restoring relationships, preserving dignity, and fostering productive relationships for the future.

- Render the decision in an objective, balanced fashion. Explain the rationale for the decision and, when possible, help doubtful parties work through any reservations. Be supportive but firm with individuals who resist. If there are winners and losers, ensure that one party is not permitted to gloat or take advantage and that the dignity of the other party is preserved. If corrective action is required, implement it discreetly, ensuring that confidentiality and privacy interests are respected.

- Set clear expectations regarding new understandings, actions to be taken, and behavior changes to occur. Establish a process for monitoring the situation or overseeing the relationship, including timelines for compliance and methods for reporting and follow-up. Monitor the situation and, when necessary, revisit to ensure that the parties remain focused on new expectations.

- Remain unconditionally constructive and instill a belief that renewal, restored relationships, positive change, and a return to a productive environment are imminently possible. Even when corrective action is required, take the attitude that individuals are capable of improving their circumstances and want to change.

Using Principles of Dialogue to Encourage Open Conversation

As a manager or leader working with a group, it may be tempting to move the group quickly through discussion about an issue in order to arrive at a decision. It is perhaps counterintuitive in the course of everyday business where decisions must be reached yesterday to slow down the decision-making process. However, the more a group is invested in the decision to be made and has concerns about achieving an outcome that addresses its concerns and needs, the greater the need to allow for meaningful conversation that provides all group members time to be heard. Managers and leaders must embrace the concept of "go slow to go fast," recognizing that the more time they give for dialogue on issues that matter to the team, the more likely they will reach high-quality, efficient decisions that are fully embraced by team members.

The Greek roots of the word *dialogue* are *dia*, meaning "through," and *logos*, meaning "word" or "meaning." Dialogue, therefore, is generally understood to involve the process of increasing understanding in relationships through the "flow of meaning." A dialogue process creates a "pool of shared meaning" in which all the beliefs, values, ideas, assumptions, and related input of all members are placed in a pool or "container" and fully evaluated and considered before a decision is reached. Lengthier processes involving group dialogue may not be practical for many business decisions. However, as you engage in decision-making processes in which group members would value the opportunity to be fully heard, consider how you may incorporate the following principles of dialogue to reach higher quality, broadly supported decisions.

> A dialogue process creates a "pool of shared meaning" in which all the beliefs, values, ideas, assumptions, and related input of all members are placed in a pool or "container" and fully evaluated and considered before a decision is reached.

CREATE AND FOSTER SAFETY

For team members to feel they can openly share concerns, they must trust that what they share will be treated respectfully and confidentiality. You must foster this sense of safety every day by consistently handling sensitive information in a careful, confidential, and ethical manner and by encouraging the same among team members. Team members are then more likely to freely share information and concerns during team dialogue meetings. When meeting, remind them of the need to respect confidentiality and to ensure safety among one other. Make it a ground rule.

FOSTER EQUALITY BY MINIMIZING THE BADGES OF AUTHORITY

In a joint decision making, you are representing that you are simply one of the team and that you want the team to arrive at an outcome that works best for all. Nonetheless, a natural barrier exists because you are the "boss." While this badge of authority may never completely go away, you must demonstrate by word and deed that you will respect the joint decision-making process and will do your part to carry out any decisions accordingly. During dialogue, make every effort not to exert your "badge," either through explicit action such as an order or command or implicit action such as statements or nonverbal communication suggesting that you will put your "manager hat" back on when you don't like the direction the dialogue is going.

LISTEN AND ENCOURAGE OTHERS TO LISTEN WITH EMPATHY

Use the skills learned in Part II of this text, teach others these skills as part of the process of forming as a group to engage in dialogue, and reinforce these skills and behaviors during meetings. It is particularly important to skillfully manage the natural tendencies you or others have to interrupt colleagues while they are sharing their views. Ensure that team members are fully heard before others are given the opportunity to be heard. Support empathic responses by which team members demonstrate to the person talking that they have understood her point of view from her frame of reference, not their own.

MAKE ASSUMPTIONS EXPLICIT

People naturally draw conclusions and make judgments based on what they have seen or heard without the benefit of having all the facts. Making our assumptions explicit is a way of demonstrating that based on what we have seen and heard thus far, we are drawing certain assumptions and conclusions. However, it is also a way of signaling to others that while we may believe, feel, or conclude x, we acknowledge these are only assumptions at the moment and that we are open to the possibility that other interpretations and conclusions may be drawn. We signal our willingness to have our assumptions explored and tested and to have different viewpoints and new information shared that may lead us to draw different conclusions or alter our judgments.

SUSPEND JUDGMENT

The natural process of dialogue involves a period of time in which team members struggle through "divergent" thinking in which multiple viewpoints are expressed and appear incompatible. Through time and deliberate effort to understand one another, the hope is that the group will achieve more "convergent" thinking by which they find ways to resolve their disagreements, realize their disagreements are not significant enough to present barriers for moving forward, or manage to minimize the detrimental effects of their disagreements so they can move forward. This process will not occur unless team members suspend their judgments about one another's viewpoints, judgments, motives, and behaviors. Help team members guard against making such knee-jerk judgments or reacting negatively to the knee-jerk judgments of others.

BALANCE ADVOCACY AND INQUIRY

Dialogue challenges individuals to move from "either/or" thinking to "both/and" thinking. It challenges individuals to see how each participant's ideas and viewpoints may be pieced together to construct a collective or "whole" result in support of a mutually supported outcome rather than as mutually exclusive in which the acceptance of one idea, viewpoint, or approach means the rejection of all others. Therefore, as much as individuals should be encouraged to confidently assert their viewpoints, they should also respectfully inquire about the viewpoints of others and be open to thoughtful inquiry about their own viewpoints from others. Advocacy skills include giving voice to your views, asserting yourself, explaining your positions and why you advocate for them, respectfully challenging the positions of others, and stating your assumptions and making your reasoning explicit. Inquiry skills include suspending judgment, seeking clarification and drawing out others' reasoning, interviewing, testing, and listening for new understandings.

PERFORMANCE CHECKLIST

- At times you must intervene and make decisions to solve problems or settle disputes affecting the individuals you manage.

- Select joint decision-making processes if you believe buy-in from the group is needed to effectively implement a decision.

- When you engage in a joint decision-making process, such as consensus decision making, you must work with the group to jointly arrive at a decision and not exercise your authority as manager to accept, reject, or modify the decision.

- Select consultative decision-making processes when you wish to reserve the right to make the ultimate decision but want to invite the group to give input.

- The level of participation and input you allow in a consultative decision-making process will depend on the importance of making a quick decision, the level of agreement or discord among the group, the amount of buy-in needed to implement a decision, and the group's comfort level with managerial decisions made without the group's being consulted.

- Select directive decision-making processes if you do not want to invite input on the decision.

- When engaging in directive decision making, you must take care to render a decision that is fair and that takes into account the best interests of the parties and the organization.

- Managers must "go slow to go fast," giving time for dialogue on issues that matter to the team; doing so increases the likelihood for reaching high-quality, efficient decisions that are fully embraced by team members.

TEST YOURSELF

True/False

For each statement below, check true or false.

TRUE   FALSE

_____ _____ 1. Anonymous idea generation is the best brainstorming process when team members fear being identified with an idea when someone in authority is present in the room.

_____ _____ 2. Roberta is the manager of a group. She asks the group to engage in a joint decision-making process. In the course of this process, she proposes a solution, which the group rejects. It would be appropriate for her to overrule the group's decision.

_____ _____ 3. In a round robin, individuals write down their ideas that may solve a problem before sharing them openly with group members.

_____ _____ 4. An effective consensus decision-making process requires that all team members agree before a decision may be implemented.

_____ _____ 5. In consultative decision making, it is never appropriate for the manager to state upfront what decision he or she is inclined to make and to then tell the group members that they probably will not be able to sway his or her decision.

MULTIPLE CHOICE

Circle the letter next to the best answer for each question. On a separate sheet of paper, state why you chose that answer.

1. *One benefit* of participatory management is that it
   a. alleviates the manager of responsibility in the decision-making process.
   b. makes the decision-making process quicker.
   c. better ensures the quality of the decision.
   d. gives complete control to the team to make the decision.

2. Consensus decisions *do not* require
   a. complete agreement on all terms by all members.
   b. acceptance by all members, even if some members do not agree with all terms.
   c. efforts to address the concerns of dissenters before reaching an agreement.
   d. opportunity for all members to be heard before reaching an agreement.

3. All the following are viable techniques for determining consensus among members of a group *except*
   a. voting.
   b. polling each member and asking if she or he will support the decision.
   c. asking if there is any reason why any member cannot support the decision.
   d. assuming consent if the group remains silent for five minutes.

4. In directive decision-making processes, when evaluating relevant information before rendering an adverse decision affecting an employee, the *least relevant* consideration is
   a. the employee's credibility.
   b. the manager's bias.
   c. an employee's length of service with the company.
   d. an employee's history with respect to incidents similar to the incident at hand.

5. Of the brainstorming processes listed, the process that is *most likely* to encourage candor and openness is
   a. full group discussion.
   b. round robin.
   c. anonymous idea generation.
   d. group rotation.

1. When thinking about the organization where you work (or previously worked), what would you say is the level of participatory management typically used? Discuss specific examples for which this style of management proved to be effective, as well as examples for which it proved to be ineffective. Why was it effective or ineffective?

2. Do you believe achieving *absolute* consensus is possible, or do most group processes result in achieving only *modified* consensus in which one or more members are not in complete agreement regarding the decision ultimately reached? Discuss.

3. Do you agree with the authors that a directive decision can and should be made in a fair and objective manner, or do you believe any decision that a manager makes without consulting those who will be affected is inherently subjective and potentially harsh? Discuss.

CASE: DECIDING WHAT TO DO

OBJECTIVE

To practice consensus decision making, consultative decision making, and directive decision making and understand the impacts of each.

PROBLEM

Jim Talent has always encouraged an open-door policy. He has made it clear that when anyone has a concern, he or she can come to him. He will listen and do what he can to address the concern. Recently, though, Jim has been rethinking this policy. While he still wants an open-door policy, he has become increasingly aware of the drain on his time this policy has created. Further, he has noticed that the policy seems to be inconsistently applied. He has noticed this particularly with Joe Newcomer's group.

Members of the warehouse team, led by Sally Ambitious, come to Jim about minor issues such as time off and overtime policies, procedures for particular job tasks and functions, and corporate policies on handling defective and returned merchandise. To Jim, it seems Sally or Joe should address such issues.

The customer service front desk is currently lacking a team leader. Members of this team are coming to Jim with actual complaints, such as being treated unfairly by coworkers and feeling stressed by excess work due to having insufficient staff. Jim believes that Joe is the appropriate person to address these issues, even though Joe seems a little overwhelmed lately with multiple tasks and is not as accessible as he should be.

Finally, Jim has been sensing growing tensions among the delivery staff, led by Fred Staid. This group includes a lot of "good ol' boys" who are not always respectful of other staff. They sit around and tell off-color jokes, which offend the two women on the team. Joe has been trying to work with Fred to correct these behaviors, though Jim has seen little change. Although the women have not been too vocal about their concerns, Jim worries that the whole situation may come to a boiling point, requiring him to intervene. Jim wonders if perhaps he should be a little more involved but has been patient, allowing Joe to work through the situation.

Jim has concluded that he needs to set new standards for his open-door policy. Therefore, he asks each of his assistant managers to figure out a process by which employees in their respective areas should communicate with management. He says, "I don't care how you do this, but please find a way to improve the overall lines of communication within your units while reinforcing the importance of my open-door policy." After the meeting, Jim pulls Joe aside and highlights his particular concerns.

PROCEDURE

Choose three students, each to play the role of Joe. Divide the remainder of the class into three groups. Each group works with the assigned "Joe" to arrive at the best communication process and action plan as directed in this scenario.

Each group must develop an action plan for employees to follow with respect to communicating their concerns, including

1. Identifying the kinds of issues that team members should address and establishing a process for how such issues will be raised and addressed with the team

2. Identifying the kinds of issues that should be directed to Joe as assistant manager and establishing a process for how such issues will be raised and addressed by Joe

3. Identifying the kinds of issues that should be directed to Jim Talent as store owner/manager and establishing a process for how such issues will be raised and addressed by Jim

To fulfill this assignment, each group is assigned a different decision-making process, as follows:

1. The first group is directed to use consensus decision making to establish an employee communication process and develop an action plan. In this case, Joe facilitates the process but shares decision-making authority with the group. The group should attempt to achieve at least modified consensus, giving due consideration to any dissenters before arriving at a final plan.

2. The second group is directed to use consultative decision making to establish an employee communication process and develop an action plan. Joe should either state up front what his preferred plan of action is and invite input, or he should allow the group to engage in discussion for a while and then announce what his decision is based on what he thinks will meet the legitimate concerns of group members.

3. In the third group, Joe is directed to use directive decision making to establish an employee communication process and develop an action plan. To the extent input is permitted, Joe should simply ask fact-based, objective questions to understand the general nature of concerns that employees need to communicate. Though respectful, Joe is less concerned about participants' feelings or opinions about any particular process and specifically does not invite such input. At the end of this process, he announces his decision. (As an alternative, Joe may choose to leave the group for a few minutes, consider a process and action plan without asking any questions, and announce his decision to the group, allowing members to comment.)

Group participants should respond to Joe's direction as they naturally would if they were actual employees in this situation. Where relevant to the discussion, participants should role-play employees in the warehouse, delivery, and customer service desk areas, respectively.

Allow twenty-five minutes for this exercise.

Case Questions

Before engaging in discussion, record each group's employee communication process and action plan on a whiteboard or flipchart. Discussion should focus on the following:

1. How did the decision reached by each group differ?

2. What impact did Joe's approach have on the ultimate decision reached?

3. What effect did each approach have on achieving the outcome requested by Jim Talent?

4. How did members of each group feel about the process, the level of participation permitted, and the level of cooperation achieved?

5. How did members of each group feel toward Joe and his methods in managing the decision-making process?

6. What were the advantages and disadvantages of each approach?

ALTERNATIVE PROCEDURE FOR ONLINE LEARNING FORMATS

Option 1: If appropriate videoconferencing capability is available, select three students to each play the three "Joes" as identified above. Divide the remainder of the class by thirds and assign one-third to each of the three "Joes." Then, have Joe facilitate the discussion as outlined above with his or her assigned third of the class, while all other students observe the interaction. Then, engage in full-class discussion of the questions above. Be sure to capture the main points of the communication plan that each group devised and compare them.

Option 2: If videoconferencing capability is not available, divide the class into thirds and assign one of the three decision-making processes to each of the three groups. Based on the decision-making process assigned, have students individually outline the communication plan they believe would be developed as an outcome of the decision-making process that Joe facilitates. Have students post these outlines within a specified time period. Then, have students offer responses and critiques to at least two posts offered by other students. Engage in additional forum discussions or online chats as time and interest allow.

PERSONAL GROWTH EXERCISE

As you consider the employees you manage, accept the challenge of new thinking and engage them in the creative process of decision making. When have you acted as the sole decision maker in the past but think that inviting the team's input would have produced a better result? When have you been reluctant to loosen the reigns of your authority in making a decision but realized that engaging in a true consensus decision-making process would have resulted in a much more creative and collaborative result?

In the next week, find an opportunity to engage your team in a participatory process, such as one of the processes illustrated in this chapter. The more you engage in such practices, the more you are likely to find that you will increase your influence with the team rather than diminish it.

TO LEARN MORE

The following resources provide information regarding various forms and practices of participative decision-making and group processes:

Ellinor, Linda, and Glenna Gerard. *Dialogue: Rediscover the Transforming Power of Conversation.* New York: John Wiley & Sons, Inc., 1998.

Isaacs, William. *Dialogue and the Art of Thinking Together.* New York: Currency, 1999.

Kaner, Sam. *Facilitator's Guide to Participatory Decision-Making.* Gabriola Island, BC, Canada: New Society Publishers, 1996.

Senge, Peter M., Art Kleiner, Charlotte Roberts, Richard B. Ross, and Bryan J. Smith. *The Fifth Discipline Fieldbook: Strategies and Tools for Building a Learning Organization.* New York: Currency, 1994.

Susskind, Lawrence E., and Jeffrey L. Cruikshank. *Breaking Robert's Rules: The New Way to Run Your Meeting, Build Consensus, and Get Results.* New York: Oxford University Press, 2006.

Susskind, Lawrence, Sarah McKearnan, and Jennifer Thomas-Larmer, eds. *The Consensus Building Handbook: A Comprehensive Guide to Reaching Agreement.* Thousand Oaks, CA: Sage Publications, 1999.

Weaver, Richard G., and John D. Farrell. *Managers as Facilitators: A Practical Guide to Getting Work Done in a Changing Workplace.* San Francisco: Berrett-Koehler Publishers, 1997.

NOTES

1. Gary Yukl, *Leadership in Organizations*, 6th ed. (Upper Saddle River, NJ: Pearson Education, 2006), 95–97.

2. Delegation is not covered in this discussion. The intent of delegation is to give control over decisions to others, whereas the intent of this chapter is to focus on processes that involve the manager directly in making decisions.

3. Sarah McKearnan and David Fairman, "Producing Consensus," in *The Consensus Building Handbook: A Comprehensive Guide to Reaching Agreement*, ed. Lawrence Susskind, Sarah McKearnan, and Jennifer Thomas-Larmer (Thousand Oaks, CA: Sage Publications, 1999), 333.

4. Ibid., 333–36.

5. Thomas Justice and David W. Jamieson, *The Facilitator's Fieldbook* (New York: American Management Association, 1999), 220–22.

6. Ibid., 216–19.

HANDLING CONFLICTS REQUIRING DIRECT CONFRONTATION

PERFORMANCE COMPETENCIES

After you have finished reading this chapter, you will be able to

- Describe a basic model for confronting individuals in an assertive and positive manner that will diffuse conflict or prevent it from escalating

- Apply the model to address performance and discipline issues

- Respond to agitated or angry reactions

When an employee's performance or conduct negatively affects his job, productivity, or the work environment, you must step in promptly to inform the employee that the situation must change or adverse consequences may result. This chapter discusses a basic model for assertively and positively confronting individuals for whom behavior change is unequivocally expected. It also provides insights for applying the model to performance and conduct problems requiring corrective action or discipline. These situations allow little latitude for considering alternatives. When handling them, you must be assertive and single-minded as you pursue behavior change, while remaining polite, respectful, and supportive toward the individual you are confronting.

SENDING THE APPROPRIATE MESSAGE

How does a parent respond when frustrated with a child's behavior?

> "Donny, stop teasing your sister right now!"

> "Marie, you are being very bad. Stop acting like a brat or I'll come over there and give you a spanking."

Some players you pat their butts, some players you kick their butts, some players you leave alone.

Pete Rose

"Leticia, I'm very angry with you. No television for you tonight."

"Maxwell, if you promise to be good in the supermarket, we'll get ice cream!"

Clearly, these methods prove ineffective for engendering change in a child. The parent's use of commands, threats, punishments, and bribes may result in resentment, anger, confusion, and fear or, conversely, encouragement to continue manipulative behaviors to receive a reward. If compliance is achieved, it is short-lived.

Yet how do some supervisors respond when frustrated with the behavior of employees they manage?

"Stop arguing with me, Michael. End of discussion. Get out of my office!"

"Jermaine, your performance is substandard. If you do not improve it immediately, you will be terminated."

"Janet, you were rude to Leonard. I'm going to have to write you up."

"Mary Ann, can I get you to work with Ginger on this project? I know you don't like her very much. I'll make it up to you."

Similarly, these messages do nothing to bring about change. Their content is vague and subjective, giving the employee little concrete information regarding the precise nature of the conduct or performance he or she is expected to change. Their manner of delivery is insensitive and accusatory, causing feelings of anger, resentment, and hurt.

Employees do not relish hearing the "bad news" concerning their conduct or performance no more than supervisors relish delivering it. Yet they expect and deserve to be treated like adults. They expect and deserve

> Employees do not want to hear "bad news" concerning their conduct or performance. Yet they expect and deserve to be treated like adults.

- Timely feedback concerning performance, including deficits in performance
- Concrete and specific details, including examples, regarding the performance problem or the nature of the offense being addressed
- A message that is direct and to the point about their performance or conduct and expectations for change
- A message that is delivered in a respectful, supportive manner and at a time and place that will ensure confidentiality and preserve dignity
- An understanding of the consequences for the behavior or performance deficit
- The opportunity to participate in a process for identifying solutions and to correct problems before consequences are realized
- A process that is fair, equitable, and consistent and that provides the opportunity to be heard and to explain, when relevant, reasons for deficits
- Support from the supervisor during the corrective process, sending the clear message that employees are valued and that a return to a positive working relationship is anticipated

THE BASIC ASSERTIVE CONFRONTATION MODEL

The process for assertively and positively confronting an employee regarding unacceptable performance and behavior is intended to soften messages that are often perceived as bad news. It is designed to shift the emphasis of the message from what the sender is feeling about the situation to what the recipient needs to know and understand about his or her behavior in a way that will best ensure comprehension and reduce negative responses. It accomplishes these objectives while maintaining dignity and respect for the individual.

Three elements are essential for conveying a positive confrontation message.

> The basic confrontation message:
> - Describe the behavior
> - Explain the impact
> - State the desired change

1. DESCRIBE THE BEHAVIOR

Describe the behavior or performance problem in objective, specific, and concrete terms. Clearly identify the behavior or performance deficit you wish the individual to correct. The behavior described should be something you have observed or that is verifiable, rather than based on speculation or wishes. Avoid general, vague, or complicated descriptions, which will confuse the recipient regarding the precise behavior being addressed. Upon delivering the message, the recipient should have a clear picture of the concern and be able to pinpoint the basic facts and circumstances to which you are referring.

2. EXPLAIN THE IMPACT

Explain the impact that the behavior is having on you, coworkers, the team, customers, productivity, the work environment, or other concerns. Again, be specific, concrete, and objective. Try to be as vivid as possible in explaining the impacts without being overdramatic so that the recipient can see the connection between the behavior or performance deficit and its impacts.

3. STATE THE DESIRED CHANGE

State the specific change in behavior or performance you want to see. These should be explicit, small, observable behavior or performance changes. The measures used should be consistent with similar expectations for others in similar circumstances, rather than unrealistic measures that only top performers can achieve.

Exhibit 15-1 presents two examples of how to deliver the basic message.

EXHIBIT 15-1
Basic assertive confrontation
message

Situation	Noticeable decline in performance in recent weeks	Offensive behavior exhibited toward colleagues
1. Describe the behavior.	Dean, I've observed a gradual decline in quality in the last three months. Your reject rate is twice that of others.	Frank, I overheard you yelling at Sammy and Peter. You called Sammy an idiot and Peter a fool.
2. Explain the impact.	This has resulted in an increase in waste and cost overruns, and has also delayed delivery to our customers.	Sammy was in tears, and Peter was fuming. In addition, others overheard your rants and felt uncomfortable and embarrassed for you.
3. State the desired change.	I'd like to see your reject rate return to acceptable levels by your next review in three weeks.	I'd like you to apologize to Sammy and Peter. I'd also like you to stop talking to your coworkers in such a belligerent tone using such offensive language.

SOFTENING THE MESSAGE

This three-part message is the minimal information necessary to assertively address behavior or performance change. Yet it may convey more of a "command and control" approach than you desire. What if you want to engage in a search for options with the individual? What if, despite the problem, you want to show some understanding of the challenges or difficulties the individual is facing, which may partly explain the problem? What if the issue is personal and your feelings and the other person's are involved? Beyond conveying the basic message, using these additional elements will help soften the message.

EXPRESS HOW THE BEHAVIOR MADE YOU FEEL

Express the emotion or the feeling that the behavior or performance concern has engendered. Note that expressing your feelings about how a situation has affected you is distinct from arbitrarily venting frustrations. One method for doing this is the "when-I" statement that combines the basic description of the behavior with an expression of emotion:

> When you don't listen to my requests and act contrary to them, I feel I am being ignored and disrespected.

Use "when I" statements to identify the behavior to be corrected in a way that is nonaccusatory and that does not place a larger burden on the individual than is warranted.

When the work doesn't get done because you are taking repeated smoking breaks, I become anxious that we will miss our quota for the day.

When I overheard you call me a momma's boy in front of the team, I felt hurt.

This keeps the message from being accusatory and from placing a larger burden on the individual for the behavior than is warranted.

EMPATHIZE (IF YOU CAN)

Empathize with the individual and the reasons that may explain why the individual acted or performed as he or she did. Perhaps the individual you are confronting is genuinely struggling with a performance issue, is experiencing personal difficulties, or made an honest mistake. Showing empathy provides a tacit acknowledgement that "hey, we are all human." It further conveys your faith in the individual that the issues can be overcome. Be sure that your expression of empathy is relevant and congruent to the behavior you are addressing. Further, if you cannot be honest, do not express empathy. You probably would not show empathy, for example, if the individual has engaged in repeated acts of sexual harassment or you are planning to terminate the individual for gross misconduct.

> Use empathy if warranted. Do not use empathy if you cannot be sincere.

CHOOSE A CONSEQUENCE

Choose an adverse consequence if the behavior or performance problem does not change or a positive consequence if it does. This requires care. If you select a consequence, particularly an adverse one, you must be prepared to carry it out if the behavior or performance problem is repeated. If the consequence involves progressive discipline, is the punishment appropriate given the nature and severity of the offense? If the consequence involves an escalation of the process, such as taking the next step of discipline or reporting to the next level of authority, will it have a more drastic impact on you or the individual (e.g., career, reputation, increased stress) than is warranted? What effect will the consequence have on your relationship?

> Stating a positive consequence if the behavior changes can be as effective, if not more effective, as stating a negative consequence if the behavior does not change.

When stating a consequence, be as specific and positive as possible. Do not frame the consequence in a way that may be interpreted, implicitly or explicitly, as threatening or coercive. Emphasize what is possible in terms of improved performance, relationships, or working environments. Remember, stating a positive consequence may be as effective as stating an adverse one. In fact, consider stating both:

> John, if you are unable to meet these performance standards by the time of your next review, we may need to discuss putting you on a performance improvement plan. However, I remain convinced that these current performance issues are only temporary and that if you work through these concerns, you will once again become one of our top performers.

INVITE OPTIONS FOR RESOLUTION AND OFFER SUPPORT

Invite the individual to suggest or explore options that will help him or her change the behavior or performance problem. Except when you must adamantly insist on a particular outcome, such as a directive to desist using foul language or to abide by a precise list of action items to avoid termination, many discussions provide room for joint problem solving. For example:

> Ted, you have heard my concerns and why I believe you will need to change the way you interact with others. I would be interested in hearing your thoughts on the matter. Perhaps we can come to some agreement on how to proceed.

A closely related message is the invitation for the individual to offer any explanations as to why the behavior or performance has not been up to par.

> Trudi, as you know, I am very concerned about this recent decline in performance. If there is anything I need to know that will explain it, I would be interested in hearing about it.

Such an invitation affords the individual an opportunity to provide a context for his or her behavior or performance. Depending on the circumstances, you may also want to express your openness to different interpretations of the facts and circumstances that led you to draw the conclusions that you have:

> Imelda, based on everything I've observed over the past month, I feel there is no other reasonable explanation for your decline in performance than a lack of interest and commitment to the work and to the company. I wish there was a different explanation but struggle to find one. However, if there is a different conclusion to draw or if I'm mistaken in my observation, I'd really like to hear how you see it differently. I would love to be proven wrong.

The authors of *Crucial Conversations: Tools for Talking When Stakes Are High* refer to this approach as "talking tentatively" and "encouraging testing."[1] The use of tentative language removes the emphatic nature of your message, suggesting that you are open to dialogue. Encouraging the other person to challenge your assertion suggests that reaching a different conclusion based on the facts and therefore a different resolution are still possible. It signals possibilities for continued conversation and helps minimize the other person's defensiveness in contrast to more direct and sometimes harsh messages that shut down any possibility for continued dialogue.

Note that use of these messages may not be best when you need to be more emphatic and have less negotiation room to give. These messages are helpful to encourage continued dialogue in order to help the individual work through the issues and return to acceptable behaviors or levels of performance. You may want to limit their use for individuals who lack the maturity to understand the helpful intent behind your message and instead take advantage of your openness to engage in endless debate.

Finally, you may wish to offer support to the individual to help him or her return to the desired behaviors or performance level:

> Jessica, if there is anything that I can assist you with, whether personal or professional, please let me know. I want to help you return to the performance level I know you are capable of. Please let me know how I can help.

Such offers communicate that you remain fully supportive, value the employee, and believe that he or she can return to the desired state you have articulated. They may also lead to the discovery of a personal, health, financial, or emotional concern of which you had not been previously aware and provide insight on how to work with the individual as you pursue corrective action.

The key with these messages is to demonstrate your openness to working with the individual. When confronted, the individual may invariably feel you have dropped a bomb. Offering support lets the individual know that she or he is not alone and that you are available and willing to help.

CHECK FOR UNDERSTANDING AND COMPLIANCE

Check to see whether the individual understands the desired change and will comply. You may wish to ask, "Do you understand what I am asking of you?" or "Have I been clear about what I expect for the future?" If you desire more than a "yes" or a nod of the head, ask the individual to repeat back the key points of what you have asked. You may also wish to ask, "Do you intend to comply with my request?" Note, however, that when talking with a mature individual who generally responds well to corrective discussions, asking for compliance may come off as condescending. Therefore, use of this element of the message may not be necessary.

PUTTING IT ALL TOGETHER

Putting these elements together results in a succinct confident statement as demonstrated in Exhibit 15-2.

Note that in each scenario, the sender has chosen not to use each element of the assertive script because some elements are not always necessary to convey the intended message. Further, the assertive confrontation message is useful not just for supervisors when addressing employee behaviors but also for day-to-day interactions such as when one employee addresses another about sexual harassment.

ADDRESSING PERFORMANCE AND CONDUCT ISSUES

The assertive confrontation model is commonly applied in settings involving performance improvement and progressive discipline. But confronting an employee in these settings involves more than simply having a

EXHIBIT 15–2
Complete assertive confrontation
message

Situation	Performance issue involving potential disciplinary action	First incident of sexual harassment experienced by an individual from another
Describe the behavior.	Margie, you have been tardy for the past week.	When you tell off-color jokes and make sexually suggestive remarks . . .
Express the feeling or emotion.	(Not used)	I feel embarrassed and uncomfortable.
Explain the impact.	As a result, you are not here when the doors open and customers are waiting. Also, others have had to pick up the slack in your absence.	Because of this, I have difficulty concentrating on my work. I also avoid you so I won't have to listen to your offensive language.
Empathize (if appropriate).	I understand you are having difficulties with your day-care situation right now, which has prevented you from coming in on time.	I understand you're used to engaging in this behavior where you worked before and that you don't consider your remarks to be sexually explicit.
State the desired change.	I would like you to work out your day-care situation in the next week so that you will be able to come in on time.	Nonetheless, I would prefer that you refrain from this behavior while in the office.
State the consequence (adverse and/or positive).	If you are unable to correct this situation soon, we may need to look at whether you will be able to continue working here. I would hate to do that because you are such a good employee and I look forward to seeing this situation turn around soon.	If you do not refrain from this conduct, I may have to talk with our supervisor about this. However, if you do stop, I believe we can have a positive working relationship.
Invite options for solution.	I would like to know what ideas you have to correct this situation, or if there is anything I can do to help.	(Not used)
Check for understanding and/or compliance.	(Not used)	Do you understand what I am asking?

discussion. You must understand the practices and policies in your organization regarding such matters and how they apply to the particular situation you are addressing. You should know, for example, your company's disciplinary procedures, workplace conduct rules, union contract provisions regarding conduct and discipline, and policies for managing and evaluating performance. Your organization will likely also require you to consult with the human resources department or other appropriate authority before making a decision to confront an employee. Together with these authorities, you will explore all the issues and facts of the situation to ensure that confronting an employee is appropriate, fair, lawful, and consistent with how the organization has applied policy under similar circumstances.

When you have determined that addressing a performance or discipline issue is appropriate, you would apply the assertive confrontation model through formal counseling. Two types of formal counseling are typically used under a progressive discipline regime:

> Hold a *formal counseling session prior to discipline* when you believe the employee will correct his or her behavior or performance and avoid formal discipline.

- The *formal counseling session prior to discipline* is intended to address discipline or performance problems before using the actual progressive discipline process. A supervisor would hold such a session in the hope that the employee will correct his or her performance or behavior and avoid formal discipline.
- In a *disciplinary counseling session*, the supervisor invokes a step in the progressive discipline process. If no discipline has previously been invoked, a verbal warning is typically the first step, followed by a written warning, suspension, and termination, as the behavior or performance becomes worse or fails to improve. Depending on the severity of the performance or behavior, however, the supervisor may choose to skip steps in the process, thus hastening the path to termination if matters do not improve. Further explanation of the discipline process is provided in a later section of this chapter.

When holding either of these sessions, keep these considerations in mind before engaging in an assertive confrontation discussion:

- **Do your homework.** Be sure that you have the facts, observations, and documentation at hand that support your case for corrective action. Has the situation been properly investigated, and is the corrective action contemplated supported by policy and the organizational culture? Conducting an investigation is discussed later in this chapter.
- **Ensure that the employee has been given sufficient warning regarding his or her performance or conduct.** The formal counseling session or discipline should not be a surprise to the employee. Has the employee had the chance to correct his or her behavior prior to taking such a serious step? Have you given the employee feedback regarding performance? Have you had previous discussions in a less formal setting in which you addressed the same issues?
- **Consider the physical setting and time of day for holding the session.** The session should be held in private and at a time you can focus solely on the employee and the issues. Do not allow for interruptions, such as phone calls, pages, or the annoying bell on

your computer indicating that an e-mail has arrived. Unless there is an immediate need to confront the individual, hold the session at a time when the employee will be most receptive and least disruptive in the event he or she becomes upset. Often, the best time to meet is the end of the day so that the employee does not have to return to work.

■ **Check your emotions before addressing the situation.** You may be so frustrated with the individual's behavior or performance that you are not sure you can remain objective and calm. If need be, put the session off an hour or two or until the next day to give yourself time to reflect on your feelings and prepare for a thoughtful session. Having another supervisor or human resource's professional present may help you maintain focus and provide a witness. When you do meet, maintain control of the discussion. Remain firm on the discipline you are invoking, the need and expectation for change, and the consequences for noncompliance.

■ **Maintain a tone that is impersonal and serious.** Be specific regarding the reasons for the discipline or potential discipline. The assertive confrontation model will help you do this. Remember to use I-statements instead of you-statements. Remember also to avoid labeling individuals or their behavior and to make statements that have some basis in observation or verifiable fact. Consider the following examples:

Instead of saying:	Say instead:
"You are always late."	"I have observed you come in five minutes late for the past two weeks."
"You are so irresponsible."	"I believe that your actions do not reflect the professional, responsible behavior that is expected of all of us in this organization."
"I can't believe how insensitive, uncaring, and disrespectful you have been to me."	"When you ignore my instructions and bad-mouth me behind my back, I feel that my authority is not being respected."

■ **Allow the employee to state his or her side.** It is important to hear the employee's side of the story in the event you have not fully considered all the issues. During counseling prior to discipline, this information may mitigate any discipline you later invoke or alleviate the need for discipline altogether. There should be no surprises when invoking formal discipline. Hear the employee out in case there is new information to consider or to better understand his or her viewpoint.

■ **Engage the employee in dialogue regarding specific action items, goals, and strategies that the employee will use to correct the behavior or performance deficit.** Despite the inherent negative connotation of progressive discipline, the intent of the discipline session is to provide guidance and direction on how the employee may return to acceptable levels of performance. If you

> If you approach an employee in a supportive atmosphere, he or she is more likely to work with you to identify specific steps to bring about change.

approach the dialogue in a supportive atmosphere, the employee is more likely to work with you to identify specific steps to bring about change. Reduce these steps to writing, including time frames, and obtain the employee's agreement to comply. You should also come to an understanding of how you will monitor progress.

- **Document the session.** At a minimum, the following items should be discussed and documented:

    - The results of your investigation, including the specific behaviors you have observed that warrant discipline
    - Your initial warnings
    - The employee's explanations and responses
    - The discipline decision
    - The consequences you have identified if further misconduct or performance deficits occur
    - A plan for corrective action

Further, you should prepare a summary letter to the employee, confirming what was discussed and the corrective action expected.

STANDARD DISCIPLINE PROCEDURES

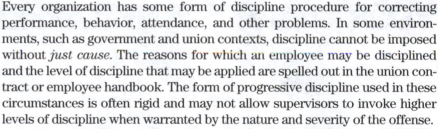

Every organization has some form of discipline procedure for correcting performance, behavior, attendance, and other problems. In some environments, such as government and union contexts, discipline cannot be imposed without *just cause*. The reasons for which an employee may be disciplined and the level of discipline that may be applied are spelled out in the union contract or employee handbook. The form of progressive discipline used in these circumstances is often rigid and may not allow supervisors to invoke higher levels of discipline when warranted by the nature and severity of the offense.

Many employers use instead progressive discipline processes that allow managers to select the type of discipline that is warranted based on the facts and circumstances of the situation. In these environments, distinctions are drawn between major and minor violations, and discipline is imposed accordingly. For example, the first instance of insubordination may result in a written warning or suspension without pay, while subsequent offenses will lead to termination. Further, for even the first instance of physical threat or violence, a manager would likely skip steps in the discipline process and terminate an employee immediately.

The typical progressive discipline process involves a four-step procedure:

1. *Verbal warning.* This is often an informal counseling session or the first formal step after an initial counseling session. Though verbal, such a session is generally documented as a memo or informal note in the employee's file. Depending on the circumstances, an employee may be issued a few verbal warnings before proceeding to the next step. The employee is also counseled that further violations may result in further steps in discipline.

2. *Written warning.* The supervisor describes in a formal document the specific rule or conduct violation and the time, dates, facts, and other circumstances supporting the warning. The document further specifies what the employee must do to correct the behavior and a time frame (thirty, sixty, ninety days) for doing so. If warranted, an action plan agreed to by the supervisor and employee may be appended to the document. Signature lines for the supervisor and employee are also included. The employee's signature indicates acknowledgment of receipt of the document but does not necessarily reflect his or her agreement with its contents.

3. *Suspension.* Suspensions generally range between one day and two weeks or more. Leave is usually unpaid. Some employers issue a series of suspensions, which escalate in length after each recurrence. In some cases, employers issue a "suspension pending termination" in which the employer suspends the employee for a brief period (three to five days) while it investigates the matter to ensure that termination is warranted. When termination is contemplated either as the next step or immediately following the return from suspension, the notice should state as much.

4. *Termination.* Before termination, the employer must ensure that the reasons for termination are appropriately documented and that the prior steps in the discipline process were observed. However, serious offenses, such as violent behavior, drug or alcohol use during work, disregard of safety rules, insubordination, theft, destruction of property, falsification of documents (such as the job application), and carrying concealed weapons, generally warrant immediate dismissal without proceeding through the other steps in the process. The employer must also review the record to ensure the decision is consistent with what has been done for other employees under similar circumstances.

Finally, some organizations adopt *positive discipline*[2] or *discipline without punishment.*[3] Such systems involve giving employees a series of "reminders" regarding their behavior with time to think about the behavior, its impacts on others and the organization, and whether they feel they can abide by the work rule or expectation violated. Final steps in this process involve "decision-making leave," whereby employees are given time off to think about whether they desire to continue to work with the organization. If they agree to abide by the rules, termination occurs only when further violations happen within a specified period. The intent of these systems is to remove the punitive nature of warnings, give employees choices, and support them as they work to correct behaviors.

A discipline system is a tool employers use to seek a change in behavior or end the employment relationship. It is not the only tool. In fact, a discipline process is often a last resort after other measures have been tried. Other tools include training, reassignment, transfer, demotion, reduced wages or bonuses, probation, and employee assistance programs and counseling. Before pursuing discipline, carefully assess the employee's situation to consider whether other measures will more effectively bring about positive change. Ideally, such exploration should occur as early as possible upon discovery of a performance deficit, such as during a counseling session prior to discipline or during the verbal warning stage.

CONDUCTING INVESTIGATIONS OF MISCONDUCT

Many situations involving misconduct require investigation before you confront an employee regarding his or her behavior. This is particularly true when one employee complains about inappropriate behavior perpetrated against him or her by another employee. To ensure a thorough and fair investigation, follow these steps:

1. *Determine the appropriate individual to investigate the matter.* Issues with serious legal implications, such as discrimination, harassment, and workplace violence, may require the intervention of others, such as human resources or legal counsel. Report such matters to the appropriate officials and assist them with their investigation. Day-to-day conduct rules violations generally fall to the supervisor to investigate. However, if there is the potential that you will be perceived as biased, consider deferring the matter to another supervisor to investigate.

2. *When possible, obtain a written complaint.* When one employee complains to you about the behavior of another, ask for a written statement. If your company has a complaint form, provide it. However, do not insist on a written complaint. Many issues, such as discrimination and harassment, will require you to investigate regardless of the existence of a written complaint. Further, some issues evolve based on your observation or through secondhand sources without a specific complainant coming forward.

3. *Interview the complaining or aggrieved employee.* Meet in private with the employee and obtain the facts, dates, places, and specific behaviors the employee finds offensive. During the initial interview, do not indicate whether you agree or disagree with the employee or guarantee any specific outcome. Further, do not make promises regarding preserving anonymity or holding the matter in absolute confidence. In many cases, such as discrimination and harassment, you will be obligated to proceed with an investigation once you become aware of the situation, regardless of the complainant's willingness or reluctance to proceed. Instead, assure the individual that the matter will be treated confidentially and shared only with those individuals necessary to investigate and resolve the complaint.

4. *Notify the appropriate parties regarding the complaint.* Inform only those parties who "need to know." Specifically, inform the appropriate authorities within the organizations who will conduct the investigation or who should be kept apprised of the situation as you investigate. Further, if you do not supervise the alleged perpetrator or witnesses to the alleged misconduct, notify their supervisors regarding your need to investigate. You may need to

work together to address the situation. In all cases, stress with others that the matter should be held in confidence.

5. *Interview the alleged perpetrator.* Inform the individual of the reason for your interview and the general nature of the complaint. Indicate that you are simply gathering information regarding the complaint and that no assessment has yet been made regarding the truth of the allegations. Then, proceed with obtaining the relevant facts and information from the employee's point of view.

6. *Interview relevant witnesses.* Both the complainant and the alleged perpetrator may have provided names of witnesses. Interview each witness in private, obtaining the relevant facts and information within their knowledge. Assure witnesses that the matter will be treated confidentially and obtain their assurance that they will keep the matter confidential. Also, share only those aspects of the complaint that are necessary to obtain relevant information from them.

7. *Obtain all relevant physical and electronic evidence.* The parties or witnesses may have relevant photocopies, e-mails, photographs, drawings, written statements, memos, and other relevant documents and physical evidence. Ask them to produce this evidence.

8. *Evaluate the evidence.* Review your investigation notes, party and witness statements, and physical evidence. Consider whether this evidence proves the allegations of the complaining employee. Also, evaluate it against the particular policy or rule alleged to have been violated. Does evidence point to such a violation? Do you have sufficient evidence to decide either way? Is further inquiry or follow-up required?

   When weighing the evidence, you will also need to consider the credibility of the parties and witnesses, their reputation for honesty, any motive either party has to lie or distort the truth, and the opportunity either party or a witness had to observe an important matter firsthand.

9. *Reach a conclusion and take appropriate action.* After you have thoroughly investigated the matter, you will draw one of three conclusions:

   a. *The employee violated the policy.* If this is your conclusion, proceed with progressive discipline, using the appropriate direct confrontation message. Further, state your conclusions in writing and indicate the reasons for the discipline and the specific corrective actions that the employee must take. Specify how the situation will be monitored and that future violations may result in further discipline. You may also notify the complaining party that you are addressing the violation with the perpetrator, but you should not reveal the manner or severity of the discipline or corrective action as such matters are confidential between the employer and the disciplined employee. Remind both parties to respect the confidential nature of the process.

b. *The investigation was inconclusive.* If a violation cannot be clearly established based on the evidence presented, notify the parties of this conclusion. You may also want to indicate to the complaining party that such a conclusion does not mean that the incident did not occur as alleged or that you doubt the veracity of the complaint (unless, of course, you do). When harassment or other clearly offensive behavior is involved, remind the parties that such behaviors are not tolerated and would be considered violations of the company's policies.

c. *No violation has occurred.* Notify the parties of this outcome. The investigation of the complaint should not be held against either party, and your investigative file should be maintained separate from the employees' personnel files. If the complaining party has particular concerns regarding this outcome, counsel the employee regarding the situation and, if deeper personal issues are involved, make the appropriate referrals. Also, when an employee indicates a desire to seek further legal action, affirm his or her right to do so while indicating that your investigation has concluded.

THE ASSERTIVE CONFRONTATION MESSAGE AND PERFORMANCE EVALUATION

> *Performance management* involves more than drafting and meeting to discuss an annual *performance appraisal* document. It encompasses a cycle of activities.

A common criticism of performance evaluation is that it is often imposed on the employee with little opportunity to provide input on defining performance expectations or how they will be met. Further, the process is perceived as nothing more than an annual or semiannual event in which the supervisor and employee meet to discuss a "performance appraisal" document. A better term is *performance management*, which is intended to encompass a cycle of activities that are typically performed on an annual basis, such as the following:

- Planning performance, including defining major job duties, developing performance standards for how these duties will be performed and evaluated, and establishing job and developmental goals and objectives
- Monitoring performance, including providing ongoing coaching and feedback to the employee as needed throughout the cycle period
- Evaluating the employee's job performance in fulfilling performance standards and meeting job and developmental goals and objectives
- Reviewing performance with the employee, including discussing what the employee accomplished, how well the employee performed these accomplishments, and progress in meeting job and developmental goals and objectives
- Renewing the performance plan for the next cycle, including establishing new performance expectations and job and developmental goals and objectives

While all phases of this process are important, it is critical that the employee understands how he or she is performing during the review period. It is through coaching and feedback, of course, that you will engage, as warranted, in assertive confrontation to encourage performance improvement. When doing so, keep these considerations in mind:

1. *Tend toward the "softer side" when delivering the assertive confrontation message.* Unless there are clear behavioral issues you need to address through the performance review, particularly recurring behaviors that have not changed despite previous warnings, craft a message that utilizes the components for softening the message. Many performance issues involve basic human error and are correctible. The employee needs support, not harshness. While remaining firm that performance must improve, strive to convey that you remain fully in the employee's corner.

2. *Base criticism on job-related criteria.* Be sure that the focus of your message is on specific, measurable behaviors related to the job and the performance factors you have identified and not on the employee's personality.

3. *Maintain objectivity.* A supervisor may make any number of evaluation and rating errors, usually with no conscious intent to do so. For example:

   - *Leniency error:* The appraiser overstates or understates performance and gives a higher or lower rating than deserved.
   - *Halo error:* The appraiser rates a performer high or low on all factors based on the impression he or she has on performance of a specific factor.
   - *Recency error:* The appraiser gives greater weight to recent performance, discounting performance that occurred earlier in the review cycle.
   - *Central tendency error:* The appraiser tends to avoid ratings at the extreme ends of the scale, such as "excellent" and "substandard," choosing instead to rate in the middle range of the scale.

   Be careful to avoid these errors when addressing a performance deficit. If necessary, consult another manager, human resources representative, or someone in higher authority for a second opinion to ensure that your decision is an objective one.

4. *Be consistent and guard against discrimination and bias.* For the performance factor in question, be sure you have or would engage in a similar discussion with any other employee with a similar performance deficit. If you let the factor "slide" in the past, you may be on shaky ground if you raise the same issue with this employee.

5. *Be forthright and honest.* Be clear about the performance factor you are addressing and how the employee can improve performance. If there is a chance that the employee will be rated negatively or that progressive discipline or a performance improvement plan may be implemented, be clear about how the failure to correct the concern may be reflected in the review or result in other adverse consequences.

6. *Allow time to correct the performance problem.* So that the employee has the chance to improve performance before receiving

a negative rating, give the employee adequate time to improve the level of performance before preparing your appraisal (usually between thirty and ninety days). If you are nearing a review period, either extend the review period or include the factor as part of the activities for review in the next cycle.

7. *Have good documentation.* When meeting with the employee to discuss the performance deficit, have the initial performance plan document in hand to cite the specific performance factor, standards of performance expected, and objectives to be met. Following the meeting, document your conversation, including specific reference to the performance factor you are addressing. For many situations, it may also be necessary to prepare a written action plan with the employee to outline how the performance deficit will be corrected.

RESPONDING TO DEFENSIVE AND ANGRY REACTIONS

No matter how sensitive and supportive you are when delivering your message, it will not always be received well. While some individuals may respond positively, others are likely to respond at some level of defensiveness and anger. When invoking progressive discipline, in particular, expect resistance. Many of these responses can be addressed in the normal course of conversation, and the individual can be brought back to seriously considering how to correct the concern after being allowed time to vent.

When you sense that the individual is becoming agitated, attempt first to calm him down. In *Anger at Work: Learning the Art of Anger Management on the Job*, Hendrie Weisinger refers to this as reducing the individual's "anger arousal."[4] If the individual is standing or pacing about, offer him a seat. If you are in an open area, suggest that you go to your office or a private conference room to talk about the situation. Suggest that you take a short break and then return to discuss the matter. The point is to try to get the individual to slow down his responses. In the process, you are also showing your intent to be helpful and to listen.

Often, individuals need time to vent their frustrations, after which they become better prepared to address the situation in a more objective manner. To help someone do this:

- Ask him to share his feelings about the situation and why it is upsetting him.
- Give him ample time to fully vent his emotions and do not interrupt him.
- Do not judge, criticize, or dismiss his feelings or reasons for having these feelings at any time while he is speaking or after he has finished.
- Exercise active listening techniques, such as sitting up, giving eye contact, making gestures, and providing other signals ("uh huh," "I understand," "I see") to indicate you are listening.
- Paraphrase his statements to indicate that you understand what he is saying. Keep working at it until he is satisfied that you do understand.

- Ask clarifying questions to help guide his telling of the story, such as

  - Why does this situation upset you?

  - Can you give me an example of how you have struggled in the past with meeting this performance standard?

  - Help me understand what you mean by "unfair" and "stupid."

  - What exactly am I doing that is so harsh and uncaring?

Once you have come to an understanding of the situation, be empathetic. Even if you cannot completely agree with the individual or why she feels as she does, let her know that you might feel the same way if you were in her position. Do not discount her feelings with statements such as "That doesn't make sense to me" or "There's no reason for you to feel that way." Instead, use validating statements such as "I can see that you are upset" or "I see you're really bothered by this situation." Ask her how she would like to resolve the situation but do not agree to any proposal that you are not prepared to implement. Work with her to clarify expectations regarding outcomes. If the individual's perspective regarding possible resolution varies widely from what is possible or acceptable to you, identify where and how your and her perspectives differ and talk through these issues until clarity is achieved. Encourage her to focus on solutions that are mutually beneficial and promote the positive consequences for pursuing such solutions. The more you show that you are supportive, patient, and understanding, the more likely the individual is to calm down. When she perceives that you are trying to constructively help her sort through feelings without blaming, judging, or criticizing, she will be more willing to engage in constructive problem solving.

REMAINING CALM AND FOCUSED

While you have planned carefully to deliver a supportive confrontation message that is objective and absent personal attacks, you should not expect the employee to respond with the same level of objectivity and professionalism. Despite your best efforts to minimize defensive responses, the employee may engage in personal attacks that may in turn cause you to react negatively. Recall the discussion regarding "fight or flight" in Chapter 2. Just as the employee may engage in "fight or flight" responses based on the perceived threat your message poses, his negative reactions may likewise trigger a "fight or flight" response in you. Consider these approaches for remaining calm and focused:

The employee's negative reactions to your assertive confrontation message may trigger a "fight or flight" response in you. Plan accordingly to avoid these reactions and to remain calm.

- **Plan for it.** As you prepare to approach the employee, know the buttons the employee may push, plan for the employee to push them, and know how you will respond when he does. Be conscious of these times when they arise in the course of your conversation with the employee.
- **Don't take it personally.** When your buttons are triggered, recognize this and do not take the attacks personally, even though that is the individual's intent. Taking in such attacks, within reason, is part of your job as manager.
- **Slow down.** If you do find yourself beginning to react, such as raising your voice in response, increasing the speed and tempo

of your speech, or engaging in nonverbal actions to express your frustration, intentionally break this cycle. Stop talking, take a deep breath, lower your voice, or suggest a quick break before resuming. Find a way to slow yourself down to give yourself time to think and refocus.

- **Don't be baited.** Refuse to engage in argument or debate with the employee. The employee may try to put you in a position in which you will feel a need to defend your actions. Instead, reaffirm that you have made your decision concerning the discipline or performance and that now is neither the time nor place to engage in such discussions. If the opportunity for pursuing recourse through formal processes is available, such as filing a grievance with HR, advise the employee of these avenues.

- **Set limits.** If the employee's personal attacks move from basic statements regarding how you execute your role as manager to deeply hurtful comments about your personal life or character or clearly derogatory or offensive statements in violation of policy, state that such discussions are off limits and that you may need to end the meeting if the behavior persists. Similarly, if the individual raises his voice beyond acceptable levels and repeated attempts to encourage him to lower his voice are unsuccessful, reinforce that you cannot effectively listen and try to help him if he continues to yell.

- **End the meeting when warranted.** As noted previously, giving an employee time to work through his anger can be a natural and productive process that can serve as a precursor the employee needs in order to begin constructively finding solutions to the issues presented to him. If this venting process becomes counterproductive and also risks making you angry, end the meeting. It is also time to end the meeting if the employee's behavior escalates to potentially violent and physically threatening behavior. Chapter 16 provides further instruction on managing workplace violence.

TOOLS TO ADD TO YOUR CONFLICT SURVIVAL KIT

Before engaging in a confrontation discussion, take time to prepare a script, rehearse it, and obtain feedback from a trusted colleague.

1. *Prepare your script.* Think of the situation for which you anticipate needing to confront an employee (or someone else in your work or life) and complete a script using the elements identified.

Situation:
Describe the behavior:
Express the feeling or emotion:
Explain the impact:
Empathize (if appropriate):
State the desired change:

State the consequence (adverse and/or positive):
Invite options for resolution and offer support:
Check for understanding and compliance:

2. *Rehearse your script.* Find a colleague you trust. Ideally, find another supervisor who may be somewhat familiar with the situation and the employee you are planning to confront. Ask him or her to assume the role of this individual and to listen as you deliver the message.

3. *Critique your message.* Ask your colleague for an honest assessment of your message and delivery. How did he or she feel when receiving the message you communicated? Were you direct, yet supportive? Was your message clear? Were you offensive in any way? How might you improve on your message and delivery?

4. *Do it again.* Go through this process a couple of times, refining your message and delivery based on your own impressions and the feedback from your colleague. Also, though your colleague may listen during only your first or second run-through, have him or her truly play the role of the employee and interrupt, argue, sigh, or engage in any other possible behaviors, given what you know about the individual. This will enhance your practice under more "real-world" conditions.

5. *Do it for real.* Having prepared your script and rehearsed it, you are ready to confront the individual in the most direct, yet supportive, manner possible. When you engage in this discussion, do not take your script with you. The point of your rehearsal is to get as comfortable as possible with your message without sounding rehearsed or as though you are reading. If you need an aid when meeting with the individual, reduce your script to bullet points to remind you of the key parts of your message.

PERFORMANCE CHECKLIST

- An effective way to confront an employee regarding a performance or conduct concern is through preparing and delivering the appropriate assertive confrontation message.

- An assertive confrontation message incorporates the following elements:
  - Describe the behavior.
  - Express the feeling or emotion.
  - Explain the impact.
  - Empathize.
  - State the desired change.
  - State the consequence.
  - Invite options for resolution and offer support.
  - Check for understanding and compliance.

- Variations of the assertive confrontation message can be used to address an employee's discipline problem, discuss the need for performance improvement, or address day-to-day issues involving an individual who has engaged in inappropriate or offensive behavior.

- Such messages are necessary when you want to make clear that change is expected or adverse consequences may result.

- An assertive confrontation message may initially be received with defensiveness or anger, so you must be prepared to address such responses in a caring manner while not defusing the gravity or importance of the message you are delivering.

- When delivering an assertive confrontation message, the manager should understand when her own "fight and flight" responses may be triggered and plan accordingly so that she does not react inappropriately to the employee's angry or defensive behaviors.

TEST YOURSELF

True/False

For each statement below, check true or false.

TRUE   FALSE

_____ _____ 1. When delivering an assertive confrontation message, it is generally best to include an adverse consequence you are prepared to implement if the individual does not change the inappropriate behavior.

_____ _____ 2. When confronting an individual about gross misconduct, such as violating a clearly established safety rule, bullying, or sexual harassment, showing empathy as part of your assertive confrontation message is not only recommended but also essential.

_____ _____ 3. When confronting a mature individual who is capable of responding proactively to your assertive confrontation message, you probably will not need to ask him or her if she intends to comply with your request.

_____ _____ 4. Showing empathy when delivering the assertive confrontation message can be helpful to the individual you are confronting because it shows that you support the individual despite the behavior you wish him or her to change.

_____ _____ 5. When the outcome of an investigation of misconduct is inconclusive, it is still appropriate to remind the parties involved of company policy and the consequences for violation.

MULTIPLE CHOICE

Circle the letter next to the best answer for each question. On a separate sheet of paper, state why you chose that answer.

1. All of the following examples illustrate elements of the supportive confrontation message, *except*

   a. "I would prefer that you no longer use such language around me."

   b. "When you tell dirty jokes, I feel embarrassed."

   c. "You're boorish, rude, and condescending."

   d. "Over the past few days, I have overheard you telling offensive jokes in the break room."

2. The basic supportive confrontation message requires that you (1) describe the behavior, (2) explain the impact, and (3) state the desired change. However, you may want to also include other elements, such as show empathy, state a consequence, and check for understanding, because

   a. the basic message does not provide the essential information that the individual needs to know in order to correct his or her behavior.

   b. depending on the circumstances, the basic message may be more direct and blunt than you intend.

   c. every situation requiring direct confrontation also requires that you have empathy for the other person and his or her behavior.

   d. the recipient of the message will not see the point of changing his or her behavior unless you state an adverse consequence for noncompliance.

3. At the conclusion of an investigation of alleged misconduct, the person conducting the investigation may appropriately draw any one of the following conclusions, *except*

   a. evidence was inconclusive to determine whether the individual engaged in the misconduct; no discipline should be invoked.

   b. evidence demonstrates that the individual engaged in the misconduct, as alleged; appropriate discipline should be invoked.

   c. evidence demonstrates that the individual may have engaged in the misconduct, as alleged; appropriate discipline should be invoked.

   d. evidence demonstrates that the individual did not engage in the conduct, as alleged; no discipline should be invoked.

4. Preparing a script and rehearsing it with a trusted colleague before approaching the individual to whom you must deliver the supportive confrontation message is helpful for all the following reasons, *except*

   a. it allows you to memorize your message and state it verbatim, which will minimize the likelihood you will overlook an important element of your message.

   b. it helps ensure that the delivery of your message will be as natural, supportive, and as direct as possible.

   c. the trusted colleague can role-play the individual you must confront, allowing you to refine your message in a "real-world" simulation.

   d. it allows you to receive an honest critique of your effectiveness in conveying the message in a manner that is least likely to create defensiveness in the other person.

5. The *halo error* is the tendency to

   a. overlook all behavior or conduct problems that any objective observer would conclude requires corrective action.

   b. be too "soft" when delivering a supportive confrontation message.

   c. rate an individual high or low on all performance factors based on an impression of the individual's performance of some specific factor.

   d. rate all performance as outstanding, in contrast to the "horns error," which is the tendency to rate all performance as substandard.

DISCUSSION QUESTIONS

1. Discuss specific scenarios wherein the supportive confrontation model would be effective and ineffective, including factors to consider in deciding whether it would be an effective tool.

2. Some practitioners believe progressive discipline is an effective tool for returning employees to acceptable levels of performance. Others believe that once you begin progressive discipline, you have essentially eliminated any possibility of ever returning to a productive, positive working relationship with an employee. What is your view? What do these views say about the possibility for resolving conflict in the workplace?

CASE: CONFRONTING AN EMPLOYEE WITH A CONDUCT ISSUE

Tamiko Timid is one of only two women working in delivery. Recently, she approached Joe and said Fred Staid, delivery team leader, has been bothering her. Specifically, she says he has been telling off-color jokes among some of her male coworkers. While these men do not seem to mind the humor, Tamiko says it is offensive to hear. Tamiko also says Fred has been staring at her. Joe has never witnessed Fred behaving in this fashion, though he is aware that Fred is a "good ol' boy" and likes to spend time with the other men during break times. Joe has no idea what they talk about.

Both Fred and Sally Ambitious have applied for the vacant customer service team leader position. Joe has not made any decision regarding this position and is, in fact, not sure either individual would be appropriate. Though excellent employees, Fred can be gruff at times and Sally can be pushy. Neither of these qualities seems appropriate for a customer service position. Joe, of course, has not shared his thoughts on this matter to anyone but Jim Talent.

Fred has made some subtle inferences lately that suggest that he believes he is not being fairly treated. He recently reacted when Joe offered praise to Sally for coming up with a creative solution to a tricky customer service problem. Fred said that he could have come up with a similar solution, but that it takes time to think through these problems. Fred has also been critical about Sally's "recklessness" in making decisions. He complains that Sally is a "newby." Joe also overheard Fred grumble to a coworker that, "I've been around this place long enough; it's about time I got a break for a change."

Finally, it is known that Tamiko and Sally are close friends and often go to lunch together. Tamiko has hinted that she would love to have Sally as her boss.

Joe has asked to meet with Tamiko to discuss her concerns further.

Case Questions

As a class or in small groups, discuss the following:

1. What specific steps should Joe take to investigate Tamiko's concern? Include in your response the facts, data, and other information that must be collected, questions to ask, and strategies to take to ensure a thorough, fair process.

2. Assuming Tamiko's concerns have merit, what script would you use to confront Fred and other men on the delivery team? In your response, be sure to consider all elements of the script.

3. What angry or defensive responses might you anticipate from Fred or the other men? How would you respond?

As an alternative to class discussion, have students pair up and practice a role-play, using the assertive script activity in "Tools to Add to Your Conflict Survival Kit."

ALTERNATIVE PROCEDURE FOR ONLINE LEARNING FORMATS

Option 1: Have students individually review the case and respond to the questions, posting them by a specified date for all other students to review. Have students offer responses or critiques to at least two other student responses. Engage in addition forum discussions or chats as time and interest permit.

Option 2: Assign students in pairs and have them engage in off-line conversation in which they practice the assertive script as outlined in "Tools to Add to Your Conflict Survival Kit." Have each student practice the role of Joe and the role of Fred or another man on the delivery team. Ideally, students should plan to meet to have these discussions. If meeting isn't possible, they should engage in such discussions via telephone, teleconferencing, or videoconferencing. Upon completion of the role-play, have each pair jointly prepare responses to the questions and post them within a specified time period. Engage in additional follow-up forum discussions and chats as noted in Option 1.

PERSONAL GROWTH EXERCISE

As you engage in assertive confrontation techniques, the temptation may be to emphasize the corrective aspects of the message and to overlook its more supportive aspects, such as expressing empathy, stating positive consequences for anticipated behavioral change, and offering support to help the individual change. Depending on the nature of the issue you are addressing, and your skill and tact in delivering your message, you may come across as more harsh than you intend and create more defensiveness and anxiety in the recipient than is warranted.

To overcome this, look for opportunities to make your assertive confrontation message as supportive and caring as possible. Practice delivering assertive confrontation messages to the point at which the recipient of your message not only understands the importance of changing his or her behavior but also feels supported and encouraged to do so for positive results in his or her life and relationships with you, team members, and others.

TO LEARN MORE

The following sources provide further insight on direct confrontation models and responding to anger and defensiveness:

Fauteux, Kevin. *Defusing Angry People: Practical Tools for Handling Bullying, Threats and Violence*. Far Hills, NJ: New Horizon Press, 2011.

Pachter, Barbara. *The Power of Positive Confrontation: The Skills You Need to Know to Handle Conflict at Work, Home, and in Life*. New York: Marlowe and Company, 2000.

Patterson, Kerry, Joseph Grenny, Ron McMillan, and Al Switzler. *Crucial Confrontations: Tools for Resolving Broken Promises, Violated Expectations, and Bad Behaviors*. New York: McGraw-Hill, 2005.

Stone, Douglas, Bruce Patton, and Sheila Heen. *Difficult Conversations: How to Discuss What Matters Most*. New York: Viking, 1999.

Weisinger, Hendrie. *Emotional Intelligence at Work: The Untapped Edge for Success*. San Francisco: Jossey-Bass, 1998.

The following sources provide additional information regarding discipline, performance evaluation, and conducting investigations of misconduct:

Aguinis, Herman. *Performance Management*, 2nd ed. Upper Saddle River, NJ: Pearson Education, 2008.

Goodwin, Cliff, and Daniel B. Griffith. *Supervisor's Survival Kit*, 11th ed. Upper Saddle River, NJ: Pearson Education, 2009.

Grote, Dick. *The Complete Guide to Performance Appraisal.* New York: American Management Association, 1996.

Lee, Christopher D. *Performance Conversations: An Alternative to Appraisals.* Tucson, AZ: Fenestra Books, 2006.

Mader-Clark, Margie, and Lisa Guerin. *The Progressive Discipline Handbook: Smart Strategies for Coaching Employees.* Berkeley, CA: Nolo Press, 2007.

Repa, Barbara Kate. *Avoid Employee Lawsuits: Commonsense Tips for Responsible Management.* Berkeley, CA: Nolo Press, 1999.

Williams, Anne H. *How to Discipline and Document Employee Behavior.* Brentwood, TN: M. Lee Smith Publishers, 2002.

NOTES

1. Kerry Patterson et al., *Crucial Conversations: Tools for Talking When Stakes Are High* (New York: McGraw-Hill, 2002), 131–36.

2. Stephen P. Robbins and David A. DeCenzo, *Supervision Today!* 3rd ed. (Upper Saddle River, NJ: Prentice Hall, 2001), 458.

3. Dick Grote, *Discipline Without Punishment: The Proven Strategy That Turns Problem Employees into Superior Performers*, 2nd ed. (New York: American Management Association, 2006).

4. Hendrie Weisinger, *Anger at Work: Learning the Art of Anger Management on the Job* (New York: William Morrow, 1995), 74–75.

SPECIAL SITUATIONS: "OPPORTUNISTIC" EMPLOYEES, WORKPLACE VIOLENCE, TERMINATIONS, AND BULLYING

PERFORMANCE COMPETENCIES

After you have finished reading this chapter, you will be able to

- Identify the behaviors of low-level maturity or "opportunistic" employees and adopt appropriate strategies for managing them

- Identify and manage employees who are aggressive or potentially violent

- Identify workplace bullies and adopt strategies for dealing with them

- Identify situations that warrant termination and end the employment relationship accordingly

As you progress in your career as a manager and develop conflict resolution skills, you will find that most individuals you encounter possess the fundamental goodwill, trust, and maturity to engage effectively in conflict resolution. You will also encounter individuals for whom no manner of encouragement, solicitousness, or goodwill will change their behavior or willingness to cooperate. These include "opportunistic" employees, aggressive and potentially violent employees, employees for whom the only alternative is termination, and workplace bullies. While working with such employees is never easy, knowing and using the right methods for managing them will help you facilitate a process for correcting their behavior, minimizing the harmful impacts of their behavior, or expediting their removal.

Fighting, to me, seems barbaric. I don't really like it. I enjoy out-thinking another man and out-maneuvering him, but I don't like to fight.

Sugar Ray Robinson

WHAT IS AN "OPPORTUNISTIC" EMPLOYEE?

An "opportunistic" employee generally operates at a low level of maturity and generally does not possess the capability to engage in meaningful, collaborative conflict resolution processes. Such an individual

- Fails to recognize how his actions contribute to the circumstances for which he is being corrected or disciplined
- Resents and resists authority, particularly of a direct supervisor
- Shifts blame to others or to circumstances, such as a lack of training, a failing on the part of the supervisor, unfair or discriminatory treatment, or coworkers who he claims are making his life difficult
- Presses to gain every advantage with no consideration for others' concerns while viewing any concession as weakness and an opportunity to exploit
- Concocts conspiracy theories to explain how and why he is being treated so unfairly, seeks to garner allies to his cause, and demonizes those who do not agree
- Engages in manipulative behaviors to escape or delay the consequences for his actions, such as

  - Avoiding discussions where his behavior will be addressed
  - Continually raising new and unrelated issues that challenge the supervisor to respond, often in writing
  - Claiming illness or disability and making claims of unfair treatment based on these considerations
  - Creating an excessive paper trail to defend against the slightest perceived injustice

- Threatens procedural and legal action if the suggested consequences for his actions are carried out and often pursues such action to the point of exhausting such processes even when it has been established that he is clearly wrong

HOW DO I MANAGE THE OPPORTUNISTIC EMPLOYEE?

> Managing an opportunistic employee requires containing the employee's inappropriate behaviors within narrow parameters.

If you have an opportunistic employee in your organization, you will generally not be successful in your attempts to achieve integrative, win/win resolutions. Instead, you will likely experience continual conflict and will, accordingly, need to adopt strategies that contain inappropriate behaviors within narrow parameters and, if those parameters are violated, lead to an end of the employment relationship.

1. *Don't hire an opportunistic employee!* If you manage such an individual, the unfortunate reality is that he or she has been allowed into the workplace in the first place! Perhaps your screening processes need to be evaluated to prevent similar

hires in the future. Next time, before hiring someone, check your processes for interviewing applicants and conducting appropriate criminal background and reference checks. Often, prior employers will give only neutral references, limiting the information to basic details such as start and end dates and salary. To encourage a prior employer to provide additional information, such as that pertaining to performance, secure a release from the applicant authorizing the prior employer to provide such information. Work with your human resources department to identify additional methods for screening applicants and weeding out employees who may present a potential performance or conduct problem. If, after taking all possible measures to avoid a bad hire, you have lingering doubts, do not hire the individual.

2. *Use the probationary period to identify potential problems and, if in doubt, do not retain the employee.* Employers generally impose probationary periods to allow the employer time to evaluate whether the employee is a good "fit" for the organization and, if not, to release him or her. Typical probationary periods range between 30 and 180 days. During this period, most or all rights afforded regular, non-probationary employees under the organization's disciplinary and grievance procedures do not accrue. Terminating employment during this period is, therefore, easier. Though some opportunistic employees may successfully hide their flaws until after the probationary period has ended, many others will not be able to do so. It is best to identify these issues early and cut your losses if you have any doubt about the employee's potential for success within the organization.

3. *Know your organization's disciplinary procedures, conduct rules, union contract provisions (if unionized), and other policies regulating employment, and follow them consistently.* You must further know the difference between a major and a minor infraction. A major infraction, such as theft, violent acts, or harassment, may be a basis for immediate termination. A minor infraction, such as an attendance problem, is not generally the basis for immediate termination, though an accumulation of similar infractions may lead to termination. You must know these policies and be determined to implement them for any employee who violates a rule, declines in performance, or engages in inappropriate behavior.

4. *Prepare for the long haul.* The opportunistic employee often treats the process of dealing with her behavior as a game. And it is a game that she is prepared to win by manipulating and outmaneuvering you until you relent. Supervisors often do not have the staying power, courage, or motivation to meet such an employee at this level of engagement. To be effective in managing such an employee, your approach must be to confront her firmly and consistently until *she* relents. You must meet the employee toe to toe until either she changes her behavior, gives up and leaves, or is terminated.

> An opportunistic employee treats the process of dealing with his or her behavior as a game. You must keep at it until he or she changes, gives up and leaves, or is terminated.

5. *Be relentless with documentation and follow-through.* Whether for the first time or the tenth, *each time* you must document unacceptable behavior, follow organizational procedures precisely, and consult the appropriate authorities, such as human resources and legal counsel. You must build your case completely and thoroughly so that you can specify the precise behaviors that are unacceptable; support them with appropriate documentation, witnesses, and observations; and succinctly connect them to the relevant policy violated or step in discipline warranted. You must also be sure that the consequences you are imposing are equivalent to, and neither more nor less stringent than, what you would impose on any other individual for similar violations. You must allow no opportunity for arguments and accusation that may weaken your case. If such weaknesses exist, rest assured that the individual will exploit them. Your efforts will pay off if and when the individual pursues legal action and you must prepare a case that can survive legal scrutiny.

6. *Maintain a dispassionate, levelheaded demeanor.* When you confront an opportunistic employee, she may try to distract you with accusations, irrelevant issues, and other actions calculated to distort your message or draw you into a quagmire of point/counterpoint. To counteract such tactics:

   ▪ Draw up a script and rehearse it before meeting with the employee to confront her about her behavior.

   ▪ Make a list of reactions you might expect from the individual and prepare possible responses, including reasoned responses to legitimate questions and more direct responses to close off discussion of irrelevancies. Examples of such reactions and possible responses are provided in Exhibit 16-1.

   ▪ Discuss your plan of action with a colleague and rehearse your script with him or her. Have your colleague role-play the individual and provide feedback regarding your approach.

   ▪ Have your colleague join you in the meeting to witness the interaction and help you maintain focus.

7. *Do not be the person's friend.* When confronting the individual, you must be clear about the corrective action you are taking and the precise steps you expect him to follow. When you do otherwise and allow room to consider options, the individual may look for ways to delay consequences or expected results or attempt to push responsibility back on you. While your natural tendency may be to show sympathy, you must instead be stingy with such expressions. The individual may use your kindness as an opening to make excuses for his behavior and pleas for leniency. He may also perceive your response as weakness and search for more "chinks in the armor." Your message should thus be short and succinct:

   [After describing the behavior]: Joe, this conduct is completely unacceptable and must change. If it does not change, we will be pursuing the appropriate steps that will lead ultimately to your termination. [Omitting expressions of feelings, support, and sympathy.]

> Your kindness and expressions of empathy may be viewed as signs of weakness or opportunities to make excuses for inappropriate behavior or pleas for leniency.

The following are a few examples of specific statements to consider in response to various reactions raised by the opportunistic employee.

EXHIBIT 16–1
What to say to the opportunistic employee

Threats of legal action:

You are free to pursue the avenues of recourse available to you. We believe our actions are appropriate and supportable and will be prepared to respond as warranted. But let me be clear—your threat to pursue legal action will not stall or deter the approach we are taking. You must either improve your performance or your employment will be terminated. The choice is yours.

Objections to the performance expectations imposed:

We feel these expectations are realistic, achievable, and consistent with the level of performance of others in your position. If you are not willing to meet them, you may want to consider looking for other employment. Please understand that these expectations are not negotiable, and we expect you to meet them as directed.

Claims you are treating the employee differently and more severely than someone else:

If I observed that any other employee was not meeting performance expectations, I would be having this same conversation with that person. As it is, you are not meeting your performance expectations and, therefore, I am supervising you more closely until your performance improves.

Raising irrelevancies, arguments, and other diffusion tactics:

The issue we are discussing is your level of performance, not whether Fred and Ginger are having an affair. We are also not talking about how unfair the new attendance policy is. I have addressed these issues as warranted. They have nothing to do with your disruptive behaviors and your failure to produce your reports on time. Let's get back to talking about those concerns.

The employee persists with irrelevancies:

I will not entertain these issues further. Fred and Ginger's alleged affair and the new attendance policy are closed for discussion. I have asked you to meet with me to discuss your performance. If you are unwilling to do this, I will have no choice but to pursue appropriate discipline.

Claims of illness, disability, or other emotional or personal concerns:

I certainly want to be sure that your needs are met and that our policies and procedures are respected. I will be happy to provide information to you regarding these matters and help you to get the assistance you need. However, I am pursuing this discipline and expect you to meet the performance expectations as outlined.

8. *Consider presenting a written performance improvement plan or action plan rather than discuss performance expectations at length during a meeting.* In your document, be explicit about measures by which acceptable performance will be judged and timelines for compliance. Indicate that while you are open to questions about these expectations, there is no negotiation about the performance expectations themselves or the fact that they must be met or further consequences will follow. You must, of course, be explicit about these consequences and your intention to enforce them.

9. *Plan for a short meeting.* When you deliver the "bad news" regarding disciplinary action, entertain only appropriate questions and comments, close off discussion of extraneous issues, and conclude the meeting. The individual may want your attention and will, if allowed, drain your energy and resources by holding you captive. You must cut off her sustenance. When she realizes she cannot have your attention, she may desist. Of course, if she seeks this attention elsewhere or otherwise continues to engage in unacceptable behaviors, you must be prepared to follow up with the consequences you outlined. If that means another meeting to impose the next level of discipline or next level of performance expectations, be prepared to revisit the issue using the same process.

PREPARING FOR THE LONG HAUL WHEN MANAGING THE OPPORTUNISTIC EMPLOYEE

With many employers, such as those in the private sector, effectively dealing with the opportunistic employee may be a relatively expeditious process. With other employers, such as public sector and unionized employers that generally provide employees more procedures for grieving adverse employment actions, the process may be more arduous. Indeed, grievance procedures and other protections are among the tools opportunistic employees use to delay the inevitable and to badger and discourage their managers and coworkers. This is all the more reason to be prepared for the long haul. You must have staying power as you patiently and professionally make all the right moves, over and over again, to insist on correct behavior or terminate employment. Exhibit 16-1 offers examples of how managers should respond in these situations.

RESPONDING TO AGGRESSIVE AND POTENTIALLY VIOLENT BEHAVIORS

Employees who are aggressive or potentially violent pose an additional level of complexity that you must manage beyond the challenges of supervising the typical opportunistic employee. To address such situations, it is important to have some understanding of workplace violence and the characteristics of individuals who are prone to violent behavior. You should also understand your organization's workplace violence policies and procedures and how the organization addresses matters such as responding to emergency situations, providing professional referral services, and making discipline and termination decisions related to violent or potentially violent behavior. A key to this understanding is knowledge of the measures your organization takes to prevent violence through supportive management systems and structures. Consult your human resources department or legal counsel regarding these matters and seek appropriate training on workplace violence.

With this in mind, you may eventually be called upon to confront a potentially violent individual regarding performance or conduct concerns. You must be prepared to handle the situation in the safest manner possible. While some of these situations will require immediate precautionary or emergency action (addressed later in this chapter), you can safely address many of these situations with appropriate planning and preparation. Consider the following:

1. *Know who and what you are facing.* In many situations, you may already have a fair understanding of how the individual is behaving and whether he is exhibiting stress, hostility, aggression, negativity, or other signs of potentially violent behavior. You must assess how these underlying influences will impact your interactions. For example:

   ▪ How does the individual feel about himself?

   ▪ Does he have high or low self-esteem?

   ▪ Are there health, financial, or emotional concerns?

   ▪ How are his relations with others?

   ▪ Is he friendly and helpful, or is he withdrawn, uptight, and angry?

   ▪ How does he feel about you?

   ▪ Have you done something, rightly or wrongly, to upset him?

   ▪ Does he trust you?

   The more you know up front, the better prepared you will be to handle reactions when they do occur.

2. *Set up the meeting in anticipation that the individual may become aggressive or potentially violent.* Consult with appropriate authorities, such as human resources, security personnel, or the organization's crisis management team, about how best to handle the meeting. In most cases, including particularly significant disciplinary events, it is a good idea to have someone join you. If you do meet alone with the individual, inform others when and where the meeting will occur. If your concerns are more serious, have the appropriate security personnel waiting nearby inconspicuously (i.e., in an adjoining room or waiting in the hallway) in case assistance is needed. Finally, in the event the meeting becomes heated, arrange for someone to call or knock on your door with a predetermined message to end the meeting.

> When arranging to meet with an aggressive or potentially violent employee, have a colleague join you, or at least let others know when and where you are meeting.

3. *Arrange the meeting space to maximize safety.* Arrange seating so that you are closest to the door in case you need to make a quick exit. You must also decide whether to leave the door closed or slightly ajar. While privacy is a concern, so is your safety. If you want the door to remain open, take measures to find a location and time where others are not likely to be nearby and overhear your conversation (except, of course, appropriate security personnel). Have a barrier, such as a desk, between you and the individual, and keep hard objects, such as paperweights or staplers, out of reach. If your office cannot accommodate these details, find a conference room that will.

4. *Proceed in a professional, supportive manner while remaining vigilant for escalating behaviors.* When meeting, give the individual the benefit of the doubt that he or she will act in a professional manner. If the purpose of the meeting concerns a performance or conduct concern, proceed as you normally would to confront the issues in a constructive, supportive fashion. When appropriate, allow the individual the opportunity to present his or her side of the story and to vent emotions and frustrations. Offer your support and ask how you can help. If the individual reacts within tolerable bounds, manage these reactions in order to restore calm and to get him or her to refocus on the matter at hand. Your meeting may thus conclude uneventfully. At some point, however, a line may be crossed that is beyond your ability to manage. You must have the judgment and instinct to know where this line is and be prepared to respond appropriately and quickly.

5. *End the meeting if behavior escalates.* Look for signs indicating that the individual is not able or willing to calm down and focus, such as the following:

   ▪ Failing to listen, not allowing you to speak, interrupting, and constantly arguing

   ▪ Animated gestures, such as flailing arms, angry or cold stares, and repeated finger pointing

   ▪ Uncontrollable crying

   ▪ Standing up and pacing

   ▪ Yelling, screaming, cursing, and name calling

   ▪ Stomping feet on the floor or pounding fists on the table

   ▪ Threats, insults, and accusations

   ▪ Raised voice and belligerent tone

If these or other behaviors persist and are making you uncomfortable, it is time to end the meeting. To do this, use the appropriate exit line:

> I cannot discuss this with you when you are [screaming at me, acting so angry, making threats, etc.]. When you can talk about this in a calm manner, we can resume this conversation. Until then, we'll need to end this meeting.

If this does not immediately close down the discussion, state, "if you do not leave my office right now, I will leave." If this is unsuccessful, state,

> If an employee's behavior escalates, end the meeting. Announce your intention to end the meeting and leave the room, but if in doubt about your safety, simply leave.

"I'm leaving now," and exit the room. On the other hand, if you are truly uncomfortable, simply leave and forgo these courtesies. Your safety is the paramount concern.

ADDITIONAL CONSIDERATIONS FOR ENSURING A SAFE WORKPLACE

Whether as an outcome of your meeting to confront an employee's conduct or based on other assessments you have made, you should keep in mind a few additional considerations to ensure a safe and secure workplace.

Referrals. If you are aware of personal, emotional, or psychological concerns that may be the cause of the employee's inappropriate behavior or that may lead to the employee eventually becoming violent, make the appropriate referrals for counseling. Many companies have employee assistance programs to which employees can be directed. Such services can assess employees' needs and further direct them to the appropriate medical, psychological, or other support professional. While encouraging self-referral may be sufficient in many cases, you may want to make a mandatory referral if the situation is more egregious and retaining the employee, absent such assistance, is in doubt.

Suspension and leave. If the inappropriate behavior must change before the employee can be returned safely to work, suspend the employee or place him or her on leave pending a mandatory fitness-for-duty evaluation establishing that the employee can return to work. If medical or health concerns are involved, place the employee on medical leave for treatment and assessment. This includes alcohol and drug abuse, which are often associated with incidents of workplace violence.

Legal considerations. Before making any referral or recommendation regarding treatment or counseling, seek legal counsel to ensure you are complying with relevant laws, such as the Americans with Disabilities Act and the Family and Medical Leave Act. Care must be taken to avoid labeling the individual, implicitly or explicitly, as "disabled," "ill," "mentally disturbed," "emotionally unstable," or other terms that run afoul of such laws designed to protect against discrimination based on actual or perceived disabilities or health conditions.

Safety first. If the individual exhibits violence or you believe violence is imminent, get out of harm's way. This may mean removing yourself from the office or floor, or even hiding under a desk or in another room. You must use your judgment as to the safest exit or hiding place when the incident occurs. Do not be a hero. If you do not have specialized training in handling crisis situations, do not act as though you do. As you seek to protect yourself, also warn others of the threat, particularly those who work in the same area as the employee or whom the employee has specifically identified as potential targets. Once you have sought your own safety and warned others, call the appropriate authorities. This may be either security personnel within the organization or local law enforcement.

Once the individual has left or been removed from the premises, ensure that he or she does not return. Seek legal counsel to pursue a restraining order preventing the employee from coming on or near the premises. If criminal activity is involved, contact the appropriate authorities, such as the police or prosecutor, to pursue appropriate action.

Preserve dignity. It is important to remember that any decision to confront a volatile employee can be traumatic for the individual. The person will often feel a great sense of loss and a blow to his or her pride and esteem when confronted with discipline or termination. If he or she is already feeling vulnerable, the act of confronting the employee may be all it takes to tip the scale toward violence. Therefore, make every effort to treat the individual with dignity while seeking also to protect yourself and others.

BACKGROUND INFORMATION ON WORKPLACE VIOLENCE

Workplace violence includes physical assault, threatening behavior, and verbal abuse. Depending on how organizations choose to define it, this can also include, among other behaviors, workplace harassment, intimidation, bullying, acts causing psychological trauma, acts causing damage to company property and resources, and domestic violence brought to the workplace.[1] Threats can be verbal, written, or communicated through electronic means and can come in the form of (1) direct threats to commit harm to another; (2) indirect, veiled, or subtle messages or statements suggesting potential harm; or (3) conditional threats suggesting that harm may be avoided "if" or will occur "unless" some condition is complied with.[2]

The National Institute for Occupational Safety and Health (NIOSH) classifies workplace violence into four categories:[3]

- Type 1: Criminal acts by individuals who have no other connection to the workplace, such as assault, robbery, trespassing, and homicide. This also includes terrorist attacks.
- Type 2: Violence directed at employees by others for whom the organization provides services, such as customers, clients, patients, students, or inmates.
- Type 3: Violence against coworkers, supervisors, managers, or others in the workplace by current or former employees.
- Type 4: Violence by someone who doesn't work in the organization but who has a personal relationship with an employee, such as a spouse or domestic partner.

Many organizations have policies that specifically address workplace violence and include, at a minimum, these components:

- A statement of zero tolerance for workplace violence
- Definitions and examples of threatening and violent behavior
- Consequences for violating the policy, including mandatory termination for actual violent acts perpetrated against others or company property
- Encouragement and mechanisms for reporting incidents of workplace violence, including contact information of the offices, representatives, and security personnel designated to assist
- Protocols and procedures for conducting internal investigations of complaints of workplace violence and threatening behaviors

In addition, many organizations incorporate other mechanisms to ensure against violence or to prepare and equip the workforce in the event of violent events and emergencies, including the following:

- Mandatory training on workplace violence, harassment, and anti-discrimination laws
- Appropriate screening devices to screen out employees with poor work records or who demonstrate the potential for violent or criminal behavior, including, as job-relevant and permitted by law, checks on employment and educational background, criminal background, job and character references, military and driving records, and credit reports.
- Searches of applicants' self-disclosed information on Internet sites, such as social media and blogs, to screen out job applicants with the potential for violence
- Employee assistance programs and related referral services
- Drug- and alcohol-free workplace policies and related treatment programs
- As permitted by law, drug and alcohol testing, including preemployment and of current employees
- Work/life programs and other services focused on assisting employees with issues like domestic abuse; stress management; child and elder care; financial management; work/family/life balance; and health, wellness, and nutrition
- A crisis management team that meets regularly to assess the potential for incidents of violence in the workplace and to develop and implement emergency response strategies
- Implementation, communication, and practice (drill) of an emergency action plan so employees will know how to respond in the event of violent incidents
- Policies prohibiting the possession and use of firearms and weapons on company premises
- Supervisory training focused on empowering and motivating employees and developing trusting supervisor/employee relationships and conflict resolution skills

While workplace violence manifests itself in many forms, behaviors can be categorized in one of three stages:

Stage one: The individual has the potential for violence but is not necessarily violent at the moment. He is often argumentative, challenges authority, swears and curses, uses derogatory and sexually explicit language, intrudes on another's personal space, taunts and shouts at others, and engages in other forms of verbal abuse and harassment.

Stage two: The individual exhibits an increased potential for violence through behaviors that have escalated beyond the first stage. He often makes threats of physical and psychological harm, can be extremely argumentative and disrespectful of organizational policies and procedures, and tends to blame others for his difficulties.

Stage three: The individual has realized his potential for violence through action. He engages in physical confrontations and altercations with others; displays and uses weapons; and commits criminal acts such as assault, sexual assault, arson, vandalism, and theft. He may also be suicidal.

In the earlier stages, there is a tendency to dismiss behaviors as inappropriate and to ignore the signs that such behaviors may lead to violent acts. Such incidents are, therefore, not reported pursuant to the workplace violence policy and addressed accordingly. The opportunity to correct the behavior and provide the employee with the appropriate support is lost, leaving the organization vulnerable to violence. Supervisors must be vigilant to the early signs of violent behavior and respond accordingly. They must also encourage employees to report incidents that concern them regarding their coworkers so that management may intervene as early as possible. Though no list can be all-inclusive, some of the early warning signs follow:

- Fascination with weapons and incidents of workplace violence (such as what is reported in the news)
- Use and abuse of alcohol or drugs
- History of past acts of violence or aggressive behavior
- Poor prior work history
- History of failed personal relationships
- Low self-worth
- Poor personal hygiene
- Recent adverse changes in personal life or career, such as divorce, demotion, or being passed over for promotion
- Marginal performance and decline in productivity
- Increased absenteeism
- Claims of injustice or unfair treatment
- Loner, detached personality, with no social support
- Poor peer relationships
- Bullying behaviors or being the target of bullying
- Personality changes, including mood swings and feelings of persecution
- Irritable, reactive, and easily angered
- Experiencing financial difficulties
- Experiencing severe stress, often brought on by recent events
- When confronted, becomes defensive, blames others, and resists change

Note that while these signs may exist in current employees, many also exist in employees who have recently left the organization, particularly those who have been terminated as a result of performance or conduct issues. Continued vigilance, therefore, is required in the event a former employee may return to the workplace and pose a threat.

The presence or absence of any one of these signs, or a combination thereof, is no guarantee that violence will or will not occur in the workplace. Each situation is unique and should be addressed on a case-by-case basis. Care must also be taken not to label an individual's behavior as potentially violent just because he or she is experiencing some difficulties. Doing so may lead to isolating the employee and limiting his or her opportunities. Rather, these early warning signs offer the opportunity to intervene in a supportive manner to assist an employee and perhaps avoid more drastic responses later on, such as corrective or disciplinary action or a call for an emergency response after the employee has acted out.

ENDING THE RELATIONSHIP

When your relationship with an employee becomes untenable, there is little alternative but to terminate the individual's employment. In addition to the strategies and techniques shared previously, termination involves special considerations:

1. *Be sure that termination is warranted.* Is termination appropriate given the nature of the behavior or performance concern, its severity, and its pervasiveness? Is termination the logical next step in discipline after previous steps have failed to bring about change? If you have properly documented the concerns along the way, consulted with the appropriate authorities such as human resources, and given the employee sufficient warning and time to correct the behavior, then you likely stand on firm ground to terminate employment.

2. *Make all severance arrangements prior to meeting.* At the termination meeting, be prepared to provide the employee his or her final paycheck, including vacation and other earned leave due, and information about retirement, continuation of benefits under COBRA, and other benefits to which the employee is entitled. Also provide information regarding any assistance the company will provide regarding unemployment, referrals, outplacement, employee assistance, and other services. This should include information on how the company will handle reference checks. For terminated employees, this policy may be limited to giving neutral references only. You should also have a checklist for return of items in the employee's possession, such as keys, phones, pagers, files, equipment, clothing, proprietary or confidential information, and computers and software. In addition, be prepared to answer any questions about these matters that the employee may have. If in doubt about specific questions, refer the individual to human resources for clarification.

3. *Arrange the meeting.* Have another manager or a representative from human resources attend the meeting with you. This ensures that another witness from management is present. It also better ensures your safety.

    Special care must be given to the timing of the meeting. Common sense may suggest that the end of the day and the end of the week are the best times for implementing terminations. However, scheduling such meetings early in the day and early in the week gives the employee the opportunity to have questions answered before the day or week ends, whether these questions are posed to you, human resources, the local unemployment office, other state agencies, or to an attorney. The earlier and sooner you can facilitate

Arranging the termination meeting earlier in the week allows the employee time to take constructive action regarding the situation before he or she has the chance to brood about it over the weekend.

the information-gathering process, the more quickly the employee will be able to move beyond the termination decision to constructive action. Holding off the termination discussion until the end of the week could be problematic if the employee truly does become upset or has the potential for violence. He then has the chance to brood over the weekend, which could lead to problems Monday morning. Of course, if there is any concern about the potential for violence or other disruption to the work environment, dismiss the employee immediately regardless of the time or day of the week.

4. *Keep the meeting brief and to the point.* Focus on the facts and policies warranting termination. The termination message should be succinct, outlining the issues that led up to and support the termination, followed by the pronouncement of termination:

> Dan, you were given a written warning on April 1 for being tardy from work for three days in the month of March. On May 1, you were suspended for three days for being tardy two additional days in April. As you know, we need our employees at work on time in order to handle customer calls. Therefore, our policy does not allow employees to be tardy more than six times in a 180-day period. You were tardy on May 5 and you came in late today. Therefore, I have no other choice but to terminate your employment, effective with this meeting.

> Milton, you were warned on December 8 that one more derogatory remark toward Jack would result in immediate termination. As you know, I sent you home early yesterday, pending the investigation of the complaint by Jack that you called him a "fag." I found that at least two other employees overheard you make this comment. Therefore, I am terminating your employment.

> Keep your emotions in check. Do not allow the employee to upset you. If the employee becomes emotional, seek to shift the focus back to the termination notice, severance details, and any assistance and referrals to other resources the company will provide upon exit. If the employee wants to argue with you about the fairness of your decision, reinforce your belief that the decision is fair and consistent with policy, and that nothing will change this outcome. Then, end the meeting.

5. *Arrange for a safe, dignified exit.* Upon conclusion of the termination meeting, decide how you will collect the items in the employee's possession that must be returned to the company and how you will allow the individual to collect his or her things and leave. Organizations vary in their policies concerning exiting employees. Because some businesses involve highly confidential or sensitive information, security personnel oversee the process for allowing employees to return to their offices to retrieve their personal items before escorting them from the premises. If you have no standard procedure for handling exits, you will need to decide the best way to handle the matter to preserve the individual's dignity without exposing the organization to increased liabilities, such as

violence, sabotage, theft, or destruction of property. Arranging the termination meeting at a time when the fewest people are around will minimize the employee's feelings of embarrassment and maintain discretion as the employee does what is necessary to leave. You could also arrange for a time that the employee can return, such as after hours, so he or she can leave the building quickly upon termination and return when people are not around.

If the employee poses no real risk and is, under the circumstances, amiable and trustworthy, you can ask the employee how he or she would like to handle leaving. At the other extreme, if there is a risk, arranging for an immediate escort may be necessary. Under such circumstances, you can either allow the employee time to collect personal belongings, under careful watch, or have someone collect these items to give to the employee upon exiting or to deliver to his or her home later. You would use this alternative when it is necessary to avoid an unpleasant scene or because the employee has become or is likely to become violent upon leaving the termination meeting.

The individual will likely have some final details to address that cannot be handled during the termination meeting, such as arranging for continuation of benefits under COBRA, returning company items that are at home, or follow-up questions concerning retirement benefits. Provide the individual with the name and contact information for the representative who can address these questions. If you are concerned about the possibility that he or she might randomly contact employees in the organization, either with legitimate questions or to harass them, be explicit that the individual should contact only this representative who will relay relevant questions to the appropriate individual in the organization. If the former employee needs to return to the premises, but you believe such a return could be disruptive, instruct the individual to arrange the visit in advance with the designated representative.

6. *Treat the terminated employee with compassion, dignity, and respect.* If you can honestly say so, let the employee know that you wish her well and that you believe she will find another position in another organization better suited to her needs and interests. But even if your support is limited, realize you are dealing with someone who is fragile. Termination is traumatic and leaves the terminated employee feeling vulnerable. Taking the right steps in termination will go far in preserving the individual's dignity and minimizing conflict and the potential for violence.

> Termination is traumatic and leaves the terminated employee feeling vulnerable. You must handle the termination with compassion, dignity, and respect.

TOOLS TO ADD TO YOUR CONFLICT SURVIVAL KIT

As you consider whether opportunistic or potentially violent employees exist within your workplace, create standardized checklists to help you gauge the following:

1. Whether an employee exhibits the characteristics described for an opportunistic employee. In addition to characteristics identified in this chapter, add your own that you believe accurately describe those

individuals for whom you must be relentless in your efforts to insist on changed behavior or take steps leading to termination.

2. Whether an employee exhibits the characteristics of an aggressive or potentially violent employee. Again, using the information provided in this chapter as a starting point, create your checklist based on characteristics that are particularly pertinent to your organization and nature of business.

It will be especially helpful if you can consult with human resources or other professionals when creating these checklists. Such tools serve merely as a starting point to help you identify at an early stage when an employee possesses the appropriate characteristics requiring monitoring and perhaps intervention.

Beyond checklists, discuss with other supervisors, human resources professionals, and legal counsel how the organization as a whole should respond when an opportunistic or potentially violent employee is identified. If training on such matters is not ordinarily provided or the organization's policies and procedures are not clear, look for ways that you and your colleagues can create a culture of understanding regarding how to address such matters.

The key to success in this area is being as proactive as possible to prevent employees who possess these characteristics from creating adverse working conditions.

MANAGING WORKPLACE BULLYING

Gary and Ruth Namie, founders of the Workplace Bullying Institute and authors of *The Bully at Work: What You Can Do to Stop the Hurt and Reclaim Your Dignity on the Job*, define workplace bullying as follows:

> repeated, health-harming mistreatment of a person by one or more workers that takes the form of verbal abuse; conduct or behaviors that are threatening, intimidating, or humiliating; sabotage that prevents work from getting done; or some combination of the three.[4]

Bullying is distinct from other forms of rudeness and incivility. Perpetrators of generalized uncivil behavior do not direct their actions on specific "targets" whereas bullies do:

> The bully puts her or his personal agenda of controlling another human being above the needs of the employing organization. That control is typically a combination of deliberate humiliation and the withholding of resources that the Target requires to succeed in the workplace.[5]

More overt bullying behaviors include yelling, screaming, shouting, and threats of violence. Bullying also includes behaviors intended to demean the target, insults and put-downs, teasing, sarcastic remarks, and hostile glares and gestures. When the bully is the boss, bullying can take the form of setting impossible deadlines and work standards, creating undue pressure and stress, overworking employees, constant criticism, and bringing up old mistakes. It can also include depriving employees of work and professional development opportunities, withholding information and resources necessary to complete tasks, and depriving employees of social interaction with others. Bullying also includes behind-the-back behaviors such as spreading malicious gossip, discrediting the target before others, and going to higher-ups with criticisms about the target.

According to survey data from the Workplace Bullying Institute, 35% of U.S. workers have experienced bullying. Men constitute 62% of the bullies while women constitute 58% of the targets. Women bully other women disproportionately compared to other bully-target gender combinations (man-on-woman, man-on-man, and woman-on-man). While bullying can occur among coworkers (18%) and by lower ranking employees against higher ranking targets (10%), the majority of bullies outrank their targets (72%).[6]

When you are the manager and observe or are informed of bullying by one employee toward another, stepping in to correct the bully's behavior is less problematic than when the bully is your boss or someone in higher authority. This text focuses mostly on providing the manager with tools and strategies for resolving conflict when he or she has the authority to directly control or influence the behaviors of others. However, many bullying and similar harassing and opportunistic behaviors are perpetrated by individuals in authority and, therefore, require different strategies, as noted next.

Put a name to it. People who experience traumatic events tend to deny their impact. By putting a name to the behavior you are experiencing, whether you call it bullying, harassment, or some other inappropriate behavior, you are putting responsibility for the situation squarely on the shoulders of the bully and not blaming yourself. You are also taking back control of the situation and a step toward finding concrete solutions.

See yourself as a target, not a victim. The Namies' use of the term *target* is intentional. When someone adopts a victim mentality, she often second-guesses herself, wondering if there is something she has done or could have avoided doing that would have kept her out of harm's way. She may also make excuses for the bully's behavior and become sympathetic toward her abuser. Rather, the target is simply in the wrong place at the wrong time and is the unfortunate recipient of the bully's venom. Rejecting the victim mentality is another means of taking control of the situation.

Avoid or minimize exposure to the bully. Whenever possible, use e-mail or phone communication rather than face-to-face interaction. When you must interact directly, consider the boundaries you will establish, whether physical such a having a desk or table between you and the bully or personal such as topics of conversation that are off limits for discussion. Seek to schedule necessary meetings so they are short in duration. Meet in locations that are more public and in which you have predetermined seating and proximity to the door. Discourage drop-in visits, limit talk time if you must engage, and remain standing or, if seated, stand and prepare to exit when the bully approaches.

Utilize support systems. Bullies thrive when their targets remain isolated. Targets who view themselves as victims may tend to keep quiet. Instead, the target can take advantage of the natural support systems around her to talk through concerns, remain grounded, realize she's "okay," and

> Whenever possible when working with a bully, use e-mail or phone communication rather than face-to-face interaction, set appropriate physical and personal boundaries, and minimize meeting time.

strategize ways to address the situation. This would include friends and family, as well as coworkers who may be experiencing similar treatment or are at least aware of the treatment she is experiencing. The target may also need to consider pursuing professional help, whether counseling to deal with psychological issues or a lawyer to consider legal options. Note that bullying per se is not unlawful in most jurisdictions, but the nature of the bully's behavior may implicate other illegal conduct, such as harassment under Title VII, slander, defamation of character, and intentional infliction of emotional distress.[7]

Do good work. One reason bullies bully is that the target represents a threat by virtue of his productivity, ability to work well with others, superior knowledge or ability, or similar traits reflecting positively on his competence and citizenship within the organization. Bullying behavior is often the outcome of feelings of inadequacy or insecurity, and the bully responds accordingly when he or she perceives a threat based on another's success or acceptance within the organization. As a target, take solace in the fact that you are doing good work for which the bully is in an odd sense complimenting you! Don't retaliate with the same kinds of unprofessional behaviors to which you have been subjected. Maintain your integrity and continue to be a model. By doing so, you avoid supplying credible evidence to the bully on which he or she can criticize you or undermine your efforts before others.

Prepare yourself to expose or confront the bully. If you do decide to confront the situation, the Namies advise that targets must first prepare themselves psychologically. They must assess whether they "have enough stamina to see the fight through to the end."[8] They must assess the reasons for fighting and for not fighting back. Reasons for fighting back include satisfying the need for fairness and equity for oneself and others and the need to move on with dignity. Reasons against include the physical and emotional toll on the target's health, the toll of dealing with a defensive employer, and potential economic (job) loss.[9] The Namies note that because HR is part of management, targets should not automatically expect HR to be supportive or responsive.[10]

Expose the bully. If you decide to expose the bully, the Namies recommend the "rule of 2," which means bringing your complaint to an individual who is at least two levels above the bully in rank, such as a high-level executive. The Namies suggest making a business case for dealing with the bully or even removing the bully because of the costs of the bully's action on the bottom line. Such a case should present an objective view of the bully's behavior and a case for the bottom-line costs and adverse impacts on the organization.[11] It should also be dispassionate. The Namies note that "[i]f you drift into tales about the emotional impact of the bully's harassment, you will be discounted and discredited."[12] As you prepare to deliver the presentation, and after you have done so, have realistic expectations about outcomes for success, including deciding what you will do for your health, safety, and future if the organization is not as responsive as you would like.[13]

Confront the bully. If you decide to confront the bully, consider the precautions discussed previously. Do not expect the bully to change or to acknowledge any wrongdoing or responsibility for his actions. Do not offer any statements that suggest empathy for the bully or excuse his behaviors. Likewise, do not make statements that suggest any responsibility on your part for the bully's actions. Remember you are a target, not a victim. Because you should not expect the bully to change or to be reflective, your confrontational tone should be strictly behavior based, highlighting the key behaviors that offend you, the expected change you expect to see, and the consequences for noncompliance. The supportive confrontational message discussed in Chapter 15 (absent empathetic overtures) provides guidance that you can adapt for this situation.

Leave. Confronting or exposing the bully may not always be the right approach. The strategies identified above may be sufficient to help you cope and weather the storm, but, in the worst case, your only realistic recourse to preserve your health and dignity may be to leave. If possible, bide your time while aggressively seeking employment elsewhere. If you must quit without securing a job first, prepare for a graceful exit, preserving the positive relationships you have and securing references.

PERFORMANCE CHECKLIST

- As a manager, you will face situations in which no manner of goodwill and encouragement will bring about a change in behavior or performance. You must, therefore, confront an employee directly and insist on a change or expedite his or her removal from the workplace.

- Opportunistic employees are either unable or unwilling to take responsibility for their actions, respond to authority, and cooperate; they shift blame to others or to circumstances beyond themselves and engage in manipulative behaviors to avoid the consequences of their actions.

- When managing an opportunistic employee, prepare for a long process as you insist on behavior change, allow no room for the employee to deviate from clearly defined expectations, and be relentlessly consistent over time in your efforts to either force a change or terminate employment.

- When addressing aggressive or potentially violent behaviors, you must know your organization's workplace violence policies and procedures, be attentive to warning signs, and be prepared to respond appropriately.

- When confronting an aggressive or potentially violent employee, take appropriate precautions to avoid creating a violent situation, and learn how to firmly address performance issues while supporting the employee to get appropriate assistance to correct his or her performance or conduct.

- When preparing to terminate an individual's employment, be prepared to support your decision through appropriate documentation, observance of company discipline policies, and consultation with authorities such as human resources.

- When terminating employment, ensure the employee's safe and smooth exit from the workplace; preserve his or her dignity; and offer support, as necessary, during a clearly difficult time of transition in the employee's life.

- Responding to a bully may require different strategies than those identified previously, particularly when the bully is the boss or in a higher level of authority. To manage the bullying, the target should put a name to the behavior, see herself as a target rather than a victim, avoid or minimize exposure to the bully, utilize the support systems around her, continue to do good work, and prepare herself psychologically before deciding whether to confront or expose the bully or to leave the organization.

True/False

For each statement below, check true or false.

TRUE   FALSE

_____   _____ 1. Escorting a terminated employee off the premises is the universally accepted practice.

_____   _____ 2. When arranging to meet with an employee who is aggressive and potentially violent, it is essential to have another manager or a human resources representative present during the meeting.

_____   _____ 3. "Tell me why do you feel I am being unfair?" is a good question to ask an opportunistic employee.

_____   _____ 4. Nick recently broke up with his girlfriend. He was in a serious car accident in which he broke his leg. His car was totaled and he did not have insurance. When he finally returned to work, he had to take a bus because he couldn't afford to buy a car. At work, he kept to himself and didn't interact much with others. These are classic signs for the potential for workplace violence requiring immediate intervention before matters escalate to a violent situation.

_____   _____ 5. Eunice asked her manager, Trevor, a lot of questions as to why he terminated her employment. Trevor patiently answered them. The meeting lasted an hour. Trevor acted appropriately.

MULTIPLE CHOICE

Circle the letter next to the best answer for each question. On a separate sheet of paper, state why you chose that answer.

1. As a manager, you might engage in all of the following responses when dealing with an opportunistic employee, *except*

   a. initiating a performance improvement plan after repeated instances of shoddy work, which you suspect is due to a serious alcohol abuse problem.

   b. documenting repeated occurrences of argumentative behavior exhibited by the employee and use these occurrences to support your decision to issue a written warning.

   c. meeting with the employee who has consistently blamed you for his failure to perform at acceptable levels and ask why he is targeting you for his failures.

   d. referring the employee to the company's employee assistance program, while insisting that his emotional outbursts will not be overlooked when evaluating his performance.

2. Samantha, who is African American, threatens to file a discrimination charge for a recent verbal warning you issued, claiming that you have overlooked similar behaviors by at least three White employees. You have either disciplined these employees in the past for similar behaviors or you are confident their behaviors are dissimilar to the behavior for which you are disciplining Samantha. In response to Samantha's behavior, the *most appropriate* response would be

   a. I would be interested in talking with you more about why you believe I am discriminating against you. However, now is not the time.

   b. I didn't realize you would be so upset. Tell me more about your concerns. I certainly don't mean to hurt your feelings.

c. I'm not at liberty to discuss with you any disciplinary action I may have taken regarding other employees.

d. I don't have to entertain your clearly erroneous perceptions of your behavior and the behavior of your coworkers.

3. All of the following precautions would be prudent when meeting with an employee you believe is potentially violent, *except* meeting in a

a. place that affords you a quick exit.

b. place that is far removed from other offices and people.

c. place where hard objects are not easily accessible.

d. private place but tell others where and when you are meeting.

4. When you have identified an employee who you believe is exhibiting "stage one" behaviors for workplace violence, you *should*

a. refrain from responding in any way because it is too early to tell if the individual has the propensity to become violent.

b. address the behaviors you have observed, noting especially your concerns that the individual may become violent.

c. address the behaviors you have observed and ask if there is anything you can do to help the employee.

d. call security immediately and examine ways to monitor the employee's movements while at work.

5. When terminating someone's employment, the following practices are generally acceptable, *except*

a. if necessary, arrange for security to escort the employee from the premises upon conclusion of the termination meeting.

b. arrange details regarding how the employee will communicate with the company to handle the return of company property.

c. arrange details concerning calls for references from prospective future employers.

d. arrange the termination meeting for 4:45 p.m. on Friday when the termination decision was made on Wednesday.

DISCUSSION QUESTIONS

1. Do you find the methods suggested for managing opportunistic employees to be harsh and lacking in compassion? Discuss the implications of using such methods to address conduct and performance problems and the place that compassion plays when managing both opportunistic employees and other employees who are affected by their conduct.

2. In your workplace today, what are the factors, if any, that cause the greatest concern with respect to the potential for aggressive behavior or violence? Share these concerns and identify concrete changes you can implement to eliminate or lessen this potential. Engage in a similar analysis and conversation regarding bullying.

3. How difficult is it to terminate someone's employment? What are the procedures? What factors affect such decisions? Do these factors vary depending on the context in which the performance or conduct problem arose, the nature of the organization, and the levels of review the decision must pass within the organization? Discuss these questions and whether a termination decision should ever be easy.

As an outcome of an investigation regarding allegations that Fred Staid and a couple other men in the delivery section had been harassing a coworker, Tamiko Timid, Joe instituted corrective action and counseled the men regarding appropriate behaviors. As an outcome of his investigation, however, he learned that Anton Knox was unquestionably an opportunistic employee.

Joe learned that of all the men who had engaged in off-color humor, Anton was the worst. In fact, some of the men said Anton constantly swore and made derogatory remarks about women. Fred Staid also said that Anton was often late to work or called in sick. Sometimes, when he came to work, Fred thought he could smell alcohol on his breath but was reluctant to say anything to Anton. Instead, Fred counseled Anton on his tardiness and other behaviors that were affecting his performance without mentioning his suspicions that Anton was an alcoholic.

In the course of his investigation, Joe learned that Anton was indeed an unstable and volatile employee. When Joe initially questioned Anton concerning Tamiko's concerns, Anton became defensive, saying that Tamiko was out to get him fired. When Joe asked about Anton's use of foul and demeaning language, Anton proved the case by swearing at Joe. Further, after Joe concluded his investigation and met privately with Anton to counsel him, Anton stood up at one point, pointed his finger in Joe's face, and yelled at Joe. Joe immediately told Anton to leave for the day. The next day, Anton approached Joe and said he was sorry for his outburst.

Unfortunately, prior to Joe's investigation, Fred had not informed Joe about Anton's behaviors. Further, Fred had not instituted any formal discipline. Fred confided in Joe that formal discipline was tricky because Anton seemed to know just when he was about to cross the line. As soon as Fred considered formal discipline, Anton would return to an acceptable level of performance and be a "sweetheart" for a few weeks until the pressure was off. Then, as soon as Fred let his guard down, another incident would occur requiring Fred to counsel Anton again.

Joe realized that he had not been as attentive to Anton's behaviors or to Fred's supervision as he should have been. He also realized that it was time to insist that Anton either change his behavior and improve his performance or face termination. Therefore, Joe met with Jim Talent and asked what he should do.

Case Questions

In class, discuss the following:

1. Based on what you have learned in this chapter, what advice would you give Joe regarding how to respond? Specifically, what steps would you take to

   a. arrange a meeting with Anton?
   b. counsel Anton and address inappropriate behaviors?
   c. implement discipline, including termination if warranted?
   d. prepare for potentially aggressive or violent behavior?

2. When you confront Anton regarding his behavior, what specific behaviors, comments, and arguments might you anticipate from him as an opportunistic employee? Discuss these specific situations. How would you respond to these behaviors, comments, and arguments?

3. Would you say that Anton has been a bully to Tamiko? Why or why not? Assume for the sake of discussion that Joe and Fred had not been responsive to Tamiko's concerns and Anton's behavior toward her continued, unabated. How would you advise Tamiko to handle the situation?

As an alternative to class discussion, have students pair up and practice a role-play in which one student plays Joe and the other plays Anton. In the role-play, Joe counsels Anton. Each responds as he or she believes the characters would based on an understanding of the scenario and the role profiles. Following the role-play, the class reconvenes to discuss specific challenges Joe faced and how to overcome them.

Option 1: Have students individually review the case and respond to the questions, posting them by a specified date for all other students to review. Have students offer responses or critiques to at least two other student responses. Engage in additional forum discussions or chats as time and interest permit.

Option 2: Assign students in pairs and have them engage in off-line conversation in which one student plays Joe and counsels the other student who plays Anton. Ideally, students should plan to meet to have these discussions. If meeting isn't possible, they should engage in such discussions via telephone, teleconferencing, or videoconferencing. Upon completing the role-play, have each pair jointly prepare responses to the questions and post them within a specified time period. Engage in additional follow-up forum discussions and chats as noted in Option 1.

PERSONAL GROWTH EXERCISE

Some opportunistic employees will play on your emotions, and it will be tempting to become sympathetic and overly compassionate so that you overlook much needed discipline and corrective action. While expressing concern and offering support for employees are important, remember that the opportunistic employee tends to take advantage of such displays.

When you are tempted to be sympathetic to the opportunistic employee, keep in mind that you are not the only individual who likely finds such an employee to be disruptive and difficult to work with. By failing to implement appropriate discipline, you are performing a disservice to those employees who are performing their jobs appropriately. These employees also deserve your compassion and support.

The next time you must confront someone with a difficult disciplinary or corrective discussion, do not waver. While remaining supportive of employees' legitimate needs, be firm in your decision to impose appropriate discipline.

TO LEARN MORE

The following resources provide information regarding workplace violence, terminations, and bullying:

Daniel, Teresa A. *Stop Bullying at Work: Strategies and Tools for HR and Legal Professionals*. Alexandria, VA: Society for Human Resource Management, 2009.

Davenport, Noa, Ruth Distler Schwartz, and Gail Pursell Elliott. *Mobbing: Emotional Abuse in the American Workplace*. Ames, IA: Civil Society Publishing, 2005.

Davis, Dennis A. *Threats Pending, Fuses Burning: Managing Workplace Violence*. Palo Alto, CA: Davies-Black Publishing, 1997.

Kinney, Joseph A. *Violence at Work: How to Make Your Company Safer for Employees & Customers*. Englewood Cliffs, NJ: Prentice Hall, 1995.

Labig, Charles E. *Preventing Violence in the Workplace*. New York: American Management Association, 1995.

Lies, Mark A., II, ed. *Preventing and Managing Workplace Violence: Legal and Strategic Guidelines*. Chicago: ABA Publishing, 2008.

Namie, Gary, and Ruth Namie. *The Bully at Work: What You Can do to Stop the Hurt and Reclaim Your Dignity on the Job*, 2nd ed. Naperville, IL: Sourcebooks, Inc., 2009.

Needham, Andrea W. *Workplace Bullying: The Costly Business Secret*. Auckland, NZ: Penguin Books, 2003.

Paludi, Michele A., Rudy V. Nydegger, and Carmen A. Paludi Jr. *Understanding Workplace Violence: A Guide for Managers and Employees*. Westport, CT: Praeger, 2006.

Repa, Barbara Kate. *Firing Without Fear: A Legal Guide for Conscientious Employers*. Berkeley, CA: Nolo Press, 2000.

Sutton, Robert I. *The No Asshole Rule: Building a Civilized Workplace and Surviving One That Isn't*. New York: Warner Business Books, 2007.

Williams, Anne H. *How to Discipline and Document Employee Behavior*. Brentwood, TN: M. Lee Smith Publishers, 2002.

NOTES

1. Society for Human Resource Management, "Dealing with Violence in the Workplace," March 29, 2010, http://www.shrm.org/Research/Articles/Articles/Pages/Dealingwithviolence.aspx (accessed April 26, 2011).

2. Alan F. Friedman, "Basic Principles and Concepts in Threat Assessment Evaluations," in *Preventing and Managing Workplace Violence: Legal and Strategic Guidelines*, ed. Mark A. Lies II (Chicago: ABA Publishing, 2008), 41.

3. Ibid., 39–40.

4. Gary Namie and Ruth Namie, *The Bully at Work: What You Can Do to Stop the Hurt and Reclaim Your Dignity on the Job*, 2nd ed. (Napierville, IL: Sourcebooks, Inc., 2009), 3.

5. Ibid.

6. Workplace Bullying Institute, "2010 & 2007 U.S. Workplace Bullying Surveys, WBI-Zogby," http://www.workplacebullying.org (accessed April 26, 2011).

7. Jason Habinsky and Christine M. Fitzgerald, "Office Bully Takes One on the Nose: Developing Law on Workplace Abuse," *New York Law Journal*, January 21, 2011, http://www.nylj.com (accessed April 26, 2011).

8. Namie and Namie, *The Bully at Work*, 121.

9. Ibid., 122–28.

10. Ibid., 93.

11. Ibid., 242.

12. Ibid.

13. Ibid, 242–44.

One of the things I learnt when I was negotiating was that until I changed myself I could not change others.

Nelson Mandela

ACHIEVING EFFECTIVENESS AS A CONFLICT MANAGER

PERFORMANCE COMPETENCIES

After you have finished reading this chapter, you will be able to

- Describe the process of experiential learning and its role in increasing your effectiveness as a conflict manager

- Describe specific traits and characteristics of an effective conflict manager

- Engage in reflective exercises to assess the extent to which you possess these traits and characteristics and to identify opportunities for further development

Our knowledge of the theories and models for managing conflict is meaningless without the opportunity to apply these models to actual conflict situations. The skills we develop to manage conflict are wasted without the opportunity to practice them.

This final chapter is devoted to helping you reflect on your practice in managing conflict, learn from your successes and struggles, and apply what you have learned as you approach new conflict resolution opportunities. True effectiveness will come only through continual guided reflection on your experiences as you grow and mature as a conflict manager.

Have you learn'd lessons only of those who admired you, and were tender with you, and stood aside for you?

Have you not learn'd great lessons from those who reject you and brace themselves against you? or who treat you with contempt, or dispute the passage with you?

Walt Whitman

PRACTICE DOESN'T NECESSARILY MAKE PERFECT

Think of a professional athlete or a master artist you admire. If an athlete, is he or she a golfer, a basketball player, or a figure skater? If an artist, is he or she a singer, a dancer, or a painter? Whoever it is, what did it take for this individual to achieve the level of mastery that you so admire? If you said practice, you are only partly right.

Indeed, to achieve mastery, the gifted artist or athlete has undoubtedly dedicated years to practicing her craft. But then, the avid amateur golfer could say the same. He may tell you about the years he has spent on the links, the dollars he has spent on equipment and lessons, and the frustrations he has experienced to achieve his current handicap. Yet his golf swing may be anything but masterful! What differentiates this amateur from the gifted athlete?

Only the rarest professional athlete or artist can say he or she has not experienced setbacks, failures, or mistakes along the way to becoming a master at his or her craft. But with these experiences come the opportunity to reflect, to apply the lessons learned through more practice, and to refine the craft in preparation for the next competition. While other factors may separate them, such as temperament, innate talent, and dedication, perhaps this ability to reflect and refine is not as well honed in the amateur as it is in the true practitioner. When the golf stroke is not working, the amateur keeps hitting the ball. The professional golfer learns what is lacking in his stroke, practices continually until he has corrected it, and attempts to use the refined stroke to his advantage in the next tournament.

So, too, your effectiveness in managing conflict depends not simply on practice, but also on refining your practice through guided reflection. Otherwise, if your practice in managing conflict has consisted in the past of berating employees, your "success" at getting them to stop arguing and return to work may lead you to continue this practice. Upon reflection, on the other hand, you may realize the devastating effects your domineering style has on team cohesion, trust, and relationships and adopt a more supportive approach. Beyond practice, you must become a reflective individual eager to learn from your experiences to increase your effectiveness with every new opportunity that presents itself.

> Effectiveness in managing conflict depends not only on practice but also on refining practice through guided reflection.

USING THE EXPERIENTIAL LEARNING CYCLE FOR GUIDED REFLECTION

Experiential learning refers to a sequence of events in which learners adapt what they have learned from a particular experience and apply it to subsequent experiences of a similar nature. It is "reflective" because learners gather information from the current experience, reflect upon it through appropriate evaluative and analytical methods, and use the lessons learned to increase their likelihood for success in the next experience. The "success" they hope to experience will vary depending

EXHIBIT 17-1
The experiential learning cycle

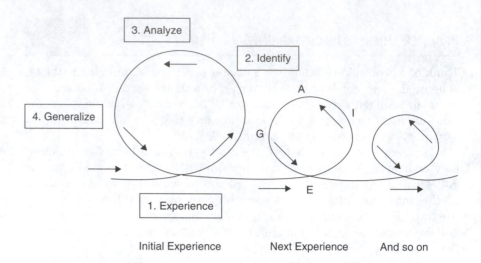

Initial Experience   Next Experience   And so on

> The reflective learner gathers information from the current experience, reflects upon it, and uses the lessons learned to increase his or her likelihood for success in the next experience.

on the situation, but it may include increased knowledge and understanding of the subject matter, quicker assimilation of the concepts involved, more adept handling of complex issues, or increased expertise and effectiveness in their roles.

One model of experiential learning is depicted in Exhibit 17-1.

As the learner (1) engages in an experience, he or she (2) identifies what happened during the experience, (3) analyzes why the experience happened as it did, and (4) generalizes what he or she can learn from the experience. The learner then applies what he or she learned to the next experience, continuing the cycle.

Let us examine each phase of this cycle as it applies to achieving effectiveness in managing conflict.

1. EXPERIENCE—WHAT WAS IT?

If you have not tried a particular activity before, your initial steps will feel awkward. As you begin your journey to manage conflict more effectively, you are not expected to be an expert or to have mastered every technique you have learned. The awkwardness you feel may continue for a while as you try out new tools and fumble through processes that seemed clear when you learned them but now challenge you as you work with actual situations. Let this awkwardness occur, do not be hard on yourself, and view these moments as exciting opportunities to learn and grow.

> *Experience:* For reflection later, choose both a few moments from the conflict resolution experience that were successful and a few moments that felt awkward and uncomfortable.

During this phase, with respect to each conflict resolution process you handle, make a note of both those moments during the process that seemed to go smoothly and those moments that made you feel awkward and uncomfortable. Focus only on a few significant events rather than every tiny detail of the encounter. Consider how the experience of handling these moments made you feel based on the level of knowledge and experience you had at the time rather than how you believe you should have handled them in hindsight. These moments will serve as a basis for deeper reflection.

Conclusion

2. IDENTIFY—WHAT HAPPENED?

For each event you identified and would like to explore more deeply, sit back and think about what occurred. Consider both the successes you experienced and the errors you made. Then, probe into the particular elements and details of the event to gain a broader perspective of what occurred. For example, as relevant, you might ask these types of questions.

If you were a party in a negotiation:

- What outcomes did you achieve? Were these outcomes satisfactory to you and the other party?
- What process did you use to evaluate whether proposed outcomes would satisfy your needs?
- What communication challenges did you encounter? What processes did you use to work through these challenges?
- What process did you use to explore options for resolution and to engage in problem solving? What worked well? Which aspects of these discussions were struggles?
- How did you and the other party go about exploring your respective BATNAs? How did the outcome achieved compare with your BATNA?

If you were mediating a conflict between parties:

- What outcomes did the parties achieve? What did you do to facilitate this outcome? What did you do that aided their decision-making process? What did you do that frustrated it?
- What skills did you employ to help the parties communicate with and understand one another? When and how did you employ paraphrasing and empathic responses? Were these efforts successful?
- What level of trust and rapport did you achieve with the parties? What did you do to build or diminish this level of trust and rapport?
- Were you successful in separating your role as manager from your role as a mediator? What did you do to ensure that you did not exert undue influence as a manager? What did you do that may have crossed this line?

If you were a decision maker involved in a conflict between others:

- How did you go about facilitating the decision-making process? What steps did you take? What did you do to involve others in the decision-making process? Which steps were awkward? Which steps were more comfortable?
- What did you do to elicit support for your decision by those affected by the decision? Were you successful in eliciting their support, or were they resistant?
- What did you do to ensure that the process was fair and equitable? Did the parties perceive your efforts as fair and unbiased? What did you do that may have compromised these perceptions?

With regard to your experience overall, irrespective of the outcomes achieved:

- From the standpoint of evaluating your efforts and the skills you employed, what were your most successful moments? What moments were less successful?
- What particular traits and characteristics did you exhibit that you believe were effective in facilitating the conflict resolution process?
- What behaviors and patterns did you exhibit that you believe may have gotten in the way of your ability to facilitate an effective conflict resolution process?

Identify: Break down experiences into specific, manageable pieces. Probe into the specific elements and details of an event to gain a broader perspective of what occurred.

The purpose of this phase is to break down the experience into specific, manageable pieces, including both those that were positive and affirming and those that were challenging and less affirming. The central focus is to ask what happened.

3. ANALYZE—WHY DID IT HAPPEN?

During the analysis phase, examine your experience and ask why the events occurred as they did.

This phase involves cause-and-effect analysis. Each action you took, or that the parties in the conflict resolution process took, led to a particular result. One action leads to another, which leads to another, and so forth. Potentially, the entire process and why it occurred as it did can be explained based on an examination of a chain of events. If you can understand this sequence, you can explain why you were successful in some instances and less successful in other instances.

When you look at the various events you identified, consider the specific actions that produced the event you experienced. For example:

- Why were some outcomes successful and others less successful? How did your efforts contribute to achieving successful outcomes or lead to less successful outcomes?
- How did a party respond to your offers or, if you were mediating, to your suggestions for possible resolution? Why were these responses positive or negative?
- If you were mediating, how did the parties respond to your efforts to facilitate communication? How did your efforts help or hinder communication?
- How did the parties respond to your efforts to paraphrase or to listen empathetically? Why were these efforts positively or negatively received?
- How did you respond to expressions of anger, disappointment, or worry? How did you respond to aggressive and passive behaviors? How did you respond to competitive, avoiding, or accommodating behaviors? How did these responses contribute to or hinder the resolution process?
- If you were acting as a decision maker, how did the parties respond when you imposed a decision? Why was your decision positively or negatively received?

The key is to make the appropriate connections between the events you identified and the causes for these events to have occurred as they did. Your goal is to consider how your actions and the skills you used contributed to the successes and challenges you experienced. It is particularly important to identify any patterns in your actions and behaviors. To the extent that you accurately identify these patterns, you increase your chances for success in the future by continuing positive patterns and correcting counterproductive ones. Knowing why events occur will help you change the outcome.

> *Analyze:* Make connections between the events and their causes. Consider how your actions and skills contributed to the successes and challenges you experienced.

4. GENERALIZE—WHAT DID YOU LEARN FROM IT?

In this phase, reflect on the experiences you identified and analyzed to consider what these experiences can teach you and what can be applied to benefit your conflict resolution efforts in the future. Use the information gathered to generalize to the future and envision alternative outcomes of similar conflict resolution activities.

> *Generalize:* How can the information you have identified and analyzed help you avoid repeating mistakes and concentrate on duplicating success the next time?

- What conclusions can you draw about yourself and your effectiveness at managing conflict that can aid your practice the next time you have the opportunity to engage in a conflict resolution process?
- How can this information help you avoid repeating mistakes and concentrate on duplicating success the next time?
- What specific skills were effective that you would want to develop further and apply the next time?
- What traits and characteristics of an effective conflict manager did you exhibit that you would apply next time?
- What are the skills, traits, and characteristics that you lack and would want to develop in preparation for your next conflict management opportunity?
- What specific patterns of action or behavior will you want to avoid or modify in order to be more successful next time?

To be effective, you do not want to repeat the same experiences each time. You want to engage in deliberative reflection on past experience to refine your practice in order to enjoy a more rewarding, richer, and successful experience each time you manage a conflict situation.

BEHAVIORS, TRAITS, AND CHARACTERISTICS OF AN EFFECTIVE CONFLICT MANAGER

As you develop your conflict management skills, it will be helpful to model the behaviors, traits, and characteristics that exemplify individuals who are effective at managing conflict. These fall under six broad categories: (1) openness, (2) self-awareness, (3) persistence, (4) consideration of others, (5) critical reasoning, and (6) integrity. For each category, consider the extent to which you exhibited or attempted to exhibit each behavior, trait, or characteristic during your last experience with managing conflict. This assessment will provide a basis for further development as you prepare to engage in the next conflict resolution process. A self-assessment tool is provided at the end of this chapter.

OPENNESS

Openness: Collaborative conflict resolution processes require individuals who are flexible, creative, and willing to explore options.

Any conflict resolution process that favors achieving collaborative solutions over competitive outcomes requires individuals who are flexible, creative, and willing to explore options. An individual involved in a difficult conflict situation often is unable or unwilling to envision positive or productive solutions. His or her thinking becomes hopelessly entrenched. A skilled negotiator or mediator is open to possibilities that will expand the pie and is effective at helping others consider win/win solutions. An open individual is

- **A problem solver:** He encourages brainstorming and examination of all possible options to resolution, narrowing down to the most workable options, then selecting the best option.
- **A risk taker:** He encourages consideration of options that may not have been considered before and that may move people beyond their comfort zones.
- **Comfortable with ambiguity and uncertainty:** He works with parties to search for answers and to make connections that had not previously been explored. He is patient with this process, especially when answers are not readily forthcoming.
- **Creative:** He brings up new and sometimes radical proposals and ways of looking at things that help parties overcome entrenched thinking.
- **Forward thinking:** He challenges himself and others to think about how various options will impact the partiesor the long-term prospects for resolution.
- **Adaptive:** He adapts his negotiating or conflict resolution style to the situation at hand. He will compromise, compete, accommodate, or collaborate, as warranted, and will alternate between modes as the negotiation posture changes.

SELF-AWARENESS

Self-awareness: You must be the first to acknowledge and attend to your own behaviors and attitudes that may interfere with your ability to manage conflict.

As you manage a conflict, you may ask individuals to change their behaviors and attitudes. This expectation requires them to take a close look at themselves to see how their behaviors and attitudes are contributing to the conflict. To be taken seriously, you must be the first to acknowledge and attend to your own behaviors and attitudes that may interfere with your ability to engage in effective conflict resolution processes. A self-aware conflict manager is

- **Calm under pressure:** She maintains her focus in the midst of pressures to settle for less than what is fair, arbitrary deadlines, manipulative behaviors and tricks, forceful or difficult personalities, emotional outbursts, and similar challenges.
- **Humble:** She is not committed to her own ideas for resolving issues and gives deference to others who also have good ideas for solving problems and settling disputes.
- **Aware of emotions and their place in conflict:** She assesses the hot buttons that may prevent the parties, including herself,

from approaching the conflict situation objectively. She expresses emotions appropriately and does not engage in personal attacks. She encourages others to express their emotions as appropriate to the situation.

- **Attentive to her message:** In the process of communicating, she is vigilant to every aspect of her message, whether sent through words, tone, inflection, body language, or other means, and how her message is received. She makes corrections, as warranted, to ensure that her message is received as intended.

- **Aware of her limits:** She addresses only those conflicts for which she possesses the appropriate knowledge and expertise to handle without the assistance of others. She seeks the assistance of others when it is appropriate to do so.

- **Confident in her position and organizational support:** She understands her job and her level of responsibility within the organization for responding to conflict. She understands the underlying policies, procedures, and other "rules of the game" within her organization for responding to conflict.

- **Self-effacing:** She can laugh at herself, especially when she makes mistakes. She acknowledges her mistakes without being unduly harsh or critical of herself. She moves forward and learns from her mistakes and does not dwell on the past.

PERSISTENCE

It takes time and patience to achieve collaborative resolutions. When faced with difficulties, some people give up and give in too quickly. Perhaps they feel hopeless and overwhelmed and want to make a quick exit, regardless of the gains they could be sacrificing. Perhaps they lack confidence in their skills and abilities to keep pressing until they are completely satisfied with the proposed solution. Persistence is essential to realizing resolutions that are most advantageous and mutually beneficial. An individual who is persistent when managing conflict is

> *Persistence:* When faced with difficulties, some people give up and give in too quickly. Persistence is essential to realizing the most advantageous and mutually beneficial outcomes.

- **Patient:** He is careful not to settle too quickly on one or two options or to lock himself into positions that may hinder meaningful exploration of more viable and long-lasting solutions.

- **Persuasive:** He can make an articulate and convincing argument for his case and why it should be believed and supported.

- **Determined:** He seeks to overcome obstacles, work through relationship difficulties, and push for a workable resolution, stopping only at the point when no further concessions are possible or further discussion is futile.

- **Thick-skinned:** He can focus on the overriding issues and interests at stake; separate the people from the problem; and resist retaliating, feeling hurt, or withdrawing when attacked, criticized, or misunderstood.

- **Probing:** He is inquisitive and will dig to get others to open up about their issues and concerns, including the underlying, often buried causes for their concerns.

- **Durable:** He will keep himself and others on task and encourage others to not give up, particularly during moments of impasse when further concessions appear unlikely. He has sufficient energy to remain positive, hopeful, and encouraging through lengthy and often frustrating discussions.

CONSIDERATION OF OTHERS

Traditional bargaining has typically involved a win/lose mind-set. The parties perceive that a win for the other side is a loss for their side. Therefore, they engage in selfish behaviors and are reluctant to share information, concede issues to the other party, or attempt in any way to address the other party's needs. Collaborative approaches to conflict resolution recognize that the more a party seeks to understand and address the other party's needs and interests, the more likely both parties will have their needs and interests met. More is to be gained by sharing information and showing concern for the other party than by not engaging in such behaviors. Someone who is considerate of others is

> *Consideration of others:* More is to be gained by sharing information and showing concern for the other party than by not engaging in such behaviors.

- **Faithful and trusting:** She believes that the conflict she is engaged in is imminently resolvable and approaches others with a steadfast belief that they will achieve a collaborative resolution. She genuinely likes people, believes in their capacity to work through difficulties, and wants to help them.
- **Interdependent:** She recognizes that she needs others as much as they need her to achieve the best possible outcome.
- **Relationship focused:** She values her relationships and recognizes that preserving and improving them is integral to the conflict resolution process. In a conflict setting, she seeks to build trust and rapport with others before engaging in discussions about the facts, issues, and details surrounding the dispute.
- **Sensitive:** She understands the sensitive nature of others' issues. When mediating, she is aware of the trust placed in her to work with the parties in a sensitive and compassionate manner. When acting as a decision maker, she understands the potential a decision has to disappoint a party and, therefore, seeks an outcome that will do the least harm.
- **Empathetic:** She exercises appropriate attentive listening skills (e.g., establish eye contact, make supportive comments, ask clarifying questions, sit up straight, nod head). As appropriate, she uses paraphrases and empathetic responses to show that she understands others' concerns as *they* view or experience them.

CRITICAL REASONING

When you negotiate with another party, mediate a dispute, or make a decision that will resolve an issue, you must manage a great deal of information, interpret its meaning and relevance to the situation, assess the merits of possible solutions, and decide on the best solution. The process of resolving conflict generally involves a number of elaborate and complex thought processes. Critical reasoning is essential to enable you to assess whether any proposed resolution is fair and satisfies your interests. An individual who is effective at critical reasoning in a conflict situation is

- **Analytical:** He is capable of analyzing the issues involved in the conflict and considering how various options and proposals may address the issues and satisfy the needs, interests, and goals of all parties.
- **Rational:** He can maintain his perspective on the conflict situation in the face of strong emotion exhibited by others. He keeps his own emotions in check and does not allow them to cloud a rational perspective on the situation.
- **Objective:** He is capable of weighing any proposed solution against objective criteria relevant to the conflict. If necessary, he will research and seek to understand the underlying values, guidelines, and other standards by which a fair and objective agreement should be based.
- **Critical:** He rigorously tests proposed agreements to ensure they are durable, will satisfy the parties' interests, and preserve or improve their relationship. He challenges assumptions that he or others have about the conflict or proposed solutions, finding "leaks" where they exist and "patching up holes" until a workable agreement is achieved.
- **Consistent:** Given the same set of facts, circumstances, and standards from which to judge a situation, he would make the same decision the next time.
- **Wise:** He possesses the judgment, common sense, and intuition to make sound decisions. When mediating or acting as a decision maker, he recommends or renders decisions that are not only "legal" but also correct based on standards of fairness, justice, and equity.

Critical reasoning is essential to enable you to assess whether any proposed resolution is fair and satisfies your interests.

INTEGRITY

When negotiating, the other party must trust you or he will be reluctant to be open with you. When trust is low, optimum outcomes are unlikely. When you are mediating, the parties must feel comfortable with you and believe you are not taking sides. When you are acting as a decision maker, the parties must trust your judgment and sense of fairness if you expect them to willingly abide by your decision, especially if the decision is contrary to the outcome they proposed. Integrity is a vital ingredient to successful conflict resolution. An individual who displays integrity is

Integrity: Others must be able to trust you before they will open up to you and entrust the conflict resolution process to you.

- **Fair:** She recognizes that a successful resolution must be based on principles of fairness and trust. She does not take undue advantage of others during negotiations. When mediating or acting as a decision maker, she does not take sides and is perceived as truly neutral by the parties. She affords the parties full opportunity to be heard and ensures that no party dominates or takes advantage.

- **Trustworthy:** She gains and maintains others' trust and confidence. Others feel comfortable opening up with their concerns, knowing she will handle the information and their feelings appropriately. When mediating or acting as a decision maker, the parties know she will carry out the process in an equitable manner and that she can be entrusted with confidential information.

- **Respected and qualified:** She has garnered respect both at an interpersonal and an organizational level as someone who can work with individuals to solve problems and handle conflicts in a professional manner. Whether negotiating, mediating, or decision making, her expertise, experience, and other qualifications to participate in the conflict resolution process are readily recognized.

- **Honest:** She is transparent in her viewpoints and judgments, leaving no doubt where she stands. When acting as a decision maker, she is forthright in rendering a just decision and in explaining the basis for her decision. She has nothing to hide or to be defensive about.

- **Principled:** Before addressing any conflict, she assesses the point at which her principles or ethics would be compromised were she to agree to a particular proposal. She is willing to engage in continued give and take, yet prepared to walk away if her principles are threatened or compromised.

Use the exercise in Exhibit 17-2 to assess the extent to which you possess the behaviors, traits, and characteristics of an effective conflict manager.

TOOLS TO ADD TO YOUR CONFLICT SURVIVAL KIT

If, based on honest reflection, you believe that you are well developed with respect to any behavior, trait, or characteristic, celebrate and use it to your advantage when you engage in your next conflict situation. If, on the other hand, you realize you need further development, take heart and patiently work toward developing it as you engage in conflict situations in the future. Consider these tips for turning these areas into strengths:

- Focus on developing only two or three behaviors, traits, or characteristics at a time.

- Consciously choose the behavior, trait, or characteristic you will work on developing and decide to use it when engaging in your next conflict situation.

- Share with a loved one, close friend, or trusted colleague the behavior, trait, or characteristic you want to develop. Elicit supportive feedback regarding his or her assessment of your use of it and how you can further develop it.

- If need be, exaggerate your use of the behavior, trait, or characteristic to be sure you exercise it fully in a conflict situation.

- Realize that practicing a new skill or behavior for the first few times will feel awkward; let it. Only through conscious practice will you achieve competence and, eventually, mastery.

1. Think about a recent conflict situation in which you were involved. For each of the behaviors, traits, and characteristics identified in this chapter, indicate the extent to which you used or exhibited the trait or characteristic, circling the answer according to the following scale:

EXHIBIT 17-2
Self-assessment: How effective are you?

N = Never   O = Occasionally   S = Sometimes
M = Most of the time   A = Always

Openness

Problem solving	N O S M A	Y N	+ −
Risk taking	N O S M A	Y N	+ −
Comfortable with ambiguity and uncertainty	N O S M A	Y N	+ −
Creative	N O S M A	Y N	+ −
Forward thinking	N O S M A	Y N	+ −
Adaptive	N O S M A	Y N	+ −

Self-awareness

Calm under pressure	N O S M A	Y N	+ −
Humble	N O S M A	Y N	+ −
Aware of emotions and their place in conflict	N O S M A	Y N	+ −
Attentive to your message	N O S M A	Y N	+ −
Aware of your limits	N O S M A	Y N	+ −
Confident in your position and organizational support	N O S M A	Y N	+ −
Self-effacing	N O S M A	Y N	+ −

Persistence

Patient	N O S M A	Y N	+ −
Persuasive	N O S M A	Y N	+ −
Determined	N O S M A	Y N	+ −
Thick-skinned	N O S M A	Y N	+ −
Probing	N O S M A	Y N	+ −
Durable	N O S M A	Y N	+ −

Consideration of others

Faithful and trusting	N O S M A	Y N	+ −
Interdependent	N O S M A	Y N	+ −
Relationship focused	N O S M A	Y N	+ −
Sensitive	N O S M A	Y N	+ −
Empathetic	N O S M A	Y N	+ −

Critical reasoning

Analytical	N O S M A	Y N	+ −
Rational	N O S M A	Y N	+ −
Objective	N O S M A	Y N	+ −
Critical	N O S M A	Y N	+ −
Consistent	N O S M A	Y N	+ −
Wise	N O S M A	Y N	+ −

EXHIBIT 17-2
Self-assessment: How effective
are you?
Continued

Integrity

Fair	N O S M A	Y N	+ −
Trustworthy	N O S M A	Y N	+ −
Respected and qualified	N O S M A	Y N	+ −
Honest	N O S M A	Y N	+ −
Principled	N O S M A	Y N	+ −

2. After rating yourself on the scale, go back through the list and indicate whether you believe your use or nonuse of this behavior, trait, or characteristic had a significant bearing on the outcome of the conflict. Circle either Y or N according to the following descriptions:

Y = Use or nonuse had a significant bearing on the outcome
N = Use or nonuse had no significant bearing on the outcome

3. Go back through the list and indicate how you feel about your response, circling either a plus sign (+) or a minus sign (-) according to the following descriptions:

Plus sign (+) = I am satisfied with my rating
Minus (-) = I am dissatisfied with my rating

4. After completing this self-analysis and thinking about your responses, complete the following:

In preparation for my next opportunity to engage in a conflict resolution process, I would like to further develop and apply the following behaviors, traits, or characteristics:
1. _____
2. _____
3. _____
4. _____

(*Note:* Focus on only a few behaviors, traits, or characteristics at a time. Do not become overwhelmed with the thought that you need to develop every trait or characteristic all at once.)

I would like to further develop these behaviors, traits, or characteristics by doing the following:

1. _____
_____
_____
2. _____
_____
_____
_____
3. _____
_____
_____

(Identify the specific action items you will take to develop each behavior, trait, or characteristic you identified previously.)

- Effectiveness in managing conflict is not achieved through practice alone, but through reflection on past experience to apply what you have learned to new experiences.

- The experiential learning cycle provides a method for assessing your successes and challenges in responding to conflict and applying these lessons the next time you have the opportunity to address a conflict situation.

- Using the experiential learning cycle for guided reflection involves (1) experiencing a situation, (2) identifying what occurred during the experience, (3) analyzing why the experience occurred as it did, and (4) generalizing what you learned from the experience to avoid repeating mistakes and concentrate on duplicating success the next time.

- Effectiveness at managing conflict involves developing specific behaviors, traits, and characteristics, including (1) openness, (2) self-awareness, (3) persistence, (4) consideration of others, (5) critical reasoning, and (6) integrity.

- You must assess the extent to which you possess and exhibit these behaviors, traits, and characteristics in a conflict situation, develop them through practice, and continually apply them to new conflict situations.

True/False

For each statement below, check true or false.

TRUE   FALSE

_____   _____   1. One aspect of critical reasoning is being calm under pressure.

_____   _____   2. In a mediation, Attila and Ivan yelled at each other. They then turned on their manager, Mahatma, and criticized him for failing to come up with any solutions to their problems. Mahatma shouldn't have to put up with such behavior from the participants.

_____   _____   3. Carly engaged in a mediation process with two employees whom she managed. It was a disaster. She was a new supervisor and hadn't ever conducted a mediation process before, nor ever observed one. Further, the employee relations manager later heard about her attempts and informed her that she had not followed the appropriate lines of authority in the organization to ensure that the mediation was handled correctly. Of the six broad categories of behaviors, traits, and characteristics discussed in the chapter, Carly demonstrated a lack of openness.

_____   _____   4. In the *identify* step of the experiential learning model, you are asking why your experience happened as it did.

_____   _____   5. When you analyze your experience, you are making causal connections between specific events that occurred in your experience and the reasons why these events occurred as they did.

Circle the letter next to the best answer for each question. On a separate sheet of paper, state why you chose that answer.

1. All of the following are examples of reflecting on past experience to apply what was learned to new experiences, *except*

    a. Juan asks Marcus, an employee he supervises, why he was so offended by a remark he made during a mediation session.

    b. Carmen reviews her file of vendor agreements in preparation for meeting with a new vendor to negotiate the price of a copy machine.

    c. During a disciplinary counseling session, Inez asks Susie, "Why do you continue to repeat this error? I must have told you a thousand times how to do this."

    d. Alicia decides that when she goes home tonight, she will spend a half-hour with her teenage daughter and listen without commenting.

2. Manuel, a supervisor, is facilitating a process in which he must decide how to resolve a dispute between two employees, Jeff and Randy, who are constantly bickering. Before deciding, he meets individually with each employee and asks each to share his side of the story. Manuel *does not* exhibit integrity when he

    a. asks probing questions of Randy, but not Jeff.

    b. refuses to consider Jeff's proposal to reassign him to another area so he won't have to deal with Randy any more.

    c. disciplines Jeff for foul language and pointing his finger in Randy's chest, but only warns Randy who raised his voice but did not swear or point his finger.

    d. tells Randy to try to be more understanding of Jeff because Jeff is having marital problems.

3. During negotiations, *the best reason* that being open and flexible is important is that

    a. the parties should be completely forthcoming about their BATNAs

    b. negotiations are tough enough without having to deal with people who are rigid.

    c. the parties need to be able to think creatively to identify the best solutions.

    d. negotiations could drag on forever unless the parties are open to possibilities for resolution.

4. Self-awareness is reflected in the following behaviors, *except*

    a. a manager laughs at herself when one of the parties in the dispute she is mediating points out that she has been misstating some of the facts involved in the situation.

    b. a new manager asks a senior manager to assist him when meeting with his team to discuss a complex issue involving realignment of some job tasks.

    c. a manager sits quietly and listens as a clearly immature employee berates him on his skills as a manager.

    d. a manager sits back in his chair and states to an employee in hushed tones how he would like to work out their communication difficulties.

5. To get the most benefit from using the experiential learning cycle, do all the following *except*

    a. focus on the broad range of traits or characteristics to improve upon for your next experience.

    b. choose to reflect upon the most significant experiences.

    c. break down the experiences you choose to reflect upon to identify specific successes and challenges you encountered.

    d. engage in a cause-and-affect analysis, asking why an experience occurred as it did.

1. Do you agree with the authors' premise that "practice does not necessarily make perfect"? Do you agree that beyond practice, it is important to reflect on your past experiences to learn from them and apply what you learned to new experiences? Defend your answer.

2. For each of the six general categories of behaviors, traits, and characteristics discussed in this chapter (openness, self-awareness, persistence, consideration of others, critical reasoning, and integrity), share examples you have observed in which (a) it was used or exhibited to the advantage of a party in a conflict situation and (b) its nonuse had detrimental effects on a party in a conflict situation. Describe these impacts. What do these examples tell you about the importance of developing and possessing these behaviors, traits, and characteristics?

3. Do you believe that each trait or characteristic is equally important as all others toward achieving effectiveness at managing conflict? If not, in your view, which behaviors, traits, and characteristics are more important than others? Defend your answer.

CASE: REFLECTING ON EXPERIENCES WITH MANAGING CONFLICT

Joe has enjoyed his Managing Conflict class and is grateful for the instruction Professor Justice has provided. While he has enjoyed learning theory, the class has been especially helpful in providing opportunity to practice what he has learned, both in class and with actual situations at work. Yet, in many respects, he still feels unequipped. In particular, over the past three months, it seems that as soon as he has learned a new tool and tried it out, it is time to learn a different tool and try it out. He has not had any significant time to reflect on what he has learned and how these lessons will serve him in the future.

After his last class, Joe asks to meet with Professor Justice. With notebook in hand, he asks the professor, "What would you say are the two or three key lessons I should keep in mind when I am serving in each of the conflict management roles we've discussed?" He then hands Professor Justice the list of roles.

Amused, Professor Justice responds, "Joe, have I taught you nothing? It is really not for me to answer this question. You must decide for yourself what the most important lessons are." He then asks Joe to open his notebook and go through the list and identify these key lessons. The list contained the following roles:

1. manager, encouraging parties to collaborate
2. negotiator
3. mediator
4. decision maker, leading a consensus decision-making process
5. decision maker, leading a consultative decision-making process
6. decision maker, leading a directive decision-making process
7. manager, required to confront an employee directly with a performance or conduct concern or to terminate an employee
8. manager, required to manage an opportunistic employee

Case Questions

In class, finish this discussion between Joe and Professor Justice. If you were Joe, how would you answer this question? Specifically, for each role, assuming that you, like Joe, have had limited opportunity to practice the role, what are the top two or three lessons you would want to take with you if you were required to serve in that role tomorrow? In answering this question, you may consider not only the behaviors, traits, and characteristics discussed in this chapter, but all the skills, competencies, tools, theories, and concepts you have learned.

Option 1: Break the class into four to eight small groups and have each group discuss only one or two of the roles. For each role, try to be as specific as possible, thinking about the tasks involved with it. For example, if you believe that communication skills are important for each role, describe the specific skills required as they relate to that role and why they are important. Try to avoid being too general or repetitive as you discuss each role. Give the groups approximately ten minutes for their small-group discussion. Have them record their responses on flipchart paper or whiteboard. Then, have each group report its responses to the rest of the class.

Option 2: List each of the eight roles on top of a separate piece of flipchart paper. Then, place each flip-chart page on a separate wall around the classroom. Break the class into eight groups, or fewer if total class size is small (recommended group size: at least three students per group). Assign each group to a separate role initially. Have groups record at least one lesson to keep in mind for that role. Give only a few minutes for this. Then, have the groups rotate clockwise to identify a lesson to keep in mind for the next role in the rotation. Challenge the groups to be creative and identify a lesson or learning that is different from what the previous group recorded. Continue this rotation for eight complete rounds or, if time does not permit, at least four rounds. After the rounds are completed, debrief the complete exercise, summarizing the key points for each role.

ALTERNATIVE PROCEDURE FOR ONLINE LEARNING FORMATS

Option 1: Assign small groups similar to Option 1 above. Have the groups meet or connect online to engage in discussion for one or two roles. Have them post their collective responses online through the appropriate forum or chat format by a specified time period. Have each group provide at least three distinct lessons to keep in mind for the role or roles assigned.

Option 2: Similar to Option 2 above, divide the class by eight, assigning each group initially to one of the eight roles. Have groups post a few lessons to keep in mind for the role assigned by a specified time period. Once these initial responses have been posted, have all students add additional posts to those posted by the initial group for each role. Either have students add additional posts to each of the remaining seven roles to which they were not initially assigned or have them add additional posts to at least two or three of these remaining seven roles. Encourage students to be creative and add content that is unique from previous posts.

PERSONAL GROWTH EXERCISE

In the next year, complete the self-assessment in the chapter after each conflict in which you are involved. Observe your patterns in addressing each conflict, consider no more than three traits, behaviors, or characteristics to focus on for improvement each time, and consciously apply these traits, behaviors, or characteristics in your next conflict situation. Refer back to the text for additional insights on how to refine your practice, as necessary. Then, periodically, celebrate your successes, as you develop into a more effective and confident conflict manager.

The following sources provide information regarding the behaviors, traits, and characteristics for effectiveness in managing conflict in various contexts:

Dawson, Roger. *Secrets of Power Negotiating: Inside Secrets from a Master Negotiator*, 3rd ed. Pompton Plains, NJ: Career Press, 2011.

Fisher, Roger, and Wayne H. Davis. "Six Basic Interpersonal Skills for a Negotiator's Repertoire." In *Negotiation: Readings, Exercises, and Cases*, 3rd ed., ed. Roy J. Lewicki, David M. Saunders, and John W. Minton (Boston: Irwin McGraw-Hill, 1999), 354–59. (Reprinted from Roger Fisher and Wayne H. Davis, "Six Basic Interpersonal Skills for a Negotiator's Repertoire," *Negotiation Journal* [April 1987]: 117–20.)

Gerzon, Mark. *Leading Through Conflict: How Successful Leaders Transform Differences into Opportunities*. Boston: Harvard Business School Press, 2006.

Lang, Michael D., and Alison Taylor. *The Making of a Mediator: Developing Artistry in Practice*. San Francisco: Jossey-Bass, 2000.

Lovenheim, Peter. *Becoming a Mediator: An Insider's Guide to Exploring Careers in Mediation*. San Francisco: Jossey-Bass, 2002.

Masters, Marick F., and Robert R. Albright. *The Complete Guide to Conflict Resolution in the Workplace*. New York: American Management Association, 2002.

Mayer, Bernard. *The Dynamics of Conflict Resolution: A Practitioner's Guide*. San Francisco: Jossey-Bass, 2000.

Phillips, Barbara A. *The Mediation Field Guide: Transcending Litigation and Resolving Conflicts in Your Business or Organization*. San Francisco: Jossey-Bass, 2001.

Rackman, Neil. "The Behavior of Successful Negotiators," in *Negotiation: Readings, Exercises, and Cases*, 4th ed., ed. Roy J. Lewicki, David M. Saunders, John W. Minton, and Bruce Barry (Boston: McGraw-Hill/Irwin, 2003), 169–81.

Raiffa, Howard. *The Art and Science of Negotiation: How to Resolve Conflicts and Get the Best Out of Bargaining*. Cambridge, MA: Harvard University Press, 1982.

Ury, William. *The Third Side: Why We Fight and How We Can Stop*. New York: Penguin Books, 2000.

The following sources provide information regarding experiential and reflective learning:

Conner, Marcia L. "Learning From Experience." *Ageless Learner*, 1997–2007. http://agelesslearner.com/intros/experiential.html (accessed June 3, 2011).

Kolb, David A. *Experiential Learning: Experience as the Source of Learning and Development*. Englewood Cliffs, NJ: Prentice Hall, 1984.

Pfeffer, Jeffrey, and Robert I. Sutton. *The Knowing-Doing Gap: How Smart Companies Turn Knowledge Into Action*. Boston: Harvard Business School Press, 2000.

The Conflict Survival Kit provides profiles featured in the cases at the end of each chapter. The main character is Joe Newcomer, who is an assistant manager with More Power, Inc. Identifying with Joe and the other characters will help make the cases and role plays more realistic and enjoyable. If you have the opportunity to play a role in a group situation, you will be expected to make decisions from the viewpoint of the character you portray. For example, if you are given the role of Joe, you should act in a way you believe an individual like Joe would act when addressing a particular conflict situation.

In addition to traditional characters employed in a hypothetical organization, a few additional characters act in the role of experts, such as Joe's boss and his evening class professor. Further, characters include at least one customer and a vendor who do business with More Power. Every attempt has been made to broaden the types of conflicts a supervisor might face in a typical day.

THE COMPANY: MORE POWER, INC.

More Power, Inc., is a large, local retail store specializing in the sale and service of hardware, tools, lawn and garden implements, and other materials for the home. More Power operates seven days a week, dawn to dusk. Approximately 120 employees work in distinct divisions within the store, including customer service/return desk; warehouse and delivery; service and repair; and three distinct sections focused on (1) hardware and tools, (2) lawn and garden and outdoors, and (3) home building and improvement. Five assistant managers who oversee these divisions report to the owner/manager. The organizational chart of More Power, Inc., includes the employees who are featured in the case studies.

JOE NEWCOMER, ASSISTANT MANAGER, WAREHOUSE, DELIVERY, AND CUSTOMER SERVICE

As Joe, you are the key figure in most of the case studies. You are an assistant manager and have been working for More Power, Inc., for four months. In your role, you are responsible for overseeing the customer service/return desk and for managing the warehouse and delivery functions. You manage approximately thirty people.

You are twenty-six and married, with a two-year-old daughter. Your wife is pregnant and works full time as an office manager. Although your current

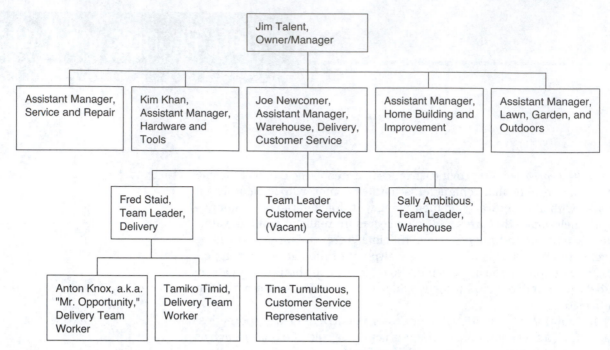

Organizational Chart for More Power, Inc.

position is not perfect, you thought it was the appropriate progression in your career as a manager. In addition, when you accepted the position, you understood that you would have flexibility to pursue other goals. Specifically, you expected the job would allow you to return to night school to work toward earning a four-year degree, adding to your two-year associate degree. The position offered more money and better benefits, which is more important than ever now that you and your wife have a child with another on the way.

Now that you are enrolled in night school, it has been difficult balancing school with work and family obligations. Although your boss, Jim Talent, is generally understanding about your need to leave early in the evening to attend school, you have been expected occasionally to stay later and either arrive late or miss class altogether. At home, you are not always fun to be around because you often have to study instead of spend time with your wife and daughter.

It has been especially difficult to balance all these obligations because of the stresses and challenges you face on a daily basis at work. You are expected to address and resolve innumerable employee, customer, and vendor problems every day. You are not always sure whether you have made the right career choice by accepting your current position. You are not always sure you have the skills to handle some of these trying conflicts.

JIM TALENT, STORE OWNER/MANAGER

As Jim Talent, you grew up in the hardware, lawn, and garden business. You worked with your father, who started the business, until he retired. You have worked in virtually every imaginable position in the store and know the business inside and out. You are forty-one, married, and have two teenaged children.

Although you have a four-year degree, which you earned the hard way through years of night school while working full time, you believe your management expertise and leadership style were developed more through the day-to-day grind of work than through formal education. You are a straightforward, direct individual who prefers deliberate action to deep analysis and talk. You can be patient with the assistant managers you supervise and are willing to coach them on how to perform their jobs and become effective managers. However, you prefer that they make decisions on their own, take ownership for those decisions (good or bad), and not always depend on you to bail them out. Your reason for this approach is a matter of both personal management style and practicality. With so many employees to manage and areas of responsibility to oversee, you rely on your assistant managers to be as resourceful and tough-minded as you are.

When you hired Joe, you thought he had a lot of promise. Though Joe seems insecure in his role, he is also task oriented and sincere about being an effective manager. You can tell he cares about his customers and the people he manages, but he often spends too much time deliberating over how to handle difficult situations. You would rather that he jump in headfirst to confront matters, as you would. He could also use a little more experience in delegating. While you support his aspirations for school, you believe all that "head knowledge" is no replacement for the hard knocks Joe needs to be successful. To that end, you believe you can provide a good balance to his college experience as a real-world coach.

FRED STAID, TEAM LEADER, DELIVERY

As Fred Staid, you are comfortable working as the team leader in the delivery section. You oversee the logistics of delivery; arrange deliveries; and direct a small fleet of drivers, loaders, and installers. You know this end of the business well as you have been in this role, in this store, for as long as anyone can remember. You enjoy the security of the position, being the resident authority over a particular area and having a job you can leave at the end of the day without thinking about it.

This security is especially important right now. You are fifty-two, married, with three kids, two in high school and one in college. Your kids are hard working, as they must be. You are encouraging them to seek the opportunities you never had, such as going to college, but are unable to support them financially in these goals. You enjoy spending time with your wife, attending your teens' football games and band concerts, and fussing with the lawn.

You are a conservative individual and not comfortable with rapid organizational change. You are analytical and good at organization and planning. You don't like making changes rapidly but prefer to think things through and move slowly. While you realize others may have input in how things should be run in your area, you are somewhat reticent to relinquish even the least amount of control to others.

SALLY AMBITIOUS, TEAM LEADER, WAREHOUSE

As Sally Ambitious, though you like your job, you have no desire to remain in your position as warehouse team leader forever. In fact, you would like to move up to an assistant manager position eventually, though this may take longer than it would others since you have only a high school diploma. At twenty-two, you have plenty of time. You want to attend college but currently are focused on raising two young children. Moving into an assistant manager position might also require accepting a position with another company in another state, something you are not prepared to do. Your husband recently started a new position so moving right now would not make sense.

You are making the most of your current role. You like the idea that More Power management, including both Jim Talent and Joe Newcomer, have given you a great deal of leeway in directing day-to-day warehouse operations. In the year that you have held this position, you believe you have streamlined functions so that products are more effectively inventoried and shelved and that depleted products are replenished more quickly. You also believe that the processes you have implemented have ensured that customers receive ordered products in a prompt manner, either through in-store pickup at the customer service desk or through coordination with Fred's delivery section. However, you still see ways in which functions between your section and Fred's may be more efficiently coordinated.

You are an expressive, creative individual with more ideas than you have time to implement. You tend toward impatience. You are prone to making quick decisions, but this is because you are more intuitive than analytical about the best way to proceed on projects. Often, your intuition has led to innovative and successful results. On the law of averages, your approach has proven no less effective than the slower, more deliberate approach others might prefer.

TINA TUMULTUOUS, CUSTOMER SERVICE REPRESENTATIVE

As Tina Tumultuous, you have a mixed employment record as a customer service representative. When you started working with More Power five years ago, you loved the work and you were quite good at it. You know the retail business and can recite chapter and verse of More Power's policies and procedures on returns, refunds, and damaged items. You know a great deal about the products More Power sells, where they are located in the store, and where to direct customers to find items or to seek further assistance. You have generally treated customers in a respectful manner. In fact, because of your knowledge and work with customers, you were named Employee of the Month a couple of times in the past few years.

But your attitude has changed recently. You are as capable as you ever were, and if asked, you would acknowledge that you are still committed to your job and to helping make More Power successful. But your personal life is in turmoil. You went through a difficult divorce. You have two kids, one in junior high and the other in high school. Your older child, a son, has been in and out of trouble in school and with the law.

Lately, Jim and Joe have talked with you repeatedly about your behavior and interaction with customers. They have used words such as "curt," "bossy," "loud," "rude," and "insensitive" in counseling you about customer interactions they have observed. On occasion, you have been disciplined for these behaviors. The stress and anxiety you have been feeling regarding your personal life may account for why you have been acting this way. However, you are reluctant to discuss these issues with management.

PROFESSOR TIMOTHY JUSTICE, PH.D.

As Professor Justice, you are Joe's professor for Managing Conflict in Work and Life, an elective that Joe is taking toward a degree in management and supervision. You are also Joe's academic advisor. You are rumpled and gray-haired, with a generous spirit and a passion for teaching. You once worked in an industrial environment but returned to school and earned a Ph.D. in industrial and labor relations. You have been a professor for twenty years and would not think of returning to a position in industry. However, you do serve as an independent consultant for various companies, and you also enjoy helping to equip future leaders like Joe to succeed in their roles as managers.

You like Joe. You find that he has a lot of intellectual curiosity about the theories of management as well as conflict and negotiation. You find, though, that Joe is having a difficult time applying what he is learning in the classroom to the real-world situations he faces at More Power. You teach collaborative and empowerment models of management and conflict intervention and insist that your students get a good grasp of these theories and concepts to apply them in their jobs. You also try hard to balance theory with practical, albeit hypothetical, case studies, exercises, and other applications to give students a picture of how these theories and concepts work on the job. With Joe, you are more than happy to teach him, to listen to his frustrations in dealing with conflicts at work, and to offer advice when you can.

VIC VENDOR, SALES REPRESENTATIVE, DO OR DYE TOOLS, INC.

As Vic Vendor, you are the regional sales representative for Do or Dye Tools, Inc., which has a long-standing relationship with More Power as one of Do or Dye's largest distributors. You have worked for Do or Dye Tools only a few months, having replaced the former sales representative to More Power, Axel Rod, who had served in that role for almost twenty years. You are young, but you have a good sales record from previous sales positions.

Since you are new to your role and are replacing someone who had a trusted relationship with More Power management, you are careful at first to respect that relationship and the "gentlemen's agreements" between Axel Rod and More Power. However, you are slowly realizing that your predecessor engaged in all sorts of unsound business practices, such as giving large volume discounts on tools; refunding More Power for defective tools "no questions asked"; and agreeing to endless rebates, "freebies," give-aways, and other deals that drastically affected Do or Dye's profit margin.

You think that Do or Dye has been taken advantage of, thanks to Axel Rod's "old boy" approach. You want to base the relationship on a pricing structure that has some reasonable basis in valuing Do or Dye's manufacturing and delivery costs, other overhead, expectation for realizing a profit, and similar considerations. You are prepared to introduce a new pricing structure but know this will not be received well by More Power managers.

MARIA SERVICE, CUSTOMER

As Maria Service, you are a professional woman who works as a real estate account manager at a major bank. You and your husband own a home and shop at More Power as your preferred retailer for tools and lawn and garden and home improvement needs. You have generally been pleased with the prices and customer service at More Power. However, you occasionally shop at More Power's competitors in town. Service is not quite as good, and prices are generally just a little higher.

At times, you have had to return a product to More Power, either because you realized you did not need it after all or because of a slight defect. Returns have generally been honored.

In your daily interactions with others, you are generally pleasant, but you are also confident and willing to press your position if you believe you are not being treated fairly. This has not always been easy for you. You are a second-generation Latina American. Your family immigrated to the United States from Mexico when you were a child. You are well aware of the struggles your family and others in the Latino community must endure to earn fairness and respect in the community and in business affairs. Your family is proud of you for having earned a bachelor's degree and an MBA. Your husband owns a management consultant firm.

KIM KHAN, ASSISTANT MANAGER, TOOLS

As Kim Khan, you have been the assistant manager in the hardware and tools section for three years. You worked for More Power in previous positions, resigned to work in the construction industry as a carpenter, and then returned. You are an expert with tools, and you love sharing your expertise with customers. In fact, in addition to working with customers to select the best tools for their projects, you offer free weekend classes on how to use tools and how to do various construction projects.

You are more effective at working with customers than you are in managing sales or people. You will spend hours working with customers and are not prone to use sales tactics to encourage customers to buy tools. You have developed a loyal customer base among a small group of customers. As a manager, your employees are often frustrated. As the expert, you spend time with customers and, therefore, do not train employees as you should or give them enough opportunities to interact with customers.

Employees have complained that you tend to assign menial tasks to them and keep all the interesting work to yourself.

You are not sure how you feel about working with Joe. There is a lot of interaction between you and Joe, as you rely on his area to keep inventory up; handle customer ordering; and work with customers regarding complaints, returns, and other matters. Often, Joe has to come to you with questions. You are a skilled tradesperson by training, not a college graduate. Joe seems to do okay with management issues but lacks the expertise you think is needed to effectively handle More Power's products and services. It irritates you that he has to come to you so often with questions and seems to do the same with Jim Talent. "Either you can do a job or you can't," you say to yourself. "If you can't, then move on." Jim is apparently oblivious to this.

Anton Knox, a.k.a. "Mr. Opportunity," Delivery Team Worker

As Anton Knox, you are young and irresponsible. You do not take your work seriously. On your best days, you are an average performer. On such days, you usually come to work on time and put in the minimally required effort to keep your job. On your worst days, you are late to work and do not pay careful attention to the work you are doing. You tend to sit around and wait for Fred Staid to give you your next assignment. You like to joke around with the other guys on the delivery team.

You are called "Mr. Opportunity" because you never miss an opportunity to get around doing your work. You also never seem to miss the opportunity to call in sick or come in late. When Fred talks with you about these issues, you find his comments to be outrageous and demeaning. He apparently does not understand all the personal issues surrounding your life that give you legitimate reasons for the behaviors for which you are accused. Nobody seems to have all the troubles that you do because if they did, they would understand.

The way you feel treated at work is enough at times to make you angry. Yet you generally avoid outbursts. You just complain a lot. You also know the store's policies on sick leave and tardiness and are a master at improving your performance at the point when discipline might be imposed. You have learned to work around Fred and convince him that you will improve your performance. You are grateful that you are not on Joe's radar—for now.

Tamiko Timid, Delivery Team Worker

As Tamiko Timid, you come to work every day and do your job. You are a consistent, average performer. You are one of only two females on the delivery team. The men on the team like to joke around, which at times makes you uncomfortable. Yet you do not complain about this.

You are not overly excited about working with Fred Staid, though you acknowledge that he knows the business of retail delivery. You respect his authority and always respond to his requests. You wish that others on the team would do the same.

You have not formed many relationships among your coworkers. You are not comfortable with chitchat and want to simply put in an honest day's work and go home. You do not like complications in your life, nor do you want to form complicated relationships at work. You also worry a lot about losing your job.

There is one person you admire: Sally Ambitious. You have occasionally had lunch with her. She has tried to encourage you to be more confident. She has especially encouraged you to be more assertive about matters that concern you and to communicate your concerns to Fred or others.

Thomas, Kenneth W., 46
Thomas-Kilmann Conflict Mode Instrument
    accommodating approach, 50–51
    assertiveness, identifying degree of, 47
    avoiding approach, 48–50
    clarify your values, using conflict modes to, 48
    collaborating approach, 55–57
    competing approach, 51–53
    compromising approach, 53–55
    conflict mode questionnaire, 57–59
    conflict strategy, 47–48
    conflict style, identifying, 47
    cooperativeness, identifying degree of, 47
    outcome, importance of, 47
    relationship, importance of, 47
    smoothing, 50
    withdrawal, 49
Threats, 312
Three alternatives rule, 146–147
Touching behaviors, 69
Traditional adverserial bargaining, 37, 336
Transformative approach to mediation, 232
Triggers, conflict, 20–22

U
Use of time, making effective, 69–70

V
Verbal channel, 88
Verbal communication, 68, 74–78
Verbal feedback, 93
Verbal warning, 288
Violent behavior, responding to, 308–311
Visual media, role of, 3–4

W
Willingness to confront conflict, 132–133
Willingness to resolve conflict, 133
Window on behavior, 144
Withdrawal, 49
Work environment checklist, 18–20
Workplace bullying, managing, 318–321
Workplace violence, 312–315
Workplace violence, defined, 312
Written warning, 289